TEN LITTLE
POLICE CHIEFS
A DETROIT POLICE STORY

ROBERT M. HAIG

Formatted by IRONHORSE_Formatting

ISBN: 1497491339
ISBN-13: 978-1497491335

CONTENTS

ACKNOWLEDGMENTS

I would like to clarify a few things before this train gets rolling. The City of Detroit provided me with the unique opportunity to join a very special group of people: The men and woman of law enforcement. So my first thanks goes out to Detroit. Although this book, at times, appears to be bashing the city I hired on to protect, nothing can be further from the truth. This book simply is that: The "truth." I make no attempt to sugar coat anything, or to write a pleasing story everyone will enjoy. This is about the real-life experiences of a police officer, set in one of the most violent and dangerous cities in the United States. It is written from the street and the heart. I know the language and realities will disturb some readers. I am sure some of my feelings and comments will not sit well with other police officers. My hope is that by the time you turn that last page, you no longer will see just a blue uniform and a badge. You will realize it takes a very special man or woman to strap on a bulletproof vest, holster a gun and hit those deadly streets. You also will walk away a little more educated, learning something about real police officers who possess that special courage to risk their lives to protect yours.

I would like to thank my wife and my kids for all their support and patience while I wrote this book. I know I wore them out at times. A special thanks to my mother for all of her encouragement, and I apologize for all the worry I put her through over the years. A kiss goodbye from her always was followed with a "Be safe, baby boy." Her eyes filled with concern and the love that caused it. Thanks to my father (a retired Detroit Fire captain) for all of his input, advice and guiding hand. Thanks to my brother and sisters for helping make me the person I am today, which ultimately influenced the type of officer I have become. Also, thanks to my first partner Jim, who kept me alive through those first few years. We learned some hard lessons, and, fortunately, survived them. And thanks to the good command officers who helped guide me as my career developed. A special thanks to my Robbery Team. It was a pleasure and honor to work with such dedicated men and woman. It was the best four years of my career.

I especially want the families of those officers who lost their lives in the line of duty to know that their sacrifices were not in vain. Working officers always will recognize what was lost and can never be replaced.

So hold on as this train picks up speed. I can guarantee, it is going to be one hell of a ride.

TEN LITTLE POLICE CHIEFS

The two marked scout cars were parked out front, freshly washed and gleaming. All four officers were seated in the small coffee shop, two at the counter, the others at a small table. The clinking of silverware, and the aroma of brewing coffee, comforted the patrons as they quietly prepared to start their day. The officers scribbled out reports, and clicked on laptops catching up on unfinished paperwork. Their radios were quiet. The bright sun had crept above the trees and the waitress quickly adjusted the front blinds. The officers spoke in soft tones. They talked about the job, home and the day to come.

A man stepped through the front door un-noticed, appearing as any customer would. He slowly walked to the counter where the first two officers were seated, and positioned himself directly behind them.

Pulling a semi-automatic pistol from his waistband, he placed the muzzle to the back of the head of the first officer and pulled the trigger. The officer slumped forward as brain matter splattered the counter, pen still in his hand. The second officer was frozen, her ears ringing as their eyes met. In a split second, her training kicked in. Her right hand automatically reached for her service revolver, and her left rose up in a defensive motion. The bark of the second shot was followed by the sound of the officer tumbling from her stool. She lay on the ground clutching her throat, as blood pumped from between her fingers. She gasped shallow breaths as she tried to hold onto her life. The man immediately stepped over her, concentrating his aim on the remaining two officers. The third officer was pulling his weapon as the first shot struck his chest. His opposite hand went up in the same defensive posture as his co-workers. The following shot pierced his hand and stuck the left side of his forehead. His weapon never cleared its holster. The last officer had now pulled his department-issued weapon and returned fire. Several rounds hit the officer, as he lunged toward the man. Although mortally wounded, and his strength waning by the second, the officer fought to subdue the gunman. They struggled and spilled through the front door, where the officer collapsed. The shooter stood up, and without looking down, he placed his weapon back in his waistband. The smoke still was clearing as he turned away. He smiled as the sun warmed his face. With no regret, he strolled past the gleaming scout cars and spit.

It was all over in minutes. Stunned customers still sat at their tables, some screaming and others crying.

All four officers were pronounced dead at the scene. Their families were going about their daily routines unaware of the tragedy that had befallen them. The suspect did not know the officers, nor did they know him. He was a criminal. To him, those were not people in those uniforms, they were "COPS." They were the police, and they died because of it.

THE ACADEMY

I was unaware of the chaos I was jumping into and had no idea how this happened. I was twenty-five years old, and just getting ready to step through the doors of the Detroit Police academy. When I was little, I never dreamt of becoming a cop. I didn't dress up as a police officer on Halloween. I actually was at the other end of the spectrum — and was kind of a handful for my mother. My father was a Detroit firefighter, and I had entertained following in his footsteps. I had taken the written and agility test for that job the prior year. I passed everything with flying colors, but apparently there were some racial issues with the applicants, and I was told they hired fifty black candidates and seven white. Unfortunately, I was number nine on the white list. Being a firefighter would have to wait.

At the time this was all developing, I was working a good job in a machine shop, but knew that wouldn't last forever. I had reached that age where I needed some security, good benefits and peace of mind. I knew my education package was lacking, with a high school diploma and about sixteen college credits. Was I asking for too much with so little to offer? I was worried about that. At the time, my youngest sister was married to a police officer, and he suggested I apply for the Detroit Police Department. I pondered that one. It had the same benefits as a firefighter, with no fire, and they give you a gun. I had seen the "Big

Four" cruise through our neighborhood before. This was an unmarked car with four burly police officers in it. They had a reputation of "fluffing up" the bad guys. Everyone understood this street term. If you got caught, they would throw you a beating. They were a scary bunch, and I knew I didn't want anything to do with them. They left an impression whenever they showed up. I have no idea if they had a count down in the car or not, but when they exited that dark car, all four doors always opened at the exact same time. Due to my upbringing, my brushes with the law were few and far between. I was more worried about facing my mother than any police officer. This made my choices easy when I was young. I knew the difference between right and wrong and where to draw the line.

I was about fifteen when I got my first sit-down in the back of a marked police car. We were playing basketball at the park, when a group of kids ran through pushing a bike. A couple of seconds later, an eight-year-old came through running in the same direction. He was crying and yelling that they stole his bike. We quit playing ball and ran after the gang. There was no concern about the fight at the end of the chase. We were all tough kids, some just tougher than others and most of us had something stolen from them at one time or another. Their escape route had run under the expressway, which was a no-no for me, per my mother. My buddy had no such standing orders and followed. I ran along the exit ramp to cover him. As I made the end of the ramp, a police car screeched up cutting me off. Without a single question, they grabbed me and threw me in the back of the scout car. They sped back to the park, accusing me of running on the expressway. I protested, but was guilty by cop. They didn't want to hear me say I wasn't on the expressway, and read me the riot act. It ceased only when they received a priority run. I could hear the radio crackle about someone being stabbed. I was told to stay off of the expressway and was released. I stood alone in the park puzzled. I had done nothing wrong, and actually was trying to do some good. Weren't these the guys that were supposed to help me? The police had left an impression on me.

My second contact with the Detroit Police Department was a traffic ticket. I was sixteen years old, driving through the neighborhood with some friends, and had just made a left-hand turn when I noticed flashing lights in my mirror. I was terrified and shaking as I pulled to the curb. Two uniformed officers approached my car, requesting my license and registration. I asked what I had done, and received no response as they walked back to their car. After several minutes, they pulled their vehicle next to mine. The officer in the passenger seat was leaning back and had his window down. He was looking straight ahead, when he handed me a ticket. I'll never forget his words, "Clean it up buddy," and they pulled off. I had a sour taste for police, and those two officers also left an impression I wouldn't forget.

Growing up, I saw the police on a regular basis, but they usually were carting off the local hoodlums. Those two incidents were my only personal interaction with them and they stunk. Even for a teenager, the police seemed so unprofessional.

But I also remember the time the police department had to deal with Butchie Carson. He was a local thug of the worst kind, and had hooked up with one of the sweetest girls in the neighborhood. Everyone knew it was a match made in hell. To complicate matters, they had a child together at the age of eighteen. On this particular day, Butchie was on the front porch and wanted to see his baby boy. Pounding on the door and screaming was Butchie's normal routine when he wanted to visit. Due to previous incidents where the police had been called, the parents of our neighborhood princess had learned not to allow him in the house. After fifteen minutes of frustration, Butchie just kicked in the front glass and wrenched the baby away from its mother. Now, mind you, a crowd had gathered and I was in it. Local entertainment like this was ever present on the streets in my neighborhood, and we never wanted to miss a thing. House fires, stabbings and overdoses were common.

Now carrying the baby like a sack of flour, Butchie headed for the park with the taunting crowd in-tow. During his run, he stopped at an alley entrance, reached into a garbage can and removed a glass pop bottle. He busted the end off against the can, and began slicing his wrist. The mob howled loudly. Some wanted him to release the baby others encouraged him to finish it. Blood began to flow. As a Detroit police car pulled up, followed by a second unit, Butchie started running, again still carrying the now-blood-soaked baby. The officers pursued as we cheered them on. Butchie quickly scaled a fence and scrambled onto the roof of a garage. This was an old turn-of-the-century garage with a chimney. Butchie now was at the peak, hiding behind the chimney while holding the officers at bay with repeated threats that he would kill the child. He attempted to cut his own throat, and blood ran down his chest. He then attempted to cut the electrical wire, which easily would have killed him and the child. He dangled his son down the chimney. The scale of the incident now was ridiculous. There were about a hundred people all screaming and yelling, and I have no idea how many police officers had responded. Several fire trucks now were at the scene, with their lights and sirens adding to the chaos. I remember how calm the officers were. One was just feet from Butchie, pleading for him to turn over the child. The officer had a flak vest on, and was using a garbage can top as a shield. He was clinging to the ridge of the roof, while he attempted to convince Butchie to give up the baby. It was easy to see the life-threatening danger these officers faced, yet there was no hesitation, and no concern for their own safety. It was quite heroic. They rescued the baby and talked Butchie down. I now was starting to get it. Same uniforms, different cops. Not different cops, different people. They weren't all jackasses.

TURN YOUR HEAD AND COUGH

So I had mixed emotions as I walked through the recruiting office doors for the Detroit Police department. I filled out the application and waited.

The first step in the process was a civil service test. I received a notification informing me of the time and location. Business attire was required, and no applicant would be admitted after 8:15 a.m. Okay, rules were good. I liked order. I chose dress pants, a shirt, tie and sport coat for my first big step. I arrived forty minutes early. The test would be administered in a large conference room, and I took a seat up front. What I saw over the next two hours amazed me. Applicants were showing up in all kinds of attire. A guy sat next to me in biker's shorts, a tank top and hair past his shoulders. Females with plunging necklines and all kinds of bizarre outfits filtered in. I guess the rules didn't apply to everyone. As I was early, I started getting anxious. Our jump off time was 8:15 a.m., and I glanced to the rear of the room to see if they were going to close the doors. Much to my surprise, they didn't. I just watched the clock as it reached 8:30, then 8:45, and then 9. They finally shut the doors, but continued to allow people in as they began to explain the test. I wondered to myself if this is an example of things to come. I passed the written exam and was next scheduled for the required physical agility test. This was a pass or fail deal. No pass, no police.

Now this was one of the most ridiculous things I had ever seen. We were given a reference sheet with certain numbers on it. This test consisted of pushups; a seventy-pound bag carry (you picked it up and ran forty feet with it and ran back); a 160-pound body drag; a grip test; half-mile shuttle run; and obstacle course (where you crawled about thirty feet through a tunnel, then jumped an eight-foot wall, ran around some pylons, re-jumped the wall and crawled back through the tunnel).

The numbers on the reference sheet would help you maintain a passing score. The key was you had to be physically capable. I was in shape and young at the time of the test, but I still was anxious.

Confidence couldn't overcome a twisted ankle if I screwed up on the course. This was it, and I wanted the job security the department was going to provide. At each station, the instructor would tell you what score you should try to achieve on each exercise. This would coincide with the numbers on your reference sheet. What I didn't know going in was that female applicants had a different set of standards to meet. All their times were significantly less then the men. Pushups were one of the more glaring differences. You would have to do as many pushups as you could in a minute. The max was sixty for the men, and it was ten for the women. Wow, I thought to myself, I knew this was going to be a physical job, so what gives? I saw a woman who did four and qualified. I did forty-eight. I thought, what if you had a weak guy who was smart as a whip but could only do four pushups? I guess he wouldn't make it. You were going to need physical strength on this job, and you would need it often. That much I was sure of. I passed with an above-average score, and was proud of it.

Everything was looking good, and my hopes began to rise. The next step was the medical exam, which turned out to be a horrible experience. I was in shape at six feet tall and 240 pounds. I was playing basketball three days a week, and still working out. My only concern was that I had major knee surgery after tearing two ligaments when I was in high school. I was worried they would question my knee's stability. The first thing they did was weigh me. I flunked. They showed me the height/weight chart, and I was fifty pounds over weight. Mind you, I just breezed through the agility test, but that chart was the medical gospel. If I didn't lose weight, there'd be no job. I was off to a bad start. Okay, I can overcome that. I'll starve myself. The next thing was the knee exam. If you ever had your knee examined, it is pretty extensive. There are lots of twisting, turning, stability and motion tests. I really couldn't hide anything as I have a nine-inch scar on the inside of my left knee. The doctor looked at me, and asked me to stand up. He told me to do a deep knee bend. I complied, and he asked for another. I banged another one out, and he told me my knee was fine. So much for worrying. Next on the list was blood work. This scarred me for the next twenty years. The technician spoke very little English, and poked me six times. Using a needle, she dug around as if she was looking for lost gold. I almost passed out, and finally stopped her. It was either the pissed off look, or the death color on my face that got me a new technician. The new girl got it on the first poke. I was needle jumpy for years after that. After taking some X-rays, they sent me on my way.

I went home with purpose. No beer, no pizza and no Mexican food at 3 a.m. I dropped eighteen pounds in three weeks. The medical section was so impressed that they listed my weight at 205 pounds and passed me.

So, I, Robert Haig, the son and brother of firefighters and a Delray troublemaker, was breaking tradition. I was going to get my chance to be the "Real Police."

THAT FIRST DAY

I was flush with pride as I entered though those doors on my first day at the police academy. I was one of the chosen few. The big plus was that I was on the payroll. I was going to get paid for going to police school. I admit that I was a bit shocked at the appearance of the place. It was run-down with flaking paint and desperately needed a thorough cleaning. The first priority for me, though, was parking. It was on the street. Being a life-long city resident, I knew this was a risk. Any local crack head would know I would be in the building for eight hours. It wouldn't take much to get into my Jeep.

I couldn't decide if I was thinking as a police officer or as a Detroit resident. I wondered who would have the audacity to break into a car so close to the academy. I would soon find out that B&E Auto was one of the first crimes I would need to learn about. Someone from the academy had their car broken into about every three weeks.

I had butterflies, but was confident. I felt I was more than street tough because I grew up in Southwest Detroit. You had to fight for what was yours in my neighborhood, and I had no problems stepping up. I also was aware that someone would put a licking on you, no matter how tough you were. It gave me good assessment traits even as a kid. I knew how to pick and choose my battles, and I knew when to run. My mouth was part of my arsenal, and many times, roaring saved the day. I eventually would learn how critical talking could be for a cop in a tight situation. I thought maybe I already had acquired some of the tools necessary to become a police officer.

Sitting in the classroom, I scanned my fellow student police officers. They were diverse some were black, others white, some were male, others were female, and we ranged from big and small. One guy looked like a kid. He was only eighteen. Hell, he couldn't even buy ammo. I did a whole bunch of thinking my first day, and believed eighteen was a big mistake. What kind of experience could this kid be bringing to the job? His high school graduation couldn't have been more than a month ago. Two white guys sitting in the front of the room struck me as funny, as they had hair down to their shoulders. We had been given specific instructions regarding grooming. Everyone had their hair cut military style. Girls cut short and boys cut shorter still. I thought to myself, "What clowns." It reminded me of the civil service test, and how people showed up in different getups and wild hair. Boy, were they going to get into trouble.

Class 86-Sam was our unit designation, and we were assigned to TAC Sergeant Green and TAC Officer Moss. We ended up calling Sergeant Green Cabbage Patch, because she was tiny and looked like a Cabbage Patch doll. They entered the room, and we learned this whole thing was going to be a paramilitary operation, which I liked. "Attention" was the command, and we all rose in unison.

Our sergeant was almost funny looking. At about five feet tall, she was short and wore a ton of ribbons. She had steely blue eyes and the stature of Curly from the three stooges. She tried to act tough, but real tough can recognize tough, and she wasn't tough. I thought she must get her ass beat quite a bit. TAC Officer Moss struck me as the real deal. Tall and lean, he spoke quietly but with authority. You hear about guys from Vietnam with the thousand-yard stare. That was him, or as I would learn on this job, my impression of him.

We reviewed what was expected of us and what would be covered during our four-month training period, and it included physical training, law and ordinances, driving, weapons, etc. It sounded like I was going to like it, and I couldn't wait to get to the range. Everyone felt the same way. When was I going to get my gun? Carrying that gun seemed like the coolest part of being a cop. We did not yet realize the danger and responsibility that privilege encompassed.

We started with a session where we all introduced ourselves and talked about why we joined and what we expected. Everyone nervously stumbled through it. It's funny on this first day how you could tell who was going to be the police and who wasn't. I don't mean just graduating, I mean doing the job. We would elect a class president, and picked a guy with a college degree and a great speaking voice. Two weeks later, we wanted to impeach him. Remember that first impression thing? We already were learning.

We were told what uniforms we would be wearing at the academy. Black tie, khaki shirt, khaki pants all pressed and creased with polished black shoes. Corframs were recommended for those who couldn't polish their shoes because they had that patent leather finish to them. I was in this bunch and bought a pair. Actually, I could polish shoes, but I was too lazy to do it.

All the classroom material would be handouts, so we didn't have to lug a bunch of books. We would have to maintain a certain grade point percentage to graduate. It didn't sound too tough and here was the big plus: If you went through the whole program and flunked, it was okay. They allowed you to recycle and you could start over. You would get paid to go through the four-month training session again. Now, I really started thinking. First, why would they allow this? Second, why would they tell you this? You really wouldn't be motivated knowing you had a safety net. You could fail and get paid. My second thought really made me wonder what I'd do if I got stuck working with a tiny woman who did six pushups and was recycled. At this point, I realized the danger of this job could come from within. It was a heck of a feeling to have on your first day. What kind of team was I joining?

So they give us a couple of days to get our uniforms together, but I make sure I am wearing mine the next day. I felt great. Only one other person has their uniform on. I was smiling and feeling like I had done something special. We were standing at attention in formation, when TAC Officer Moss comes over to me. I thought he was going to praise me because I was looking squared away. Lines and creases of my uniform were pressed and tight. My Corframs were gleaming. He was very loud and had his face close to mine. I could feel his spittle spray my face as he chewed me out. He gave me the business about if I was going to wear the uniform, wear it right. Apparently, I forgot to button the button on my right rear pocket. That never would happen again. Maybe this paramilitary discipline thing would weed out the incompetent. Either way, this was going to be quite the experience.

SEPARATING THE WEAK FROM THE STRONG

We soon fell into a normal routine. We attended class and participated in physical training. The paper work was easy and I was in shape, so the PT was just a pain in the ass. Some people were unprepared and struggled.

I was amazed at people who flunked tests. They seemed so simple. You were given all the needed materials — it was just a matter of studying a little bit. Heck if you paid attention in class, even the studying wasn't necessary. I know the guy next to me couldn't spell worth a lick. We had regular spelling tests and he would get fifteen wrong. How in the hell did he get hired? Besides the physical end of the job, I was pretty sure there was going to be a whole bunch of writing.

PT was a different story. Training to defend yourself separated the meek from the strong. Some people didn't want to mix it up. The instructors would press them, but they wanted none of it. They sure picked the wrong line of work. I knew there would be fighting out there.

I got whacked pretty good by a female student police officer during baton training once. There were two lines facing each other. One rank armed with batons the other would pose as the bad guy. The student police officer would simulate a strike to the thigh of the suspect. I was in the bad guy line and extended my leg. On command, they were to take a huge swing to simulate the strike, but stop just short. But on the command, my girl never slowed down. You would have thought someone shot a rifle in the gym it was so loud. I was now hopping around on one leg, while being restrained by my classmates. She was one of the meek and ran.

We began growing close after a couple of days. I don't know if this was attributed to the label 86-Sam or the simple fact we were all new. There were other classes in the academy and maybe it was the competition with them. We never interacted with them, and we wanted to leave our mark — the mark of being the best. At least, that is the way I felt at the time, and I was sure there were others who felt the same.

We conducted a daily roll call and inspection every morning. Just like the military, we stood in ranks as our TAC officers walked down each row, giving us the once over. It was best that you were squared away, or you would be taking a lap around the block. This would be followed by drills.

Our TAC officer must have been an ex-military guy because he sure could march and bellow a cadence. All the classes marched every morning, and each one tried to out yell the other. In the beginning, we were like cattle on skates. I must have heard, "Your other left, idiot," a thousand times. We eventually gelled, and at the end of training, 86-Sam won the best formation class. I must admit that we were pretty slick.

But everyone made mistakes, and most of those landed you in the "Lean and Rest" position. This covered everything from talking in class to poor uniform appearance. Lean and rest was your basic push up position. You'd stay there until you were instructed to get up. Some of my class spent a whole bunch of time in that position. My other favorite penalty was to recite the police code of ethics to the fire extinguisher in the hall. It really was good when several classes had goof-ups, and you ended up with three or four guys on different floors yelling at fire extinguishers. It sounded like a birdhouse.

PRIDE, PERSEVERENCE AND TEMPERANCE

I had motivation to do well. Every test, I could hear my mom's voice along with one of the nuns from my Catholic education saying, "Bobby just doesn't apply himself." Hey, I was an honor roll student, but they were right. Girls and sports seemed to be at the top of my priority list. But those voices now helped push me. I didn't need to be the top dog in academics, but I wasn't going to let mom or the Haig name down. I finished sixth in the class, and still had fun. Pride is what they instilled in me. It would be important in this line of work.

All of us were different, but the majority of us were all striving for the same thing. It brought us closer, but we still butted heads at times.

The only time I lost my cool with my classmates was during PT. Now, I didn't mind working out, but I'd rather play hoops or lift weights. I never liked running, even during football practice (and I loved football).

I remember we were jogging through downtown Detroit in formation. One of the "runner looking guys" decided to start kicking a can, which TAC officer Green immediately went ballistic over. He added five laps and another severe ass chewing. I always felt why make things hard when you can make them easy. When we got back in the locker room, several guys still were cutting up. I told the nearest guy how I felt, but loud enough for everyone to hear. I screamed I was going to beat the fuck out of the next motherfucker I caught kicking a can. They may like running, but I don't. The locker room was quiet as we dressed for class. I had some tough guys in my class, and I'm glad I wasn't called out on that one. The roaring helped.

BULLSEYE

Training was training, but what we were all looking forward to was the range. We all just knew our first trip there was going to be awesome. Gunpowder and targets — just like on TV. I was excited but scared (I think we all were). I couldn't wait to get my very own police gun and start shooting. I knew how to handle weapons, and was very confident in my shooting abilities. I had been hunting since I was twelve, and I was pretty good at it. As I observed the firing line and targets for the first time, I realized something: I was not going to be shooting alone. I would be with thirty other people, and most of them had never even held, let alone fired, a gun. I hadn't thought about that one. I now could see the headlines: "Student police officer killed by classmate in accidental shooting."

When we first received our guns, I was a bit shocked. They came in a very small gray cardboard box. I opened it and discovered a nickel-plated

S&W .38 caliber revolver. My service weapon looked like the type used by officers during prohibition. It was pretty ancient compared to the modern firearms being carried by other agencies. I thought some type of semi-automatic would be much more effective. After all, this was Detroit. I felt the more firepower the better. But what the heck, this pistol was mine and mine alone. I did think often about its history, as it was a hand-me-down. I only could imagine what it had seen, what it had done. I cherished it.

The first trip to the firing line was not good. We had received plenty of instruction about handling and shooting the weapon. It was obvious by their posture, plenty of my classmates were afraid. This frightened me even more. With shaking hands, we all loaded our weapons in unison. We had all put on safety glasses and ear protection. The range officer instructed us to get ready. The range officer now was on a microphone, stating, "Get ready, they're coming at you." The targets turned and all hell broke loose. It wasn't the steady firing of thirty people; it sounded more like a war zone.

Some were clipping off rounds in rapid fire, and others were slow. The wood in front of the targets was being shredded with misses, and some of the targets were shot off of their stands. Trees above the targets lost leaves and branches, and smoke and debris were everywhere. After we fired six rounds, we were instructed to, "Make safe and holster." Looking down range reminded me of one of those old pirate movies. The firing was like a broadside being unleashed over and over. Branches still were falling amid the smoke, and targets were creaking as they fell over. We obviously needed work, and we would get plenty of it.

The other weapon we would be using was the Remington 870 pump shotgun. For those of you unfamiliar with weapons, this is a shoulder-mounted long gun. It shoots a large round, and is very loud. It is quite intimidating just to watch someone else fire it, let alone fire it yourself. Most everyone was terrified of it the first time around, and most officers never overcame that fear. It was a shame, because it was a very good weapon. It didn't happen in our class, but I heard some student police officers fired it and it flew out of their hands. Believe it or not, many officers would get medical deferments so they wouldn't have to fire the shotgun. Everyone knew these deferments were bullshit, but the department allowed it. How about if you are not capable of firing a department weapon, you get fired?

I did get a chuckle out of this gun. I really thought the pistol aftermath was something. Brother, it paled in comparison to the shotgun. It really looked like Lord Nelson had unleashed the full fury of the British navy on those targets. Smoke didn't clear for twenty minutes.

The range was part of state-required qualification to become a police officer, and everyone would have to obtain a passing score. Eventually, everyone qualified (some barely after repeated efforts). You sure wouldn't want to be in a firefight with some of them. I ended up in a shoot-off for the best marksman and came in third. I was pretty mad, as I shot horribly that day. Maybe it was the pressure. And it made me think: Would I crack when the chips were down? I didn't want to be just a target shooter. I was nervous during the shoot-off, and no one was shooting back.

After we started working at the range, I began having police dreams. I was chasing bad guys, and they would shoot at me. I would return fire, but my bullets would come out of the gun very slow or not at all. Some of my classmates had the same type of dreams. Very haunting. I had these on and off for a couple of years. To my relief, they eventually stopped.

Despite all the shaky shooters, the range always was fun. The two big drawbacks were the mosquitoes and floods. The range was at Rouge Park, dug into a deep hole near the Rouge River. Any significant amount of rain would flood the range. I'm not talking a couple of inches; I'm talking as high as six feet. Something is not right when you have a rowboat near the firing line.

So, any significant rainfall would cause the range to shut down. It made me wonder who picked that spot. Later in my career, they updated and remodeled the classrooms that were fifty feet above the shooting range. The firing line still was in the swamp hole. I wondered, why put money into it — why not move?

HOLD YOUR BREATH

One of my favorite incidents at the range was the day we were gassed. The range staff was going to deploy the department-issued tear gas to educate us on the effects it had on suspects and responding officers. Our entire class was instructed to all lock arms in a circle. They now would deploy a canister of gas into the middle of 86-Sam. We were informed that if anyone broke ranks, we would do it over and over until we stayed together. We locked up and braced ourselves. We could hear the pin being pulled and the hiss of the can as it was released. It no sooner hit the ground when Student Police Officer Kit broke ranks, screaming. He ran about ten yards and scaled a six-foot fence. Holy shit, I thought, he must have been gassed before. I could hear his screams trailing off as he put distance between himself and the deployment area.

The rest of us held tight and it was pretty bad. There was lots of burning, tearing and snot. We all wanted to kill Kit, but we lucked out and did not have to do it again. Kit eventually was recycled (flunked the first time through the academy), passed the second time, but eventually was fired.

With the issuing of our weapon, I naturally thought we would get a ballistic vest. When I asked about one, I got a whole bunch of chuckles. Oh, you could buy one and wear it, but the city didn't provide one. Our pay wasn't much, and most of us couldn't afford one. This bothered me, as I asked myself, wouldn't any company want to protect their investment, let alone a life? I had been on the job for about five or six years before the city started providing vests. Even at this young age, I was beginning to learn about the department.

THE NEW REALITY

The academy flowed pretty well for most of us. No one dropped out, although TAC Officer Moss always was on Student Police Officer Kit. He walked in the room one day looked right at Kit, stated, "I hate you," and then walked out. We all had a good laugh, except Kit.

A priority was staying out of trouble when off duty. Any type of criminal offense or arrest would get you the boot, and believe me, that was a real risk for some. Most of us were young and wild. It took a bit of that for this type of job. But it was about choices, choices and more choices. We would make these for the rest of careers, and we knew it. In the beginning, most of us always would make the right ones.

I was living the single life, and had bought a two-thousand-dollar house with my fireman brother. Yes, that dollar figure is correct. The top-of-the-line house in our neighborhood wouldn't have cost more than ten thousand dollars. The combination of the railway yards, overhead expressway and stench from Wayne Soap had a direct impact on the market prices. It was on the southwest side and came with a truck and a dog. We fixed the truck and sold it, but kept the dog. We also fixed up the house, and the highlight was a bar with Christmas lights in the front room. The first party I had for 86-Sam was a bring-your-own-chair party, as we only had one chair. I learned my classmates could drink. Lots of singing and dancing brought us closer.

Most of 86-Sam were Detroiters, which allowed us to mesh much easier. We were pretty much all ages 22 to 25. I made friends easy, and still remain friends with all of my classmates. We developed a bond, and it would be the first of many for me. We all couldn't wait to be confirmed and graduate. I felt I was part of the police team, just not a complete part.

It was at this point, I heard of the loss of one of our own. A street officer was killed in the line of duty. I must admit that it didn't make much of an impact on me. I thought, how did he allow himself to be killed? He was trained and armed. My "not-even-out-of-the-academy" mind couldn't grasp it. I now can look back and attribute those feelings to my age and certainly my inexperience. Little did I know that I would face this tragedy thirty-three more times during my career. Each one that followed would change me, not only as a person but as a police officer. I have placed them as they happened.

> **Police Officer**
> **Everett Williams, Jr.**
> **End of Watch:** Saturday, September 27, 1986
>
> Detroit Police Department Officer Williams was shot and killed while responding to a breaking and entering call at a residence. As he approached the home, he was shot by the homeowner who mistook him for burglary suspect.

DEVIL'S NIGHT

Our first police action would be at the end of our academy stay. We would be assigned out for Devil's Night. It was three days of walking a beat in the Gratiot Conner area near city airport. We were eager to get out and be the police. I must admit that we looked ridiculous. They gave us our blue hat with silver police cap shields. We also wore a blue uniform jacket, our khaki uniform with tie, and our utility belt with cuffs and nightsticks. We were given one radio per team. We all hated the khakis, and while the little bit of blue made us feel more like the police, we looked all mismatched. We also looked squeaky-clean brand-new. My partner for the three-day event was the guy who couldn't spell. Now I have the non-speller, one radio and I'm dressed like a clown. It didn't seem like a good plan.

So they release the mighty 86-Sam on the city. We spent three days walking the Gratiot corridor, with strict instructions to not wander off of Gratiot. No need to instruct us; I think we all were terrified. We were not ready to wander off into the dark. The big event for the three-day detail was when one of the beats locked up a guy stealing a bag of chips. They requested assistance over the radio and soon were surrounded by a sea of khaki. All of us had run to their aid. It is one thing that has never changed over my career. No matter if you are a worker or not, when an officer needs help, everyone goes.

POMP AND CIRCUMSTANCE

With the Devil's Night Detail behind us, we needed to start preparing for graduation, as our academy stay was winding down. It looked like everyone was going to pass, though Kit didn't. One guy need a twenty-three percent on his last test, and he got twenty-four.

A graduation party was in order, and several classmates stepped up and located a hall. I'll never forget the menu discussion. Main course choices were filet mignon and chicken. This immediately brought responses from three of my classmates. They didn't like fish and would not go if it was chosen. It took a while, but we finally got through to them on the filet-fillet fish thing.

Our party went well and the pressure was off. It was the first opportunity for us to really unwind. Both of our TAC officers showed up for the festivities. I was sitting at a table with TAC Officer Green and several of my classmates. We all brought dates, one of which was wearing a very low-cut and revealing dress. Green asked Jim what was up with his date's titties. Jim didn't know how to respond, but we all had a good laugh. It made us feel part of the Real Police Team.

Graduation day came and we all were excited. This would be our first time in full uniform. I took great care while dressing that day.

I had made it. They were going to present our badges on stage. Our families and friends along with department personnel would be in attendance. We all wore white gloves that made our blue uniforms pop. My family was there, including my dad and brother in firefighter uniforms. I was proud of myself and proud of my class.

Chief Hart gave us our badges, shook our hands and snapped a salute as we marched across the stage. The crowd thundered its applause. Maybe, just maybe, this was going to be a great choice for me. I was ready.

1ˢᵀ COMMAND - NEW CENTER

We all were anticipating assignments. Some of us wanted the busiest and most dangerous precincts. Others were honestly hoping for desk jobs. We soon discovered 86-Sam would go to the same command: Mini-station section New Center Patrol.

Mini station? That didn't sound exciting. I immediately wondered, who the heck were we going to learn from if we all went together. I knew I wasn't prepared to be the police. Yes, the academy taught me the law and everything the state required to certify me as a police officer, but working the street was going to be a whole different ballgame. We eventually found out what this unit was all about. The city was looking at the New Center area as a starting point to revitalize the city. It had the Fisher Theater, GM Headquarters, St. Regis Hotel and Henry Ford Hospital. Several blocks north of the Fisher were reconditioned homes and apartments. These were big-dollar items priced at more than 100,000 dollars. I guess Detroit needed someone to protect them. Sending rookies was a great idea because they listened and did what they were told. Rookies didn't have enough experience to be smart mouthed, so you would get a bunch of "Yes, sir" and "Yes, maam" responses.

The problem with the area was that one block north of these great homes were adult foster care residents and drug houses. It was big-money people living with no-money people, which didn't sound like a good mix to me, but I was ready to dive in. I was apprehensive, but ready.

The only thing good about our assignment was two shifts. The entire department was on a twenty-eight-day swing shift. It was twenty-eight days of days, followed by twenty-eight days of afternoons, ending with twenty-eight days of midnights. Who came up with that great idea? It would take an officer about fourteen days to get used to one shift and then you switched. Mix in court dates and you can imagine the nightmare. You get off midnights at 8 a.m., head straight to court and, on average, would be there until noon. You could be there as late as 5 p.m. How about afternoons? You're off at midnight, and would be so wound up that you might get to bed by 2 a.m. Then you're up at 7 a.m. for court. It's tough squeezing in family time. I learned it would be a juggling act, as well as a huge emotional and physical strain, for a number of years.

New Center would be days and afternoons only. We basically had one-square-mile to patrol. On average, there would be four beats in the area, and we all would be walking a beat.

The first thing we learned after a couple of weeks is to quit running to everything. If they gave a police run within our area, all the beats ran to the location. After some false alarms and bullshit runs, we learned fast to be steady and slow because there's no need to kill yourself. We would rotate with different partners, and you soon learned everything about that person. Being in the academy and working with someone were two totally different things. Sometimes, an eight-hour shift seemed like a month. You also learned who the workers were. Some people wanted to walk out of the base and hide. Others would want to go to a restaurant. The gratuities you were taught not to take were taken on a regular basis. I walked into a place one time and the girl asked, "Can I help you?" My partner responded, "What do I get free?" I walked out.

Immediately, you pleaded with the bosses to pair you up with someone who had your same work ethic. We didn't know much at this point, but we were willing to learn and wanted to be out there. The same thing worked for the non-workers. They wanted to be paired up with a slug, and if they were, it made their day that much easier. I was standing on a corner with my partner one day and the radio gave a run on an accident half a block away. It was not in my beat area, but I could see it was a minor accident. I watched the two cops who were assigned to that area, walk out of the alley peek around the corner and walk the other way. These were brand new officers walking away from a police run. We volunteered and took the accident report.

Our bosses were okay. The lieutenant seemed like an arrogant ass, but the sergeants seemed all right. Once I had some time on the job, I realized that would be the last place I would go if I were a supervisor. It was a do-nothing location. There was no action, but it was a good place to go if you wanted to study for promotion. All the supervisors moved up the promotion ladder.

The sergeants were strict on your appearance and wanted you on your beats. We were young, so we followed the rules. All this gave the public a very good impression of the police.

The first action we were willing to nibble on was parking tickets. We mastered them pretty quickly and, believe it or not, it felt like police work. I was writing tickets with my partner next to New Center One Building when I walked up to a car in a no-standing zone. As I approached the driver, I realized it was the chief of police. I snapped him a salute and he asked me if he could park near the front door. I informed him it was posted as no standing. I thought it was a good answer and was nervous talking to the head cop. He pulled off and I went about my duties. Several minutes later, I got a call over the radio to return to the base. I was met at the door by my sergeant, and all he said was, "don't forget the chief parks wherever he wants." First lesson for Officer Haig.

"MY BABIES ARE IN THE TREE"

We learned at a much slower pace compared to the rookies who went to precincts. They had groomed us for a very specific job, and we were happy with what we were doing. Walk around, be polite, and be seen. It certainly wasn't much help in gaining the experience we needed to work the streets of Detroit. So each incident was vital to our street training.

One Sunday, I was walking my beat in front of the Fisher Theatre. It was drizzling and both my partner and I were wearing our raincoats. We observed a female standing on the sidewalk, looking up into a tree. We approached her and naturally looked up into the tree too. My partner asked her in a polite voice what she was looking at. Mind you, it was a very quiet Sunday morning with no one on the street. She looked him in the eye and said, "My babies are in the tree." My partner replied, "There are no..." He didn't get the opportunity to get the rest out, when she swung a looping left at him, hitting him in the shoulder. He grabbed her and they began spinning in a circle, all fists and kicks.

I approached the circle, attempting to punch her, or pull her off of him. Realizing the moving ball of fists and kicks was whirling around much too fast to just grab her, I grabbed them both and we went down in a heap. We rolled in the mud for a moment, as we shouted our standard academy instructions, "Don't resist. Put your hands behind your back." After a minute of futile order yelling, I knelt in the middle of her back, grabbed a handful of her hair, pulled it back and said, "Bitch, get your hands behind your back." It worked and she was cuffed. I had to go a little bit ghetto, but it worked. I looked at my partner who was all in tatters with a couple of scratches. He was complaining I had thrown them down so hard that I had hurt his shoulder. Georgia Ann Spiller was on the ground calling me a "Mother-Fucking-Titty-Squeezing-Brewster-Project Nigger." I was getting a preview of what my job was going to be all about.

We requested a scout car for transport and two senior officers showed up. They looked us up and down and didn't ask a single question. They pointed to the rear and we piled in the squad car. They flipped on the lights and sirens and did 90 to the hospital. When they screeched to a halt, they hollered "OUT." We scrambled out quickly, towing Georgia with us. No delay by them, they screeched off. They had dropped us off at the Crisis Center, where we learned how to do our first commitment into the facility. Welcome to nut central.

We were inexperienced and considered the step-children of the precinct. Patrol officers didn't like us because we were not attached to the radio. Meaning, we did not get police run after police run. In their eyes, we had a cushy job. If we brought an arrest into the precinct, the doorman would make us wait to process our prisoner. If it was a felony arrest, the clerk would make us type out our print cards. The desk boss always gave us a hard time with a lockup. This hassle always amazed me because I thought we were on the same team. We were disliked because we were creating work for those manning the precinct. I thought that is what the city had hired us to do. Make it safe. We were young, so it didn't matter to us, we would bring them all the arrests we could muster up. Some officers were helpful, but the majority always gave us the evil eye when we came in. So not only did we have to deal with the criminal element, but we constantly fought our own department.

HOW TO COVER YOUR CHEST WITH RIBBONS

We eventually had two scout cars assigned to our unit. This gave us a bit more freedom and allowed us to learn at a quicker pace. Mind you, they always wanted us to stay in the New Center area, but we pushed the boundaries and strayed outside our borders whenever we got the chance. We still had beats walking, but the cars made us a bit more self-sufficient. We could transport our own arrests, and this seemed to ease the precinct tension some.

It was about this time I got my first lesson in how to earn ribbons (Remember, Cabbage Patch had a bunch of them). It happened on the day one of our beats made an arrest. A suspect had thrown a rock through the front window of a shoe store. We had no idea if he was going to steal anything or not. The bad guy ran and they caught him. They received a meritorious write-up and a ribbon to display on their uniform. I was new, but really didn't think that a ribbon was warranted. They caught a guy for throwing a rock. If that was it, I knew I was going to cover my chest with ribbons, just like Cabbage Patch.

SAVED BY THE SAFETY

There were several incidents at this command that would have an impact on my career. The first was a simple traffic stop, which always is one of the most dangerous actions. Two officers from our command approached the car. The driver ran and one officer pursued him. The next thing we knew, the officer was screaming for help on the radio. I was in the area and I found him about a block away in the alley. The bad guy was on top of him, and had disarmed the officer. He was straddling the officer, holding the muzzle of the gun to the officer's chest. He was repeatedly squeezing the trigger, but the weapon would not fire. He didn't know how to get the safety off. While the officer had purchased his own vest, a .45 caliber pistol at that range would have blown right through it.

This incident gave me my first, "Oh shit, this job is dangerous," moment.

POLITICAL SCIENCE 101

I also had my first taste of politics while at this command. I was walking a beat when we received an accident run for Cass and Baltimore. It was winter and very cold. We responded to the scene, finding a minor accident, but both cars were disabled. There was an eighteen-year-old white female standing around crying. She was driving a Ford Escort.

The second party was a well-dressed black male in his sixties. He was driving a BMW. I suggested we all step inside a building because of the weather, and they could both warm up, while I got their information. I spoke with the male and my partner talked to the female. Once we were done, I compared notes with my partner. While we were talking, a scout car pulled up. Without saying anything, the male exited the building, got in the scout car and they drove off.

The first thing I said to my partner is, "Apparently he knows someone." The following day, I was asked to report to an inspector's office downtown. Now, this is a pretty big deal, and I had no idea what it was about. Maybe I was going to receive a ribbon. Upon entering the inspector's office, he began questioning me about the accident. The male apparently felt he was not treated equally and had made a complaint. It was obvious he knew someone or I wouldn't be in the inspector's office. I was steamed, as I had treated him very professionally — the same way I would have treated anyone else. I guess because he knew someone, he wanted extra special treatment.

The funny thing was, two weeks later, I received a letter from the parents of the girl thanking me and my partner for how well their daughter was treated (which was the exact same way we had treated the male).

HOW THE STREETS AFFECT EMOTIONS

Another street incident that affected me was a chase involving a carjacker. It was around 4 a.m. when we spotted a Toyota Camry driving south on Third Street at a high rate of speed. We attempted to stop it and it took off. We notified dispatch that we were in pursuit, and gave a description of the vehicle. This was in the old days when they didn't call off chases. The pursuit bent back and forth through the neighborhood, and he attempted to hide the vehicle several times. He would cut the lights and pull back in someone's driveway. This cat-and-mouse game continued for some time.

He eventually drove the car onto the sidewalk attempting to make it to Woodward. As he came off the curb, he blew all four tires. He jumped from the vehicle while it still was rolling and ran. He entered an alleyway and my partner began chasing him on foot. I drove a half block and entered the same alley from the east. What I saw terrified me.

The suspect, who was about 6'2" and weighed 240 pounds, was on top of my partner assaulting him. There was no light except the scout car headlights. I had no idea if my partner was dead or alive, as the suspect completely covered his body. I leapt from the car and jumped on the suspect. I began punching him in the head and back with all my strength. I had no idea what I was saying but he gave up. I was in a rage.

I cuffed him, and began checking my partner. He was bruised but unhurt. I picked up the suspect and, as rough as possible, put him in the scout car screaming the whole time. I returned to my partner who had now taken his shirt and vest off. He had thrown up.

I went back to the scout car pulled open the door and began screaming profanities. I wanted to drag the suspect out and beat him. I immediately caught myself, wondering what I was thinking. I knew these types of incidents were part of my job, and I would have to control my emotions. I was okay, but more important, so was my partner. My partner told me I was punching the suspect so hard, it was hurting him. This bad guy had carjacked the vehicle twenty minutes earlier.

I was learning about the stress of the streets and how they affect a police officer's emotions and actions.

THE FIRST "LUCK" LESSON

Another incident that shook me up was a simple investigation. It looked like a guy was selling dope on the corner. We stopped to check him out, and he took off running. My partner pursued on foot, chasing him into a house. I pulled up in the scout car, and the woman who owned the home granted us permission to search the house. We cleared the first two floors, and several other units arrived to help. The only place left to look was the basement.

There was a stairway leading down, but the first set of stairs was gone. We had to jump the six-foot gap. My partner, myself and two other officers headed down. No one else wanted to go because it looked too dangerous. I think they were concerned that they could jump down but not get back up. There were no light switches, so we would be searching by flashlight only. We fanned out and began checking the few rooms we found. The furnace was located in the middle, so we had a limited view of the entire basement.

After several minutes of searching, one of the officers began yelling, "Let me see your hands." I ran around the furnace to see him kneeling on a guy's back, who was face down on the floor. Right in front of him was a Thompson submachine gun with a drum magazine. He was hiding under a mattress, positioned in the doorway of a small room, and had a clear field of fire. The weapon was pointed right at the bottom of the stairway. He could have slaughtered all of us. My adrenaline was roaring at this point, and we arrested him and hoisted him out of the basement. Once we were back in the car, I got a chill. It only lasted a couple of seconds, but I realized how lucky we had been. Luck would play a big part in police work. This was my first "Luck" lesson. I was learning and learning fast.

STREET SMART VS. CRIMINAL SMART

We did have some good days at the New Center. It wasn't all doom and gloom. The Detroit Police Department used to hold a field day at

Tiger Stadium. We were volunteered to represent our command. There would be a platoon inspection by a marine major and our formation would be marching and given a score. I took pride in being chosen for the detail, and because the best marching class in the academy still was together, we won hands down. I often wondered if our commander bragged about us.

Our education continued on a daily basis. You get tested quite a bit as a new officer. In the street, it is called, "getting played." I thought I was street smart, but I wasn't a criminal. The first time I stopped a person with a plastic cap gun, I didn't know what to think. I quickly learned he was a hold-up guy. You don't get a carrying a concealed weapons charge for a toy gun. In the heat of the moment or in the dark, it looks like the real thing. There is a reason why they put a red tip on them. We weren't taught these things in the academy and with each new incident you had to log them into your street file.

I also soon learned how to recognize the walking nut cases. My first week, I had a guy run up to me, yelling, "they killed him, they killed him."

I tried to calm him down, pulling out my notebook as I was going to solve my first murder. Things were going good until I asked the question, "When did this happen?"

He told me 1941 — right around the start of World War II. I'd experience many similar incidents throughout my police career.

Police Officer Freddie Lee Jackson
Detroit Police Department, Michigan
End of Watch: Monday, October 6, 1986

Officer Freddie Jackson was shot and killed while working a plainclothes detail in an area that had been experiencing a high level of automobile burglaries. He and his partner had observed three men tampering with a car. As they approached the men, they all fled the scene. The two officers began examining the car for damage when a man stepped out of a building with a shotgun and opened fire, striking Officer Jackson in the chest. The man was the vehicle's owner and thought the two officers were breaking into it. He was convicted of involuntary manslaughter in connection with Officer Jackson's murder.

Officer Jackson had served with the Detroit Police Department for thirteen years. He is survived by his wife and four children.

"WHERE IS THE KNIFE?"

My first trip to court also was a learning experience. I had arrested a person for a knife ordinance violation. I received a subpoena in the department mail. Court really wasn't covered in the academy, so I asked one of my sergeants where was I supposed to go. He directed me to 36th District court located downtown on Madison Street. I got myself all polished up and off to court I went. Upon my arrival, I had no idea where to go, and just followed the other officers. They handed their subpoenas to a sergeant who stamped them. I did the same. They seemed to be looking at some courtroom sheets, and I again did the same, finding my defendant's name and courtroom number. So far, so good. I sat in the courtroom and watched the proceedings, trying to learn as much as I could. Our prosecutor asked if I was prepared, and I told him I was. I was feeling nervous but confidant.

They called my case and I walked to my position and was sworn in. The prosecutor asked me several questions and I felt I nailed them. I'm sure the defense attorney recognized me as new guy, and asked the simple question, "Where is the knife?"

I was puzzled, and said I didn't know. That was a really good question. He asked it again, and I replied with a slower version of "I don't know."

He moved for the case to be dismissed, the judge concurred and smacked his gavel down with a loud a bang. I stood there dumfounded for a few seconds then I shuffled off. I felt like someone had pulled my pants down. I soon learned that we are responsible for our own evidence in misdemeanor cases. I had no idea, and just thought the evidence appeared in court when your case was called. Rest assured the first lesson I taught when I became a training officer covered this procedure.

THE NUMBERS GAME

We also had to learn about the police department's numbers game. Mind you, we did not have a quota for tickets but you had better write some. The bosses tried to keep the workers paired up together. That could be both good and bad. Good workers, good numbers. Bad workers, bad numbers. They also decided to post statistics for the month, which allowed officers to see what their co-workers were doing. Supervision also assigned a point value to any type of work the crews accomplished. Tickets were worth a point, parking violations were only a half point, misdemeanor arrests counted three points and felonies were seven. This created some friendly competition, but it also caused some problems.

Two female officers wanted to be at the top of the list, so they would write up to 130 tickets a month. The average for the unit per officer was about ten. My partner and I would keep the ladies out of the top spot by averaging twenty felony lockups per month. They didn't like that one bit. They got their revenge and embarrassed the crap out of me one day. They didn't know they were doing it, but that didn't ease my pain in the least. I was in court, waiting on the traffic docket. There was a line of people waiting to fight the female team's tickets. There always was. The first person up gave the following testimony: A person would have to be crazy to run that stop sign near the New Center. Everyone and, I mean everyone, who works at New Center knows those two officers hide behind that dirt mound every morning. No one comes to a complete stop at that sign, as it is positioned on a curve. Apparently, they write tickets until they get tired because they never are hiding later in the day. The judge asked for a show of hands to show who was there for tickets written by those two officers for that specific stop sign. Twenty people raised their hands. He told them all of their cases were dismissed, and they were free to go. Like I said before, people see uniforms, not individual officers. I now was the guy behind the dirt mound, whether I liked it or not. It was the revenge of the ticket writers.

AN EMBARRASSING RIDE-A-LONG

Black and white always has been an issue with the department. No one wants to talk about it, but it is there. I experienced it with my application and tests for the fire department. I will work with anyone as long as they work. I was called into the supervisor's office one day, and was told I would not be working with my regular partner. I was going to be working with John Jemiss, a black officer. The reason given was that we would have a Detroit Free Press reporter riding with us on our patrol. They were doing a story on black and white officers working together. Now, mind you, this officer was not my cup of tea. He worked harder at avoiding work then he did at working. I thought, "what a bunch of crap." My supervisor knew this, but he paired us up anyway. So we make introductions and get ready to roll. The reporter has a video camera and he had just returned from Sri Lanka. He had once won a Pulitzer Prize for a story he did. He struck me as a pretty smart guy. We roll off the ramp and my new partner says, "I got to get my three."

"Three what?" I ask.

He says "tickets," because he likes to get them out of the way. Remember we previously talked about tickets and quotas? If the department didn't have a quota, we sure did now. Our Pulitzer Prize winner wasn't stupid. My partner writes a violation for a broken taillight, another for a failure to signal, and the last one is a doozey. He cites a dump truck for parking in a construction zone.

On this third ticket, the reporter leans forward and asks if we ever give anyone a break. Notice, he said "we." How do I explain to him that it is not me but my temporary partner writing tickets? Now, not only am I the officer behind the dirt mound, but also the dump truck in the construction zone guy. I try and salvage the morning and make a couple of arrests. We locked up a prostitute and scored a misdemeanor traffic violation. Before I knew it, the day was over. Thank goodness.

Several weeks later, a three-page spread appeared in the Free Press with photos (several good ones, I might add). The article went on and on about the working relationship and how the department had changed. Could you imagine if I told my side of the story?

ONE THAT MARKS YOUR SOUL

Our patrol area was soon expanded to the entire 13th Precinct. We now began learning at an accelerated pace. I saw my first tortured infant and it left a mark on my soul. The little kid couldn't have been more than a couple of months old. It had curling iron and cigarette burns all over its body. Lying on a full sized gurney, he looked so small. Tubes and monitoring leads crossed his body, and his breathing was shallow as I watched his tiny chest rise and fall. It was obvious he was fighting for his life. He was in critical condition when I left the hospital.

All this pain was suffered at the hands of his parents who were supposed to protect and love him. Who does that kind of thing to their child? I knew to leave this type of thing at work, but it was impossible. I was starting to understand the emotional end of police work.

THE GRAY AREA

All officers have their own methods and tactics. Some of it is learned, and some of it isn't. When you are new, everything is by the book. With experience comes that grey area. One day, we got a run to Fisher Service Drive and Cass Avenue. A man was attempting to jump off the overpass. When my partner and I arrived, we found a man hanging from the top rail, threatening to jump. We pleaded with him not to end it all. We told him that life still was worth living. We didn't want to approach him for fear he would plummet to his death.

Seconds later, the booster car from the Thirteenth Precinct comes screeching in. The car almost hits the rail the guy was dangling from.

The booster car is like the big four I described earlier. The officers jump out, grab him and turn him upside down. They are holding him by his legs, dangling him high over the freeway. The man is desperately pleading with them to not let go. He now agrees with us, and starts screaming that life is worth living. They held him in that position for several seconds, pulled him back over the rail, and dumped him on the sidewalk. He was left whimpering in a fetal position as they screeched off.

Stunned, I had my radio in my hand and really didn't know what to do. I conferred with my partner and we determined no one was hurt, and the best course of action was to just leave.

Apparently, the guys from Thirteen knew how to handle this guy's act. I concluded no report was required. Later, I learned this guy had been threatening to jump for years.

UNHAPPY DRIVERS

While at this command I also received my first citizen's complaint and found what would be a common attitude among a minority of people. No matter how well you handled their situation, they felt they were mistreated or disrespected. A woman had double-parked her vehicle on West Grand Boulevard in front of a liquor store. She was blocking traffic on a busy street and her vehicle narrowed the road down to one lane.

I could see there was available parking a mere forty feet away, so it wasn't necessary to double park. Not wanting to give someone a civil infraction, I began writing a parking ticket. As the woman exited the store, she began running toward her car. She was about six months pregnant, and began screaming and yelling at me. She got in my face and lectured me about her pregnancy and how I should be locking up real criminals instead of picking on her. I explained to her the hazards of blocking a moving lane of traffic and how I could have written her a civil infraction.

She stormed off, in a profanity-laced huff, and screamed back that she would see me in court. I never lost my cool, but found out at the precinct that she filed a complaint, claiming I mistreated her. This would be the thankless part of the job.

I never got much satisfaction in writing tickets. The majority of violators I stopped in Detroit didn't have a license anyway. An incident I still smile about also occurred while I was at this command. I was working alone, and stopped a female driving a station wagon. Her license plate was in the rear window and had slipped down so you could only see part of it. Displaying it in a rear window is a violation, but being from Detroit, I understood why it was there. Criminals would steal your plate if it was posted on the outside of the car, or they would take a pair of tin snips and cut the yearly sticker off. This could be sold in front of any local party store for five bucks. As I approached her vehicle, I got the, "Why the hell did you stop me?" routine. Mind you, I was just going to tell her to pull the plate up where it would be visible. When I attempted to tell her, she began lecturing me. She knew what the law was and she repeatedly said that I must be a new cop. After several minutes of listening to her, I gave up.

Figuring I would get my point across with a ticket, I returned to my car and wrote the appropriate ordinance violation. When I returned to her car, she was madder than a wet hen. I told her it was against the law to have the plate in the rear window, and the plate must be affixed to the rear bumper or trunk lid. Now she really knew I was wrong and she knew all about the law. She informed me she couldn't do that because she didn't have a rear bumper. Now, silly me, I attempted to tell her that too was a violation. She was having none of it, and continued to tell me all about the law. I did not utter another word, but walked back to my car and wrote her up for no bumper.

When I approached her window, I cut her off before she could say anything. I handed her the second ticket and told her if she wanted to continue to quote me the law, I would continue to writer her tickets. She sped off, hollering, "I will see you in court." I could hardly wait to see her interact with a judge, but she never showed up in court.

Was I a smartass? A little bit. But she deserved it.

FAULTY PERCEPTION

Everyone's perception of a police officer is different. Mine was filled with old TV clichés. My idea of a cop was a person who was upstanding, honest, trustworthy, faithful and pure of heart. There is a code of ethics for police officers and I held it in high regard. I soon learned everyone didn't think the same as me. One of the guys, assigned to our unit was arrested for sexually assaulting his young daughter. He eventually was fired from the job. That will blow your perception of the police. Add that to the dump-truck, hide-behind-the-dirt-mound label.

We had an incident where we chased some bad guys who had stolen an EMS truck. When we caught them, one of the officers from an assisting unit jumped out and beat the suspect with a flashlight. It split his head open. The officer tried to blame the assault on us. The majority of the time rookies learned about this type of officer and their behavior is the hard way. It was a tough lesson for us, but a subject that was never touched in the academy.

Intelligent, controlled conduct should apply to every police officer. You are walking around with a loaded handgun and have the option of using deadly force. The opportunity to use this force is waiting for you just around the next corner. You need to be able to make sound and just decisions, not only to protect yourself but also others. Knowledge gained through street work is critical.

A good example of lack of knowledge about how to manage a dangerous situation came on a summer day in the late 80s. It was an incident where we had responded to barricaded gunmen. I was corporal for the day, and was assigned to drive my sergeant. We pulled up to the location and found several Wayne County Sheriff's deputies standing in the middle of the street about five houses from the target residence. When we asked to be briefed, they explained a court officer had responded to the location to evict the resident. The suspect had answered the door, and was informed of the eviction. He agreed to comply with the order and asked the officer if he could get something from the front room. The suspect returned to the door with a loaded M-1 Garand rifle. The court officer ran for his life.

After hearing all this, my first suggestion to everyone was to move off the street and get out of the line of fire. I couldn't believe they were standing there in clear view of the house. The guy with the rifle had an open shot and was only fifty yards down the street. We took cover and reported our situation to our dispatcher.

At this point, I decided to play scout and crossed the street. This block had no alleys, so I had to jump a number of fences to position myself in the yard directly across from the suspect's house. I was almost there and would have to cross one more driveway. Knowing the suspect might be able to see me, I pulled my weapon and sprinted toward the last fence. My young legs allowed me to vault the fence easily. My eyes had held steadily southbound, watching the suspect's front door. I eased through the yard, concentrating on the suspect's house. I reached my destination point, which was about two-thirds into the yard, right at the corner of the house. I holstered my weapon, and uncapped the binoculars I had so carefully carried with me. I now had a perfect view of the front door of the suspect's house.

Suddenly a chill ran through my body. Something was wrong, I just didn't know what. I slowly lowered my binoculars and quickly surveyed my surroundings. I was now focused as my "Police Danger Radar" was going bonkers. I could see the ground I was standing on was bare, except for several patches of weeds. There were at least half dozen large holes, with dirt mounded around the edges. Bleach white bones were strewn about. Things began clicking as I locked on several large piles of crap. I was so fixed on the suspect's house I hadn't noticed any of this. My head quickly swiveled to the shed positioned at the back of the yard. It was elevated from the ground and underneath I could see two sets of eyes. The eyes almost appeared to be boiling red, and the distance between them, assured me whatever was under there was huge. As my brain was processing this threat, my legs already were churning as they headed toward the fence. My upper half was listening to the low guttural growl, when it decided to try and catch up to the lower half. Dodging bones, holes and poop, I could feel the beasts closing. I made a desperate leap for the fence and clipped the top as I tumbled over. My pursuers crashed into the fence, bending it. The fence sprung back, sending both dogs to the ground. I was up and running, realizing the suspect could now see me. Safely behind the next house, I took a deep breath. Looking back at the yard, made me laugh. It looked like one of those old World War I pictures of no-mans land. There were holes and debris everywhere. How had I not noticed?

The dogs now were pacing back and forth, heads hung low. It wouldn't be the last time I would see dogs smiling. Rookie lesson learned. Always check for dogs. I worked my way back across the street finding several command officers had showed up along with a SWAT team. A tense and dangerous situation had now changed three times for me. Dangerous, funny and back to dangerous again. I needed to stay focused.

They attempted to talk the suspect out, even having his brother show up to plead with him. He gave a warning that he would kill anyone who approached his house. This negotiating went on for about an hour. We were positioned eight houses down on the same side of the street. The only things we could see from our position were the large hedges in front of the house. They were six feet tall and extended all the way to the sidewalk. The hedges concealed the front of the house except for the three-foot entrance into the yard. We referred to this as a kill corridor. There was no other way to go in except through that entrance. This was the last place you would want to be.

At this time, several blacked-out vehicles pulled up to our location. Eight guys got out, including our department chief. Everything got quiet. He was a very serious looking man. He huddled with several command officers and I figured this would be over in seconds. The chief of police was here and obviously would make the proper calls to end this standoff. I had put on a flak vest at the start of this fiasco, as did everyone else. An

M1-Garand could definitely put some hurt on you.

As they were formulating their plan, a regular vehicle pulled up and someone helped a very old lady out of the car. She was standing with the other officers and I did not pay it any more attention. The next thing I knew, the chief was walking the old lady down the sidewalk. Someone told me she was the suspect's mother. The chief wasn't wearing any type of protective vest, and he and the old woman were moving at a tortoise pace. My mouth was agape as I watched him approach the front of the house. I looked at the deputy next to me and his face was identical to mine. I watched as they slowly turned up the death corridor and disappeared.

It almost seemed like a dream, and I wasn't really seeing what I was seeing. No one could be that stupid, let alone the chief of police. I was incredulous that he wanted to jeopardize his own life, but he also was stupidly putting the old lady's life on the line. After a minute, the lady began screaming and crying for help. I pulled my gun and began running toward the house. Funny thing about cops, the dedicated ones always run to danger, not away. If you saw someone with a gun, which way would you run? You sure wouldn't chase them.

Everything was in slow motion. Every step I took, I kept repeating, "This is bad. This is bad." I turned the corner of the hedges, and found the old lady on the ground screaming. The chief and the suspect were struggling with the rifle. The suspect now had three pistols stuck in his belt and two bandoliers of ammo crossing his chest. It would have been comical if wasn't so dangerous. The suspect looked like Barney Fife. The chief was a big guy, but he had his hands full. The deputy had followed me in. We were dumbfounded by what we saw, but immediately tackled the suspect and brought him under control.

He was disarmed and his mom was rescued. The chief walked off the porch entered his car, with his cronies and drove off. There was no "thank you" or even a nod of acknowledgement to the officers who had rescued him from the dangerous situation he had created.

The suspect was conveyed to the Crisis Center and I was left with all the paperwork. He had four guns, tons of ammo and dynamite. I didn't have to handle that, and I was stuck with hours of paperwork.

The next time I saw the chief was months later on the street. He told me to put my hat on.

BECOMING SEASONED

They eventually extended our patrol area from the Detroit River to

Highland Park. We now covered the Cass Corridor, which is an experience every officer on the department should have. Lawlessness is the perfect word to describe this area of Detroit. The Corridor covered three square miles near downtown. Prostitutes were everywhere. On Friday night, the working girls would stand naked in the doorways of the motels. You could buy narcotics on almost every corner. Mix in a number of homeless shelters, and you had a bowl of Satan soup.

Folding all this in, the job was becoming more exciting. I was transforming into a seasoned and experienced police officer. Oh, I had a long way to go, but my confidence was growing. Each new incident supplied me with a little bit more knowledge. As time passed by, everything became easier — paperwork, testimony in court, and most important, recognizing a crime before it happened.

My first experience in spotting a crime that was about to occur happened when I was walking a one-man beat. I was strolling through the Fisher Building and began exiting through the north doorway when I observed two "bum-looking" guys entering the building to my left. I slipped around the corner of the entranceway and began watching them through the door. They walked into a drug store located in the building. I reentered the building and positioned myself so I could look through the interior glass window of the store. What caught my attention were the suspects' behavior and their dress. They were "rubber necking," which meant they were looking all around in a suspicious manner. I watched them walk by the cashier and walk to the rear aisle of the store.

It was near lunchtime, and the store was crowded. Really crowded. I had a clear view of the suspects, as I was looking directly down the aisle they were walking in. They stopped in front of a large earring display. One of the suspects immediately pulled a black garbage bag from his coat, while the other put a 2-foot-by-2-foot earring display board in the bag. He also picked up another large basket full of earrings and dumped it in the bag.

There were customers in this same aisle, shopping, and they seemed totally oblivious to what was transpiring. The suspect placed the bag in his coat and the two walked out, passing the cashier who didn't even look up. I was a bit shocked. This was in the middle of the day in a crowded store.

Having already radioed for backup, I stopped the suspects coming out of the store. When I asked where they got all the earrings, they claimed they bought them from a store at Northland. They had no idea I saw them steal the items. My heart was racing.

I felt a rush just watching them. It was an accumulation of these types of incidents that seasoned me as a police officer. Crime didn't always happen in a secluded dark area early in the morning. It could happen anywhere at any time. I knew this wasn't a big arrest, but I had done it on my own. I was hoping to make more.

KNOW YOUR POST

A close call I had also made an indelible impression on me. We were working uniformed patrol and had gained enough experience to start doing some narcotics work. My partner had dropped me off a block from a corner that was a known dope hot spot. I went into the backyard of a nearby house, and watched the activity from a distance. If I could see a transaction, we would make an arrest.

There was some action, but it soon slowed to a crawl. Our schedule was tight, so I could not stay long. Remember that being mobile, we now were attached to the radio. After about thirty minutes, I called my partner to pick me up. We didn't travel more than a mile, when we made a traffic stop that resulted in a felony warrant lockup. We were sitting in the precinct doing paperwork, when we heard the department radio dispatch cars to a shooting incident. When the address was given, I realized it was close to the house where I had been standing in the backyard. I made a quick call, and discovered it was the house I had been posted behind.

When officers arrived, they found the house engulfed in flames. Apparently, it was the home of a high-level drug dealer. I had no idea about this fact when I had used the yard as an observation post. It was a well-maintained house and blended perfectly into the neighborhood. Responding officers discovered a body that was shot multiple times in the front doorway. The killers apparently had knocked on the door and when the victim answered the door, they shot him dead. They doused the hallway with gasoline and set the place on fire.

This was a good example of how luck will sometimes influence your survival on the job. I had no idea what type of house it was when I started my surveillance. I always would check after that. It was another lesson that only could be learned on the street. If I had posted myself in that yard only a few minutes later, I would have been involved in a very dangerous situation: I would have been only thirty feet from the front entrance when the hit men started shooting. More than likely, I would have run toward the gunfire. I would have ended up face to face with several killers armed with semi-automatic weapons and gasoline. I shudder to think how my inexperienced ass and my Detroit six-shooter would have fared. I filed that incident in the survival room of my memory.

STEP AWAY FROM THE HYDRANT CAP

Working the streets also was teaching me the horrible effects of narcotics on drug addicts. We were driving through the corridor on a bitter cold day. There were almost six inches of snow on the ground and the temperature hovered around ten degrees. On the corner of Ledyard and Cass, there was an open fire hydrant. It was blowing water twenty feet into the street. A black male, wearing only underwear, was standing near it. As we approached, I saw him lift up the hydrant cap, and attempt to place it over the jet of water blasting out into the street. He instantly was knocked off his feet and landed about ten feet from the hydrant.

He got up laughing, and told me, "I got it. I got it, officer."

He grabbed the cap again, and ended up with the same result. After he was blown into the street again, I noticed blood on his arm near track marks of drug injections and understood what had made him so confident. We called for an ambulance, and he continued to yell for another chance to replace the hydrant cap as they took him away.

OFFICER NEEDS ASSISTANCE

There also was an incident that taught me how police officers are dedicated to protecting each other. This all started with a routine traffic stop. We activated our lights and siren, and our suspect vehicle pulled into a liquor store parking lot. It was a hot summer night and the lot was alive with activity. Music was playing from a boom box and people were drinking and loitering in the area. The vehicle had four occupants, and all four suspects had started to exit the vehicle.

We placed them at the rear of the car in a leaning forward, legs spread stance. I looked into the vehicle and informed my partner that there was a handgun on the floorboard. As we started handcuffing them, the crowd in the parking lot began taunting us. There were about thirty people, a mix of different ages and all of them were drinking. We quickly loaded our four suspects into the squad car, and I recovered a total of three handguns from their vehicle. The crowd had now closed in on us. They told us we were not leaving with the prisoners. I keyed the radio asking for assistance.

There are two priority runs for police officers. One is officer needs assistance and the other is officer down or in trouble. The second one means you are taking an ass beating or are shot. The first one means you're going to just need some help. It is funny how much you can interpret from someone's voice on the radio.

Dispatch must have noticed a squeak of urgency in mine, and she asked if we needed assistance or were in trouble. I replied we needed assistance, but if someone didn't get there quick, we were definitely going to be in trouble.

The crowd was now about ten feet from us and people were surrounding the squad car. I told you earlier about roaring. I was now at full roar, yelling orders and threats, hoping it would keep them at bay long enough for the cavalry to arrive. It seemed like hours, but it was only minutes before seven cars arrived. Three were from other precincts. I already had singled out the loudest clown in the group and targeted him as the instigator. I waded through the crowd and drug him by the scruff of the neck to waiting officers. It was amazing how quiet he got. His silence did not spare him a night in jail. I thanked all the crews for risking their lives. They had come to our aid within minutes. I didn't know a single officer who responded. They risked their lives coming to possibly save ours.

This incident taught my partner and I some important things. Make the stop on your terms if possible. Do not let your suspects pull into a crowded area. Call for backup if they disregard that order. Don't be foolish and act brave thinking you can handle it just because you have a uniform on. Once I saw that first weapon, I should have walked back to my partner and started locking these guys up. I can't tell you how many times I've watched young officers hold up a gun or some dope they found, showing it to the suspects and asking, "What is this?"

That usually ignites a sudden explosion of everyone fleeing in different directions like a covey of departing quail, including any witnesses who may have been standing around. At this point, I was one of those young officers. I was scared and so was my partner.

Lieutenant Johnnie C. Shoates
Detroit Police Department, Michigan
End of Watch: Sunday, December 7, 1986

Lieutenant Shoates succumbed to a gunshot wound sustained ten years earlier when he was shot during a robbery. He was off duty, waiting in line at a fast food restaurant when a man entered and announced a robbery. Lieutenant Shoates identified himself and ordered the man to drop his gun. The man turned and opened fire, striking Lieutenant Shoates in the head. Lieutenant Shoates remained in a coma from the time of the shooting until his death.

Lieutenant Shoates is survived by his wife and three children

UNHEEDED WARNINGS

I was hearing the same thing from senior officers over and over: Leave the Detroit Police Department or you will regret it. Go before you have any time invested, they urged. The department would give you nothing and take everything. Years later, I would realize they were right. Your first few years, you know nothing and simply go with the flow. After five years, you become somewhat comfortable. I didn't know everything, but was confident enough to handle whatever came my way. These were the good years. I was young, in shape and everything was an adrenaline rush. Money was not a factor. I was married, but we had no kids and I wasn't overly concerned about the gunfire in the neighborhood where we lived. Why would I leave? My viewpoint on this issue would change just a little bit every year. In the end, I would be one of those old timers telling the young guys the same thing.

Learning on the street was a big part of an officer's career, but learning about department policy and discipline is just as important. Discovering what our union could and couldn't do also was part of the game. This was another subject not taught in the academy. I soon learned our three-year contracts always would be six. The city never would settle after three years, and we always would go to arbitration. This would drag on over three years, and once we settled, the length of the contract would actually be six years. I received retroactive pay only once in my career. We were risking our lives, wasn't that important? These were things I would have to start paying attention to.

HERE'S YOUR CUP

About this time, the department started random drug screening. I was all for it. I had nothing to hide. Procedure was, you would receive notification from your supervisor. Then you'd fill out the appropriate paperwork, and make it to the testing site within an hour. My first trip down, I was shocked to find a command officer at the site sitting at a desk. He was there to give you an opportunity to "come clean." If you told the command officer you had a cocaine, heroin or marijuana problem, they would not fire you but get you assistance with your drug addiction.

I was puzzled, believing it was some kind of prank. I thought drugs were illegal by themselves, how in the world was it OK for a Detroit Police officer to use them? Who made that decision? I immediately thought of the hiring process and the test I took, where contrary to written directions, people could be dressed any way they wanted to and it was no big deal if you were late. I thought about the academy and how you could be recycled if you flunked. Didn't this department want the very best? Now it wanted drug addicts to remain on the job.

Well, for those of us who were not addicted, you completed some paperwork and went into a bathroom to pee in a cup. You would give the cup to a technician when you finished.

Turns out, I guess the whole process worked. The department fired five officers for testing positive for cocaine. One of them was from our unit. You knew something wasn't right with the guy, because of his highs and lows. He didn't need to pee in a cup for everyone to see that.

Our union protected them, and got all of them their jobs back by citing a flawed drug-screening test. The officer from our unit returned to work. Can you imagine being assigned to a scout car with this guy?

The department soon revamped the test and the same guy tested positive for cocaine again two years later and was fired. The new test would allow a technician of your gender to watch you fill the cup, so no one could provide someone else's sample.

Several officers sued the department and it turned into a class action suit. They didn't appreciate someone watching them pee. I jumped on this bandwagon and got a small payout. It was about forty bucks. The officers who started the suit each received $5,000.

Someone eventually put their thinking cap on. They revamped it one more time. The current test is this: You change into a paper gown and slippers. Great idea, but if I wanted to supply someone else's sample, it wouldn't be very difficult. You enter the bathroom, provide your sample and return it to the technician. Now you still are in a paper gown and slippers. You have to seal your sample, placing tape over the lid. You need to sign the tape and place the sample in a plastic bag. You seal the bag and sign it. You sign several more forms, then you are allowed to dress. This whole process is horrible and done only wearing a paper gown. I always walk around with my gown untied, allowing my caboose to hang out. It makes me feel better about the whole process.

There was one incident that really sums up the system. A female officer who tested positive for cocaine was fired. She contacted the union and they fought for her job. Her claim was she didn't know it, but her boyfriend was sprinkling cocaine on his penis before she gave him a blowjob. He claimed it would heighten the experience. Do you believe she got her job back? Even if her story was the truth, what was she doing with a boyfriend who was using or had access to cocaine? The department was starting to amaze me.

THE DEPARTMENT'S NOT ALONE

I learned my department was not the only business out there that was making idiotic decisions. One day, we received a run for a shoplifter at Penke Drugs. We all hated shoplifter runs. The arrest itself belonged to the business and a security company. We basically just transported, but we were required to do a report. As busy as we were, it was the last thing you wanted to be tied up with. We arrived at the scene and were directed to the rear of the store. We entered the storage area, and I observed a security guard handcuffed to a pole. He is in full uniform, wearing his hat, and has a nightstick hanging from his belt. The first thing I do is remove his nightstick. As I told you before, I was getting some experience. Then I started asking questions. According to the manager, he witnessed the suspect/security guard remove a small can of juice from the cooler and drink it. I'm shocked and ask if that was it. He says this guy has been doing it for some time. I inform him that without documentation or video, none of the previous incidents matter.

The standard question when dealing with a shoplifter is: Did he try to leave the store without paying? It's a question we must ask. Provability is the whole thing with police work. I asked if the manager had asked him to pay for it. He told me no, but he was tired of this behavior and wanted to press charges. I informed him this was not the best course of action, and said he might want to call the security company. They may want to fire this guy. Nope, he wanted to press charges.

So we made the arrest and transported the thief, but this really was bothering me. This wasn't my norm. I could easily move onto the next case. This was their arrest, their decision. I just couldn't let it go and I called Penke corporate headquarters and told them what was going on. I felt it may be in their best interest to let this case go. They told me that they had the utmost confidence in their manager and his decision-making abilities. Yikes. Okay, I won't beat a dead horse. We completed our paperwork and went on about our business. Several weeks later, I was given a subpoena for court. When I arrived, I discovered the security guard was suing everyone except me. He was suing Penke Drugs, the security company, the manager and Mr. Penke himself for $5,000 apiece. Since there really wasn't a criminal case, it was looking good for the guard. I had an opportunity to talk to Mr. Penke, and told him my story. He seemed to have the same attitude as the other corporate guy. He would stand by his manager's decision. Well, the court got an opportunity to think about that manager's decision, and awarded the guard $20,000. All this over a 60-cent can of juice and a bad decision. It really reminded me of my department.

EVERYONE'S GOT AN ANGLE

I also was learning most people have an angle or a line of bullshit. I was working late one night, and saw the same foreign car cruising in an area known for prostitution. I told my partner if we saw the guy again we would pull him over. Sure enough, about twenty minutes later, we found him sitting in the middle of the street with his lights off. As we pulled up behind him, someone left the passenger side of the vehicle and walked between the houses. It looked like a classic drug transaction. We pulled the guy over as he tried to speed off. He claimed he was from Ann Arbor and was staying at a motel in Southfield. He said he came out to get something to eat and got lost. Of course, this was a line of crap, and he was out trying to get laid, or cop some dope. I gave him the standard riot act, and told him he was going to get robbed or shot. He assured us he would head back to his motel.

About an hour later, a unit received a shooting run, down on the edge of the Cass Corridor. We volunteered to back them up. Upon our arrival, we found the same blue Toyota Camry that our lost guy had been driving. He had been shot and had been transported by ambulance to the nearest hospital.

The scene told the story. He had been shot through the open passenger window. There was blood and chunks of flesh all over the driver side. The initial unit knew nothing more than that the victim had been shot. We told them we had warned the guy earlier and went on our way.

About two years later, two guys in suits who were carrying brief cases showed up at my base. They asked if I was officer Haig. They had a subpoena for me to appear in Lansing. I asked what it was about, and they said it was a workman's compensation case. They gave me a few details, and I learned it was about our lost boy in the blue Camry. He claimed he was working when he got shot. His stay in Southfield had been true, and he said he was at a work conference representing his company. Since his attendance was work-related, he felt he should be covered, even if he was down in Detroit looking for the dirty deed and got shot. I thought this was hilarious. I was going to be paid for court plus mileage. I was there for three days and made six hundred dollars. He lost the case.

KEEPING UP APPEARANCES

My shoes always were polished and my uniform creased. I took great pride in being professional. Knowing I always was in the public eye helped me maintain that attitude. With that came a flip side to that coin. It seemed everyone always was trying to catch you in an awkward position. A bird dropping a load of white poop on a blue uniform always was a good one.

That uniform attracted girls like you wouldn't believe. I was patrolling my one-man beat when I noticed several girls across the street. They had put their eye on me and I immediately puffed up like a Thanksgiving turkey and began strutting. I adjusted my belt, checked the volume on my radio, and pulled my hat down tight. In the middle of this exhibition, I lost track of where I was heading. I walked right into a no parking sign. Of course, the sign began bonging loudly like the bells of a cathedral. I slid off of the sign and slunk away down the sidewalk. I could hear the girls giggling, which caused me to giggle too, and it helped sooth my ruffled feathers.

Being in the public eye never was more evident than at the scene of my first critical accident. This incident easily could have cost me my job. We had just picked up several pizzas for our base and were en route back when several cars came off a side street at high speed, nearly hitting us. The first vehicle was a Mustang, the second a Mercury Marquis. The driver of the Marquis was pointing at the Mustang and yelling they just robbed him. I hit the lights and siren and picked up the radio. My partner accelerated around the corner and we could see the Mustang about a block away. He must have been doing about 70, and had smoke coming from the rear of his vehicle. I never had the opportunity to tell dispatch about the chase, as the fleeing Mustang immediately hit another car. The suspect had blown the stop sign at the first intersection. We could see both vehicles enter the picture, then nothing but smoke.

We quickly pulled up to the vehicle he struck. It had come to rest in the middle of the intersection, and its front end was almost sheared off. The impact was so violent that the oil filter was blown off the motor. The elderly lady driving was sitting calmly behind the wheel. My partner would cover her.

The Mustang was about a half a block down and must have rolled eight or nine times because it was almost flat. I ran the short distance to the vehicle. The suspect was sitting just inside the passenger side. The vehicle was on its roof, and you really couldn't tell it had been a car. The suspect was just sitting there putting his shoe back on. It was visible he was bumped and bruised and possibly suffering from a concussion. His first words to me were, "Fuck you."

We notified dispatch and requested ambulances for both parties. We also ordered a couple of tow trucks and an accident investigation car.

Another unit made it the scene to transport the suspect. EMS checked our bad guy out, and besides the bumps and bruises, he was fine. Our elderly victim didn't have a scratch on her. We then assisted the accident car with the investigation and measurements. This whole thing had taken several hours.

The location of the incident was in a fairly deserted area with a number of vacant lots and abandoned apartment buildings. We realized we still had two pizzas in our trunk and felt it would be okay if we had a bite. No one was around and daylight was disappearing quickly. We opened the trunk and started our ghetto picnic. We shared what we had with the accident investigator, and I was just starting to bite my second piece of pizza when a guy walked up to me. He asked what I was going to do with the other person. It irked me momentarily, and I asked, "What other person?" Couldn't he see I was eating?

"The other person who came out of the car," he said.

I lost all color realizing we had missed something. He pointed to the vacant lot about mid block. We ran over there and found a female who had been ejected from the Mustang. Her arms were twisted and pointing in the wrong direction. She had severe trauma to her head but was alive. She was in waist high weeds and was so far from the vehicles we never even thought of looking over there. Luckily, this man had witnessed the whole thing.

Again, this is where luck is a factor on the job. I thought I was a very professional by-the-book guy doing my job with extreme diligence. Obviously, I was not that cop on this night. I could see the headlines: "Cops enjoy pizza party while female lies dying forty yards away."

Fortunately, we got her in an EMS and she survived. The guy we arrested never even mentioned her. You can bet I completed one serious canvass of the area at my next accident scene. Lesson learned.

RUN FOR YOUR LIFE

That last incident re-enforced what I already knew. Wearing a police uniform has always been a tough row to hoe. As you are a representative of all law enforcement, I always felt it was imperative to look my very best no matter what the circumstances. Not only do you represent yourself, but also everyone else willing to put on a badge. Unfortunately for me, the uniform of the Detroit Police Department was navy blue in color, which allowed it to show every piece of lint and dirt you came into contact. No matter how much time you spent polishing and ironing for your appearance, it could be quickly ruined with the splash of a puddle, or simply rubbing up against a dusty shelf. Once this happened you immediately would be forced to go into cat mode, licking and brushing in an attempt to return to that gleaming appearance you started the shift with. Maybe it was because of the effort we went through to maintain this appearance, but for some reason, the public always enjoyed viewing an officer's misfortune when it came to those uniforms. Watch a cop, slip and fall in the mud, and I can guarantee his picture will be plastered over every media outlet available. The laughing is loud and deep, and many people will scream at the top of their lungs, to bring more "laughers" to the scene. Who wants to miss a cop looking like he just emerged from a pig waller?

So not only are we trying to catch bad guys, but we also are on constant alert to avoid these other slap stick mishaps. All cops at one time or another throughout their careers will experience one of these moments. One of my personal favorites are split police pants. There is simply no way to cover that one up, and it usually happens at an outdoor scene where you have to stand with your drawers flapping in the breeze for hours.

The most dreaded of all is bird droppings. Now when you think about it; the odds of being hit by bird crap are about the same as hitting the lottery. A load of well-placed pigeon crap on a navy blue cap or shoulder is funny no matter who you are. The worst part is it just does not cleanup easily and even if you can remove most of it, ingrained in the back of your mind is the smell. It can make for a very long day wearing a soiled cap. Although I've never been hit by our airborne friends, I have had two partners who took incoming poo. The look on their faces definitely was worth a few giggles.

Experience has always been critical to police work, so every incident holds a valuable lesson. Obviously we cannot control when a bird has to dump or where, but we can try and dodge puddles, and wear looser pants to avoid some of these misfortunes. I received part of my education one day, when they were going to implode a five-story building near my precinct. It was old and ready to go anyway, so the quickest route would be to blow it up. I think everyone in the neighborhood wanted to see just how this was done, as it was surrounded by other buildings. My partner and I were two of the curious. To ensure safety, the construction crew had barricaded off several city blocks surrounding the target building. Detonation had been set for 10 a.m. and the gathering crowd could get no closer than a hundred yards. Everyone was anticipating the explosion as they counted down. A series of loud booms signified the start of the collapse. Eagles searching for prey, proud and professional, my partner and I had positioned ourselves as close as possible. The building began

43

to tumble in on itself, and we realized something bad was going to happen.

The structure was coming down but rising out and up from it was a debris cloud, which began to boil. Like an avalanche racing down the Matterhorn, it thundered in our direction. Momentarily stunned, the crowd had been frozen in place, but now they began screaming and turned to run. We never attempted to stop anyone, as we went from eagles to gooney birds just like the rest of the crowd. All of us were flapping and stumbling in the same direction in hopes to take flight from certain doom. Unfortunately, none of us stood a chance and we were soon overrun by the thick dust.

It was all over in minutes. I stood there in my now-white, navy blue uniform, which completely was covered from the top of my hat, to the tip of my toes with dust. To make if even more comical, my thick eyebrows and mustache now matched my uniform. Everyone around me also had been dusted like a biscuit and we all stood laughing. Now here is the lesson part. Before the detonation, I had noticed quite a few construction workers gathering at the site. What struck me odd was that most of them were inside vehicles, which were positioned facing the crowd. I now understood why and was positive this hadn't been the first time they enjoyed such a show. I had to admit it was pretty funny, and the opportunity to laugh with the crowd seemed to breakdown that ever-present wall between us. That memory would stay with me the rest of my career. If my hat blew off and was crushed by a passing car, I would flash back to that crowd stumbling west bound, fleeing for their lives while, just like a cheap disaster movie, a debris cloud would swallow them whole.

My laughing immediately would temper my frustration, which made it much easier to pick up that bent hat and place it back on my head. With the slightest of motions, I would tip it in the direction of the squawking gooney birds, smiling as I squawked right along with them.

CRIME HITS HOME

I had entered this profession street smart, but soon realized I was not criminal street smart. My family had been victimized by criminals a number of times. My grandparents had owned a small meat market in Delray. They were robbed by armed suspects three separate times, eventually driving them to close the store and move north. They left a neighborhood they had lived in all their lives. They left it, knowing it was dying.

My aunt had tended bar at the Dragoon Saloon. It was a small neighborhood joint. One night, four armed suspects entered announcing a robbery and opened fire. My aunt was shot through the abdomen, and the owner and a patron were shot through the chest. My aunt survived, but the other two died.

I had another aunt who lived in the same house she was born in. A suspect knocked on her door one day and when she answered, he forced his way in. He demanded money, and when she didn't have enough, he beat her with a chunk of concrete. She survived and soon after moved to the suburbs.

We had cars stolen, our house broken into, and everything from bikes to Christmas lights were taken. Incidents like this change you as a person. When you bought a car used or new, you had to make sure the tires did not come off easily. If not, the second day you got that baby home it would be up on milk crates. My sister had her tires and rims stolen. She promptly replaced them, just to find her car back up on cinder blocks the next day.

You learned to assume a defensive posture all the time. Making it safe would seem the obvious answer to anyone who grew up in Detroit.

RESIDENCY REQUIRED

To be the police in Detroit, you had to live within the city limits. Residency had to be established before you could be hired. There were no exceptions, no matter how bad it got, and no matter how many times you heard gunshots in your neighborhood. You had to live in the city. I was a lifelong resident and hadn't given it much thought. To me, all of this was just the normal way of life. I knew of no other way.

I was newly married when I hired on, and had no kids. I began house shopping and wanted to find the safest area. I had resigned myself to the fact that when I did have kids, they would end up going to a private school. I watched my parents struggle to put all of us through parochial school, and I wasn't going to risk the lives of my kids by sending them to public school. The safest area on the west side was known as Copper Canyon. It was on the far western edge of the city, and was somewhat separated from the rest by a large park.

My wife and I drove through the neighborhood and were delighted to find small homes with well-kept yards. Police officers and firemen owned the majority of the homes. We found several that were on the market and made some calls. We were shocked at the prices — $60,000 to $100,000. This was for a house in Detroit: The Murder Capitol. This obviously was out of our price range, so we had to travel east and continued shopping. We wanted to stay as close to this neighborhood as possible. We located a very nice three-bedroom bungalow less than a mile away. It was on the opposite side of the park, deeper into Detroit. The price was $19,000, and it was in better shape than a number of homes in Copper Canyon.

In Copper Canyon, you bought the neighborhood, not the house. I wanted to be on the other side of the park for the safety factor, but couldn't afford it. Lack of money would cost me the security blanket I so desperately wanted. After we purchased our starter home, they robbed the butcher shop at the end of the block. A mom and pop business, it had been in the neighborhood for decades. The perpetrators made three of the employees lay down and executed them. Like many of the Detroit businesses, it was soon boarded up.

I knew I was going to have to make some decision if we had kids. There was no way was I going to raise them in this war zone.

A DIFFERENT TYPE OF PROMOTION

I had about four years under my belt when the first promotional test came up. Plenty of people were taking it, and you basically got the day off to participate. My partner and I figured we'd take the test, go out for lunch and have the rest of the day off. What a great deal. Neither of us studied, but why would we? I figured I was not remotely prepared to be a supervisor. I felt I did not have enough street experience. I eventually would learn I was very wrong on this point. I was learning how certain people were promoted and what type of street experience they had.

I learned of charter promotions. These were promotions were a command officer just gave you the rank. The reason for the charter promotion as listed in our general orders was so a command could promote officers with special skills or experience in a certain fields. These were skills other officers had not obtained.

The chief of police has to submit a letter of recommendation to the Board of Police Commissioners. This would explain who the officer was and the reason for the promotion. Once it was reviewed, the board would render a decision. To this day, I never have seen anyone with special skills promoted this way. I've seen plenty of charter promotions, but no one with special skills. Some horrible supervisors were generated through this system.

I also learned there were a certain number of officers who were promoted and may have worked the street for a very limited time or not at all. Some officers came out of the academy and went right to clerk jobs or worked in some office position. I wanted the streets, I wanted the experience. It was part of the reason I joined. How would you learn anything about police work being a clerk?

I was once working a beat with a brand new female officer. We were standing in front of the Fox Theater, when a blacked-out police vehicle pulled up across the street. A sergeant got out and motioned us across the street. We began walking, and the sergeant said, female officer only.

I walked back to my post and watched her talking to someone in the car. She came back and seemed confused. I asked her what that was all about, and she said they asked her to work in the chief's office. She had been on the job a week. She asked my opinion, and I asked her what were the reasons she joined the department. If she wanted to be a secretary, take the offer. I was off the next two days, and when I returned, her locker was cleaned out. She took the spot. I'm sure she needed only one thing to get that position: Good looks — and she had them.

I can sum the whole promotion thing up this way: You could feasibly come out of the academy and never work the street. Someone of rank could give you a clerk's position or assign you some type of inside duty. You would have an ideal position to study for the test on duty. No sirens blasting and no one shooting at you. No court to drag out your day and wear you out. You could take the sergeant's test within three years, as long as you had a degree.

Once you made the rank of sergeant, you could take the next test for lieutenant. This would be about five years. Now, if by chance after your promotion to sergeant you ended up on the street, within weeks, your friends in high places would find you a spot to hide. It's the perfect time to study for the next test. Once you passed the lieutenant test, the next rank was inspector. No test, this was an appointed position. Perfect. Since you knew people, you could start stroking them. The next step was commander, then deputy chief, assistant chief and, finally, chief. These are all appointed positions. You see where I'm going? I knew an officer who was charter promoted to sergeant, lieutenant and appointed up all the way to the rank of assistant chief.

It's a great system we had in place. Much later in my career, I had to attend a city-wide crime briefing meeting that was attended by all the higher ranks.

I looked around and saw a commander who had wrecked his take-home police car drunk. He called another command officer to help him at the crash site, and this command officer eventually was fired for removing liquor bottles from the car. Another commander had been driving drunk and fled on foot from Detroit Police officers. There were two female commanders who had gotten into a fistfight in front of officers at the precinct, and an assistant chief who stalked his girlfriend. Also at the meeting was a commander who was out drinking and emptied a clip at some guys. He said he was being robbed while out with a girl (who wasn't his wife). These were our leaders. It really made you question the code of ethics we all took.

Police Officer Richard L. Fortin
Detroit Police Department, Michigan
End of Watch: Friday, June 19, 1987

Officer Richard Fortin drowned while attempting to rescue four people from a boat that had capsized.

Officer Fortin had been with the agency for twenty-three years, and he is survived by his wife, daughter, two sons and mother.

THE MALICE GREEN BEATING

One of the most important incidents for the Detroit Police Department was the Malice Green beating. Malice Green was a person known to precinct personnel. He was a drug user and easily could be found on West Warren near a dope house. On this particular evening, he and several other persons were stopped and investigated by the police. The officers pulling him over were veteran plainclothes officers from the Fourth Precinct. They knew Green and the location he pulled up in front of. During the investigation, Green attempted to hide something in his hand and began struggling with the officers. During the struggle, Green was hit in the head with a flashlight. An EMS unit had pulled up along with several other scout cars and assisted the plainclothes officers. After several hours, Green was pronounced dead at the hospital.

Later that evening, the mayor and chief of police appeared on the news. They stated to the world that the officers had murdered Malice Green. Seven officers at the scene were fired that night. Fired! There was no investigation or suspension. Now I had enough time on the job to know that the actions of one police officer affected everyone in law enforcement. The public does not see an individual officer, but the entire police community. I was being labeled a murderer. The mayor and chief had just thrown gasoline on a fire. Didn't they realize the potential they had created for the city to riot?

I was eight in 1968 when the city came apart. When the Detroit Riots began, I was sent home from school, and my entire family moved in with my aunt and uncle in Livonia. My father, a firefighter, had worked nonstop for a week. I remember returning to the city and my friends telling me that tanks were stationed at the park. They were so excited, and I was so disappointed that I missed tanks and soldiers. The reality of all of that came rushing back.

After the statements by the mayor and chief, it was quite possible we would relive that. I would have to move my family out. I would be on the front line with the soldiers and tanks. Are you kidding me? The officers may have been wrong, they may be guilty of murder, but let's investigate the incident. Suspending them would have been a good first step. The city was simmering, and we all were waiting for the lid to blow off.

I had been off for several days after the incident and, upon returning, was matched up with my regular partner. We were servicing a shooting run at the hospital when dispatch told us we were to report to the police gym at headquarters. Our orders were to not call our base, just immediately report. I looked at my partner and asked what he might have done when I was off. He was as bewildered as I was. The ride down was quiet. Was the war starting? If they could fire officers on the spot, were we next for something someone may have accused us of? When we arrived, we found the gym full of white uniformed police officers. We were all milling about not having the slightest idea why we were there. Several command officers finally showed up and explained why. We would be standing in lineups. Lineups? For what? For the Malice Green murder we were told. Great. Now I ran the risk of being picked and fired. I wasn't even there.

We were downtown for several hours. We were all uncomfortable, to say the least. To make matters worse, my partner was identified as one of the officers at the scene. He was pretty upset about the whole thing. But he was off that day, so he had a good alibi. After this whole thing played out, all of the officers but the two in question were found innocent and regained their jobs. The fired officers also all settled large lawsuits with the city. The two accused were convicted of second-degree murder and sent to prison. I am all for justice, police officers or not. What bothered me most were the blanket accusations against everyone who was at that scene: The stupid decision to fire all of the officers, and the money it cost the city to settle those lawsuits.

I realized at this point I would be fighting the system. It also was at this point in my career that my attitude began changing. I had grown to love police work, but now knew there was so much more to it. Can you imagine doing your job, then being on trial for your life?

THE ACADEMY NEVER COVERED THIS

With each new experience, I learned something more about the department and more about myself. I was becoming better prepared to handle people and critical incidents on the street.

Learning to handle the department was a whole different category. You are taught things in the academy, but what you are taught is basically just to get you to pass the big test. This is what the state required. The academy didn't cover precinct operation, personnel issues, or department practices and procedures that do not go by the book.

Take headquarters, for example. It is located in downtown Detroit. Probably an ideal location when officers were riding horses. It is completely surrounded by one-way streets and very little parking is available. When we were brand new, my partner was tasked with dropping some paperwork off at HQ. Now, when you are new, you shut your mouth and do as you are told. If you didn't know where headquarters was, you better find out. To give you the mindset of a rookie, I'll give you an example. Two officers were taking the bus to their beat area. They just got on a bus and didn't realize it was a SMART bus. It drove them to the suburbs and dropped them off. They were too afraid to tell the bus to stop that they had to call it over the radio to get picked up. They didn't have enough knowledge or experience to handle a simple bus ride. This should give you a rookie officer's state of mind.

My partner didn't want to admit it, but he had the same mindset. He drives to HQ, parks in front and goes in to drop off the paperwork. He exits the building with a sense of accomplishment to find his scout car missing from in front of the building. Panic sets in. He frantically searches for the keys and finds them. He stands there puzzled, and figures he is going to get fired for losing the scout car. How can an officer let his police car get stolen? (Although it's more common than you think). After five minutes or so, he calls our base. The sergeant asks if he parked in front of HQ. He tells him yes. The sergeant then tells him to go inside to see if they towed the scout car.

Young officer he was, he follows orders and marches in, wondering why they would tow his car if it wasn't disabled. He asks the desk boss and, sure enough, the Detroit Police Department towed a Detroit Police Car. He is informed they tow it about three blocks away and leave it on Gratiot. You have to walk over and get it. The desk boss reads him the riot act, telling him everyone knows you are not supposed to park in front of headquarters. Well who would have thought a Detroit Police officer in a Detroit Police car is not allowed to park in front of Detroit Police headquarters. So he made the walk and recovered his police car. The only good thing about his misfortune was that he came back and told all of us. So we learned if you went down to HQ, you had to take someone with you so they could circle the block. Better to have one lemming get his car towed, than for all of us to follow him over the cliff.

Later in my career they issued administrative messages informing you that if you were towed from in front of headquarters, the department would issue you a ticket and you would have to pay for it. It was bad enough if you got caught out front, but the spots along the west side of the building were numbered for command officers. Get caught parking in one of these spots and you were in a world of hurt. The royalty would request the gallows for the peasant police officer who dared park in their spot. It was quite ridiculous.

Your only option was the parking garage under headquarters. There probably were only thirty available parking spots inside the building, as space was very limited. This garage was set up for horses back in the day and had very low ceilings. It had a civilian employee guarding the gated entrance. Half the time, he was drunk and he felt he was the king of this fiefdom. He had ultimate control of who entered. Now you only would use the garage when you had a prisoner. You would get the green light to park, so you could convey your arrest to the eighth or ninth floor.

One day, I pulled up to the gate and the drunken troll was not on his toadstool. My partner got out and lifted the gate and we drove in. We had a male suspect for armed robbery. The gate guard now suddenly appeared on a dead run, yelling and waving his arms.

"What do you think you are doing," he shouted.

I had some time on the job at the time of this incident, so I was not afraid and couldn't be bullied anymore. I told him we were dropping off a prisoner for armed robbery.

"Like hell you are," he said.

"Watch me," I answered.

He screamed that I could drop off my partner and prisoner, and park on the street. Yeah, so I could get towed. I heard that one before. I told him I would not leave my partner or prisoner, and we were going up. This whole conversation is taking place, while he is hanging on my door. I parked and we got out. His brash and loud tactics were not working, so he flipped his approach. He told me he was going to call "Benny," the chief.

He picked up a phone located on one of the support pillars. I told him go ahead, I'll wait and talk to him. He hung up the phone, tucked his tail between his legs, and walked off. I just knew I was going to come back to the van and find one or two flat tires. That's how Detroit was.

Luckily, no flats, and we didn't get towed or issued a ticket. Once you have some experience, you don't frighten as easily.

ANOTHER LESSON LEARNED

There were two critical floors at HQ. One was for male prisoners the other was for females. The male prisoner floor was like entering the Spanish inquisition, complete with bugs and rats. Prisoners had been up there for days or even weeks without being charged. As soon as you stepped out of the elevator, you were again at the mercy of civilians. There were more than one or two fights up there between officers and "turn keys," as the civilians were called.

The Female floor was the worst. Those girls just never wanted to work. They would have you waiting forever, and were always pissed off because you brought them some work. There never was a "Good morning, how are you?" Everyone dreaded going up there.

The first female I took up there was a prostitute. Once the elevator doors opened, she refused to walk and slumped to the floor. Me being new, I tried to coax her up. She refused. I felt my only option was to carry her. I picked her up, carried her twenty feet and plopped her down at the check-in desk. Ms. Grumpy filled out the paperwork I handed to her, never looking up or saying a word. When she was done, she called for one of the girls from the back. I told her I would get it because the prisoner had to be carried.

"Unh unh baby, ain't nobody carrying that bitch," she said.

She then walked around from behind the desk, grabbed the prisoner by her long hair and twisted it into a rope. She then began dragging her down the floor to a cell. The prisoner now wanted to get up, but was told, "Bitch I thought you couldn't walk, so you can keep your broke ass on the floor."

After the prisoner was placed in a cell, the girl walked up to me and said, "That's the way you deal with that shit, baby."

Another lesson learned. It would be the only time, I ever felt good about dropping off a prisoner at HQ.

"OOPS, NOT NOW."

HQ was a haven for most of the non-workers. There were very few police runs, and not much violence in that district. I had been working this district once when I made an arrest and recovered a weapon. The suspect was wanted for armed robbery. I completed the paperwork and went to the front desk for a supervisor's signature. A lieutenant was the officer in charge, and I handed him my report and evidence envelope with the handgun in it.

I was holding the gun for fingerprints and had written in large bold black marker "Hold for Prints" on both sides of the envelope. I watched him, untie the bag, pull the gun out with his hand, and start examining it. The envelope was right in front of him. I told him the gun was being held for prints.

"Oops, not now," was his response.

That guy kind of summed up my attitude about HQ's. He later was appointed through the ranks of inspector and commander.

The lessons were piling up both on and off the street, and I was like a sponge. I wanted to learn everything yesterday. I couldn't wait to go to work.

CHECK THE ENGINE

I just really couldn't figure out why most lessons we learned always were learned the hard way. So one day we found a confirmed stolen vehicle parked right in front of a party store on Linwood. It had all the classic stolen car clues — one mini spare, license plate with one screw holding it on and right rear vent window busted out. Usually, one of these was a good sign, but three was the trifecta. We ran the license plate through LEIN, and sure enough, it was stolen. We figured we would get in a position to watch it, and when someone got in, we would swoop down and make the arrest.

First off, we have to be far enough away and in a spot where no one would see us. Any criminal seeing us in an alley would be like a rooster in the barnyard. The classic signal would be a loud whistle. It would put all the bad guys on alert letting everyone know the police were around. They might not be able to see us, but they now knew we were in the neighborhood.

We picked a good vantage point and begin watching. The vehicle is parked at a busy location and plenty of people are looking at it. Several sit on the hood, and one opens the door. Now understand that in the stolen car world, if no one gets in it for several hours, it is open to anyone. So if you need a ride home, in you go. The only way this won't happen is if everyone in the neighborhood knows a heavy hitter stole it. Basically, the bad guy is the neighborhood bully or someone willing to pull the trigger on you (i.e. shoot you).

We have been watching the car for some time, and are playing the milk the run game and hoping it works out. Milking a run means dragging a police run out to give you more time to do police work. Example being it takes ten minutes to investigate a suspicious person run, but you do not call back in service for twenty minutes. So ten minutes for the run, ten minutes of milking to find bad guys. If you don't milk a run, they are going to give you another one immediately. We actually milked a run, and then requested a code (thirty-minute lunch) to give us an hour. No lunch, we just stayed on the stolen ride. Knowing we had to go back into service soon, we decide to just recover it. As soon as we roll up, I know we've made a mistake. I can see the hood slightly ajar. I walk to the front of the car, lift the hood and I find the battery missing. This car was going nowhere. Lesson learned, and it would not happen to me again. I've seen rookies set up on cars with no engines or transmissions. I wouldn't let them set up for very long, but we always got a laugh out of it. They loved to hear the "been there done that" story.

YOU'RE UNDER ARREST (FOR SOMETHING)

In the academy, you are taught a number of laws and it was obvious you were not going to use them all. Once on the street, you may use about ten charges on a regular basis. When you arrest someone, you complete a preliminary complaint report and that is just what it is: preliminary. Keep it thorough but simple. As a rookie, about the only charge you know is murder.

I was walking a beat with my partner in the corridor one day. It is late, and we see a guy carrying a four-foot-by-four-foot box. The box is new, and whatever he is carrying is very heavy. We know the first step is to stop and investigate. We tell him to put the box down and he complies. We didn't know at this point, but usually once a suspect puts something down, they run. Luckily, he didn't and we begin questioning him.

He tells us he has no idea what is in the box and that he just found it. Even my feeble rookie mind can figure he is lying. Why carry a box if you don't know what is in it. Could be rocks. I asked where he was going with it, and he says home. We know this isn't happening, because he could barely lift it. On the outside of the box in large letters is Fox

Parking Garage. Now, we know they are building a new parking deck for the Fox Theatre. With keen police logic we determine he took it from there. We search for the next step. We are less than a block from the parking garage, but figure we had enough to lock him up. He has property that does not belong to him. That's got to be something.

We request a car for transport, and two officers with some time on the job pick us up. They ask what we have, and we tell them the story. They say nice job, and tell us they will drive by the garage to see if they can find a point of entry. Great, we figure point of entry for a breaking and entering. We check and can't find any damage. They drive us to the precinct and drop us off. We now are in a terrible position because we have to fill out and type print cards that have a big box asking for "Charges." We have no idea what we are charging this guy with and thought we caught a break with the B&E thing. We couldn't find evidence of a B&E, so that flew out the door. One of us also had to tell the boss what we have. We now are kind of hanging out in the garage with the suspect and the property (it was a big gear, weighing 170 pounds).

Everyone who walks by asks what we have, we tell the story, and finally, someone says, "Nice R&C arrest." Damn it. What is R&C? Luckily, his partner asked me, "Is that Receiving and concealing over one hundred dollars?"

"That sure is," I replied, and we completed the cards, talked to the boss and rushed back to tell class 86-S of our adventures. You would have thought we just solved the Lindberg kidnapping.

MR. NEAT GETS A SURPRISE

We also are learning about bosses and department procedures. Paperwork is extremely important, as everything you write can end up as a legal document in court. Some officers could not write if they tried. We already had spelling issues. Some of the reports looked like straight up chicken scratch. I was a nut about it. If you made a mistake, on any document, you would have to draw a line through it an initial it. This way, everyone could see what you wrote, and that you were not attempting to hide something. If I made a mistake, I would do the whole thing over. I didn't like mistake lines.

One day, I am working with the worst printer in the world. His paperwork looked horrible. He is doing our daily log sheet, which chronicles everything we did that day. We review it together and then both sign it. I comment to him about how messy it is, but he says it is good. The content is correct, but you can barely read it. This guy has been turning in the same crap since he got out of the academy. I, on the other hand, am Mr. Neat. About a week after I worked with this guy, I get a call up to the supervisor's office. I am told they have a negative administrative counseling entry for me to sign. I am crushed. I was unaware of anything I might have done wrong. I read the entry and in very technical terminology it says my paperwork is messy. Now, I'm pissed. I take great care in my paper and want to know what this is all about. They pull up the run sheet from a week ago. I look at it and start laughing.

"Are you kidding me?" I asked. "You have a guy that for the last year has been turning horrible paperwork and the day I work with him, you are going to correct him?"

They told me by signing the activity log, it was as if I had done it myself and I was responsible for what was on it. I asked why they did not write him up on the days he worked by himself, and that I take great pride in my paper. They already know this, as they have to check my log sheet every day. They told me sorry, but I was responsible. This was the first time I really wondered how supervisors got their positions, and who picked them.

AVOID NEEDLES WHILE IN THE HAY STACK

Everyone knows police work is a dangerous profession. You would think most officers are concerned about being shot. I never really thought too much about it. My worst fear was being pricked with a hypodermic needle or bitten by someone. Some of the street people you deal with can be pretty skanky. You constantly ask when you are searching someone if they have any needles. You grab the outer clothing or pockets to feel through the material before you reach in.

I came close a number of times but was never poked. A guy who worked in our unit was walking through a vacant lot, when a needle went through the toe of his boot, puncturing his big toe. It made me sick just thinking about it. These are the other risks police officers run into. Don't forget about air and blood borne pathogens. I can carry those home, not to mention every other creepy crawler I come into contact with.

The closest I came to being bit was while I was working the corridor. We had locked up a prostitute and she was fighting. I had forced her into a sitting position on the ground. I was standing behind her with my hands pressing down on her shoulders. We were waiting on a car to transport her, and I was talking to my partner. I could hear a clicking noise and looked down, and saw her chomping at my wrist. She couldn't reach it so her teeth were clacking together. It made me furious. I assured her if she bit me, it would be the last time she bit anyone, as I would relieve her of any future dental issues by knocking all her teeth out. There were a few profanities laced in that threat including the mother of all bad words.

Now, I obviously couldn't knock her teeth out, but it was part of your reputation on the street. Everyone could hear what I said, as it was profanity-laced and left an impression. Throw a couple of drunks in the mix and you could hear them say, "Man, did you see Officer Haig was going to knock that bitch's teeth out?"

You could never trust anyone on the street, but a reputation carried some weight.

FEARING THE ONES YOU PROTECT

Probably the incident that had the biggest rookie impact on us was a shooting that two of our guys were involved in. They responded to a mental run, and were let into the house by the mother. She told them her son was out of control and had locked himself in the bedroom. He was about thirty years old, and on a number of medications. The officers went upstairs and attempted to talk him out. He was refusing, so the mother opened the door with a key. Their intentions were to take him to the Crisis Center. When they entered the bedroom, the suspect pulled a folding knife out, slashing at one of the officers. His partner pulled his weapon, firing twice, and hit the guy in the chest. He fell dead.

What followed was something I learned would be very common for us. The family wanted to kill the officers. They wanted help, not murder as they put it. Their feelings were understandable in the heat of the moment. The problem was that officers had been to this house a number of times for the same thing. It was just a matter of time before something like this happened. The officers began receiving death threats.

All officers were warned about servicing runs in that area. People protested at the precinct. This went on for months. It started to seem like we always were the bad guys in the public eye. And now I have to be afraid of the citizens I'm trying to protect.

FELINE DISTURBANCES

Early on, you learn that being scared is part of the job. One day, I was looking for a suspect responsible for a critical shooting. Other officers had lost him in the area, and we were out on foot assisting. I ended up in an old garage and was looking for any recent disturbance, like items knocked over, dust missing, hand or foot prints. It never is a good feeling when you have to go into a place where you know someone may be pointing a gun at you. I enter the garage cautiously.

In these situations, you learn to be very quiet. You may hear some movement, or even the bad guy breathing. It was deadly quiet. Next thing I know, an alley cat tears across a large shelf to my right. He knocks over every can and bottle on the shelf, breaking several of them. I never had a chance on that one. I froze. If I were a horse, I would have dropped a load of road apples right there. It was a good first cat lesson. I survived and was uninjured. I didn't shoot the cat, and another unit caught the bad guy.

I never was a cat lover, but did have sympathy for one once. We received a run on person handcuffed. We responded to the run, fully expecting to find either some sort of sexual situation gone bad (lost key), or some kids just fooling around after they found some cuffs. We pull up finding a guy holding a cat. I get out and ask him what the problem is. He says the cat has been cuffed. I look down like an idiot expecting to see a small set of cuffs on Mr. Patch's paws. The cat actually was cuffed around the neck. Both cuffs locked around his throat. It is not restricting his airflow, but it didn't look comfortable. We uncuff kitty, and the crowd applauds us.

I guess we are not always the bad guys. I would learn these little incidents of recognition and praise by the public would be few and far between. The clapping crowd did make me feel good.

THE BEST KISS I EVER RECEIVED

Probably, the most satisfaction I ever got out my job was on a shots fired run. We responded to the listed address and talked to several distraught women. One is the mother the other the grandmother of a mentally challenged fifteen-year-old.

Apparently, someone tried to rob him, and fired a shot at him. Terrified, he ran and was hiding somewhere. Both women were sobbing and pleading for help. I assured them we would find him, and that everything would be okay. We begin searching the area, and after about twenty minutes, found him hiding under a back porch. He was very frightened.

When we walked him back into his home, you could see the joy and relief on the faces of his family. They truly loved him. They could not thank us enough. As I was walking out, the grandmother motioned for me to come to her. I did and she leaned over wanting to whisper something in my ear. I bent down to her and she motioned me closer. As I leaned in she softly kissed me on the cheek and said, "Bless you."

To this day, the love in that old woman's teary eyes has never left me. In all my years on the job, it was the best kiss I ever received.

Police Officer John James Fitzpatrick
Detroit Police Department, Michigan
End of Watch: Friday, October 9, 1987

Officer Fitzpatrick was struck and killed by a drunken driver while on patrol. He is survived by his wife, daughter and two sons.

WHEN THE SIZE OF THE BULLET MATTERS

Things were starting to flow for us, as we began to pile up arrests and experience. I felt more confident with every run. My street tools were increasing and it was a great feeling.

Our area covered a large hospital and we had the opportunity to respond to a number of different shooting runs. All new officers wanted to see this and it also weeded out the ones who couldn't take the sight of blood.

Many times, we would have to enter the area where doctors were working on our victims. I watched them crack open a person's chest and massage a heart to keep them alive. You see emergency physicians try to staunch the flow of blood as major arteries try to pump the body dry. I really didn't enjoy this, but it was part of the job. You were there in case a victim gave a dying declaration, identifying their assailant.

I was quite shocked the first time I serviced a run where the guy was shot in the head. I showed up fully expecting to just be getting some dead on arrival information. They directed me to an exam room, where my victim was lying in bed. His head was wrapped and he was talking to a nurse. I thought I had the wrong room, and asked the nurse where the guy shot in the head was. Right here, she instructed. I'm thinking, "What did he get shot with a BB gun?"

I asked what happened. He said several suspects had approached him, and one was armed with a handgun. They announced a robbery and ordered him to lay face first on the grass. They demanded his money and he turned over two dollars.

"That is all you got?" the armed suspect hollered.

"Yes," the victim replied.

"This is one broke-ass nigger," the suspect said, and he then fired one round into the back of the victim's head.

The bullet entered the scalp but did not penetrate the skull. It ran under the skin and exited near his left eye. A small caliber bullet usually is the most lethal as it bounces around in the body ricocheting off of bones and organs. In this case, the small bullet saved his life.

I would see this type of thing three more times in my career. Three very lucky people. This incident also told me a little about the disregard for human life on the street. Two dollars wasn't enough to keep this guy alive.

IS IT LUCK OR SMARTS?

As we learned more, the whole luck thing kept popping up. I was very, very lucky one morning. On this day, I was assigned to a one-man car. Detroit was dangerous, and you only were allowed to work a one-man car on the day shift. I was heading back to my base, and saw a guy standing near the street. He was waving his arms about. We had tons of mentally challenged people in this area, and I didn't really think too much about him. It was not unusual to see people dancing, barking or flapping their arms. He seemed to be minding his own crazy business.

I caught a red light two blocks north and as I was waiting for it to change, I heard a car call Priority Shots fired in a very urgent voice. The location they gave was two blocks south of me. I hit the lights and bent a U-turn. As I pulled up and jumped out, I could see the guy who moments earlier was waiving his hands in the air, was now lying on the ground. A pool of blood was appearing beneath him and a large butcher knife was lying about ten feet away.

I asked the officers what happened, and they said they had pulled up to him to tell him to get out of the street. He pulled the knife from under his coat and rushed them. They were forced to shoot him. I thought about that one for a long time. Was I lucky or smart? Was I developing a weird police sense? Whatever it was, I was glad I had it on that day.

Better arrests began to come as we learned all the tricks of the trade. I was working by myself one morning and spotted a car with four people in it. They gave me the "I'm not right look," and I pulled them over. I knew this was dangerous, but I was well equipped with the confidence of youth. When they were loading the landing craft for the assault on fortress Europe on D-Day, if they tried to load the landing craft with forty-year-olds, they probably would have mutinied, commandeered the ship and sailed back to the ole US of A. It was good to be young. Wars are fought by young men, and I was a soldier and this was a war.

As I walked up to the car, there was a towel draped over the steering column. This was another stolen car sign. Everyone sees the classic hot wire on TV. I've never seen that. Stealing a car was not that complicated. You either punched out the ignition cylinder and inserted a screwdriver as a key, or you peeled or broke the left side of the column. This allowed you access to the ignition slide. When you turned the key on the right side of the column, it engaged this slide on the left. Once it was exposed, you just pulled up on it and the car started. I figured I had four people in a stolen car, and I better get some help.

I'm talking to the driver and acting like I never saw the steering column. I gather identification from everyone, and say I'll be back. The driver has no license, but I tell him as long as he doesn't have warrants, I'll let him go. I was attempting to put them at ease, but you could feel the tension. My heart was thumping. Once I was in my car, I felt a little bit more secure. I call for backup and the other car out of my base responds. Unfortunately, the guy and gal manning it are not workers. I run the names through the system, and discover all are wanted, including one of the males for armed robbery. I'm excited.

But as the minutes tick by with no backup, this excitement fades. The suspects were fidgety to begin with, and the longer we wait, the worse it gets. It takes almost fifteen minutes for them to arrive. When they do get there, I get out and arrest everyone. Once they are secure, I cut into my coworkers. This is built up, as I know they are slugs. If they want to drive out of their district to eat, or visit, or shop, that is on them. When my life is in question, I won't stand for it. I told them next time, don't even answer and another car can respond.

THE PUPPY DEFENSE

Detroit has many criminals and there are different categories for all of them. We had to learn about everyone single one of them. One of my favorites would be the misdemeanor, repeat offender. They have learned to play the system, knowing well the manpower and prisoner housing issues the department is facing. Most criminals learn early on that if the police stop you and you're wanted for a felony charge, you go directly to jail. Now if you slip into the misdemeanor category, the officer can practice a little discretion. For me, the attitude of the suspect always was my number one factor when considering this discretion. Throw me a bad attitude and I'll give you a free ride. Tell me to do my job, and I'll oblige you. Either one, will guarantee you a trip to a Detroit dungeon. You will be treated to the very best: a concrete bed, or floor if you prefer complete with roaches, and your menu for the day includes a yummy breakfast of bologna on white bread with a cup of water. The lunch entrée will be bologna on white bread and water. Mmmm. For dinner, let's make it a trifecta: bologna on white bread. Criminal or not, this is not a good setting for anybody. Hence, staying out of jail is a priority. The misdemeanor repeat offender knows this all too well. They know you can possess a get-out-of-jail-free card if you know how to play the game. Always traveling with a child is the very best. Make it an infant, and it's even better. Open sores or festering wounds are a close second. Poor hygiene, combined with the smell of urine, wine and body odor, will pretty much get you a pass. A deep guttural, tuberculosis sounding cough, repeated over and over will have an officer covering his own mouth, and backing up.

On this particular day, I was working a one-man car, and had effected a traffic stop at the Boulevard and Second. The vehicle, which was occupied by a lone male, had expired plates and a cracked windshield. As I walked to the driver's side window, the vehicle itself told me the driver did not have a license. I already was calculating the number of warrants for his arrest, when he leaned out the window, and informed me his license has been suspended for years. My discretion meter was bending toward jail.

I asked him to step from the vehicle, at which time he added he was wanted on traffic warrants in several jurisdictions. My meter needle entered into the red, and I slipped my cuffs on him. He began to cry and plead as I led him to the patrol car. My short lecture was standard for traffic offenders. I advised him that when he got behind the wheel this morning and turned the key, he knew the risk he would be running. Don't drive, don't go to jail — it's rather simple when you think about it.

The suspect now is seated in the back, pleading for mercy. I run his name through the system, and he is wanted on multiple misdemeanor warrants. His license has been suspended for the past six years. I look over my shoulder and inform him he is under arrest.

His response was quick and without hesitation.

"Officer, what about my puppies?" he asks.

"Puppies? What puppies?" I stuttered.

"The puppies in the backseat," he replied. "They are in the box."

Scrambling, I asked if they were alive.

"Of course they are alive," he whispered.

He slid forward on the rear seat, pressing his face against the cage and told me to go check for myself.

I slowly walked to his vehicle, and saw a cardboard box in the rear seat. I had heard no noise previously, and held hope he was lying. I flipped the top of the box open, and the puppy symphony began — there was yapping, yelping and whimpering as nine of the cutest puppies in the world attempted to scramble over the sides.

I reached in to gently push them down as they nipped and scratched at my hand.

I began to pick one up to cuddle… Wait a minute, I have a handcuffed criminal in my backseat. I quickly closed the box up and stomped back to my vehicle, mad that I had allowed myself to be overcome by the cuteness.

"Why didn't you tell me about the puppies?" I asked.

"I didn't know you were going to arrest me," he responded.

I quickly uncuffed him. What in the hell was I going to do with a box of puppies?

As he walked back to his car, I hollered to him.

"I don't care if you have a baby elephant in the back, next time you are going to jail," I told him.

"Sure, officer," he yelled back and waved.

He pulled off, and I sat there, stunned for moment. He got me. Had he deliberately loaded those puppies up before he left the house? Then I started thinking maybe I shouldn't have said baby elephant. Baby elephants are pretty cute.

"YOU AIN'T RIGHT, YOU AIN'T RIGHT"

If you were a worker, you quickly became an excellent judge of human behavior. Eyes always told the complete story. Every police run or incident involved this simple assessment. The bad guys did it to us, and we did it to them. If I showed up with a quiet, 105-pound girl wearing nail polish, things could get dicey. You could see it in criminal's eyes. This also applied to male officers: The bad guys always factored in their size and demeanor. A big angry guy with wild eyes means call for backup. If you carried yourself in a firm and authoritative manner, the criminals could see this. They knew you meant business. Basically, it was just like the animal world. He shows his antlers, you show yours. Yeah, we could fight, but why? Mr. Miyagi said it best: "Always look (at the) eyes."

In the beginning, you wrote tickets and serviced runs. It's all you were capable of. With experience, I began to investigate things. My partner and I had serviced a holdup run at a local Kentucky Fried Chicken. The business had been robbed at gunpoint by a lone suspect. A month later, the same suspect robbed them again. We did some snooping and eventually identified the suspect. He also had robbed a grocery store down the block. We turned this information over to the detective bureau, and they obtained a multiple count warrant on the guy.

We wanted more, and this now gave my partner and I a daily task. We searched for this guy every morning. It almost became routine. Well, for the life of me, we couldn't find this guy, and days soon turned into months.

We knew he would be easy to spot, as he was a black male with a reddish complexion and freckles. He was 6'1" and very thin. During one of the robberies, he was wearing a three-quarter length Detroit Pistons basketball coat. This search went on for almost a year.

One Sunday morning, I was working with a female officer because my regular partner was off. I headed down the boulevard as I always did for a quick check for our holdup man. I must admit that I had given it some thought, considering whom I was working with. I knew she would not get out and chase anyone. She had established that early in her career and everyone knew it.

But what the heck, remember that confidence of youth thing? As I bent the corner several blocks down, I could see a male and female crossing the street. At this distance, I could see the male was tall and thin and wearing a Detroit Pistons basketball jacket. They were walking off of our suspect's street, and I immediately knew it was our man. My excitement quickly dissipated as I looked over at my partner. I had to hatch a plan and quick. It's funny how you change. As a rookie, I would have accelerated the car up to them (usually from a great distance), jumped from the car, identified myself (as if they didn't know), and we would have been off to the races.

We were almost to them now, and I told my partner we were going to arrest this guy, and to just follow my lead. I didn't want to tell her what he was wanted for because I figured she would never get out of the car.

I pulled up to both of them and asked if they were from the neighborhood. I told them I was looking for a wanted suspect and had a picture of him. They said they weren't from the neighborhood, but were willing to look.

Now, "Chris," our suspect, was young, and the female he was with was at least twice his age. I guessed it was his mom. I didn't want Chris to run, so the whole ploy was just to get close enough to get my hands on him. I exited the scout, and my partner followed suit. I walked to the trunk and opened it and Chris and his mom followed. I pulled out the picture of Chris and showed it to both of them. Before it could click, I had him by the arm and one cuff on him. When I thought about it later, my plan had probably trumped their plan. Once I saw them, I am sure they saw me. They had formulated what they would do if I stopped to investigate them, and probably discussed it as I pulled up.

My partner stood there puzzled as I arrested Chris. No one on the street likes to be duped, and both Chris and his mom kept saying, "You ain't right, you know you ain't right." They were more upset about me showing them the picture of Chris then they were of him going to jail.

Now at off-duty roll call, all my partner kept talking about was this great arrest we made. Everyone was lending her an ear, and all I could think of is that they were going to decorate us for the arrest. If you were paired with a slug and made a spectacular arrest, no matter what they did or how involved they were with the arrest, they would receive the same citation or commendation you would get. So my partner and I look for this guy for a year, the day he is off I find him with this girl. She gets a ribbon on her uniform. He gets nothing. Nice.

THE FIRST DEAD BODY

Every officer wants to get that first dead body out of the way. Some look forward to it, and others dread it. Will it stink? Will it be so horrible, I might pass out? Will I throw up? Apprehensive but excited were my first feelings.

In the academy, we talked about procedure and how a dead body scene should be handled. But like everything else in the academy, this was the book version, not the street version. The street version always seemed to come with an infinite number of variables. No two were the same.

My first one definitely was a learning experience. We met the ambulance at the front entrance to a large apartment building. The run was a person discovered dead. We made the apartment and discovered the front door was open. Before we entered, I plugged my nose. Better to be safe than sorry, I thought. My partner laughed, and was going to iron man it. Inside, we found an elderly male deceased on his bed. It was very hot in the apartment, but the body was in good shape. It retained some of its natural color, and I decided to take a quick sniff. It wasn't unbearable. I actually touched the body with my finger. I don't really know why, but I did. Mind you, this is our first one, and I'm sure the EMS personnel could tell. When they prepared to move the deceased, one of them looked up at me, and said, "This is going to stink."

My rookie mind could not figure out why. The body really didn't smell, and it looked okay. Again, better to be safe than sorry, so I re-plugged my sniffer. My partner laughed at me. As soon as EMS pulled the body, the skin on the dead guy's arms and legs came off. Both technicians turned their heads away as fluid ran onto the bed. My partner barely made the door, losing his breakfast on the first landing. He left a little something on each stair as he headed for the front entrance and fresh air. We both learned something from that scene, and neither of us would soon forget it.

Sometimes the simple circumstances of finding the body were amazing. I once had a body that was found by a homeowner in his front yard. He had a three-foot fence around the yard and a row of bushes along that fence. It was the first thaw of spring and he discovered a body between the fence and the bushes. He was located on a main road, and people must have been walking by this body for months. The homeowner was sure the body was not there in the fall when he cleaned under the bushes. These bushes were right on the sidewalk. The body was in good shape because it was frozen solid. There were no signs of trauma, and I guessed he must have been a drunk, who tumbled over the fence, died and immediately was covered by snow. He wasn't visible until the snow melted months later. This incident in any other city would have made headlines. But not in Detroit.

The big plus, though, was there was no smell.

FELLOW WORKERS IN THE WAR

On another occasion I was working by myself and got the dreaded, "one down run." This was my last day before furlough, and usually you worked half a day and the boss sent you home to start your vacation. I was at the end of my half-day, and this would be my last run. I would have preferred a parking complaint. I responded to the run, finding an obviously deceased person in an alley. It looked like she had been dead about ten hours. I'm not a medical examiner, but you can tell. EMS arrived at the same time and I was upset. The Detroit Police Department is at the mercy of the morgue. This did not look like a homicide scene and once I called them, they officially cleared the body for removal. This meant I now had to wait for the morgue. They may have one or two trucks available for the entire county. I went on the list and would get serviced when a truck became available. It could be hours.

I was just starting my furlough and didn't want to wait. Luckily, I knew the EMS crew that showed up. I immediately began whining to them. Their job was to assess the patient, provide medical assistance and transport when necessary. It wasn't necessary in this case because she was dead. But I began really whining because if I could convince them to transport her to the hospital, I would not have to wait. She would be pronounced DOA (dead on arrival) at the hospital, go in the cooler, and the morgue could pick her up from there. Now, when I first proposed this plan to them, they gave me the fish eye. They sarcastically asked if I would knock the dust off of her so they could transport. They asked how could they explain to the emergency room staff that they detected signs of life?

Now, I knew this crew, and had been in some tight spots with them. I promised them I would return the favor someday. I must have lucky dust, because they transported her. I wish I could have been in the hospital when they wheeled her in.

It always seemed like working crews operated that way. Once you had shared danger with someone, you developed a bond. I'm sure they knew a few tricks to get her in. I now owed them.

Our emergency medical service personnel (EMS) worked the streets with us. They saw most everything we did, and sometimes worse. At times, I wondered how they did their jobs. Now, I have seen some EMS crews do some incredible things, and I've also seen them do some pretty crappy things.

We had a run on a man down. It was a bitter cold day hovering around zero. We found our guy under a shelter in the park. He was lying on his side, alive and shivering. His right hand was in his mouth. Spit and vomit were running down his hand and onto the concrete. We discovered we could not get him up as his exposed cheek was frozen to the cement.

EMS had responded and made their assessment. I was first aid qualified, but this was their case. My thought was to put warm fluid under his cheek and up he would come. The location of this guy was about forty yards from the road, and to get to him, we had to walk through knee-deep snow. I guess the walk back to the EMS truck was going to be too much for the crew, so they just pulled him off the concrete. He let out horrible screams as he left some of that cheek on the ground. My first thought was these guys were assholes. But I also know what these guys go through. This might be the tenth time they have dealt with this same guy. You become calloused working the streets of Detroit. The nature of the job starts to empty you of compassion.

GO WITH THE FLOW

Cockiness comes with experience and sometimes you just have to flow with certain situations. We pulled a guy over for a minor traffic offense. Pulling someone over in Detroit who didn't have a license was very common. Many of the people we stopped were wanted on warrants, and what would begin as a simple arrest, would tie us up for over an hour. We eventually learned to put a dollar amount on those we would take to jail. No license and up to five hundred dollars in warrants would get a trip to the pokey. Anything less than that wasn't worth our time.

It sounds like we weren't doing our job, but it was the nature of the beast. We couldn't lock up everyone we stopped. One Halloween night, my partner and I decided to see how many people we could stop who had outstanding warrants against them. We had investigated thirty-two people in a row when we broke our streak. Thirty-two people were wanted for some type of misdemeanor warrant. This was the makeup of the city. This behavior by the police helped contribute to the lawlessness. It's not that we wanted to let these people go, we just didn't have a choice.

As I walked up to the car during this particular traffic stop, the lone driver put his hands out the window, palms together as if they had cuffs on. I never hesitated, pulled my cuffs out, and clacked them on. I removed him from his car and placed him in the back of the scout. I sat back in the car and waited. After several minutes, I asked him what he was locked up for. He said he didn't know. I said, well you put your hands out like a wanted felon, so I just did what came natural. Now he got upset, and said he didn't have a driver's license. He figured I was going to arrest him no matter what. I replied, well it sure looked like you wanted to go to jail — I just thought that's where you wanted to go. He pleaded for mercy, and I obliged. I lectured him a bit about his behavior and sent him on his way.

One of the more comical traffic stops occurred when I was in the corridor. I got behind a car that had a cardboard plate on it. Not a dealer-issued type but the kind made out of a shoebox. It looked neat, as the letters were printed in black marker. It even had the year sticker drawn in the corner. I pulled the guy over and walked up to the driver's window. I asked about the plate, and I got the standard Detroit answer. The original plate had been stolen. He didn't have time to go to the Secretary of State and he didn't want to bother the police with such a minor issue as not having a plate.

So he simply created his own plate. Correct dimensions, and proper numbers were a must, according to this guy. I told him I appreciated the effort but he needed a real plate on his vehicle. I requested his driver's license and this is where it got really funny. He handed me an index card with all of his license information on it. The card was cut out the size of a driver's license and had been duplicated with all the appropriate lines filled in including his signature. There was even a block for a picture but no picture.

"Let me guess, you lost your license?" I asked.

He replied yes, and I immediately cut him off. I told him I was not going to stand for such shoddy work. Next time, I'm going to need a recent picture attached to the index card. Without a picture, how could I possibly know if this was the correct information? It could be anyone's license with no picture.

I handed him his index card back and walked back to my scout. He thanked me and left with his cardboard plate flapping in the wind.

Police Officer Andre Barksdale
Detroit Police Department, Michigan
End of Watch: Monday, November 2, 1987

Officer Barksdale was shot and killed with his own weapon while responding to a domestic disturbance. He is survived by his son and mother.

FROM THE RODEO TO THE POLICE FORCE

Lessons on human behavior were learned simply by walking a beat. Police partners can be a Freudian delight sometimes. You quickly find out if they are workers or not, and whether their mouth will get you in trouble. You also learn about their personal issues and goals. Eight hours is a lot of talk time.

One time, I was paired up with a talker/exaggerator type. She wouldn't shut up for anything. If you started talking, she would cut you off and turn the topic back to her. For all her accomplishments, I was amazed she was a police officer. She was a "been there, done that" type of person.

I decided to have some fun and see how far I could go with her. I was going to talk and not let her cut me off. We were discussing her previous employment and I cut her off. I began to explain my work history. First, I had worked the California coast as a marine salvage welder. I had dove on some pretty significant wrecks, and was once even bitten by a shark. I then got caught up in a pretty big narcotic thing, which I lied to the police department about, and I had to leave the country for a period of time.

When I returned, I ended up being a rodeo clown at the Calgary Stampede. I had done this for several years and had to quit after being gored by a Brahma Bull. After all the wildness, I finally settled down and graduated from Michigan Tech with an engineering degree. I got the break I needed and was hired by NASA. Things worked out for several years, until the Challenger disaster. I had worked on the suspect tiles that had separated from the shuttle.

The end of my story coincided with the end of the shift. I appeared to be a pretty serious guy to people who really didn't know me. She bought most of it, and what she didn't buy, she had to think about it. She didn't talk to me very much after that.

I also turned the tables on a mental case the same way. One of my first days on the job, this loony guy motioned me over. Like the rookie I was, I rushed over to help him out. He explained the hardships he was having, and asked for any change I could spare him. I tried to reason with him and explain his options. We talked for about ten minutes, and I couldn't get away from the guy. I was walking a beat and he followed me. What a mistake. Over the next week, he would lay in wait and tie me up whenever he could.

This went on for some time, so I decided to turn it around on him. The next day when I saw him, I rushed up to him. I told him my wife had left me the night before and I was distraught. I didn't know how I would cope. She was suing me and I was broke. I asked if he had any change so I could get lunch. He tried to walk away but I followed him, actually faking some sobbing. He bolted out the door and began trotting away. The next day I saw him, we spotted each other at the same exact moment. He was on the second floor of a building and I would have to get upstairs to catch him. By the time I made it up the escalator, he was gone. Boy, was I learning.

WATCH YOUR MOUTH

The way you treated people on the street was very important. You had to come up to speed quickly or it would get you hurt. Lots of officers thought the badge and uniform gave you the right to talk down to people. They also thought it made them bigger and more powerful than they actually were. I always treated people exactly how I wanted to be treated.

I had no idea what brought the people I encountered to their present position in life, and I did not try to judge them. Treat them with respect and the majority of the time you would get it in return. If you had a rude, loud mouth officer as a partner, he could get you into trouble in a hurry.

For example, I was working with a female officer in the corridor and we came across a transvestite working one of the corners. Mind you, this was back in the late eighties, and the sex trade had girls and guys working everywhere. This particular suspect was 6'2 and about 240 pounds. He wore a bad dress and a worse wig. His makeup was okay, but where he got high heels to fit those feet I have no idea. I knew this guy, and his name was Tommy.

We always were respectful of each other, and when I asked him to move on, he did. When he spoke, he used a very high-pitched squeaky voice. As we walked up to him, I asked how was business. He gave the standard, "You know how it's going."

I told him he was going to have to shut it down for the night. Usually, Tommy respected this and would stop working until we left the area. Today, he objected a bit, which set my partner off.

She pushed him up against a fence and said, "Bitch, you are going to get off the street or get locked up."

Now my partner was no small girl, but she was seventy pounds lighter and about a foot shorter than Tommy. Tommy went from all girl to all man in about a split second. He said in a deep voice that sounded like the devil himself, "Bitch, I will beat your mother fucking police ass if you don't get your pussy hands off me."

I could see Tommy's muscles tighten and the veins in his neck bulge. I knew my partner was in trouble, and it was what she deserved. I stepped between them, and could see the fear in my partner's eyes. Her bluff had been called big time. Her reputation on the street had been negatively established in an instant. It would follow her for the rest of her career.

I calmed Tommy down, and he morphed back into his working girl persona. I sent him on his way, and we winked as he glanced over his shoulder. That high squeaky voice had returned, chirping a "Have a good night officers."

In the early days, every run was a puzzle. You tried to prep yourself en route. What if this happened, what if that happened. You talked with your partner about your options for each situation. The problem was, we didn't know much. Every run was a learning experience. My regular partner and I responded to a domestic violence run. We pulled up and could hear screaming from inside. We quickly exited the car and ran onto the front porch with our guns drawn. The five-foot-by-six-foot front window was broken out, apparently from the couch being thrown through it. There were several other pieces of furniture on the front lawn along with clothing and groceries.

We entered the house cautiously, finding the wife huddled in a corner. She looked no taller than five foot, and was sobbing. In the front room, we found the reason for her fear. Her husband stood seven feet tall and weighed close to four hundred pounds. He was pacing and screaming. The house was dark and only lit by our flashlights. He stopped pacing looked directly at us and said, "I'm going to fuck you both up."

I looked at my partner and I think we both immediately agreed he was right. Now, I'm not afraid of a fight, but this was a big boy. You learn early on that in a police street fight, you are at a disadvantage because it seems the bad guy always is grabbing for your weapon. Not only do you have to watch out for that move, but you have to watch for a grab at your partner's gun. This is where the power of talk is so important in police work.

We ordered the wife out to the scout car, removing the object of his anger. We could now talk man-to-man, husband-to-husband. My partner and I began circling and talking. I thought of a heavy antlered bull moose, turning with the wolves that were trying to pull him down. We talked and circled for some time. We finally got him to sit down, and eventually agreed with him that his wife had led him to this.

This was before domestic violence laws were in effect, so we had some options concerning his arrest or release. His wife was uninjured, and she didn't want to press charges. We helped him gather some clothes and drove him to a friend's house. This was a situation where working with the wrong partner could have been deadly.

YOU DRINK, YOU DRIVE, YOU LOSE

You also learn quickly about drunks — especially the ones driving. I was working midnights and we rolled up on a car stopped at a green traffic light. The driver was slumped over to his right leaning on the console. We positioned our scout behind his car and activated the lights. We walked up to his car, and my partner tapped on his window. There was no response. Flashing a light in his face had no effect, and several more taps on the window elicited no response.

I told my partner I had this one, and began rocking the car side to side. Many times on this job, I would experience the "You shouldn't be doing this" moment. This was turning into one of those moments. As his body was rocking back and forth, I noticed something peculiar. His right foot was on the brake pedal. Yep, I forgot to check if the brake lights were on. I watched as his foot slowly slid off of the pedal, and the car began slowly heading down Woodward Avenue. Like cartoon characters, my partner and I held on to the side view mirrors, leaning back in attempt to use shoe friction to stop the runaway vehicle. It began gaining speed as our "Fred Flintstone" brakes were failing.

He now was headed for a row of parked cars. Thinking on his now running feet, in one swift swing, my partner broke out the window with his flashlight. He pushed the gearshift up, bringing the vehicle to an abrupt stop. This finally woke the driver up, and he began protesting about the ruckus. We locked him up for drunken driving, and were later accused of beating and robbing him. Apparently, he was unaware we saved his life.

We once pulled a guy over driving a 1966 Pontiac Catalina in mint condition. It was about 4 in the morning. The reason for the stop was he was dragging the driver's side molding, which caused a spark shower as it skipped along the pavement. It was accident damage that looked fresh, and we assumed he was drunk. He stopped, and as I walked up to the car, he jammed the car in gear and raced off.

We chased him into another precinct where he entered an alley that ran along the back of several old businesses that had loading docks. As he roared through the alley, he drove right off one of those docks, dropping about six feet, bring the chase to an end.

We hustled up to the accident and drug him out of the car. Both he and the car were totaled. We cuffed him and placed him in the back of the scout car, when he reminded us why you shouldn't drink. He was leaning up in the back seat, separated from us by a cage. He now could see his smoking wreck of a classic car.

"Oh my god, what happened to my baby?" he screamed.

He asked us what we did to her, and I told him the whole story. But he was not buying any of it. He was so drunk, he had no idea he was chased by the police and crashed his car.

Drunken drivers were not a common arrest for us because it seemed we always were busy with other more pressing runs. We did lock up a guy in the middle of the day, and that caused all kind of issues. It started off as a police run where people were detaining a person.

We made it the location to find a large crowd gathered. They had a guy pinned to the ground. It was obvious he had been roughed up, and people were screaming and shouting. I picked the calmest of the bunch and tried to get the story. Apparently, the drunk had been driving down the street and almost stuck a child. He then ran off the road, hit a fire hydrant, and attempted to flee the scene. The crowd ran him down and gave him the business.

We found out he was an on-duty mailman, but he wasn't wearing his uniform. We locked him up, but probably would have been better off letting street justice do its job.

He could barely stand as we walked him through the police garage. I told my partner that if he took him into the cellblock, I would give the desk boss the story. He agreed, and was about five feet from the door, when I saw our mailman stop and just stand there. I then saw my partner get visibly upset and start dragging him into the back. Neither of them said a word, and they both disappeared. I found out what all the commotion was about when my partner came out of the cellblock. Apparently, the guy couldn't wait or bring it to anyone's attention that he had to crap. He just stopped and filled his drawers. Keep in mind my partner previously had been soiled by stepping in bum shit. This was a tough one for him.

Now, the precinct did not provide clothes for bad guys, so he was going to have to walk around like that until he could make it to court. Good for him, but it would give us a poor grade with the cellblock personnel. There was no Breathalyzer in the precinct, so we would have to transport him to the state police post for a test. If you think baby crap stinks, you should ride in a scout car with a drunk who just filled his pants. With heads hanging out open windows we made I to the post.

We were directed to the Breathalyzer room, sat our guy down, then waited in the hall, watching him from the open door. A squared away trooper we knew came bouncing down the hall, shouting a cheery hello. She turned the corner into the room, and got all the way to his chair, before he stood straight up and said, "You mother fuckers."

She came out of the room like a scalded cat. All three of us started laughing at the situation that was forced upon us. Our state cop friend eventually conducted the test, holding her nose. She forgave us, but I knew those troopers were going to get even. Now I had to add them to the list of people to watch for.

HE WAS EATING FROZEN PIZZA

Each of these incidents pours experience into your brain. If you can survive them or handle them properly, it helps you move one step up the ladder. One of my more tragic cases was a shots fired run my regular partner and I responded to. We pulled up one door down from the given address and found a guy out front. This was a no-no in police work because we should have stopped several houses away and walked up.

You service so many shots fired runs in the city that you sometimes grow complacent.

We asked the guy if he heard any shots fired. He nodded yes. When asked where, he pointed to our given address. I now backed the car up several houses and we got out. It would have been too late if someone came out firing, but it refreshed our heads concerning shots fired runs.

As we approached the house, you could see the front door was about half open. Working hard at learning your trade helps you develop those senses that keep you alive. This didn't feel right and we entered with guns drawn. I yelled, "Detroit Police," as we crossed the threshold of the door.

It was eerily quiet, and I scanned the room to my right and found it unoccupied and dark. I could hear a TV and advanced further down the hall. As the first doorway on my left came up, I could see the reason we were called. A woman who was about twenty years old was lying on her back. She had on some type of silk pajama top, which was completely open, exposing her upper torso. She had a large hole about the size of a golf ball under her left breast. She had coughed up lung matter, which now hung from her open mouth.

As I turned the corner into the room, I was startled by a male who was about sixty years old. He was sitting quietly in a lounge chair, and the victim's feet were touching his. He was holding a paper plate with a frozen pizza on it. He had cut it into squares and was eating it as he watched TV.

At gunpoint, I told him to put the pizza down and stand up. He complied, and stated, "I killed the bitch, I told her to leave the house and she didn't. The shotgun I used is behind the door."

I advised him of his rights and he ignored them as I cuffed him. He told me he was her sugar daddy and had been taking care of her for sexual favors. Tonight, she wanted twenty bucks and he told her no. She kept going on and on, and he wouldn't budge. He warned her that if she didn't leave, he was going to do something about it. Apparently, heeding his advice, she went upstairs to gather some things to leave. At some point, she changed her mind, and came back downstairs to argue.

Unknown to her, he had armed himself with a single shot twelve gauge shotgun. As she turned the corner to enter the room, he made good on his threat. He shot her at point blank range under the left breast. He must have sat there and watched as she struggled for her life.

The part that bothered me was the way he told the story. There was no emotion or no tears — nothing. He never went to trial, as he had terminal cancer and died four months later. For the experience file, I entered the room the same way she did. Luckily, I didn't leave it the same way.

THE ONES THAT GOT AWAY

A new officer has to overcome many hurdles. You go into it having this pre-perception of how things are going to happen. If a guy is going to pull a robbery, he walks up to someone pulls a gun and takes their money. We acquire these perceptions from the academy and, to be honest, TV. Our first big caper at New Center was for B&E. Several high-end homes were broken into in the middle of the day. As the city was trying to portray this as the new epicenter, we couldn't have two-hundred-thousand-dollar homes being broken into. The 86-Sam was going to be assigned the task.

The first big plus for us was we were going to be wearing plain clothes. This was pretty exciting for us, as it usually took several years to get a plain clothes assignment. We would be positioned in two spots to watch one block of the New Center area. One position was at the top of a four-story apartment building. The other was in a home up for sale at the west end of the block. The premium pick was the apartment building. You could carry a lawn chair and lunch to the rooftop and had the opportunity to soak up some sun while you worked.

We did have a brief stint in a borrowed narcotic surveillance van. Many of us were excited about this, and were hoping to get that assignment. Our dreams came crashing down as we discovered it was empty except for a periscope on the roof. There were no infrared cameras, listening devices, radar screens or high tech electronics. It was summer time, so about twenty minutes was the max you could take inside of it. It didn't take long before the van turned into a toaster oven.

Now, we had been working this detail for about two weeks when the suspects hit. We had experienced sergeants, but our briefing basically was if you see someone breaking in, call for our roving car to make the scene and arrest them. It sounded simple enough. Everyone figured they would see them walk up, break a window and be inside for about ten or fifteen minutes, and we'd arrest them when they came out. Just like TV.

I guess the bosses forgot they were teaching infants. I was on the apartment building one morning, when I saw two suspects turn onto the block, looking like they didn't belong. I radioed my partner in the west house.

I knew enough that these may be our guys, but should have called for the roving car to make sure they were close — and not eating, shopping or paying bills. I watched as they walked down the block, rubber necking (i.e. their heads on a swivel, as they scan the area for police).

They walked up to a house about mid-block. One of the suspects sat down on the porch as the other knocked on the door. Knowing what I know now, everyone should have been about twenty feet away from these guys. They would knock repeatedly on the door to see if anyone was home. No answer, so they walked around the back.

Again, I knew something wasn't right, so I called the guy in the west house to meet me at the location. I also called in the rover car. By the time I got downstairs, ran the half block (my partner didn't think it was anything important), and made the back of the location with the rover, it was too late. The rear door was kicked in and the suspects were gone. They had been inside less than three minutes and had stolen jewelry, money and a camera. I had no idea they could be in and out so fast. It was two weeks of work down the drain.

That day, I promised myself, if I ever worked with rookies, I would lead them through each crime step by step. I would have them way better prepared than I was. Six weeks later, a marked unit caught the suspects breaking into a house about a block away.

THE BUZZER TRICK

Every single run now was a learning experience. I needed more knowledge and the streets would willingly supply it. We responded to a felonious assault run, finding the female victim beat to a pulp. She had missing teeth, large purple knots all over her head and a busted nose.

Her ex-boyfriend had come over in a rage, broken the dining room table up and beat her with one of the legs. It was an old-school leg that was about six inches around in some spots. We gathered information about him, and found him to be staying in an apartment building near the hospital complex at the south end of the precinct. The victim told us he had no transportation and he walked off after the beating.

Being the crack police officers we were, we headed to his home. We found a spot near a dumpster in the parking lot. Our plan was to arrest him when he arrived home. It was simple enough. We had a good view of the front door, but knew we had an issue. You needed a key to enter, and if you didn't have one, you needed to be buzzed in. If he got in the door before we grabbed him, he could make good his escape. Well, we figured we could hopefully catch him before he got in that door. Sure enough after about ten minutes, he came walking through the lot. He must have caught the "Iron Pimp," (which is what normal folk call the "bus"), and he still was dragging the bloody table leg.

We snuck out of the car, and attempted to close on him. Criminals also have a second sense, and he spotted us coming through the lot. The race was on, and he had a ten-foot head start. He made the door first, key in hand. He pulled the door shut, as we ran up guns in hand. He hesitated for a split second, smiled and ran. I looked at the buzzer panel and pressed the first button. No response, and thinking like a true police officer, I ran my hand down all three rows of buttons, buzzing about two hundred apartments. I got a bunch of buzzes and a couple of "Who the fuck is its?"

We both entered the apartment building and were running down the hall when we encountered our first "Who the fuck is it?" guy. This was early morning, and he wasn't going to buzz anyone in without checking first. He was groggy-eyed and scratching himself as he made the corner. I'm sure he had no idea he was going to bump into a chrome revolver. His eyes immediately dilated to the size of saucers, and he began stuttering in what seemed like some Latin gibberish. His legs already had turned around and were heading back to his apartment, when the rest of him decided to try and catch up. I was chasing a guy for assault with intent to commit murder, and who still was armed with the same weapon he had just used, but I just couldn't help from laughing as I ran down the hall, thinking of that poor guy in pajama bottoms sitting in his room wondering what just happened to him.

We caught the bad guy, recovered the weapon and had learned a buzzer lesson. It was funny, but it wouldn't have been if the groggy-eyed guy had checked the door armed with a gun.

Some apartments or buzzer panels only had a few buttons. In those cases, we learned to be pizza delivery, a gasman, the fire department, phone company or escort service personnel — basically whatever it took to get inside. You learn as you go. How to get into a building never was taught in the academy. Neither was what type of knock to use.

Police Officer
Linda G. Smith
Detroit Police Department, Michigan
End of Watch: Saturday, November 28, 1987

Officer Smith was killed in an automobile accident while assisting other officers during a pursuit. Her patrol car struck a truck and burst into flames.

THE REGULAR KNOCK VS. THE GHETTO KNOCK

You learn there is a regular knock on the door and then there's a ghetto knock. Once, I was working with an ATF agent from the Bureau of Alcohol, Tobacco, Firearms and Explosives on a homicide case. Bless their souls they have an education, and lots of cool toys, but some do not have much street sense.

We used to dangle the federal guys like the black plague. Criminals know if the feds prosecute you, you go to prison for a very long time. If you were interrogating someone, you could take a federal agent in with you and just introduce him. This would perk the bad guy up like he was stuck with a pin. They would ask why the FBI was sitting in, and you could tell them they are just concerned that this may parallel something they were working. It would change the whole makeup of the interrogation.

So I'm with this ATF agent one day, and he begins tapping on the steel screen door like any normal person would do. I asked him to step to the side of the door, so no one would blast him through the door, and then told him he could continue to knock. He tap-tap-tapped, and there was nothing but crickets.

After several minutes, he informed me no one must be home and turned to walk off the porch.

"Okay, watch this," I said, and began kicking the metal screen door at the base as hard as I could without damaging it.

I continued for about thirty seconds until I got the desired response. I heard a loud "Who is it" from inside. I hollered back in a loud voice, "The police, open the door." Someone peered through the front curtain and opened the door. I was hoping the agent was taking notes, as this was pretty standard for us.

I am not saying all agents are walking around in a haze, as I have worked with some pretty good federal guys. It's just tough to come from Boise, Idaho, and the FBI academy to working the streets of Detroit and hoping you can relate to the people and the culture. Hell, I was born here and I was struggling. You can't learn this stuff in a book, and you can't get a late start. The streets will eat you up.

MEET THE ADAMS FAMILY

Working police officers always are looking to service a run as quickly as possible. It gives you time to get back out there and prowl around. You don't want accident scenes or a dead body because they can really burn up some of that time. One day, we responded to a run of Meet the Gasman. We pulled up to the address and found a man in a shirt and tie, standing next to a white Chevy Impala. In front of his vehicle was a Carson consolidated gas work truck. The man had a very concerned look on his face.

I asked him what we could do for him, and he responded, "One of my men is missing."

Missing? Missing from where? He pointed to the work truck and told us one of his guys had responded to the listed address on a complaint of a gas leak. They had not heard from him in sometime, and couldn't raise him on the radio.

I asked which house, and he pointed to the lone building on the north side of the block. It looked like the Adams Family house, and was very dark and spooky. I asked how long since they heard from him, and he said four hours. Four hours? This didn't look good. We told him to wait in his car, and we would check the house. We creaked up the steps, and used the ancient knocker to announce our presence. After several seconds, a crooked eye peered out the dirty glass portal. The door opened and, to be honest with you, I had my gun out. A man who was about forty years old allowed us in, and we got that immediate dank smelling rush as we entered.

The man was dressed in mismatched clothes and had an unkempt Afro that gave him a clownish appearance. We asked if the gasman was in the house, and he said he didn't know. Okay, that was not a good sign. He informed us his mother might know, and he would lead us to her. I instantly thought of the movie Psycho, and was fully expecting to be led to a mummified corpse. I wasn't putting my gun away.

The house was that of a hoarder, or in this case, hoarders. There was nothing but narrow aisle ways leading from room to room. You had to sidestep as you moved about. He led us to the kitchen area, and found his mother quite alive. She was old and bent, with hands that had been changed by severe arthritis. The house and her fit, I thought. I asked if she had seen the gasman, and she replied yes. I was frightened to ask, but I did. Where was he?

"In the basement," she cackled back.

This was getting worse and worse. I asked her if he was okay, and she responded, "of course."

I knocked on the basement door, which looked like one of those dungeon doors, complete with big thick boards and hand forged hardware. I yelled, "police," and could hear a feint "help."

I opened the door slowly, and was almost run over by the gasman as he sprung from the basement. He was sweaty and dirty. I walked him to the front door so he could get some air. Shaken, he began to stammer through the story. He was allowed in the house by the mom and son. When he entered, he had the same uneasy feeling as I had. He followed them both into the basement, where they pointed out the furnace.

A large Rottweiler was chained to the wall, surrounded by large bones and plenty of dog crap. He quickly inspected the furnace and informed them he was not allowed to work on this brand. It was gas company policy. The mother already had gone upstairs, and the son was going to head upstairs to inform her. The gasman heard the chain and bolt as soon as the son left the basement. He began pounding on the door to no avail. They informed him he would be released when the furnace was fixed.

He wasn't going to stand for this, and began pounding harder. This began to send the dog into a vicious frenzy. Fearing the dog would break its chain, he quit pounding on the door. He took a seat amidst the poo as Fido watched his every move.

Unfortunately, he had left his radio in the truck and could not call his central office.

The mom continued to yell that she would release him when he fixed the furnace. I asked him if he wanted to press charges, and he said he was just happy to be out of the basement.

I sent him and his boss on their way, and went back in to talk to the mom and son. She informed me the gas company got what it deserved because it had been gassing her for the last thirty-seven years. It was a slow deadly process that had been sapping her life and will to live. Her son agreed, and he still was talking as we shouted the standard, "Have a nice day," and left.

PARTNERS IN GOOD TIMES AND BAD

After about three years on the job, my regular partner was going to get a divorce. So now throw that into the mix. It was tough, as you spend more time with you partner than you do a spouse. So I felt for him. I felt he was wrong, but he still was my partner. Our wives were close friends, and he was leaving her pregnant. It made a tough working environment for both of us. Needless to say he was a bit grumpy.

It's tough enough to control your emotions without all the extras. On this day, we got another "convey the mental" run. The location was Children's Hospital, which was about a hundred yards from the Crisis Center. Mental runs seem to accomplish absolutely nothing and are very time consuming. We all hated them. When we show, the people who are holding her are hospital security guards. She is about fifty years old, and has blown-out hair, large red circles of makeup on her cheeks, three coats on, a skirt with corduroy pants underneath, gloves and rubber galoshes. She has two garbage bags of property.

At this time, my grumpy partner loses it, as he starts yelling at the guard. Why did he not just direct her to the Crisis Center? She could walk — and it was only a block away. I was with my partner on that one, but like us, maybe he was a rookie guard. Now that we responded, we had to do something about it. The guard stammered some excuse as I walked the lady to the car.

You try to keep your distance, as most mentals always want to touch you. Holding your hand when you are not looking is my favorite. Avoiding contact, I pile her in the back seat, placing her property up front with me. My partner is livid. We don't have time to deal with this bullshit, and he hates these nut jobs. They are dirty and stinky. They have jumping bugs on them. He tears out of the drive of Children's doing 90. He wants this over as quickly as possible. We only have a 100 yards and a quick commitment sheet.

I look into the rearview mirror as he straightens the wheel. What I see gives me the giggles, which turn into outright laughter. Our girl has slid all the way to the front of the back seat. Her face is pressed against the cage and on her head is my partner's hat. She is wearing it in that rakish style of the forties. Kind of down in front and tilted to the side. I bring this to my partner's attention, and he almost crashes as he pulls the vehicle over. The combination of the nut wearing his hat and the divorce may force me to commit him. I wouldn't have given it a second thought if he started crying.

He jerks the door open and pulls his hat off of her. He is convinced she has lice, crabs and every other creepy crawler you can imagine, and he announces he can never wear his hat again. I calm him, down and get him back behind the wheel. Poor guy. I'm still giggling as I attempt to search her property. No weapons or contraband are allowed in the Center. I'm trying to do this quickly and with no dome light. Still giggling, I pick up a white heavy item. I can see it is some type of plastic and attempt to open it. I find a corner and begin to peel away. My giggling ceased as I become furious. I discover it contains baby poop. She was carrying around a soiled diaper. The only consolation for my misfortune was that my partner now was laughing, and he was laughing hard.

It seemed he couldn't catch a break, as we had a series of push-him-over-the-edge type incidents. We observed a car traveling south on Woodward. The plate was in the rear window. This was common, but this plate was from New York and it was all bent up.

Before even stopping the car we knew it probably didn't belong on this vehicle. There were three people in the car: A male driver, a heavy-set female in the front passenger spot and a male in the rear. As we walked up, the suspect in the back dropped something from the rear window. It was small and could have been anything — from a cigarette butt to narcotics.

As my partner questioned the driver, I asked the rear suspect what he had dropped. The female motioned for me to come to her window and I expected her to tell me he had some mental issues or was deaf. I was shocked when she told me she didn't appreciate how I was talking to them. She also didn't appreciate my partner talking to them that way. She said the only reason why we stopped them was because they were black.

My partner and I always remained professional, and I always attempted to avoid the whole racial issue with people on the street. I stopped you because you were breaking the law, not because of the color of your skin. I attempted to explain this to her, and she was not having it. She became loud and said we were just looking for some niggers to stop.

I stopped my explanation cold, walked to the driver's side of the vehicle, told my partner we were locking up the driver because the plate was stolen and he had no license. For us, this was a standard "stop, investigate and send them on their way" stop. We didn't have time for this crap. We had no intention of arresting anyone, black or white. She changed all that. I now was forced to do my job.

We now wanted to document everything we did because we were being accused of racism. All three were dressed in African-type outfits — with very colorful hats. The woman continued to rant and rave as we arrested her husband and got her and the other guy out of the vehicle. A small crowd had gathered, which I'm sure was her intention. We pulled away and on the trip to the station, I felt bad for the guy. I told him we were going to let him go, but his wife got him arrested. He said he knew that was the case, but he loved her. That was his "Queenie."

It was no sooner that we got to the precinct when she walked through the door, continuing with the same loud, attention-getting behavior she displayed on the street. She was going on and on about those white motherfuckers who arrested her husband. Now, the desk lieutenant was black, and he sat and listened for about a minute. He then informed her that Detroit police officers, not white or black officers, arrested her husband for breaking the law. He said if she wanted to continue with this behavior, she could join her husband in jail. She stormed out.

Now here is the part that really got my partner. Several weeks later, we were on patrol when this same female drove by us in a pickup truck.

We knew she had no license and was wanted on traffic warrants. My partner swung around and activated the lights. I actually asked him why he wanted the headache.

"I don't mind her being an ass, but I'm not going to let her flaunt it," he said.

We turned the siren on and she continued to drive, ignoring us. She wasn't speeding. She just wasn't stopping. I had to inform dispatch what was going on, and they were sending another car.

We followed her for about ten blocks, when she pulled up in front of her house. She jumped, as quick as a four-hundred-pound-woman can jump from a vehicle, and began running for her front door. My partner's door bolted open, and I grabbed him before he could get out. I asked him what he was doing. He said he was going to arrest her. I asked him why he wanted to be rolling around on the ground with her over some traffic offenses. I told him I had a plan.

She got in the front door and looked out from behind the shade. I picked up the radio and requested a tow truck because we had the right to impound her vehicle. I was quite sure she couldn't afford to get it out of the pound and would be restricted to walking. Hence, we would solve her driving issues.

Now us sitting in front of her house made her antsy. She came out on the front porch and asked us what we were doing. I informed her about the tow and this set her off. We didn't have a right to do that, blah, blah, blah. Knowing I had a good boss working that day, I asked her if she would like me to request a supervisor. Of course, she did. When the sergeant showed up, he immediately could see they type of situation we were in.

He was white, along with the both of us, and she didn't like it one bit. Her first question was posed to me, and she wanted to know what gave me the right to tow her truck. I informed her the law in the State of Michigan did, at which time the sergeant repeated what I had just said. She looked calmly at me and said, "Let your daddy know when I want to hear from him I'll ask him a question."

Now staying calm and professional in this type of situation is critical. It actually infuriates the suspect when you don't lose your cool. I told her we were not related at all, and that my father was a fireman. Although we may favor, we are not blood related. The sergeant replied, "I have no sons, but would be proud to have Officer Haig as one if I did have a son."

She now was pissed and at a loss for words. We towed her vehicle without incident. No one was injured, and that would be the last time we ever saw her. Even my partner was happy with this ending.

My partner's drama continued with his first accident. We were rolling down the street in full patrol mode, when we heard several whistles. We couldn't see anyone on the street, so we flipped around into the alley. As we crept along, a young male suspect stepped out of a garage and closed the large swinging doors behind him. We now were about four feet from him, and he never even looked at us. He took off like a shot heading east in the alley. I jumped from the scout and began chasing him. Like many foot chases, I had no idea why I was chasing him, except for the simple fact he ran. Ninety-nine percent of the time, you would go back and find some type of illegal activity. As I was running, I could hear the screeching of the scout car tires as my partner tried to negotiate out of the alley. Seconds later, I heard him come onto the radio and say he was chasing one. He then comes back on the radio, saying he was involved in an accident. No one was injured.

I stopped chasing my guy, and ran the half block back to check on my partner. I found the scout car piled into a large maple tree. Now my partner always drove a little bit too fast and a little loose, but I couldn't figure out how he ran into a giant tree. I asked him if he was injured, and he stated no. He then looked at me and said, "This is your fault."

Really, how could it be my fault? I wasn't divorcing him.

"You're stupid flashlight did it," he said."

This was going to be a good story, as my flashlight now was responsible for him running into the biggest tree on the block. I told him, "Go ahead, I got to hear this."

He explained that as I began chasing the first suspect, he pulled the car back and a second suspect appeared and began running west bound. He followed in reverse and then swung the car around as he exited the alley. The suspect ran across the first lawn on the corner, and my partner (I told you he drove loose) decided to follow. As he skidded across the lawn, he went to hit the brakes and they wouldn't go down. He began stomping on the pedal so hard his leg hurt. With no brakes, he crashed into the tree.

Now in a high-speed chase, no matter how careful you are, the car always ends up a mess. Ticket books, papers and coffee, if you had it (you quickly learn to throw it out the window) end up all over. In this case, my flashlight came out of the passenger door slot, rolled across the floor over the transmission tunnel, around the mobile data computer, and came to rest directly under the brake pedal.

Most of us had purchased somewhat expensive Kel-lites. They were very durable and made of aircraft aluminum. Mine now had a large gash in it, as if someone took a grinding wheel to it. He really must have been trying to get those brakes to work. Both bad guys got away, and they had been stripping a stolen ride inside the garage. We got a recovery and a bunch of paperwork for our trouble.

Another incident during my partner's dark time set him off. We pulled a van over for a traffic offense and as we walked up, we could see two people in the back seat, and a driver. This was strange because normally someone would be sitting in the front passenger seat. My partner could see the two people in the rear fumbling around, and he pulled the side door open. One appeared to be male, and had his pants down around his legs. The other was female and had apparently been giving him the works. My partner ordered both of them out, and I brought the driver around to the passenger side.

All three were drunk. Both males were from the suburbs and had come into the city for a little action. Well they sure found it, as with a little closer inspection, the female was a male. Remember, the feet and Adam's apple give it away every time. If both of these parts of the anatomy are large, you better take a closer look. My partner started lecturing the guys about the dangers of Detroit. He brought them up to speed quickly, telling the one guy that the person performing fellatio on him was actually a male and not a female. He started yelling, "No way" — insisting he knew the difference between a girl and a guy.

"You do? Well what about this?" my partner asked, as he then snatched the wig off of the "female's" head, exposing a small Afro. The truth now was evident. Our guy who knew male from female began puking, while his buddy began laughing. The whole situation had my partner wired, as he was very homophobic.

The story could have ended there, but my partner had to search the car. Taking into consideration what they were doing, I would have let this one go. He rummaged through the back seat, lifting a pink piece of plastic. I knew what it was before he illuminated it with his light. It was a soiled condom. He threw it down with as much authority as he could possibly generate. I could see his teakettle lid about to blow, and advised all parties to leave immediately. I snickered under my breath, but kept it to myself. My partner was having a rough stretch.

My partner's behavior had become pretty erratic, and I felt for him. We responded to a domestic run and as we arrived, we found a male and female pushing and shoving on the porch. We ran up and quickly separated them.

The male took several steps down, and we could both see the look in his eye. He was going to run, and we couldn't stop him. You always try to position yourself to block any escape route, but this happened so fast we didn't even think about it. So, he is slowly backing down the stairs, and we are both saying, "Don't do it." Bang, he is off.

Like I said, my partner was going through some rough times, and I never knew what was going through his head. One thing about him is that he could run like the wind. He missed all the stairs as he jumped from the porch and began chasing the guy. I was running for the scout, when I saw him skid to a halt. I was puzzled and knew it was not in his makeup to quit chasing a guy. I saw him cock his flashlight up in his right hand, and hurl it like the hammer of Thor. No way is this department policy and, like I said, I had no idea what was in his head. Not only could my partner run, he was one heck of a baseball player and had a cannon of an arm. The suspect was about forty feet away when the light caught up with him. As his right foot was coming up, the light struck him right on the heel. My partner could have killed this guy, but I must admit, I yelled, "yes," when the bad guy cartwheeled down the sidewalk.

One thing about chasing suspects is that they could get hit by a train, fall in an alligator pit or get clocked by a wrecking ball, and they still get up and continue running. He did, but didn't get far. My partner ran him down. The suspect probably was stunned by the whirling ninja flashlight. I caught up with the scout car and we arrested him for assault.

We returned to the Olympic flashlight throw ring to try and locate the light. Once it hit the suspect's heel, I could see it launched about thirty feet in the air. I heard it hit the ground, but was zooming by in the car. What we found was pathetic. The head of the light was broken off, cracking the lens and shattering the bulb. The screw cap on the bottom holding the battery was knocked off, dumping the rechargeable battery out. I felt this was my partner's lowest point and again, if he began crying, I wouldn't have been shocked. He didn't, and gathered up his broken light attempting to reassemble it like a bad jigsaw puzzle.

He didn't fix the light or his marriage. I talk about my partner, not to justify his actions, but to help you understand what a cop goes through. Always keep in mind police officers are just everyday people. Imagine having a bad stretch at home, and when you get to work, someone spits in your face or you step in bum shit. How about being at work, and one of your co-workers would walk by and poke you with a stick. This goes on for months. Imagine this happening every day. At what point would you crack? In our line of work, you just can't crack. The end result could be deadly.

MONSTER ENCOUNTER

Even the simplest of runs, can help load up your experience hopper. We both got the crap scared out of us on an open door run. It was to an apartment in an old run down building. I came from a family of scarers, and always was a bit jumpy. I'd fight anyone, and didn't fear many, but throw a monster into the mix, and I was a baby.

We made it the fourth floor of the apartment building and exited the elevator. The whole place had an odor to it, and it was deathly quiet. We located the apartment and found the door slightly ajar. We both pulled our weapons, and I motioned my partner behind me, as I would enter first. This had a creepy feel to it. As I pushed the door open, I yelled, "Police department!"

The apartment was completely dark and had a damp odor, which was different from the hallway. I took another step in announcing police for a second time. I now was positioned several feet inside the apartment, with a long kitchen counter running to my left. My partner still was in the hall. I sensed movement to my left and heard a gurgling ARGHHH. Something was moving toward be from behind the counter.

Whatever it was, it was no taller than three feet, and it was closing in on me quickly, as it continued to make loud grunting noises. My mind desperately searched for identification. Dog? No. Man? No. Monster? Yes — run for your life. If it reached me, I would quickly be pulled down, and dragged into its lair, where it could consume me at its leisure. I stumbled back into the hall yelling, "Monster, monster!"

My partner was in full panic. There were no lessons in the academy about monsters. He had no idea what was in there, but whatever it was, it wasn't good. My partner had bolted for the elevator, and was banging the down button. His finger was pistoning like a sewing machine needle. His other hand was sweeping his gun in all directions, not sure where the monster attack would come from. I stumbled into the hall, turned and pointed my gun at the apartment doorway. Around the corner came something.

Wait a minute. It wasn't a monster. My eyes focused and it appeared to be a very short and round man. He was missing both his arms and legs. His head appeared to be twice the normal size with a very poor complexion and patchy hair. His grunting continued with an occasional wheezing sound. He looked like a large mushroom. My mind had difficulty, but clicked from monster to man.

As my heart settled back in my chest, I called my partner back. Between hand signals and grunts, we determined mushroom man had just left his door open. We escorted him back in and I watched in amazement as he shot down the hallway disappearing into a backroom. As I pulled the door behind me, a chill ran down my spine. Backroom my ass, that probably was his lair, filled with bones. I quickened my step to the elevator and began working the down button same way my partner had.

The moral of that police run was don't let your imagination get the best of you.

Lieutenant James L. Schmit
Detroit Police Department, Michigan
End of Watch: Monday, October 17, 1988

Lieutenant James Schmit was shot and killed while he and several other officers attempted to remove a mentally disturbed man from the location. The suspect opened fire on them with a 30-30 rifle. The suspect also shot and killed Officer Frank Walls as Officer Wells led a special operations team into the home during the standoff following Lieutenant Schmit's murder. The entry team had secured the lower level of the home and as Officer Walls moved to the stairs, he was shot and killed.

Lieutenant Schmit is survived by his wife and children.

Police Officer Frank E. Walls
Detroit Police Department, Michigan
End of Watch: Monday, October 17, 1988

Officer Walls was shot and killed as he led a special operations team into the home during the standoff following Lieutenant James Schmit's murder. The entry team had secured the lower level of the home at 2:14 p.m. and, as Officer Walls moved to the stairs, he was shot and killed. The suspect was shot and killed by other SRT members after he shot Officer Walls.

Officer Walls is survived by his parents, sister and two brothers.

FENCE JUMPING

My partner lost his senses one more time on a B&E run. We made it to the back of the location and could only get in by jumping the six-foot privacy fence. My partner vaulted over, and said he would check the door. I was standing on a garbage can watching him. He checked the rear door, which was secure, and then wanted to look in the rear window, which was about six feet off the ground. He had to grab the ledge and do kind of a pull up to look in. As he hoisted himself up and his eyes reached the window, he immediately shouted OHHHHH, and dropped from the windowsill. He tumbled back into the yard, trying to run backward.

His reaction caused me to lose my balance, and luckily, I grabbed the top of the fence or I would have gone down. I asked him what it was, as I feared it might be a monster. He said someone was in there. After several minutes or so, a young woman opened the door. She lived there and her alarm accidentally was set off. We loaded back into the scout and I started laughing. I told my partner, "You should have seen yourself."

"If you thought that was funny, you should have seen that girl," he said.

He explained that as he was lifting himself up and began peering into the house, the female homeowner was doing the same on the other side of the window. After hearing a noise in the backyard, she positioned herself right under the window so she could peek out. As she began peering over the edge, they met eyeball-to-eyeball. It scared the crap out of my partner, but he said she hit the ground with her legs going a hundred miles an hour. She couldn't get any traction with her footies on and began upending everything she grabbed onto. The kitchen was a disaster as she made it to the safety of the next room.

Even the simplest task of jumping a fence is a learning experience. I would get mine chasing a guy selling dope.

As we turned a corner one day, a suspect was pulling heroin out of a brown lunch bag and handing some to a waiting customer. He made eye contact and was off. I was out and after him. He ran into the alley and jumped a six-foot, wood picket privacy fence. As police officers do sometimes, I was locked on him and attempted to jump the same fence. I weighed about 240 pounds at the time, and as I grabbed the first picket, I snapped about two feet off of it. In quick succession I snapped off about four more before I realized I was going to have to find a different way over. Hanging from the fence like a monkey, I looked to my left and saw an old man watering his grass. He was only four feet from me and I never saw him. The kicker was there was no fence where he was standing.

"You can go this way, officer," he calmly told me.

I dropped from the fence, stepped four feet to my left and continued the pursuit. If I hadn't been so locked on the suspect, I would have run right around the fence. I found the bad guy in some bushes, and recovered the narcotics. The old guy still was watering the lawn as I walked back. He was throwing me the evil eye for the fence.

Note to self, look around, stupid, there may be another way.

OFFICER LONG COLT

Being careful around your co-workers also was a priority. I had talked about the old six-shooter we started with. The department gave you an option to buy a different weapon. Most of us couldn't afford it, but some did. One of my academy mates bought a .45 Long Colt. It was a Big Dirty Harry looking gun that looked funny on him, as he was tall and skinny. The gun looked bigger than him.

My precinct bordered with Highland Park, which was the only city more violent than us. We shared a channel on the radio, along with the seventh precinct. This allowed you to monitor the activity in the adjoining districts. On this particular day, Highland Park had their Burger King robbed. They were in foot pursuit of the bad guy, and Long Colt and his partner responded to back them up. Highland Park officers observed the suspect jump into a steel dumpster. Long Colt now was at that location, as the officers demanded the suspect throw out his weapon and surrender. The suspect lifted the lid of the dumpster and attempted to drop his handgun.

Every officer's interpretation at a scene is different and apparently someone felt he wasn't giving up and started shooting at the dumpster. For some reason, when one officer begins shooting, quite a few figure this is a green light and they can all shoot. So all the officers on the scene are shooting at the dumpster. They all have .38's and the rounds are bouncing off zinging ricocheted rounds everywhere.

Long Colt opens up and begins punching neat holes into the dumpster. This is bad news for the suspect, because not only are they punching through, they don't have enough velocity to exit. So now the rounds are buzzing around like bees inside the dumpster. The bad guy is screaming for dear life, and someone finally yells for a ceasefire. The suspect is hit four times and loses a finger.

All he wanted to know was why they started shooting. They asked him to give up and he was trying too. Police always can put a twist on it, and they told him they felt he was pointing the gun at them.

GET A DIFFERENT TRADE

Developing a street reputation also is an important part of police work. If it is a good one, you have more freedom talking to bad guys.

You can't trust them, but you can talk to them. They are more willing to rat out their competition or give you solid intelligence concerning crimes.

Now, this is nothing to play with, as the information you receive could get someone killed. We had previously locked up a mid-level narcotics dealer several times. He drove a decked-out Mustang convertible that had chrome everything. It was quite an attention-getter. There's nothing like being a drug dealer and drawing attention to yourself. On this particular day, we received a shooting run to the hospital. Once we and arrived, we were informed two people were shot. I told my partner I would take the guy in pod three and he could have the guy in pod one.

A good practice is to talk with the doctors or attending nurse before speaking with the victims. They told me that of the two victims, only one had been shot. They were told the second victim had been shot, but could find no injuries at all. His blood pressure was through the roof, and he had defecated in his pants. They could find no medical explanation for either. I pulled the curtain back, finding our drug dealer. He was wide-eyed and sweating. I asked him what happened, and he refused to talk. I convinced him I would find out anyway, and told him to just give me the truth.

My partner came into the pod and saw our dealer. He informed me that he had talked to the dealer's partner, who had been shot in the foot. He gave us the "heard noise, felt pain" standard story. This is the explanation criminals give police when they are shot. "I was just standing there, or walking down the street, when I heard a gunshot and felt pain." This way, you don't have to give the "I was in a shootout" story.

Now, I knew our dealer wore a bulletproof vest, and I figured he had been shot. After some coaxing, he gave us the story. Both of them had just walked out of a house party, when they were confronted by five suspects. One was armed with some type of automatic rifle, and he opened up. Our dealer, who had his vest on, took multiple rounds to the chest. His partner was hit in the heel. The dealer picked himself up and ran. The five suspects then produced axes and chopped his Mustang into pieces. The dealer and partner met up, called a girlfriend, and had her drive them to the hospital. He felt he had been shot multiple times and was going to die. The vest had five hits on it. He left the vest with the girl, and she dropped them both off at the hospital. I have seen some pretty scared people, but this guy was terrified. Heck, he shit himself.

I lectured him about the dangers of the narcotic trade and his gaudy vehicle. He told me he was done. I believed him. Several years later, he was arrested for a string of business robberies. He had quit his trade, just not the criminal trade.

AN EVENTFUL POTTY BREAK

We also learned trying to find a secluded restroom for some privacy can lead to a scary surprise. There are a number of homeless people who make every attempt to conceal themselves if they have to go to the bathroom. There also are a number who don't. We had a dead body run once, and after arriving at the listed address, we found a homeless man standing by a vacant building. He had that "I just saw a ghost" look on his face. We asked him what had happened, and he explained he had gone into the basement of the building to go number two.

He lit his lighter as he worked his way down the stairs, and because a disposable cigarette lighter does not cast a very bright light, he moved slowly. He entered a room at the bottom of the stairway, pulled down his pants and started the process. He turned off the lighter and relaxed. As he told it, after a minute he felt uneasy, as if someone was in the room with him. He flicked the lighter on and scanned the room. At this point, he could see some sort of skeletal beast lying on the floor. This immediately triggered the fear, flight mode in him. Skipping the wipe and the repositioning of his pants, he crab-crawled at light speed out of the building. He then tidied himself up and called us.

Skeletal beast. Great. I don't like monsters. We crept down the stairs, using both of our lights to illuminate the basement. We entered the room he had been in, finding what has caused his quick exit. We moved close, and I reminded my partner to watch out for the bum shit. What we found was a female body that appeared to have been there for about nine or ten months. She was positioned on her back face up. Her head, hands and feet were nothing but bleached white bone. Her mouth was open, giving the skull that horror look. Her hair was in a pile underneath her, and you could see what appeared to be a bullet hole in the back of the skull. The rest of her body still was covered by skin. It had shrunk and now was a yellow color and very leathery appearing. Animals had eaten her nipples and pubic region. It was no doubt the best dead body I had ever seen. We were laughing when we went up and talked to the guy reporting it. I told him that it must have been quite a surprise when he flicked on that lighter.

"Officer, you have no idea," he said, adding that he felt he hadn't touched a stair on the way out.

When the evidence Tech arrived to take picture, he placed the scene into his top five of all time.

DON'T GET ME WRONG

I don't want everyone to get the wrong impression. A female victim executed and left for animals to feed off of is nothing to laugh about. That is someone's daughter, sister or mother. Remaining professional in the face of daily tragedy is a must. As you gain experience, you have to let some of that human aspect go. Do your job. Express sympathy and supply comfort. Stay in that moment. When it is over, you better be ready to move onto the next one. You can't carry the burden of all the victims and their families around with you.

Think of an entire career and the emotional devastation that would cause. In this case, there was no family or media, just the poor guy taking a crap. We laughed together, but can you imagine how it would play if it made the news if we had been caught on camera? Our actions would again reflect all of law enforcement. Something, again, you have to be aware of.

I learned quickly to leave the job at the precinct. Never carry it home. There are things we see and experience that no one should. There is no special training for this. How can you watch an infant takes its last breath and then go home and hold your own child? How can you leave a homicide scene where a husband just blew the top of his wife's head off, then go home and take your wife to dinner? Just like the soldiers we are, some handle it differently than others. I was watching a documentary on World War II and they conducted interviews with combat vets. Sixty years after their experiences, they would weep while discussing the tragedies of war. Some handled it much better than others. There is no way you can compare the two, but how the individual handles those tragedies is part of police work. It can weigh heavy on the soul.

THE WRONG PLACE TO PARK

Sometimes even experienced cops can make mistakes. My partner and I had gotten to the point where we were pretty confident — even a little cocky. If we didn't know how to handle it, we could figure it out.

We responded to a shooting run at a rundown motel. It was positioned on the northeast corner of the expressway and Clairmount. The front door was facing Clairmount opening south bound. While we were en route, dispatch updated us several times. They said they had several calls on shots fired, and EMS was ordered. This probably was going to be a good shooting.

As we rounded the corner, I drove east past the location, so we could look up the driveway that was positioned on the east side of the building. The parking lot was in the rear, and we couldn't see it. I stopped several houses down from the location, and hadn't taken my eyes off of the location. As we exited the scout, we saw a guy standing on the south side of the street. We asked if he heard shots fired. His response was yes. Okay, did he see someone shot? He replied yes. Okay, where did he get shot? He pointed to the front of the scout car.

I looked down and saw about a three-foot round pool of blood directly under my right front tire. I had parked on the crime scene. I backed out of the pool and positioned my car about twenty yards west of the scene. I could now see that I had left a perfectly neat tire tread mark in the blood. After questioning several people, we discovered that a person had been shot in the back, and already had been transported to the hospital.

We had another unit make it the hospital, and they found our victim DOA (dead on arrival). We made our notifications and would have to stand by for homicide. The first guy on the scene was the evidence Tech. We knew this guy, and he asked what we had. We pointed everything out, and sent him forward to the spot where the victim had collapsed. He slowly walked up with his camera. He took several pictures of the pool of blood and walked back slowly. He looked up and, with a wry smile, and asked if that was my Goodyear Eagle GT plus four tire track in his scene.

I responded yes, sir. He opened his mouth as if to berate me, closed it and walked back to his truck. He must have thought lesson learned, and I wasn't worth the wasted breath. It took a little of the stuffing out of us anyway.

YOU THINK YOU KNOW

I cannot stress enough how working the street and attending court helps you develop into a good officer. We had done enough narcotics work in the corridor to think we were pretty well versed.

We had obtained keys to several apartment buildings that allowed us to go up on the roof. We could scan several blocks of the corridor without fear of being disturbed. We learned quickly, as one of our first trips up there, we observed a car pull up in front of a liquor store. The driver got out and opened the trunk. A crowd of about fifteen people immediately gathered at the rear of the vehicle. With binoculars, we could see him handing out small brown lunch bags.

Now the behavior of the people was not screaming "Lunch." We figured it was a narcotics drop, and we hustled down all ten stories. By the time we got down and out, everyone was gone. Picking up a few empty lunch bags, we confirmed our suspicions, finding crack residue in the bottoms. Experience, experience. It never ended. Still, we thought we had a good handle on the narcotic trade in the corridor.

But that all came to a crashing halt one day.

A local prostitute would give us information on a regular basis. Keep in mind any informant we had got paid out of our pockets. Five or ten would have to cover it. We didn't make much, and they didn't need much. She would give us regular information on who was out selling that day.

One day, she told us Hunkie Joe was out. I asked who was Hunkie Joe. She said we knew him and talked to him all the time. I told her I had no idea who she was talking about, at which time she pointed out Joe, who was standing on the corner of Temple. I looked over, and she was right, I did know him. He was an old white Hungarian guy who was about sixty years old, spoke broken English and lived over the party store. He always was dirty and smelling of liquor. I always thought he was an accident waiting to happen. Someone eventually was going to beat and rob him. I told her this and she began laughing.

She informed us he was one of the bigger street dealers in the corridor. I asked how long this had been going on, and she said for years. Interesting. We now started to keep an eye on Hunkie Joe.

About two weeks later, we rolled around the corner and caught Joe handing something to a guy in a car. We jumped out and snatched him up. He had a bag with eighty-eight $20 rocks of crack cocaine in it and six thousand dollars in cash. Boy, had he fooled us. In police work, things don't always appear how we want them to. The worst part about Hunkie Joe was that he went to court, took the plea and got lifetime probation. For all that dope and cash, he got probation.

Now, my partner catches him three months later with 126 $20 rocks and cash. He went to court again, took a plea and got double lifetime probation. We never saw Hunkie Joe again, and I wondered if street justice evened things up for us.

Our informant eventually was murdered, probably for running her mouth. She had a tendency to do that when she was high. They found her beaten to death one morning under the expressway.

IN THE CORRIDOR

The corridor had a complete life of its own and was a real training ground for us. Catch it on a hot summer night and it had a dangerous buzz to it. Prostitutes used to stand on the service drive waiting for customers. They could talk to them when they caught the traffic light. When it flashed green, they would turn ass-end, lift their skirts and bend over so westbound traffic could check the sale items as they cruised by.

Street dealers were everywhere, and moved about like an army of ants that's constantly shifting and moving. Gunshots would echo through the buildings. There were female and male screams, and a steady stream of barking dogs and meowing alley cats wove an urban symphony. This place was not made for the weak.

Every now and then something unusual took place. One afternoon, we saw a black stretch limousine parked in front of the Temple Liquor store. This was a raggedy place, specializing in wine and lottery tickets — both ghetto staples. There would be a long line that started forming about twenty minutes before they opened, waiting to get that first drink. Local favorites were Wild Irish Rose and Night Train.

As we pulled up to the limo, I could see three beautiful girls in spike heels and evening gowns at the front door. There was no doubt they were going to get robbed or worse. We stopped, and the storeowner had just stepped outside.

We asked him what was going on and he replied with a smile, "We are celebrating."

"Celebrating what?" I asked.

He informed me his store was the No. 1 seller of Wild Irish Rose in the country.

The models and limo were accompanied by a corporate bigwig from Wild Irish Rose. He would be presenting the award.

Well, a number of locals had gathered and, amazingly, enough were remaining under control. As they presented the award, the crowd began to clap. The owner received several kisses from the models and a firm handshake from the corporate suit. The surrounding winos almost looked like some type of honor guard as they cheered. You would have thought the storeowner had just one the Noble Peace Prize. He was beaming.

After I thought about it, in his small world, his liquor award probably carried the same weight.

WE GET NOTICED

I guess all our hard work finally got us noticed.

Our first meritorious award came on a B&E arrest. I thought it was just regular police work, but would learn the ins and outs of awards as my career stretched on. We stopped to investigate a guy riding a BMX bicycle in the street. He was attempting to carry a stereo, speakers and a bag of clothes, and he was very drunk. We asked him where he was coming from, and he had no idea.

The property was newer, and it didn't appear that he just found it. I headed west a few houses down, and found some kids sitting on a front porch. Kids are the best source of information, and usually give it up willing. You have to be very careful with it though, as it could get their family hurt. Many times, I have had a mother or father drag a kid away, hollering, "Don't talk to those motherfuckers."

Well, there were no parents around, so I asked if they saw where the guy on the bike came from. They pointed straight up. I asked again, knowing he didn't fall out of the sky. They again pointed up, and I asked them to show me. They were sitting on the porch of a two-family flat. One of the kids pointed to the upper porch. He said the guy pulled up on the bike, climbed the pillar and kicked the door in. He came down the pillar like Santa with a bag full of stuff.

We checked the flat and, sure enough, it played out like the kid said. One of our supervisors submitted a meritorious write-up and we received our first ribbon. That lone ribbon looked tiny on our uniform, but we wore it proudly. We now were decorated, but we still were learning.

GETTING A LEG UP ON THINGS

Your mind constantly has to be working on the street. Jumping to conclusions never was a good thing. I have brought this up before, but sometimes we needed things pounded into our heads to remember them.

One day in the corridor, we were flagged down by a guy. He was yelling, "He just stole my car." We could see the tail end of a smoking vehicle turn east onto Charlotte. It only was about a block away, and we closed in on it quickly. As soon as we made the corner, we could see the suspect had crashed into a telephone pole. It was a pretty bad wreck.

My partner was on the radio for an ambulance as I ran up to the stolen ride. I could see the suspect slumped over, and I pulled the driver's door open. I jumped back gasping. His left leg was gone. I hollered to my partner tell them to hurry because his leg is cut off.

I attempted to rouse him and sat him straight up. I began wondering where all the blood was. As a matter of fact, I was wondering where his leg was.

I frantically looked under the car and in the surrounding vacant lot. Flash backs to the girl in the field and me eating pizza incident still shook me. Unable to locate the missing limb, I looked in the backseat and discovered a prosthetic leg. It had a tube sock and shoe neatly tied on the end. I called to my partner that I had found his leg, and to slow the ambulance's roll. I didn't know whom I was madder at: The one-legged car thief or the victim with two legs who let the one-legged car thief steal his car. As usual, I really was just mad at myself.

KINKY MOVIEGOERS

The corridor at times could be like Sodom and Gomorrah. The Pussy Cat Theatre was located on Woodward and showed only the finest XXX movies. There was an upstairs theater and a tiny one downstairs. Downstairs was for the male gay community. Upstairs was for whomever. The seats in this theater all were sticky and damp. It smelled of urine and wine and who knows what else.

On occasion, we would walk through to check for illegal activity. Actually, we would walk through to see what we could see. On this day, we were in the upper theater. In the second row, we find a black male who was about forty years old. In the seat next to him is a thirty-year-old white female performing fellatio on him. Next to her is a thirty-year-old white male who was holding her free hand and watching. I know there are all kinds of people out there, but I just had to know. I asked the owner when we walked out what that was all about. He said the white couple was from Alpena, Michigan. Once a month, they would catch a bus to the city, which is about a five-hour ride. They would come to the Pussy Cat and the husband would watch her do things.

For some reason, I could picture them in the front pew at church singing. They'd be all pressed and fresh. Then, they'd transform on that five-hour bus ride into the devil's children. I always wondered if their families knew what they did when they traveled south.

SPOILED FRUIT SALAD

One of the things it takes you a while to learn is that time rank or ribbons don't mean a thing. I felt my first ribbon wasn't warranted, but still wore it proudly. Your boss could have twenty years on the job and a mess of ribbons on his chest, but still not know diddly-squat. That boss could have worked a year or two on the street or maybe not at all, land a cushy job, have someone do him favors for the ribbons, and now he was running the show. It sure looked good when someone walked up with all that fruit salad. I fell for it as a young officer. I warned others not to. I bring this up again, as it is easy to be swayed by appearances on this job.

Depending on senior officers bit us in the ass one day. We still were young and learning when an armed robbery run came out at a local deli. We volunteered to back up the primary unit and went to the scene. We were told the suspects had robbed the victim at gunpoint and escaped in checker cab #124. Having worked the precinct for a while, we headed north, knowing holdup men liked to escape into Highland Park. We were headed that way and about three streets from the border, when I looked east down a side street, and could see a checker cab parked on the south curb. We backed up and headed east.

Our hearts began racing as the adrenaline rush kicked in. We pulled behind the cab that only was occupied by the driver. The numbers on the trunk read 124. I could feel the thumping in my temple as we notified dispatch and approached the driver. He was the actual cab driver, and confirmed he picked up the three suspects after they ran out of the deli. When asked where the suspects were, he pointed to a brown brick house. He said they walked along the side and would be returning to the cab. I told my partner I would head to the back if he would cover the front. He positioned himself near the front porch as I went south one house west of the target location. Here's a little tip: Always turn your radio all the way down, so it doesn't key at the wrong time (I had learned this lesson the hard way). I jumped the fence to make it to the alley and walked toward the rear of the house.

I could hear men talking. I peered around the edge of the garage and could see the three suspects on the rear porch. My heart was now thumping so loud I feared the bad guys would hear it. I was formulating a plan when something spooked them and they came running to the alley. I had to figure out what I was going to do in a hair of a second. If they made it the alley, we would lose them.

The path was narrow along the garage, and if I could stop them there, we might get them all. When they were almost on me, I jumped around the corner and yelled, "Get the fuck on the ground!"

They were looking down the barrel of my gun and it worked. They all went down. I hollered for my partner, who ran to the back. We cuffed all three and I started to calm down. All of a sudden, another unit gets on the air, and says they have the suspects inside an address several blocks away. We ask for confirmation, and the officer says the cab dropped them off at the location. They are inside now. We must have the wrong guys. Was the cabbie in on it? We take information from the three guys we cuffed. We found no gun or money. We must have the wrong guys so we uncuff them. I'm not feeling right, but we let them go. They walk east in the alley and as they reach the split, one pulls his sweater off and they run. I know immediately we had the right guys. We get the cabbie's information and make it the house with the suspects in it. Two cars are out front, and I ask the officer who was on the radio and where were the bad guys.

He looks at me and says, "false alarm," and explained the cab had dropped off a legitimate fare at the address. I was pissed. I asked if he was acting on what he saw or what he heard, because I just let the bad guys go. He told me to relax, that it was no big deal. These were officers with time on the job. Because of that, I thought they knew what they were doing. I wouldn't make the same mistake again.

Police Officer Charles E. Beasley
Detroit Police Department, Michigan
End of Watch: Tuesday, November 22, 1988

Officer Beasley was shot and killed while working an undercover narcotics operation. He had gone to make a large narcotics purchase from a dealer. The dealer, however, went with the intent of robbing Officer Beasley. Officer Beasley was shot and killed during the transaction.

Officer Beasley had served with the agency for twelve years. He is survived by his two children.

THE SERGEANT AND THE BANK ROBBERY

The day's activities could quickly swing from bad to good in a blink of an eye. Frustration disappeared quickly one day when the bank located about two blocks from our base got robbed. We had learned that if we made a call to the armed robbery unit, they would give us surveillance pictures if they had them.

We made the short ride downtown and picked them up. To our surprise, one camera had caught some very interesting pictures. It had a decent shot of the suspect at the teller window, but it also captured the first guy waiting for service. It was our sergeant. Well, one of them, as we had three. This sergeant was on restricted duty and appeared in plain clothes. He claimed to have been hit by a bullet fragment at the range and was having trouble seeing.

In the photos, he is standing in line oblivious to what is going on right in front of him. Remember, a police officer always is on duty, and to me, staying alive is a priority. He had no idea the bank was being robbed until the suspect walked out, and they locked the front doors notifying the police. We all got a good laugh, but it was a very dangerous situation. And it was a lesson in what not to do.

The picture of him on the bulletin board did not stay up long, and I suspect the sergeant tore it down. He probably was upset that he wasn't paying attention. He eventually took a duty disability with his bad eye. Remember: Time, rank and ribbons do not mean a thing.

ONE SCARY PARTNER

I came in one day and had been paired with the scariest girl in the unit. Some of the supervisors felt that if they paired the non-workers with the workers, the workers would inspire the slugs, or at the minimum, make them do some type of work. I spoke to them myself, and it was the exact opposite. We just wanted to survive the day. I always made it a police run day and would service them one right after another. I normally would volunteer for any priority run, but would avoid them like the plague when working with a Lazy Susan or Lazy Larry. Now, most working police officers can't just close their eyes completely. So it happened to me as we cruised down John R.

I saw a young male pick up something from the bushes in an alley entrance. I thought he was picking up narcotics and told my partner we were going to investigate him. She gave a slight sigh as I pulled behind him. Before we got out of the car, I walked her through everything I was going to do. I placed his hands on the hood of the car and began searching him. I was on the passenger side, and my partner was at the front of the car. As I patted him down, I could feel a handgun in his front waistband. I pulled my weapon, and pushed him face down on the hood. I told him not to move.

Now I looked over to my partner, who was standing there with her arms folded. I told her he has a gun, and she might want to get hers out. She drew her weapon and I holstered mine. I was pissed because she was daydreaming. And I was pissed at myself for even getting into this situation.

As I pulled the loaded .38 out of his waistband, I looked at my partner. She had her weapon pretty much leveled at both of us. Her hands were shaking so bad, I have no idea how she held onto her gun. Flashbacks to the range raced through my head. I was hoping she was such a bad shot that if she squeezed one off, it would miss both of us. I made the arrest without incident and completed all the paperwork at the station. She never had arrested anyone with a gun before. In our city, this was amazing.

SHE'S GOT IT

There was an incident where I was really, really happy I was working with a female officer. I was paired up on a Sunday morning with a girl who was super nice, though super nice did not necessarily equate to good police worker. I was in full "service all the police run" mode, and planned to put on some blinders and get through the day. I had learned my lesson with the pistol arrest.

Highland Park had given a description out of a stolen vehicle that had been just taken out of the victim's driveway. It was a gold Grand Am with a license plate of 156 BKH. I just couldn't completely stay away from it. I figured I would head north, and by the time I got there, someone would be chasing it and we could have a little action. We would be acting only in a back-up capacity. I even avoided the main drag, and went north on a side street. Two blocks from Highland Park, I pulled up to Woodward. This was early Sunday morning and there was no traffic out. As I scanned southbound, here comes a lone vehicle. It is gold, and I'm thinking, "you have to be kidding me."

It rolls buy, and I catch the plate 156 BHK. I turned behind it and tell my partner that's the car they just gave out. I told her to pick up the radio and let dispatch know we are following it. She looks at me and says, that's not our car the plate is wrong. This went right back to the non-worker not knowing. She actually thought there was an identical car to ours, same year color and one letter off on the plate. I told her just to get on the radio. She did, and repeated what I told her to say. The Grand Am picked up speed and was off. We began the chase. The whole time, I'm thinking, "What are you doing, Dumbo? What are you doing? You really shouldn't be doing this."

They dip down an alley and lose control, striking several fences, a telephone pole and a garage. The suspect bails from the vehicle and I screech to a halt. I look at her and already know she is not getting out. I jump from the car and give chase. As I exit between the houses, he has smoked me and is gone. I return back to the stolen vehicle, finding we are in Highland Park and several of their cars show up including a K-9 unit. We attempt to track the suspect, and follow the dog for about four blocks, at which point, Fido loses the scent. I am dreading going back to the car. We are going to be tied up for hours doing paperwork. The chase was not a big deal, but all of the accident damage is going to take a ton of work.

As I re-enter the alley, I see my partner talking to two Highland Park officers. They are almost face-to-face, and she has one hand on her hip as she smiles at them. I am not going to stand for this flirting, as she already should have started the paperwork. I walk up to her, ask her what she's doing, and say she should be knocking on doors and getting information. She tells me it is all taken care of. Now, I know she couldn't have done anything, given the time I was gone. Well, all that eyelash-batting convinced the Highland Park officers to handle all the paperwork in exchange for my partner's phone number.

I wanted to hug her myself, and actually gave her a "good job" remark on the way back to the precinct.

Early in my career I had the opportunity to work with a number of female officers. Every time I was paired up with one, I must admit the agility test we all took during the hiring process lingered in the back of my mind. I also saw how certain female officers were treated by command staff, simply because they looked good. Some females used this to their advantage and it was sickening. Like any other officer, in the end, some were good and some were bad. I had plenty of incidents involving female officers that turned out horrible, but I also had plenty with male officers that turned out the same.

As my career progressed, I had the opportunity to work with some great female officers. They were intelligent, tough and possessed a work ethic rivaled by any officer. Even mine. I said, this story would disturb some and feel no need to explain myself, but I would never want to tarnish the courage and heroism displayed by some of my female co-workers. The working cops, both male and female, would know this without me saying a word.

Many female officers have lost their lives in the line of duty, and that speaks for itself.

THE FOOD STAMP CENTER

You have to learn quickly about the local businessmen in your districts. Most of our party store or gas station owners are a bit shady.

They all have an angle, and are the biggest stolen property processors in the city. Some allow guys to sell narcotics for a cut of the profits. If a guy is selling out front and they see the police, they just walk in the store. They will place the drug and/or weapon in the cooler, potato chip rack, or, on occasion, the trash can. They then just circle back out. After you investigate them, they go back in and retrieve their property.

The storeowners also take a cut for lottery winnings. If you win ten grand, they will take the ticket from you and cash it themselves for a payout. Their tax is not as severe as the state's, and everyone is happy.

Their biggest moneymaker used to be food stamps, and now it's the bridge card. People having these government aid devices only are allowed to purchase certain items. No alcohol, lottery or cigarettes. What the storeowners will do for you is take $100 in food stamps or $100 off of your bridge card, and then allow you to purchase $50 of whatever you want and they'll pocket the other $50. It's quite a moneymaker.

When food stamps were in use, we used to set up on Grand River at the food stamp center. As the people would get their allotment and exit the building, an enterprising dope man would wait just around the corner. The food stamps now would turn into trading stamps, allowing you to purchase crack, heroin and other assorted controlled substances.

Everyone in the city had to have an angle on the streets. It was part of their survival. As I learned about police work, they learned about the street. I was trying to survive, and they were trying to survive. I never held it against them.

THE UNUSUAL IS THE NORM

The unusual always was the norm in Detroit. In the beginning, I was shocked at some of the things I saw. After a while, it just seemed natural.

One day, we were inside of a house talking to lady about a noise complaint. The house was a mess, with clutter everywhere. I glanced over to her couch and had to jump. There was dog standing rigid but not looking very healthy. He was kind of leaning to the side, and his fur was matted and dirty. Upon closer inspection, he was not alive. Again, brilliant police observation. He actually was stuffed. I asked her what the deal was, and she told me it was her dog, Stanley. She had him for many years and loved him dearly. When he died, she just couldn't stand to be without him, so she had him stuffed.

Well, she must have really loved him to go through all the trouble, but she was severely lacking in his upkeep and appearance care. He was missing a glass eye, and had some sort of paste stuck in his fur on the left side. He was dusty and stained. I have no idea if he came with a base, but he was now displayed on an old two-by-four. Several six-penny nails had been used to mount him, and several were bent over.

She gave him a pat on the head as she told me the story, which I found touching. I stretched the truth a bit and told her he looked good, almost lifelike. A little white lie sometimes went a long way, as she looked down at her dog and smiled.

Some of the characters you meet can be almost cartoon-like. I had two brothers who lived on the street. Both were alcoholics and penniless. Somehow, they came into possession of a car. With all that these guys were up against, they always were smiling.

The car soon broke down and they had it parked across from an old apartment building. It now turned into their home. The rear was the bedroom, and the front was for dining and entertainment. The amazing thing about this whole arrangement was they spent an entire winter in this car. They had acquired a number of blankets, and at night, cocooned themselves in. We would go by every morning and check on them. All of the glass would be covered from the inside with a thick coat of ice. We would tap on the window and soon a small hole would be scraped out. A smiling face would confirm they were okay and we would go on our way.

One day, the car and brothers disappeared. I never knew what happened to them, but they always reminded me that no matter how tough life could become, you always could stay upbeat.

One of the more unusual living arrangements I ran into came as a surprise while we were working narcotics. We had a large vacant apartment building we utilized as birds nest to watch guys sell narcotics. It overlooked a small park, right in the heart of the corridor. It was five stories tall and completely gutted. We took a third-story apartment and had a good view of the daily activities. One of the suspects who sold dope in the park even supplied paraphernalia for the use of his product. Stems and crack pipes were stored in the drain downspout of a building. You could make your purchase, walk behind a wall and fire up. The surroundings were no cigar bar, but proved to be more than adequate for someone needing an immediate high. Several milk crates provided seating.

On this particular day, we are in the apartment when I hear a loud crash. I walk down the hall to investigate and find a closed door on one of the apartments. Now, all the doors were either missing or kicked off their hinges. I slowly open the door and find a guy sitting on a bed. This apartment is fully furnished (well ghetto-furnished). There is a bed, which is neatly made, a large easy chair, and a number of books jammed on several shelves that are made out of boxes. There is a cooking area, with a small grill, and the place even had a small round piece of carpet. It honestly looked rather homey.

Apparently, this guy had been living there for about eight months and had slowly moved all of this in. He put the door on to prevent intruders. We had been using this place for about three months, and he told me he had seen us before but he didn't want to say anything for fear we would make him leave. Far from it — I congratulated him on the fine remodeling job and told him not to worry about the lease. He had the place indefinitely.

This, again, was a case of people making do and over coming.

Each new police run gave us the opportunity to meet a new character. One of my favorite people was an old lady who ran an apartment building in the corridor. We met her while servicing a "person down" run.

When we arrived, she met us on the first floor. She was about sixty years old, had a large beehive hairdo that was dyed bright red, and wore cat-eye glasses with the chain around them. She was wearing a dress that bordered on an evening gown. She informed us that she had gone to check on one of the tenants who hadn't been seen in a couple of days. She found no response at the door and had opened it with her passkey. The door still had the chain on it, but she could open it enough to see the tenant lying on the ground unresponsive.

So up we go, and she is going to point all of this out. We get the lecture from her about world peace and the price of cat food all in the same conversation. As she begins to unlock the door, she turns, looks at us, and asks if we are ready. We nod the affirmative, and she opens the door. The chain still is in place, and we can see an older woman on the floor. She is unresponsive, as we force open the door and enter the apartment, and our escort follows us in.

It is obvious the tenant is deceased, and has been for several days. Her eyes are clouded and lifeless, and she has that death color to her skin. The landlady then gives me one of my favorite lines of all time. She looks up from the body and states, "Officer, she doesn't look well."

Stifling a laugh, I ask her to leave the apartment. As she leaves, she continues talking, telling me the lady hasn't looked well for some time. I have to really hurry her out as I am going to lose my self-control. I recomposed myself, and we stood by for homicide.

IT'S NOT ALL LIGHTS, SIREN AND SPEED

When I first got on the job, young officers always wanted to be in a car chase. Lights, sirens and speed. We had no idea how dangerous this was. First off, your scout car was not the best-maintained vehicle — complete with bad suspension, and bad tires. You learned this quickly after your first trip over a set of railroad tracks doing fifty miles per hour. If you didn't lose control, you usually lost a tire or two. Secondly, the roads in the city are not a racetrack that has groomed banks and level asphalt. Toss in a whole bunch of other cars and pedestrians, and it could be a mess.

In the early days, before policy changes, you were allowed to chase just about anybody for anything. Other scout cars would block traffic at upcoming cross streets for you. You took a driving course in the academy to prepare your for this, and it was fun. But they never told you all the things that could happen during a chase, and exactly what you should be doing. First off, when a car takes off on you or you spot a wanted vehicle, your adrenaline goes through the roof. You need to control that so you can talk on the radio and get help.

The driver of the scout will call out travel direction and streets, and the jump man (officer in the passenger seat) will be communicating this through the radio. Some officers just let the jump man do the whole thing, but my regular partner and I did it our way and found it to be the best. We were not taught this, but later learned it.

The second thing we were never told is that all kinds of things — like drugs, money, guns, etc. — would be tossed from the car during the chase. If evidence did come out the windows, you had better mark it as you flew by. This way, you could direct another unit to that location so it could be recovered. How about bodies jumping out of the car? I chased a stolen car once for about a mile. A guy jumps from the passenger side, and I call it out for someone to pick him up. The car travels a full block, and then crashes into a building. I run up to the driver's door and no one is in the car. The driver's door wouldn't open, so the lone occupant jumped from the passenger side.

Last, and most dangerous, were other scout cars. Many officers are killed or injured by responding officers. Officers feel the need to get there as fast as they can, no matter what. After some close calls, you learn right away not to chase a chase. Get the suspect's direction of travel, and head that way at a safe speed, and more than likely, the chase will end up coming your way.

I almost was killed once by another car from my command. We had chased an armed robbery vehicle all through the precinct. They finally turned down a dead end street and decided to bail out. I was the jump man and quickly exited the scout. Another scout car skidded by my side of the vehicle with locked brakes. He had lost control and nearly clipped me. My injuries would not have been minor. Officers sometimes fail to realize they are driving a two-thousand-pound missile. You have to control that missile. As usual, our lesson would be learned the hard way

"SIR, SIR — I'M UNDER THE CAR"

We were working midnights once and I was with my regular partner. We were slow rolling down a street with our lights out. Not department policy, but many officers did it. On the corner of Euclid and Second, we could see three guys breaking out a traffic light. They were using a large piece of concrete. They would pick it up and toss it into the pole-mounted light. My partner asked if I saw it. I smiled at him, and said yes. What else am I going to be watching at 4 a.m.?

The bad guys saw us, which immediately stopped their destructive behavior. It's surprising how we have that effect on some people. All three suspects began walking north down the middle of the street. We closed in behind them, and as I opened the door, they bolted. One ran north down the street, the other two ducked into the first alley and ran west. We were closing quickly in the scout car when the two suspects split up. One suspect turned the corner at a garage and the other continued west in the alley. My partner bent a hard right at the garage, skidding into a vacant lot. The suspect was gone and we were sitting in three-foot-high grass.

This was mid-summer, and our scout cars did not have air conditioning. Imagine a police uniform, bulletproof vest and computer in between you and your partner. We already were sweating with both our windows were down. My partner yelled, "Where did he go?"

I did not get a second to respond when I heard, "Sir, Sir, I'm under the car."

I jumped from the vehicle following the voice. I began searching at the front of our car. No luck, and the voice continued, "Sir, sir, I'm under the car."

I followed the voice to the rear of the scout and found our suspect. All I could see were two legs protruding from under the car, positioned directly behind the right rear tire. Remember the scene from the Wizard of Oz — the one where the house is on the witch? It looked the same, sans any ruby slippers on the suspect.

The suspect continued with the, "Sir, sir, I'm under the car."

I confirmed that for him, and told him I knew he was under the car.

I had called the brief chase out over the radio, and dispatch was asking me what I had. Now, I'm really sweating. Okay, they never taught this in the academy either.

I told dispatch to stand by, as panic set in for my partner and I. We had run someone over. How did that happen? I thought we better prioritize, and the first priority was to get him out from under the car. My partner figured we could just drive off of him, and as I was suggesting this might not be the best idea, he already was behind the wheel. He touched the gas, and the, "Sir, sir," stopped, and it was replaced by horrible screaming.

Plan A was not going to work. My partner jumped from the car, and I suggested jacking the car up. Our suspect went back to the, "Sir, sir, I'm under the car," which I took as a good sign.

We retrieved the jack from the trunk and went to work. After a number of pumps on the jack, our suspect sprang up from under the car. He was standing between my partner and I. He was filthy, covered in a combination of dirt and scout car grease, and matted with grass and burrs. He had papers and what appeared to be a Slo Poke stuck to his shirt. He looked at my partner, hugged him and said, "You saved my life."

My thought was, "He just parked a scout car on you, pal — you should be a little more upset than that."

Dispatch still was hollering, and I finally got myself organized enough to talk to him. I told him he we needed a supervisor, tow truck and an ambulance. I couldn't imagine what he was thinking on the other end. He immediately clicked me out of repeat. This is where no one else can hear what we are saying. He asked, "What the hell is going on over there?"

I explained that we had accidentally parked on our suspect. He said he didn't even want to know, and would send everything I requested.

My partner had pulled the scout out of the vacant lot, allowing us to reconstruct the events. As soon as the suspect turned into the lot, he only made it about three feet, and he tripped over a large log, and fell face first into the grass. My partner turned into the lot, hit the log, and was travelling at a speed that lifted the front of the scout over the suspect and allowed the car to stay in the air for about three feet. The front end of the scout dug into the ground, slamming the rear axle down onto the log. This pinned the suspect in the position we found him. This log had saved his life.

His only injuries were a gash on his caboose, and all the skin had been removed from the palm of his right hand. That horrible screaming we heard was when my partner tried to drive off of him, as his hand was under that right rear tire.

THERE GOES THE NEIGHBORHOOD

As things were changing at work, they also were changing at home. My wife was pregnant, and my neighborhood was getting worse. When I moved in, a number of lifelong residents still were in place. They were older couples that were unable to move out of Detroit. As they passed away or their families forced them out, renters moved in. Loud music and cars racing up and down the street now were common. Nobody cared for their property, as grass went uncut and trash was strewn about. My quiet neighborhood was turning into a war zone. I could see it was in transition just like the neighborhood I grew up in.

When I was little, the main street where I lived was lined with businesses. There were barbershops, cleaners, bars, bakeries and grocery stores. Everyone knew each other and cared for each other. If someone couldn't cut their lawn, someone did it for them. If someone couldn't shop for groceries, someone jumped in and took care of it. Every summer night was a community meeting. Everyone was on their front porch talking. Fall was special, as everyone raked and burned their leaves in the street. It had the air of a county fair. There was no fear of getting robbed or being hit by a stray bullet. I remember at my grandparent's store, they had a large box with a book in it for credit. They would extend it to many of the customers. The customers always paid them back.

They key to all of this was safety. It was safe, and you knew it. My old neighborhood now is a prostitute-infested vacant wasteland. Its images are portrayed on the cover of this book. There only are a few houses standing on my block. The majority of them burnt to the ground. Is this what my new neighborhood was destined for? I knew it was. I had to consider where I was going to send my kids to school. Private school seemed to be the only answer.

A turning point came after the house next to me had gone vacant, and was purchased by a young man living in the suburbs. He threw some paint on it and rented it out. A Welfare Wanda moved in with her three kids, all who were under six years old. The welfare would allow him to collect his rent guaranteed.

I was accustomed to this renter's behavior, as I had seen it before when my old neighborhood deteriorated. There would be no care for the children, and babies would be roaming the neighborhood dressed only in a diaper. Her boyfriend would show up drunk at all hours, pounding on the door to be let in. When denied entry, he would sleep on the front porch. One day, her family, in a fit of rage, fired several shots at him in the front yard. It no longer was safe, and my own department could not provide protection for my family. This would be the final straw for me, and I began house shopping.

Police Officer Vikki Elaine Hubbard
Detroit Police Department, Michigan
End of Watch: Sunday, March 12, 1989

Officer Hubbard was killed when her patrol car was struck by a vehicle being chased by other units at 0220 hours. Officer Hubbard was assisting the units when the patrol car was broadsided by a vehicle that was traveling at an estimated 90 miles per hour. Officer Hubbard was killed at the scene, and her partner was injured. Both suspects were arrested at the scene, convicted and sentenced to life.

Officer Hubbard had served with the Detroit Police Department for eleven years.

WATCHING THE CITY BURN

Work details or being assigned out always was a learning experience for us. No one liked them, because it took you out of your comfort zone. Our most important detail assignment was Devil's Night. This is the same detail I had worked while still in the academy. It actually is three nights, from October 29 through Halloween. The entire department is mobilized to prevent the city from burning down. These three days are restricted days for the entire department, which means no one has them off, and everyone works. They have been restricted my entire career. This means no police officer had Halloween off. If you have children, you better hope you are assigned to a day shift. If not, for the next twenty-five years, you won't be making the trick-or-treat deal.

These days are restricted because every arsonist — from the professional to the amateur — feels this is the opportune time to practice their trade. For these three days, the city is ablaze. Detroit supplies the vacant structures for these individuals to utilize. The police are not the only ones to be mobilized. The fire department also restricts those three days. Neighborhood watches and church groups patrol the streets.

Can you imagine living in a community that is set on fire and, to prevent it, you have to go on the street and patrol your own neighborhood? The only good thing for the police is that crime is drastically reduced. It proves the point that if you have enough police officers on the street, the city becomes safer.

It always tugged at my heart to watch the city ablaze. It looked like some sacked city the barbarians had just invaded.

Several years ago, the powers to be decided to rename it Angel's Night. What a crock. They felt the name Devil's Night just gave the wrong impression. Funny, all those years I worked the detail, I never saw one angel. I saw plenty of devils though. Crime is cut drastically for that three-day period, but crime still does happen.

On one of those nights, we received a stolen car chase lesson. We were assigned to the detail and had just lost a stolen vehicle. The suspects shut down their lights and sped from us before we could even react. We found the car unoccupied about a block from where we lost it. I have no idea why we were trying to do any type of police work, as the department supplied only one radio for the two of us. It was super dangerous. The problem is that working cops are going to work, no matter what. We were waiting on a tow truck with another unit from our command, when a Chevy Caprice roared past us.

One of the guys had been studying a hot sheet (which is a list of all the stolen vehicles taken in the last couple of days). Now we have two scout cars and two radios between four officers. We scramble around like we are playing musical chairs. My partner yells, "I'm taking this one."

"This one" is the stolen ride he is sitting on. He tears off with our only radio. The other unit jumps off with both officers in it and I'm right behind them. I have no radio, but I'm doing it. I can't leave my partners. The other scout is the primary unit, and it closes in on the Caprice. Luckily, my partner's stolen ride clunks out. Thank goodness he didn't hit anything.

The primary unit chases for several blocks, when the stolen ride does exactly what you don't want it to do. It hits a dumpster coming out of the alley and then Plinkos its way down the street, managing to hit every other car. The bad guys bailout, and we lose every one of them.

I have no idea where my partner is and no radio to find him. I abandon the primary and begin the blanket search of the area, locating my partner in the original sitting position on the hood of the stolen ride. It was another lesson learned with no one hurt.

DOWNTOWN DETAIL

On this job, you quickly learn that being low man on the totem pole is going to get you assigned to every special event or detail. All I wanted to do was be the police, not a traffic cop at the parade.

When I was a young officer, I always felt they should send the old timers. They never seemed to want to do any work. Well, there was a reason they sent young officers. Same reason we all went to New Center. It's because of the "Yes, maam," "No, Maam," "Follow orders" types of officers.

My first downtown detail opened my eyes. I went to roll call and immediately reported to my post. I was the only one there. I could see one or two officers along the parade route, and assumed they were new like me. Most of the senior people I didn't see for the entire detail. The problem is that they are needed. Oh, they would make off-duty roll call, but they'd leave you to the mercy of the crowd during the entire detail. There never were any repercussions for their actions. Everyone knew this.

There are close to a million people who show up for the Detroit Fireworks. Traffic is a nightmare. I once worked this detail and had two other officers assigned to my corner. I never met them, and I never saw them. They just never took their post. When the fireworks let out, it was unreal. Like the spokes of a wheel, I had six streets that converged on my corner.

Everyone wants to go outbound so they all go the same direction. Everyone keeps inching and inching to my corner. When they get to the intersection, they are all nose-to-nose with no room to go back and no room to go forward. There's lots of horn honking and yelling. If the other officers had been on their post, this would have been averted. It took three hours to sort it out. It happens every year. Accountability is one of the biggest problems in our department. It never is more evident than at a detail.

One of my favorite radio requests that I heard was at a detail. This also folded into the poor promotional system we had. A sergeant who was sent to assist officers at a parking complaint called dispatch requesting a supervisor. Dispatch asked them to repeat the request, and then denied it. Dispatch informed them they are a supervisor, and asked why would another one be needed. It probably was one of our charter-promoted bosses. You think they would have had enough sense to call someone on the phone if they couldn't figure it out, instead, they call over the radio where everyone could hear what a dunce they were. I really was starting to learn that part of the job. The majority of the time, you were better off not calling a supervisor. There's less frustration that way.

LIKE A MOTH TO THE FLAME

Early in my career, I realized, I was going to be one of those special police officers who attracted the absolute looniest people out there. It must be a gift, because over the years, it also spilled into my personal life.

I once serviced a run on a noise complaint. We knocked on the door, and got the "I'll be right with you." Cops are paranoid, and the longer it takes to answer the door, the more dangerous the situation can become.

I could hear a strange noise being repeated over and over right at the door. Almost like tearing paper. I told the lady to just open the door. She told me she was trying. I asked if she was all right, and she replied fine, just a minute. She eventually opened the door, and I discovered the weird noise. Her entire house was masking taped shut —there was regular household masking tape over everything, including the windows, vents and front door. As young officers, you would enter this place awestruck. It's funny how when you get some time on the job that this doesn't seem unusual. Sometimes it is just better not to ask.

I addressed the noise complaint and was walking out the door when curiosity took over. "Maam, the tape?" I asked.

She started with, "You know they are out there, trying to get in."

I told her enough said, and suggested she switch to duct tape for the front door because it would make things a little more secure. She agreed, and told me if she ever went out of the house again, she would be sure to pick some up.

WHY A GOOD GAG REFLEX IS A MUST

Every single aspect of the job came with a lesson. The art of handcuffing and handling of property was not covered in the academy. I'll correct that. It was covered, but not street-covered — and there is a huge difference between the two.

They taught us how to safely handcuff someone, but did not inform us of all the extras that might come with it. I always like to give credit to bad guys when credit is due. Several have been able to hold a fart in until that exact moment when I am cuffing or uncuffing them — bum shit, bum farts. There's not much you can do but take it. I've been given several apologies when they flatulate, but it always comes with a smirk. Good gag reflexes are a must for street officers.

Some of these incidents have stayed with me longer than the deadly ones. We were working the south end of the precinct on a Sunday morning when we spotted two white males in a very clean car parked in front of an apartment building. This was screaming, "I am from the suburbs and I'm buying dope."

We set up about a block away to watch them, and after several minutes, a raggedy looking black male exited the apartment building and entered their car. We let them roll for about two blocks and then pulled them over. I watched the black male toss eight rocks of crack cocaine out the window. We got all three suspects out and separated them. You want them far enough apart so they can't hear each other's story.

The black male admitted to buying dope for the other two. The white males gave the standard story that they got turned around and were lost. Unfortunately, I couldn't prove that the white males had given him money and asked him to buy crack for them. So the black male was the only one making the trip for violation of the controlled substance act. We lectured the other two on the dangers of Detroit, and sent them on their way.

It was a very hot morning, and we were all sweating. Our suspect was wearing a coat, just to ease the task of carrying it. He had the wine-body odor-urine-combo smell cooking. I pulled a small pocketknife from his pants pocket. It was about four inches long with a yellow handle. I held it in my hand as I continued to search him. After a minute or two, he glanced over his shoulder and told me something that froze me in my tracks.

"Be careful, officer, I be picking my feet with that knife," he said.

A slight bit of nausea hit me as I glanced down. I knew it wasn't going to be good. He had very large feet, both covered in what were once sneakers. One was wrapped in tape, the other had newspaper coming from the side. They were once white, but now were a soiled black. They appeared to have years of wear, and the right one had a large hole along the sole and upper portion. From this hole peeked several dirty toes. One was leaning completely on its side and was a different color from his brother, probably due to the constant exposure to the elements. Curled and uncut yellow toenails topped them.

I now opened my hand exposing the feet-picking knife. My palm was sweaty, and now had an oily black fluid in the creases. I hadn't realized it, but my hand had instantly removed itself from under the knife. The brain must have sent the "Oh my god" signal as soon as my eyes locked on it. My hand now was extended away from my body and slightly behind me. Almost in a panic, I searched the scout for the industrial hand cleanser I kept. I doused the now-diseased appendage as if I was preparing for surgery, making sure to clean from the elbow to the tips of my fingers. We locked him up and completed the paper work.

For the next four days, I washed my hands whenever I could. I couldn't eat buttered popcorn for a year, and to this day, I don't like feet.

THE SILENT AK-47

We all had learned from the incident where two of my coworkers were forced to shoot a mentally disturbed suspect. I was faced with a similar situation, and the problem with police work is that you are forced to deal with these situations. There is no choice. We can't just walk away. Our circumstances were almost identical, as the mother had the mental son locked in his room. She wanted him to go to the hospital because he quit taking his prescribed medication.

We used every precaution as we quietly talked to him through the door. You are taught to never stand directly in front of the door or near the jam, because there are not many doors or jams that will stop a bullet. After about forty minutes, the son would not comply, and the mother wanted us to kick the door in. This is never good, as you have no idea what is behind the door.

Again, we had no choice because she feared he would kill himself. Not only do we not know what is going on behind the door, we have to warn him we are coming in, so he is not injured as we enter. I covered my partner as he kicked the door. The son was standing in the corner, wearing only his underwear. He told us we weren't taking him, and stood in a fighting stance. Talking always was better than fighting, but it was time to fight. As street officers, you know this. I told him he absolutely was going with us, and he replied, "Come get some."

At this point in my career, we had no secondary weapons, no mace, and no PR-24 baton. This was going to be done the old fashioned way. Let me make one thing clear: Police work is not about beating people up. It's far from it. I never have really had to fistfight anyone. There have been plenty of physical confrontations, but using your mouth instead of fists always has worked for me. You learn quickly that when it gets physical, fight like you would on the street: Strike first and use force, because it usually ends everything quickly.

So, if he wants me to come get some, I'm his guy. He tries to jump the bed as I grab him. We both hit the center of the mattress and blow the legs and head board off as it crashes to the ground. We tumble over the side, knocking the end table over and breaking the lamp. I have him pinned and my partner is right next to me. After several minutes, we cuff him. We stand him up, and his mother is in the room crying. She tells us he is okay if he takes his medication. Sorry mom, but he has to make the trip to the Crisis Center.

As we walk him to the bedroom door, I get that police chill. Propped in the corner next to the door is a loaded AK-47 assault rifle. It makes you wonder if he was pointing it at the door as we talked to him.

We were doing our duty, making it safe for the mother and neighborhood. Unlike our coworkers' incident where they were forced to shoot a mentally disturbed man, our police run wouldn't be making the news. This is the type of police work the public doesn't see.

THE CHASE IS ON

Our lesson on stolen vehicles never seemed to stop. We had a run to the north end of the precinct on a stolen vehicle. The appearance of the vehicle can tell you if someone is going to get back in it. Is it parked properly? Is it clean? Is it intact, meaning tires, radio etc.? Does it have a battery?

We discovered the vehicle in question, legally parked at the curb. This one looked ready to roll. We positioned ourselves in an alley across Woodward and waited. Sure enough, two suspects entered the car, started it and drove directly south of us.

I already was on the radio informing dispatch and providing clothing and physical on the suspects. They zoomed by and immediately saw us as we pulled from the alley. The chase was on. They got it up to about 50 and tried the first left turn they came too. They missed the street completely, driving up onto the corner and striking a tree, which now redirected them back cross the street.

Their tires were spinning as the rear end regained traction. When the tires caught, it slingshot them across the road, tearing through an eight-foot cyclone fence which stayed with them as they skidded through a backyard garden and struck the rear porch of a house. This sheared the porch from the house, shattering the pillars supporting the second story porch.

It looked like one of those building imploding. I must admit when something like this happens, you kind of take your eye off the bad guys and just sit there with your mouth open for a second.

Well, their car rolls on its side and the driver scrambles over the passenger through the cocoon of fence wrapped around the vehicle and runs. I chase him and after several fence jumps, I catch him a block away.

I walked my suspect back, finding the farmer, pulling in his crops early. He was placing turnips in an old wood bushel basket. He also gave me the fish eye. I'm sure his first thought was, "Police sure can tear some shit up."

THE CORRIDOR REGULAR AND FOREIGN DOCTOR

Working police officers always are impatient if they are going to be delayed on a non-critical run. You want to get back on the street and get after it. We were walking a beat in the corridor, when I heard tires screeching. Looking over my shoulder, I could see a vehicle fishtailing on the service drive. It would have been hard to miss because it only was about thirty feet from us. It struck a corridor regular who was crossing the street. The car must have been going about 45 and launched him into the air. I'm guessing he hit about the six-foot mark, and crashed to the pavement. It was almost artistic in a sick type of way.

We rushed to him and found him face up, clutching his forty-ounce beer. He was unconscious and we requested and EMS. After several minutes, his eyes fluttered open. His first question concerned the location, and condition of his forty-ounce. I informed him he still was clutching it. Now people from the corridor are almost indestructible. He was in pain but had no visible injuries. This is the impatient part. As it was a pedestrian accident and he was older, I had to ride to the hospital with him. Due to the age of the victim, there always was a concern he could die. You didn't want to release a possible homicide scene until you were sure the victim would survive. All I needed from the hospital was a condition from the doctor. If it was nothing critical, we could release the scene and be on our way.

Grumpy, I wait for the doctor to look him over and catch him as he exits the examination pod. First off, this is not the top-of-the-line hospital, and my doc is foreign. No offense, but I think you should have to speak understandable English to hold a position of some importance in this country. I ask him what the patient's condition is, and he says it's serious. I want to be sure he understands what I'm asking. I say, so his condition will be listed as serious on his chart. He looks at me like I have three heads. He is responding to me, but I can tell he only is doing so because I am in front of him. You know when someone responds to you, but their answer has that question tone at the end, like they are waiting for you to confirm what they said.

119

My frustration is building. I just need a damn condition. I ask again, so he will be listed in serious condition? He still is puzzled and asks, "What happen to him?"

I'm steamed now and yell, "He was hit by a car!"

He looks down at the floor as if searching for the answer. He then looks at me and says, "Car hit him, that is very serious."

Determining I was fighting a losing battle, I got the doctor's name from his tag, and listed the guy as serious, releasing the scene.

CATNAPPERS

I was walking a beat when that guy got hit. He was only feet from me when it happened. Every police officer should start their careers walking a beat. It puts you in direct contact with everyone and everything in your precinct. Mix in smells and sounds, and you become part of the street. You actually could feel it breath.

As a young officer, I was paired with a good partner one day, and we hit our beat ready for action. As we patrolled down Woodward, we saw a Siamese kitten cut across the road. Kittens were not rare, but a Siamese cat was. You learn quickly not to touch people or animals unless you absolutely have to. They carry way too many passengers. Cuteness took precedent, and my partner picked up the kitten. It purred and climbed his jacket, perching on his shoulder. It rolled under his chin, caressing his face with its tail.

My partner was in love, and said he was keeping it. I asked what we were going to do with a kitten. He tucked it inside his coat and said we could walk to the base. He would call his girlfriend and she would come and pick it up. It sounded okay to me because we had five hours of walking left. We might as well burn up some time. We had gone only several steps, when a local prostitute began yelling at us and ran across the street. She stumbled several times, and a swerving car just missed her. She put the evil eye on us, and asked where we were going with that cat. Felix (he had been named after the famous cat, moments earlier) peeked through my partner's zipped jacket.

My partner informed her he was going to give the kitten a home.

"You can't do that," our girl said.

I asked her why not.

"I saw you take that cat from the momma cat," she answered.

No, we told her, we found it.

"No you didn't," she screamed. "I saw you take her from the momma cat."

She began circling us, and flapping her arms, vehemently accusing us of breaking up a family. Her volume increased as we pleaded our innocence.

"These officers took that baby from the momma cat," she trumpeted.

No we didn't, was our response.

This battle of accusations and innocence went on for several minutes. A small crowd had formed, and traffic began slowing. Suddenly and at the same moment, my partner and I realize what in the hell are we doing. We are police officers for crying out loud, trying to do a good deed. We quickly turned from the small crowd and our accuser and stomped off. I glanced over my shoulder to confirm we weren't being followed. I could see her standing there, still pointing a finger at us, and informing everyone who could hear, "There they go. There they go, right there. They done took that baby cat from the momma cat. Done took that poor baby from her momma. Lord, have mercy."

We made it back to the base, and my partner's girlfriend met us. She took Felix home and my partner kept that cat for fifteen years. Felix outlasted the girlfriend by ten years. In the end, I never felt so bad about doing something so good.

Police Officer Sherdard Raymund Brison
Detroit Police Department, Michigan
End of Watch: Monday, March 5, 1990

Officer Brison was shot and killed while attempting to arrest an armed robbery suspect. He and his partner stopped a cab after an area armed-robbery. Officer Brison was patting down the passenger when the passenger pulled a pistol and shot him in the throat area. The suspect then shot his partner below the vest and ran. His partner killed him with one round as he ran away.

Officer Brison is survived by his wife and daughter.

OSCAR SAVES THE DAY

During my stay at New Center, I had my first incident where a department K-9 was used. I had seen it on TV and the dog tracked right to the bad guy. I figured how different could it be? A local restaurant had been robbed and the suspect had dropped his hat. The hour was late, so a K-9 unit had to be recalled because Detroit can't afford to have one on duty at all times.

After about forty minutes, the officer and dog showed up. He let the dog out on a long thirty-foot lead, and let him sniff around and do his business. He left his mark on a set of bushes. The officer then brought him over to the hat. The dog sniffed it over, and then began tracking. We walked west, following the dog. He then went onto a porch, and I drew my gun. He came off of the porch and I reholstered. Several doors down, he went onto another porch and out came my gun. He came off the porch and I reholstered.

After the fifth time, the K-9 officer gave me my first lesson. He informed me that when someone was walking or running, his scent drifts. The dog will not be tracking on the same line where the suspect walked, but to his left or right as much as thirty feet. This is where the suspect's scent lands. He told me to relax, and he would let me know when the dog had something. Good, I just thought we had a dog that needed to go to the Crisis Center. We tracked for about five blocks when the dog began circling in a vacant lot. The officer produced the head of a doll and gave it the K-9. He praised him and said good boy. Still looking like Boo the Fool from the porch incident, I was going to stay quiet. Doll head, good job? Maybe the officer needed to go to the Crisis Center.

The dog and his handler had led us to nothing. About half way back I just had to ask. The K-9 officer informed me that although you couldn't see the tracks in the lot, the suspects must have had a waiting getaway car. That's why the dog stopped tracking. There was no more scent. He had done a good job. It was the first dog lesson I learned. I wanted to ask about the rest of the doll, as the dog only played with the head, but my rookie mind was confused enough.

During my career, I have requested a K-9 about a half a dozen times. It seems like every suspect is terrified of the dog. We chased a vehicle once where two of the suspects had jumped from it and escaped on foot. We had a third suspect we caught inside of the car. We now were waiting for the K-9 unit to arrive. As the suspect sat in the rear of the scout, I explained to him why we requested the dog. I also started to spin a story about the dog. I told him he had been a former fighting dog and was a reclamation project for the police department. His favorite technique was to disembowel opposing dogs. He had to be kept on a very tight lead, as we had not had an opportunity to see how he reacted with people yet. I informed him the dog would have to sniff him to eliminate his scent. As the K-9 pulled behind us in the alley, you could hear the dog barking. My story must have really hooked the suspect. He looked back wide-eyed and started yelling, "I'll tell you anything you want. Please! They ran to a house three doors down. They hid in the basement!"

Apparently, there is no honor among thieves when you are about to be sniffed by a rabid killer. We found the other two guys in the basement without the need of the K-9. The mere thought of him had gotten the job done.

My very favorite K-9 lesson involved a dog named Oscar. He is the only canine that ever caught someone for us. On this day, a school officer had been searching a student as he entered the building. In the Detroit school system, you need to pass through a metal detector to attend class. It's not the safest environment for kids. The school officer pulled a loaded .45 cal automatic from a kid's book bag, at which time the student ran. The officer gave chase, losing the fleeing felon several blocks away.

We had responded to the chase and found the suspect's coat in an alley. It was a slow day and we decided to request a K-9. We were in luck and the few dogs the city had all were on duty because they had just completed a training session. So the K-9 car shows up and we go through the routine. He gets out, does his business and he gets to sniff the coat. The dog begins tracking and after several blocks, ends at a vacant row house. We formulate a plan. I am going to stand by outside in case they flush the suspect out, and my partner and the K-9 are going to go inside in an attempt to locate the bad guy. We communicate over the radio, and after about ten minutes, they exit empty handed.

I ask the K-9 officer what happened, and he figures the guy may have somehow slipped out, or the dog just couldn't find him. No need to worry, he will call for a second dog — just to be on the safe side. It seemed to me he lacked a little confidence in his dog.

The second K-9 shows up, goes through the doing his business routine and enters the row house. Ten minutes later, nothing. I tell the officers, don't worry about it; we can identify the kid through school records. But they inform me they are not giving up. They are calling in Oscar. Expecting the same results as the first two dogs, I agree and will stand by.

When Oscar and his handlers show up, it is a totally different ball game. As they pull up, I can see Oscar biting the side of the cage inside the scout car. When the door opens, he bolts out, with no apparent need to do his business. He wants to get right at it. His lead is stretched tight as his handler walks him to the front of the row house. The officer commands "Find."

Oscar drags the handler in, with my partner and the other K-9 officers behind him. Within two minutes, I can hear the suspect screaming. Maybe the story I told was true, and Oscar is disemboweling the poor guy.

Several minutes later, they exit with our suspect. He only is wearing his underwear and is very dirty. There are no signs of bite marks or scratches. We thank the K-9 officers and they have to drag Oscar back to the car. As we pull off, I ask my partner what happened. He tells me Oscar is the real deal. He says Oscar ran to the second floor and into a room. There's no sniffing around, he just begins jumping against one of the walls snapping at the ceiling. He is peeling some of the old drywall off with his claws.

This is the point where the suspect began screaming. He wanted to give up. He had removed his clothes so he could fit in the soffit of the roof. This is where the roof meets the attic and the gutters hang from. By squeezing in this spot, he was not visible from the attic access. It didn't seem to bother Oscar any.

I told my partner next time we request a canine, if Oscar is off, we won't even bother. Oscar made me a believer.

THAT IS NOT A BOBCAT

Another big issue in the city is animal control. We don't have enough police officers let along dogcatchers. When you get tasked with a stray dog, you may have to handle it on your own. That means catching and conveying it. My first week on the job, I watched an animal control officer clamp a dog stick on about an eighty-pound dog. This dog flipped himself completely over, and broke off several teeth biting the stick. It was very violent. The catcher could not control him, and he broke from her grasp and bit her. He ran off with the dog stick still attached. There was no class on that in the academy.

On this day, we responded to a stray that was hiding in a garage. We located the dog, and requested animal control. They had no one available, and dispatch informed us they would contact our precinct and have someone bring out a dog stick. That was great. They might as well send someone out who knows how to use the dog stick, because I sure don't. A dog stick is a six-foot metal handle, with a wire cable fashioned in a noose at the end. The idea is to slip it over the dog's head and cinch the noose tight. You then should be able to control the dog with the stick. Like everything in Detroit, the equipment was old and not cared for. Most of the time, if you could cinch the noose, the animal ended up choking to death because you couldn't get it to release.

Fortunately for us, the officer who brought the stick out had done this once or twice. He snagged the animal and guided him into our scout car. We made the trip to the dog pound, and pulled our captive out. We were met by a security guard who directed us to a cage where we deposited the pooch. The guard was male, about sixty-five years old. He was 5'9" and a sloppy three-hundred pounds. His hat was worn back and almost falling off of his salt and pepper hair. His uniform shirt was stained and one side was untucked. His black belt was worn brown, and his pants did not match his shirt. He smiled at me and asked, "You want to see something?"

I wasn't really sure, as he took a syrupy drink from a half-pint of gin he retrieved from his back pocket.

"See what?" I finally asked.

"A bobcat," he said."

"A bobcat," I said. "You don't have a bobcat here."

"Shore doo, they brought him in yesterday. He wild," he replied."

My partner and I were curious, but we agreed to take a look. I was positive he didn't have a bobcat, but this was Detroit. I know they recovered a live lion out of a dope house once.

The dog pound is a scary dark and damp place. All the animals are loud and vocal. He unlocked the rear door and we entered. The metal door had a dungeon squeak to it, as it swung open. I had my flashlight out as we walked in. He took several steps toward the first cage, and looked back.

"He wild, be careful," he said, as stopped short of the cage and pointed inside.

I have to admit, the hair on the back of my neck was standing up and my heart was racing. I began creeping around the corner, clicking on my light. I illuminated the cage and heard a loud hiss that made me jump back. Positioned in the corner of the cage was the biggest possum I had ever seen. He was standing upright on his hind legs and snapping his teeth. I looked at the guard deflated.

"That's an opossum," I told him.

"That be a bobcat," he slurred back. "I know what an Ohh-possum look like, and that be a bobcat. He tear you up if you get close."

He was rambling on about being from the south and how southerners could tell the difference between an Ohh-possum and a bobcat. He still was rambling about animal genus and species as we walked out.

Knowing Detroit, I'm sure seventy percent of the people he showed it to would agree with his identification that "That be a bobcat."

COURT: THE SECOND SOURCE OF INCOME

Court was becoming easier. You learned with each bit of testimony, and by watching others. I think a trip to court in the academy would have been the first step to better preparing us. Court was a moneymaker for most officers. It was tough to earn extra money when you are the police. If you wanted another job, you needed approval from the chief's office for outside employment. Even with the approval, how could you find a job? We were working that days, afternoons and midnight rotation. So court was a second source of income.

There are two courts for us: District and circuit. District court handles traffic and preliminary exams. Circuit court handles the trial portion. There are three tickets an officer can write: Parkers, movers and miscellaneous ordinances. Parkers will not get you in court. Movers will, if they are contested. Write enough of them and you can secure a court date once a month. Miscellaneous ordinances can land you in court anytime. The problem with them is that they are time consuming on the street. They usually come with an arrest and evidence. As I had learned the hard way, you are responsible for this misdemeanor evidence. Write a miscellaneous ordinance ticket and it will give you another day in court for the month.

A felony narcotics arrest was about your only guaranteed date. You could kind of time it, as after an arrest, the defendant had to be in court within fourteen days. Even if you made a great arrest, say for B&E or even armed robbery, you were at the mercy of the investigator assigned the case. If they made no effort to complete the case, then there's no court. There was a lot of animosity between guys on the street and the detective bureau because there were plenty of lazy investigators. Investigators could handle a case, and get everyone in the detective bureau in court. Instead of completing the case themselves, they would have everyone do a small task to get on the list to go to court.

For example, say a prisoner is arrested for B&E. The arresting officers bring him in and complete a preliminary complaint report. At least one of these officers is going to court. The arresting officers can ensure they both go to court by splitting evidence. Say they recover a crowbar and a bag of tools. One takes the crowbar, the other the tools. That way both of their testimony is needed. After this preliminary complaint report is completed and the prisoner is processed, the clock starts running. The department has 48 hours to arraign the suspect. The case is assigned to an investigator, and he will be the officer in charge of the case. He will be submitting a warrant request for review by the prosecutor's office. He is guaranteed court as the officer in charge.

So instead of him interrogating the prisoner, he will send someone else. It doesn't make a difference if he confesses or not, by interrogating the suspect, this officer is needed in court. Now, the officer in charge will allow other investigators to take witness statements pertaining to the case. Say someone saw the suspect break in. This statement is critical and this officer is needed in court. It's easy to see how the numbers of officers needed in court can go up. Think of the cost. In some cases, you need all of the help you can get. The majority, you don't. The department is aware of this practice and has tried to curb it several times. It still goes on today.

ALL IN A 4.5-HOUR DAY'S WORK

Once you received an appearance notice, you would sign for it and get yourself prepared for court. I would keep copies of all my reports so I could go over them well before court. The prosecutor always would provide you a copy at court, but I liked to have my own. You then would go to the appropriate court building with your appearance notice.

There was sign-in room, where you signed a sheet, and an officer punched in your notice. It now was stamped with an arrival time. The way court was paid out was by time. By punching in, you would get a minimum of four-and-a-half hours. A good day is when you punched in and your defendant was capias or the date had been rescheduled. You could punch out and were guaranteed four-and-a-half hours. You were required to punch in by 8:30 a.m., and the majority of court was scheduled for 9 a.m. This was quite a joke, as the majority of judges of magistrates did not take the bench until 10 or 11 a.m. So, you would have to sit around for two hours. I always thought this was ridiculous because if you weren't in the courtroom when they called your case, most of the judges would dismiss it right there. There was a lot of arrogance on the bench.

So, you would punch in and know you would have some time. Officers would go get breakfast, pickup evidence or just kill time. I know of officers who would go home, go back to bed for an hour and a half, and then return to court. Playing this court game cost the city a ton of money.

LET 'EM LOOSE BRUCE

The majority of the judges and magistrates were professional and carried themselves well. Others wanted everyone to know they were the kings and queens of their fiefdoms. They wielded their power when given the chance. A magistrate left an impression on me when I wrote a speeding ticket. I was north bound on the expressway doing the speed limit, when a female zoomed by me like I was standing still. She was well dressed, and driving a Mercedes Benz. It took me four miles to catch up to her, and I paced her doing 90 miles an hour.

I pulled her over, and was willing to listen to her explanation. She informed me she didn't have time for all this and to just go ahead and give her the ticket. I wasn't a ticket writer but if you asked for it, you were sure going to get it. She requested a court date, and we both showed. We are soon called forward and sworn in. I testified first, and was thorough and accurate. When I finished, she had an opportunity to contest the ticket. The judge asked her what happened, and all she said was, "I wasn't speeding." The judge replied, "Case dismissed."

I immediately realized she apparently knew someone, whether it was this judge or someone in the court system. Can you imagine how I felt? I knew she would speed again, and why not? There were no repercussions for her actions.

One judge was known as Let 'Em Loose Bruce. I had an armed robbery case with him once. The suspect had robbed an auto parts store in our city. He was armed with an assault rifle. One of the employees recognized him and provided his identity. A photo lineup was conducted and the suspect was positively identified. A warrant was issued and officers began attempting to locate him. It took several months before he could be arrested. He was arraigned on the charges, but went capias (didn't show up) at his first court date. Now they had to try and find him all over again. This took an additional four months.

They finally located and re-arrested him. His court date was set, and officers picked up our crucial witness. They had been delayed by traffic and were late arriving to the courthouse. The judge called the case, and the officer in charge advised him that the witness was on his way up in the elevator. The judge informed the officer in charge that everyone should be in the courtroom when he calls a case, and dismissed the case without prejudice. This allowed the suspect to go free that morning.

We reissued the warrant and went through the process of relocating and arresting him. The problem with all of this was that the judge couldn't wait a few minutes for a robbery case involving an assault rifle. Not even for a suspect who was capias the first time around. The witness was driven home by the officers and dropped off.

About an hour later, he exited his home and was shot by a masked suspect. He wasn't robbed, just shot. Luckily, he survived. We couldn't prove it, but we knew who shot him. The victim knew who shot him. And it was all thanks to Let 'Em Loose Bruce.

THIS ISN'T LAW & ORDER

Court was not like TV, with all the great testimony and banter back and forth between attorneys. For the officers, it was sitting and waiting. The longest I had to be in court was five days, from 8:30 a.m. to 3:30 p.m. It was a homicide trial and I never testified. The longest testimony I had given was about twenty minutes.

You learned early to be prepared. Bring your report or review the one provided to you. You are not allowed to discuss the case or testimony with anyone, and if you are caught doing so, it could cause a mistrial. You can fall into many traps as a young officer, and one of my favorites is the "Who was driving?" question. I am sure it is obvious to attorneys whether you are new or not when you take the stand. This helps them choose what line of questioning to use. The standard first question is, "Do you recall this incident?" Everyone says yes. The trap is now baited and ready. You are allowed to take your report up on the stand with you. You will be asked many questions, and may not recall all of the answers. You then can ask to refer to your report to freshen you memory. Once or twice may be okay, but anything more and you are going to get the, "I thought you said you recall this incident" response from the defense attorney. If the officer responds, "I do," the trap is ready to clamp shut. The attorney's response is, "I've asked you three questions and you can't answer one without looking at your report. It appears your really don't recall this case at all." This is the reason you really need to go over your report and testimony.

You learn quickly on about the "who was driving?" question. You may be testifying several months after the incident. Once you testify, you cannot talk with your partner. You already have been asked the "Do you recall this case?" question. Defense attorneys will drop in the "Were you driving?" question. That is a good one. Now, if you say you don't remember, you are really going to look like you can't recall the case. The defense is going to say, "You can't even remember if you were driving or not? Seems like the simplest thing in this whole case." If you say yes, and you weren't driving, well you know how that would look. If you were driving and can remember, will your partner testify to the same? Many preliminary complaint reports list driver in parenthesis after the officer's name. That lesson for many was probably learned the hard way.

I had only run into a few TV-type defense attorneys in my career. They always were a challenge, and you had better be prepared. They could eat you up. The remainder, were everyday attorneys, and with experience, you could almost toy with them. Keep in mind they could recognize experience and would avoid dangerous questions.

Once you had some experience, you could easily determine who the weak ones were. I have watched many crash and burn, just as they felt they have set the victim or witness up for that trial-changing question. You can actually watch it build. Their chest swells up a bit and they begin pacing. It's like a symphony orchestra ready to reach its crescendo.

I was working a pigeon drop case with the Dearborn Police Department, and my victim was in her seventies. On one hand, the elderly can be horrible witnesses, and on the other, they can be deadly. She was on the stand and answered all the prosecutor's questions without hesitation. Now it was the defense's turn. Being experienced, it now was easy for me to see the route he was taking.

He was going to contest the identification of his client. More specifically, he was going to attack the height the victim had given. The victim had listed him as 6'0" and the suspect was about 5'9." You could see it as he built the question. "Ma'am, are you sure you got a good look at the suspect? How tall are you?" It was so evident what road he was taking. He began his strut, and dropped it on her. "Ma'am, do you know my client is 5'9," and you stated over and over that he was 6'0" tall? How can he possibly be the man who robbed you?"

She looked him in the eye, and quietly said, "I don't know about all that, but I know he was taller than your short ass."

You know when you lose control of one of those skinny party balloons and it squeaks all over the room and deflates? That is exactly what he looked like. Now, she didn't really answer the question, but he couldn't gather himself quickly enough to fire back. The long pause and his frustration with being called a "short ass" torpedoed his efforts. I wanted to go up and give the old bird a hug.

The very best line I ever heard in court came from my own aunt. She lived alone in the same house she was born in. It was in a vibrant neighborhood that was full of immigrants. Well that's what it used to be. It now was a seedy block, dotted with vacant and burned out homes. She responded to a knock on her front door and when she cracked it open, the suspect forced his way in. He demanded money, and when she didn't have enough, he beat her. She located some additional change and gave it to him. Still not satisfied, he produced a chunk of concrete and beat her about the head. She was seventy years old. I knew the investigator handling the case, and the suspect eventually was identified and arrested. There was no question he was going to prison, as he had a number of charges against him. One was assault with intent to commit murder.

His attorney didn't like this one, and believe it or not, it was debatable. EMS had responded to the scene on the night of the incident. Although she was bloody and beaten, she didn't want to go to the hospital. Elderly victims are like that sometimes. As the defense questioned her, you could see it building. As his symphony began thundering, he dropped the question, "So Ms. Ianotti, if you were so severely beaten, can you explain why you didn't go to the hospital?" He had just laid down his full house.

She looked up at him meekly, and replied, "I knew I was dying, and just wanted to die in the house I was born in."

You could hear crickets in the room. Aunt Mo just laid down a straight flush.

He mumbled, "No further questions," and his client was found guilty on all charges.

Picking up a victim for court also can be an experience. Sometimes the elderly can turn on you, as was the case when I picked up one of my seventy-five-year-old victims. She walked with a cane, and there was no parking around the court building. I advised her I would drop her off at the door, park and then escort her in. It would be a several-block walk from the parking area. She argued back and forth with me, so I agreed to let her walk. As I parked the vehicle, and opened her door, I pleaded with her one more time. As she stepped from the vehicle, she shouted, "No, I told you," followed by, "Your big ass needs to walk anyway." At that moment, I felt like the party balloon. I quit asking questions, and followed her slowly to the courthouse.

There weren't many days in court that were enjoyable. Long hours of sitting and stale testimony can become very monotonous. I did have reason to perk up one day, when I had an armed robbery exam. Due to manpower shortages, we had several visiting judges presiding in our circuit court. Our judge was from a small Upper Peninsula town. It was late in the day, and only two cases remained. I had been sitting there all day, and was very grumpy. My case would be the last, as they took a narcotics case first. The court officer quickly retrieved the defendant from the back. He came out with his head bandaged. The Gang Squad arrested him and he had a kilo of cocaine. Evidently, they had "fluffed him up" during the arrest — hence the wrapped head.

As he was led to the table, three guys entered the courtroom. Two were wearing sunglasses, and all had baggy clothes on. They slumped into a bench several rows behind me. As the defense attorney questioned the officers, he got a couple of digs in that caused these three to start laughing. I didn't like it, and neither did the judge. He demanded order in his court.

After testimony was completed, the defense attorney wanted to discuss bond. As this was a non-violent crime, bond was low $50,000/ten percent, meaning five thousand dollars would get him out. Detroit was notorious for low bonds, no matter what the crime. The defense attorney got in another dig against the prosecutor and our three began laughing again. The judge immediately told them to stand up. They stood, or I should say, slouched up. The judge asked them whom they were there for. The question wasn't needed, as they were the only ones in the courtroom. The judge already knew.

The one pointed to the defense desk and said, "My boy, there."

"You are?" the judge asked. Apparently, to get his point across, the judge slammed his gavel down announcing, "Million dollars cash bond. Next case."

I wanted to standup and cheer. The defendant wanted to vault the rail and fluff up his boys. I left the courtroom thinking, if only every judge was like that.

Police Officer Rodney L. Bennett
Detroit Police Department, Michigan
End of Watch: Monday, May 28, 1990

Officer Rodney Bennett was killed in a motorcycle accident while en route to the police garage at the end of his shift. Another vehicle pulled in front of him, causing him to lose control.

Officer Bennett had been with the agency for eighteen years, and is survived by his wife and four children.

I CAN STILL FEEL THAT PULL

Back on the street, lessons still were being learned. Close calls were not an everyday occurrence, but when they came, they left a deep impression.

I was a young officer when I came close to using my gun for the first time. The incident shook me to my soles. We responded to a family trouble run, and were met at the door by a thirty-five-year-old female. You could hear screaming, and things being broken in the background.

As we stepped into the town house, I was looking down a long narrow hallway. It was about thirty feet long and ran the length of the residence. I could see four or five people through an opening to my left. They were physically fighting. As I began to ask what was going on, a female who was about sixty years old entered the hallway at the far end.

She had a large butcher knife in her hand and began running toward me.

As trained, I immediately pulled my gun and leveled it at her. She would be on me in seconds. I had no idea what was going on, or what caused her actions. In that split second, I had to determine if I was going to use deadly force. Everything slowed down and I began squeezing the trigger. To this day, I can still feel that pull.

Suddenly, a family member dove on her, from an opening about a third of the way down the hall. She was knocked from her feet, and dropped the knife. The entire family began yelling at me. "What were you going to do, kill our mother? We called you for help. Her behavior was caused by her refusal to take her medication."

I was stunned. Being a young officer, I had put myself in a bad spot. I should have stayed in the doorway entrance and could have stepped out. Or I simply could have slammed the door on her. It was a lesson well learned, and one I wouldn't forget. I was lucky. In those types of situations, you always wanted a good partner.

JUST WRITE THE REPORT

Sometimes being paired with a slug was worth the price of admission. This is an angle of the job you also have to learn about quickly. It could get you in serious trouble. As I said before, they would work harder at not working than if they just did the work to begin with. We responded to an accident, finding two vehicles heavily damaged. The drivers and/or passengers were gone. This would require several tow trucks, impound cards and an accident report. Policy in the scout car was the driver drove, and the jump man did most of the paper. I would, of course, help — but he would have to do the accident report. He could see this scene would require a bit more work than normal.

So the plan he hatched was this. We would call for two tow trucks and just have them move both vehicles around the corner. They would be off the main street, and they could get private tows when they returned. Brilliant. How in the world did this guy get on the job? We were dispatched to this run, so we would have to give radio a disposition. It would be entered on our log sheet describing the action we had taken. There also would be the record of the tow trucks responding. He said he didn't think of all that — he just wanted to avoid the accident report. This guy later would be promoted to sergeant.

SHATTERED PERCEPTIONS

I talked about the guy in our unit who was fired after testing positive for cocaine. This is how bright he was. He abandoned one of his cars about two blocks from our base — just left it on the street and took the plate off. None of us had seen the car before, and some of our guys had it towed and impounded when they found it. The supervisors had a conniption fit over it.

Again, I wondered how this guy got hired. My whole perception of police officers had been shattered. The biggest problem was, these officers were interacting with the public they swore to protect. They left quite an impression on me, and I could only shudder to think what the public thought about them.

Remember, they wear a uniform. I wear a uniform. I think you get it. All of this was folding into my education.

BUT WHY LEAVE?

As I had done in the academy, I really started to scrutinize my co-workers. That brotherhood we had developed in the academy now was fracturing. The line between workers and non-workers was clear. These types of incidents just confirmed my fears. We all were changing and would continue to do so.

For me, at about five years, I felt pretty comfortable. I knew what the job was about, was in shape, and wanted to chase bad guys. Why would you want to leave the department? These were the fun years. At eight years, you've had to deal with bad bosses, union issues, disciplinary charges and start developing a sour taste in your mouth. You begin wondering why you didn't heed that senior officer advice and leave for another department. By ten years, you want to survive, and are looking for a good unit. You can't leave now — you have too many years invested. By fifteen, it's a struggle. Once you clip twenty, you start looking at the end, and you're happy just to have made it this far.

At this time, I could feel my changes. I liked it, and I felt that need to be around the other risk takers — the officers who showed up at every dangerous run. I wanted more.

OUR OTHER PARTNERS

My lessons continued, and they helped fuel me. Medical emergencies also were a chapter in the street textbook. Everyone has a certain perception of emergency medical personnel. Those perceptions can be dead wrong. It's the same as the perception of police officers.

I had an eighteen-year-old shot through the face with a carbine. This is a .30 cal rifle round. The bullet went through his right cheek and exited his left. He had been standing in the alley with several other guys when someone opened up on him. He ran to a house about a block away and this is where we found him. He had a blood-soaked towel covering the entry wound. The side of his face was swollen and had completely closed his right eye. He could mumble responses, but not much more.

EMS showed up, and we took a step back so they could render aid. The tech asked him to remove the towel, and the tech said, "Oh wow, are you in pain?"

The young man cocked his head toward me, and mumbled, "Is he kidding?"

Some of those techs were not the brightest.

I did learn quite a bit from the EMS. We became close with several technicians in our precinct. They also had workers and non-workers. Workers always were at the most violent scenes.

My first EMS lesson was on an intoxicated man who fell into the street. He was about sixty years old, and looked unconscious when we arrived. Now, young officers immediately want to render first aid. You check the pulse, and ask in a loud voice, "Sir, sir, are you okay?"

You use the training you were taught.

We requested EMS, and they arrived several minutes later. They both got out and quickly assessed the patient from a standing position. One then knelt over the man, and started knuckling him in the chest. This is where you form a fist, leaving your middle knuckle raised, and grind that knuckle into the breastbone of the patient. It only took about five seconds when the patient jumped to his feet and started swinging. EMS already had given the drunk plenty of room, and I had to quickly duck several jabs.

Apparently, he was an alcoholic ex-fighter well known to this EMS crew. They sent him on his way and I had another entry for my street experience education.

The EMS personnel also learned some lessons in street education, particularly when their truck was stolen. When they responded to a run, they would leave the truck running and open in front of the location. I never thought this was a good idea in Detroit, but it's what they did.

We received a run to the south end of the precinct to meet the EMS crew. We find them standing in front of an apartment building with no truck and looking lost. They brought their patient out on a gurney and had nowhere to put her. Even though this was years ago, their truck had a GPS. Dispatch notified us they were tracking it and gave us the location, but warned the truck was on the move. The problem with the old equipment was it was about a half mile off. So when dispatch would give us a location, it wouldn't be there. Luckily for us, the suspects jumped on the Lodge Freeway, which gave us an opportunity to catch up to it.

Once we closed the gap, I activated our lights and siren. This caused the suspects to activate their lights and sirens and the chase was on. They exited the expressway, and bailed out several blocks later. We caught the driver and recovered the truck intact. We were pretty excited, as there always was a friendly rivalry in our unit on recovery amounts. When you recovered a stolen vehicle, you had to call it in to a recovery unit. They would give you the blue book amount on the value of the vehicle, and this was part of your monthly stats. We just knew we were going to have bragging rights for the month. A recovered EMS truck had to be worth some coin.

In my excitement, I had forgotten the department policy and they gave me only the bluebook price for that year truck. The dollar amount was six thousand. Being the investigative officer I was, I was not going to put down six thousand dollars. I called the fire department and they gave me a dollar amount of $150,000, which was much better. We were beaming over our catch and recovery.

The scariest part about the whole incident was the EMS crew showed up and we were going to return the truck to them. Keep in mind these were guys we knew. The one tech enters the truck and returns with a handgun. He had a look of relief on his face, and I now had a look of shock. He said he keeps it hidden in the truck for protection. I told him with a tone in my voice, it might be in our best interest if he told us that he stored a pistol in his EMS truck.

SCOOTER COPS

It was about this time that the powers-to-be felt it would be better if we were a little more mobile. We had a couple of cars, but they had a better idea.

Now, the only thing funnier than the range, was 86-S at motorcycle training. Department scooters would have to fit that "Mobile" bill. They really weren't scooters, but Honda 250s. The department's other bikes were the big Harleys. They required extensive training, and the 250s only needed a week of instruction. So off to scooter training we went. It would be held on Belle Isle, which I thought was a great idea because it's contained and has minimal traffic.

When we first showed up, I could easily see what was coming. All of the training bikes were bent and damaged. When they asked for a show of hands for whom had ridden a bike before, there only were four of us who raised their hands. This was going to be interesting. I wasn't as worried as I had been at the range, but I still did not want to get run over by a motorcycle. Remember that first day when someone took off your training wheels? Same thing. There was a lot of clutch stalling and dropped bikes the first day. No one was seriously injured and by the third day, everyone was doing okay.

I felt like Easy Rider, as I could do circles around everyone. I did get chopped down to size by one of the instructors when he asked me a question. He wanted to know how far my helmet would fly without me. I was driving around with it unstrapped. It's always good to have the stuffing knocked out of you every now and then. It kept me grounded.

Soon, the big day was upon us and we were going to leave the island. We would drive the length of Jefferson into the downtown area. Up to this point, we were practicing without any type of traffic. I could see the apprehension as we cruised over the bridge. Not only would we have traffic, but plenty of traffic lights, meaning lots of stops and starts. You actually could feel the tension in the air.

We turned off the bridge in unison, just like a flock of birds. It was pretty awesome. But it all fell apart at the first light. We caught the red, and were waiting for it to turn green. As the east west light was changing to yellow, the guy next to me had his rpms red lining. I knew this wasn't going to be good, and had no time to warn him. He was preloading the engine and I feared it would explode. When the light flashed green, he popped the clutch. The bike made one complete rotation as it dumped him off the back. How it missed the officer in front of him, I have no idea. I don't know who looked worse, him or the bike. EMS responded, and the officer survived with minor injuries. This now heightened the anxiety for everyone who had witnessed this spectacular feat of scooter cartwheeling.

We had several more drops and stalls before we reached downtown. Our first required decision came as we approached a Y in the road. Bikes began peeling left and right. An officer several spots in front of me began wobbling. Her legs came off the pegs, and widened as her feet skipped off the pavement. She couldn't decide left or right. For some reason, this indecision always caused the right hand of the indecisive to crank the throttle wide open. As the wobbling and speed increased, her thought process was going in the opposite direction. She Evil-Knieveled the curb, striking the fire hydrant that was conveniently positioned on the corner.

The collision sheared the windshield as she rocketed over the handlebars. The officer looked like an out-of-control gymnast as she headed west bound. Equipment and broken bike parts followed as she flew through the air. It was a very spectacular sight. Fortunately, she wasn't seriously injured.

We eventually all passed our scooter class and obtained our cycle endorsements. This would be the last time many of the officers ever would ride a motorcycle. They avoided it like the plague, and I really couldn't fault them.

NOW THAT'S ELECTRIFYING

Those first five years in Detroit allowed me to gain more experience than officers with thirty years seniority at smaller departments. The runs we serviced came in all shapes and sizes. I responded to a run of a possible fire. When I arrived at the location, I found it to be a large warehouse covering about half a city block. The third floor had a grey smoke leaking from all the windows. It wasn't much smoke and just kind of slowly rolled out and up the sides of the walls. The problem was it was coming from every window on the third floor.

An EMS truck was positioned out front with the side door open. I stepped on the side of the rig and looked into the open door. I had to step back out as I started giggling. What had set me off was a white male laying on the gurney. He appeared about thirty years old, and his hair was blown out like "Buckwheat's." It actually was standing straight out and was black at the tips, blonde at the roots. His face looked like someone had smeared ash on it. He had on a white dress shirt that was shredded at the sleeves. His hands were sticking straight up in a claw like posture. They also were black. Amazingly, his tie still was positioned around his neck. He could only mutter a "Glahhhh, Glahhhh."

I collected myself and asked the techs what had happened. I was told he had electrocuted himself. I told them it looked a little extreme for someone fooling around with an outlet. They told me I could find my scene in a third floor office located in the north corner of the building. They told me not to worry; they found no fire, just smoke.

I radioed for fire anyway, and we worked our way to the third floor. We located his office, and I couldn't believe what we found. It really wasn't an office at all but a desk and coat rack positioned in the corner of the third floor. Apparently, his lamp wasn't working so he was going to do a little electrical trouble shooting. He had walked over to a large transformer box, opened it and started poking around with a screwdriver.

Now, you could almost walk inside of this transformer box. Being the great investigative officer I was, I had put this whole thing together. The lamp on his desk had no shade, and the bulb was lying next to it. The transformer door was dusty, but clean around the handle. The door was open, and exposing raw cable as big as my wrist. I deduced he used a screwdriver, as one was lying on the ground near the two black footprints that now were staining the concrete floor. The driver had a thick handle, but the shaft had been torched off down to a nub. It was another case of simply brilliant police work. As this now was a medical run, and I was so pleased with my investigation, I made it a log sheet entry only and went on my way. And the man did survive.

GARY TEACHES THEM A LESSON

Every precinct has its regulars and my first command had several. One was Gary Fitzinski. He was a small guy about, 5'5," and 140 pounds. He was black, which was unusual with that last name. I liked it, and it kind of gave him uniqueness. He was a drinker and started as soon as the sun came up. He was pretty harmless, but every officer picked him out of the street once or twice. He was pain in the butt, but we never locked him up. No one did.

Well, every precinct also has several officers who believe the gun, badge and uniform make them holier than thou. They feel it gives them the right to talk to people any way they please. Whether it is degrading or abusive does not matter to them. They feel everyone will comply, because they are the police. This couldn't be further from the truth, and these officers would find that out.

They were a male-female team, which is a bad mix to begin with. Slap a big mouth on both of them and that spelled danger. They were going to let those alligator mouths get their canary asses in trouble. Now the story unfolded this way. We were on patrol and heard the female screaming on the radio, "Officer in trouble!"

We hit the lights and sirens and headed their way. We knew who the officers were, and it was a shame to be thinking, "What the hell did they get themselves into now?"

We arrived at the scene finding the male officer at the hood of the car doubled over. His uniform was not being worn properly as it was all twisted, front to back and back to front. He had a dazed look on his face. The female was struggling with someone in the back seat, and we saw it was Fitzinski. We separated them, and her uniform looked just like her partner's.

She turned to us, and I had to turn away. Her hair looked like the electrocuted guy's, but she was missing two large tufts, one right at the forehead and the other just slightly back of that. I'm talking three stooges — Moe pulls Larry's hair out — tufts. Both tufts are near the scout car, but are in dire need of recovery as it is a gusty day. Fitzinski sees us and stops fighting. He is drunk, but alert. I grab him from the car and cuff him. He does not struggle.

My partner has checked both officers and besides the poor uniform appearance and the two tufts, they seem to be okay — a bit dazed, but okay. I ask Fitzinski what happened. He explained he had his "drink on," when the officer told him to get out of the street. He said he did as he was instructed, but apparently wasn't moving fast enough for the officers. They got out of the car and began calling him bitches and hoe ass. He said he started to give it back to them, as he felt this was unnecessary.

They must have thought ole Fitz was going to be an easy win due to his stature. He said when they grabbed him, and threw him against the car, it pushed him over the edge. In his words, "He opened a large can of whoop ass."

I agreed with him on his opening the large can, but informed him he would be making the trip to jail for assaulting the officers. He apologized to me, but felt that if his whipping some ass corrected the rude behavior of the officers, he was satisfied. I told him not to spread it around, but I agreed with him. The female wore her hat for several days, and the male officer was quiet as a church mouse for weeks. I guess Fitz's lesson plan worked.

THE CASE OF THE MISSING DANISH

I probably really have had the most fun with all of the mentally challenged people I have come into contact with. I have said previously it is our worst type of run and can turn deadly in seconds. But that being said, it also can be the most entertaining run to service.

The majority of them are housed in adult foster care homes. The issue is these homes cannot physically prevent any of them from walking away. You open up an AFC home taking in a certain number of clients. Now you are supposed to have a monitor for every three people you have. The state pays you say one thousand dollars for each client. So you load the house up with twenty, with one or two people to watch them. It's quite the little moneymaker.

Once a person walks away from one, the police are called. It is very frustrating for officers to go to an AFC home to do a missing report. The responding officers already know the AFC home personnel are just trying to cover themselves. They don't want to lose their license if something happens to one of their clients.

The staff would get these people up in the morning, send them out on the streets, and hope they returned before dark. All of the fast food locations would have several clients inside for the day, smoking and drinking the same coffee or pop for hours.

I responded to a break-in at McDonalds at about four one cold morning. It was snowing, and I found the back door open, but it was undamaged. I knew McDonalds has a delivery truck making a drop off about this time, and I guessed he just forgot to lock the door. There were several inches of snow on the ground, and I could follow a single set of footprints to the basement. The tracks wandered about, then stopped at a locked cage that held buns, dry goods and other miscellaneous items. The lock was broken off and lying on the ground. I entered the cage to inspect the items, finding only one thing missing: A single apple Danish.

This particular item came in a large box of twenty-five, covered with cellophane. My suspect had carefully cut one corner of the box, and removed one Danish. Given the hour of the morning, the single Danish and wet prints, I knew it had to be someone from one of the AFC homes. We went outside and began tracking. We went several blocks and arrived exactly where I expected. Was it worth a knock on the door and a possible fistfight over a donut? Or maybe even a missing report if he snuck back out? I looked at my partner, and we both agreed it wasn't worth the trouble.

As we pulled off, I couldn't help thinking what a hero our suspect would have been if he took the whole box. Could you imagine him showing up with a late night snack for the house — a sugar rush at 4:30 a.m.? That one monitor would have had their hands full.

OFFICER TO THE RESCUE (OF WHAT?)

I got taken in by a mental when I had about a month on the job. I responded to a kidnapping/person being held against their will. I located the address, and found a respectable looking five-story office building. I went to the front desk, and asked if anyone had called the police. The clerk responded no, and I supplied her with the phone number dispatch had provided me. She placed a phone on the counter and informed me I was free to use it. I dialed, and a whispery voice answered. I asked if she had called the police, and she whispered, "Yes. They have me. Please hurry."

A rush of adrenaline hit me.

"Where are you?" I asked.

"They are torturing me," she responded.

This was a medal of valor type of case, and I pictured the mayor shaking my hand. My partner and I were going to rescue her. My partner could hear our conversation, and asked what was going on. I told him, "They have her, and are torturing her."

"Where is she?" he yelled.

"Where are you?" I asked again.

She said, "They have had me for several days and ..."

I now could hear someone in the background. The voice was yelling, "Susan," and getting louder. I then heard a brief struggle and the name, "Susan."

"Oh my god, they are killing her," I thought.

I could hear the phone receiver hitting the floor and then being picked up. I waited for a voice to tell me she was gone, and that I should have acted quicker. Instead I got the "Who is this?"

"Officer Haig," I responded.

The voice asked if I had been talking to Susan. I thundered in a loud voice, "Yes, and where is she? Is she alive?"

"Of course she is alive," said the voice on the other end. "Why wouldn't she be?"

"She claimed she was being held against her will," I answered.

The female on the other end now put the whole thing together.

"Officer, Susan is a mental patient at this facility, and she most definitely is being held against her will," she said. "She is currently being treated for a mental disorder."

The staff had no idea how Susan got access to the front desk phone. My brain could not scramble together an intelligent response. Explaining me being a rookie and an idiot could not prevent her from laughing out loud. I tucked my rookie tail between my legs and walked out. The girl who supplied us the phone giggled, "Have a nice day," as we walked out.

Officer Charles L. Pope
Detroit Police Department, Michigan
End of Watch: Friday, October 19, 1990

Officer Pope was shot and killed during a robbery. He was found slumped behind the wheel of his parked car.

WHERE DID I PUT THAT UNDERWEAR?

Some people we deal with are borderline mental. Once, we had a run where a wanted suspect was inside an apartment. Dispatch had given us the suspect's name and warrant information. It was a felony, and I was more than happy to go lock him up.

We arrived at the apartment and knocked on the door. The door cracked open, and a guy who looked like Danny DeVito poked his head out. Without telling him our purpose, we asked if we could come in. He said sure, and stepped back from the door. We entered, finding him naked, and it wasn't a "Good Naked."

You never want to shut a door behind you, but my partner did for the simple fact the guy was naked. We now are in his apartment with him, and he's naked. The apartment is no bigger than a prison cell, and I'm feeling super awkward. I tell him he needs to put on some clothes because he is under arrest. This doesn't shock him, and he says OK. He then states, "Where did I put that underwear?"

Now, I don't know if this was deliberate or not, but he had to search every inch of that apartment for his underwear. He kind of hopped when he walked, allowing his junk to bounce like a little spring. At one point, I pushed a small table in front of me as he approached the corner I had backed into. If his "Google" touched me, I was going to lose it.

He finally located several pair of faded white briefs drying on the radiator near the window. Yes, drying wet underwear on a radiator has an odor. Of course, the first pair he put on was not quite dry enough, and he had to take them off and try the other. I informed him that my nerves were shot, and if this pair was wet, that was how he was going. They apparently were dry enough for him to travel, and we made the trip.

I had no idea if he was mentally challenged or just enjoyed putting us through that. It's very tough to stay professional in those situations.

You always ran the risk of a fistfight when you serviced these types of runs. As an officer, you had to remember that it was simply a case of them not being able to control themselves. One of my first-fighters was a guy named Tim. We had a run to an Adult Foster Care home and discovered the staff down stairs was quite upset. They informed us Tim had not taken his medication and was upstairs tearing the place up.

Expecting the worse, we crept up the stairs. We could hear noises in the back bedroom, and entered through an open door. The room was in shambles, with furniture overturned, windows broken, etc. Tim was positioned in the corner, wearing only underwear. He was all of 5'2 and 120 pounds, and he was balding with long hair dangling from the sides. His chest was heaving up and down with every breath, and he scowled at us with clenched fists. I asked him if everything was okay, and he responded yes. I informed him he was going to have to come with us, as his medication had run out. In a very calm voice he agreed.

Getting them to agree with you always was the first hurdle. Now, each request after the first would require its own attention. I informed him he would have to put some clothes on. Tim reached down and picked up a pair of pants that would have fit an elephant. They had to be a 55 waist. He slipped them over his legs, then looked up at me. "See this is what I mean," he yelled.

He was holding the waist of his pants out and it looked like four or five more Tims could have fit in there. I could see his little teakettle lid starting to go. I thought maybe his belt would help, and asked where it was. He pointed to the top of a dresser and I picked up about six feet of clothesline that he had been using to keep his drawers up.

My assistance seemed to keep him calm, and I quickly trussed up his pants. I couldn't help but think that if I had to wear giant pants and a rope belt every day, I probably would be just as loony. We conveyed Tim to the Crisis Center, but I informed the staff that a proper fitting pair of pants may help prevent our need to return. They had to fight him, but we didn't.

A little understanding went a long way.

WHAT YOU GET FOR VOLUNTEERING

One of the first runs I ever volunteered for was a mental. These were in the early days and we ran several blocks to the dispatched address. I knew I had possibly made a mistake when a lady answered the door, and quickly slipped outside. She glanced back inside as she exited, and whispered, "He is upstairs."

"Who? I asked.

She said it was her son, and had not taken his medication in days. I asked if he was violent, and she replied, "very."

I asked how big he was, and she told me about 6'4" and 290 pounds. Hmm, this was looking like a bad thing. I figured better to be safe than sorry, and called for backup. I was hoping for some battle-scarred senior officers, but I could hear running footsteps approaching and knew the best I was going to get was some of my academy mates.

The mother tugged on my shirt as we entered, and said one more thing, "He hates the police."

Great, senior officers already had told me to never volunteer.

Amazingly, he went quietly. By showing him respect and talking in soft tones, we avoided a donnybrook.

"HE GONE!"

Some mental runs really can push you over the top. As I have said before, you already are primed, feeling you are spinning your wheels. We arrived at a facility and were met by one of the workers. No offense, but she was Oriental, and I could barely understand her. I already was mad, and her inability to speak proper English started to fan the flames. She yells at me, "He gone!"

I'm mad, so I say, "Who gone?"

She bounces back with "He gone," and I ask, "Who is he?"

She says, "He gone."

I take a deep breath and realize this "He gone"-"who gone" crap can go on forever. I calm down and ask for his chart. I'll get the information myself. She goes to retrieve the chart as we wait at the counter.

I notice something on the floor crawling toward me. I jump back as it is a patient in a gown. He is clawing his way toward the elevator. He looks up and in a raspy voice says, "Help me."

Several staff members grab him, and drag him into a back room. I think to myself, maybe there is a valid reason "he gone."

She returns with the chart and tells me, "You hurry up, he gone."

Oh, I'm going to hurry up, all right. I record the information and ask if she has a picture. "Oh, we have good picture," she states.

She fetches the picture and hands it to me. "That him," she says.

It is a Polaroid picture and not the best. All I can see is the top right portion of a face. This is in the lower right corner of the frame. I can see an eye, part of a noise and the top of a mouth, which appears agape. I pause and think better of asking her any more questions pertaining to the picture or the nut job who took it. I ask about a clothing description, and she tells me, "He have clothes on."

I understand that, and ask what type.

"Man clothes," she tells me.

Okay, I'm back into the "he gone"-"who gone" thing. I continue down the same road and ask for color and style. I hit a bingo as she tells me, "He wearing pastamas."

I quickly use my oriental interpretation skills and come up with, "he wearing pajamas."

I return the picture and head out to begin searching. It's November and about 2:30 a.m., and someone should notice a guy walking around in "Pastamas." Then again, in Detroit, that is not that out of the ordinary.

We searched for several hours, and never did find "He."

Giving it some thought, "He" may have fled for his life.

MERRY CHRISTMAS

The hits just kept rolling, and my assigned command was a training ground for the mentally disturbed. We responded to Herman Keifer Hospital on a walkway mental. It was Christmas Eve, and even this type of run couldn't dampen my holiday spirits.

Herman Keifer was one of the bigger, mental treatment centers in Detroit, and I had to admit we didn't get many runs there. They kept them locked down pretty good. Once you exited the elevator, you would pick up a phone and could be buzzed into either the south wing or the north wing. This day, we exited the elevators, finding both security doors propped open. I figured this could be the reason they were missing one. Not letting this dampen my good mood, we turned to enter the north wing. At that exact moment, a patient trotted through the doors, brushing against me. We were nose-to-nose for a second, at which time she yelled, "Fuck you," and she continued through the exit door.

My Christmas spirit and attitude swirled down the staircase with her. Putting on my game face, I entered the north wing and prepared myself for the inevitable: Another missing report.

WHO WOULD HAVE THOUGHT IT WAS THIS GUY?

I have stressed about experience and how this betters you as an officer. Some things do not appear as they seem, and as your career progresses, you learn to scrutinize everything more thoroughly. We were inside a vacant storefront, watching a young guy sell dope. You not only have to watch the dope man, but everyone in the neighborhood. If someone spots you, they will rat you out.

About a block away, I noticed a male who was about seventy years old coming to the corner just about every ten minutes. He needed a walker and his progress was slow. I thought this guy cannot be out exercising, and figured he might be a lookout. I put the binoculars on him, and after several minutes, I discovered his purpose: He was selling heroin.

He kept it in a bag attached to his walker. Customers would have to leave their vehicle to approach him, but it didn't slow the flow at all. We dropped the surveillance on the young guy, and locked up the old timer and one of his customers. He had twenty-three packs of heroin and a wad of cash on him. I would have passed him a hundred times and never given it a second thought. You'd think I would have learned with Hunkie Joe.

ONE TRICKY SCENARIO

In the early days, even a traffic accident made you put your thinking cap on. We were turning onto the service drive one day, when we heard a large crash. Looking off the overpass, we could see the northbound lanes of the Lodge expressway. There were three northbound lanes and an exit lane north bound, which would bring traffic up out of the ditch. I could see a vehicle partially in the far left fast lane, pushed against the barrier. It was positioned under the overhead viaduct, which was eight lanes wide. It was pointing north toward the far end of the overpass.

We hustled down to the expressway, and activated our lights, positioning ourselves behind the vehicle. We exited the scout, finding the female driver inside the vehicle and shaking. She appeared uninjured, but couldn't speak.

We ordered EMS and began inspecting her vehicle. It was strange that the car appeared bent from the bottom, with no exterior damage. We eventually found there was a small bush or tree lodged under the car. It must have fallen from a garbage or landscape truck. I assumed she had hit it, lost control and came to rest in her current position. EMS arrived and began checking her. I walked about thirty yards back, looking for anything that may have caused her to swerve.

I now was at the entrance to the exit ramp, and someone yelled down from topside, asking if the lady was okay. I shouted back that she was going to be fine, and asked if he saw what happened. He said yes, and I trotted up the ramp.

My mystery soon was solved, as he told me he witnessed that the female had exited the expressway and was almost to the top of the ramp when she lost control. She veered left, jumping the curb and launching herself across the expressway. There was a steep embankment, which she flew completely over, clipping the tree I found under her car. She had enough air under her to clear two lanes of zooming northbound traffic. She landed on her tires in the far lane, rolling the width of the overpass. The landing had caused her undercarriage damage.

The scene on the expressway looked like she had swerved to avoid a road obstruction, kissed the west barrier, and skidded to the far end of the overpass. If the witness had not been there, we might not have figured that one out. Some things just don't appear as they seem.

THE POWER OF ADDICTION

Dealing with the effects of narcotics also is an eye-opening experience. My guy trying to recap the fire hydrant was my first introduction. The power of drugs is overwhelming to those who are addicted. You learn as a young officer to quit lecturing people in the vain attempt to help them.

One day, we stopped a guy coming out of an alley entrance. He quickly dropped two packs of heroin, which we recovered. This guy was about thirty-five years old, and had the rough appearance of someone living on the street. I began my standard narcotic lecture, at which point he began sobbing. He looked up at me, still sobbing, and said, "Officer Haig, I'm out here sucking dicks to get high."

I had no response or advice. I left the heroin on the ground and walked away. As if there was any chance I could relate to what this man had been through or what brought him to his current state. What about my eighteen-year-old academy mate? How would he deal with this?

We also had a prostitute named Angel, who worked a very specific corner. Her sole purpose for hooking was to get high. You could see her fiending on the street as she started her day. After her first trick, she only had to go about half a block to get her fix. Once she got high, she returned to the same corner. Now, she would work the corner flying. She had not a care in the world but for that next fix. This would go on all night. She then would disappear for a few days, and then the whole cycle would start over. I hated to see her down, and almost was happy when she was high.

One day, she just disappeared. I have no idea what happened to her. I always hoped she got out, but knew she probably didn't. She probably was just another number in Detroit.

WHEN YOU RUN OUT OF USEABLE VEINS

We once checked a vacant house, and as I came up to the second floor, I could see into the bathroom. A male was sitting on the toilet, his pants down around his ankles. He was attempting to inject heroin into his penis. The lack of usable veins anywhere else was his explanation. The problem was that there was a male and a female watching him, waiting to use the same needle. They had no concern of where he was injecting the needle, nor were they concerned of its dirty appearance. They were sitting so close that it bothered me. You easily could see that need in their eyes. These incidents all were part of my narcotics learning experience.

At this point, I was becoming a seasoned officer, and still was eager to learn more. My aspirations were to become the best felony cop on the street. I had accomplished that at my command, but that was like being a division II All American. I knew I needed to be in the bigger game.

Several of my classmates had left the New Center Command and told wild stories about precinct life. Their experiences always got better when they had a few cold beers in them. Precincts were filled with experienced officers, but we didn't have much contact with them.

They would pick us up if we had an arrest and drop us off at the precinct. The senior people in the precinct all appeared miserable. If we brought in a prisoner to the Thirteenth Precinct, the clerk would make us type our own print cards, which is something she would do for her own people. The bad thing about this was the supervisors knew all about it. It was like, "What do you think you are doing, bringing arrests in here? We are too busy for that nonsense."

NAP TIME AND MACHINATION

My classmates who left would go on and on about lazy senior people. The 18 year-old kid had a terrible experience. His first day in the precinct, he is assigned to a scout car with a guy who had about twenty-five years on the force. They get in the car at the start of the shift, and the senior officer doesn't say a word. They are working midnights, and the senior guy is driving. Rookies never drove in the precinct. They had to learn to write reports and run.

He immediately drives out of the precinct and down to the Detroit River. He tells the kid not to touch anything or answer the radio. He gets out, opens the trunk and pulls out a pillow. He gets in the backseat and falls asleep. The poor kid sat there for two hours staring at the river. That is the life of a rookie. If you opened your mouth, you got the old, "Get some time on the job, rook. I've put more time on my lunch break than you have on the job." You pretty much walked around scared of the street, senior officers and the command structure.

We had several senior officers transfer into our unit. I couldn't understand why. More action was what I was looking for, not less. They appeared worn out, and always were full of stories and complaints. They didn't follow the rules and didn't seem to care about the repercussions. I loved their confidence, but hated their work ethic. They did bring years of experience, but they just didn't want to apply it. Later in my career, I would understand why.

One day, I was assigned to one of these old timers and he told me a tale. Gruff and loud, he tells me, "Kid, this is what you need to do and do it now."

I sit there all scrubbed and polished, listening intently.

"You need to get a partner you can trust — trust more than your life. Then you do this: Midnights, you and your partner take the scout car to a secluded spot. Be thorough and check, making sure no surveillance cameras can spot you. No citizens or passing traffic. About 4:30 in the morning, you get on the radio screaming, 'Oh my god, dispatch, I've never seen anything like it. The lights and noise are incredible. It's hovering right over us. It is long and cylindrical in shape about a fifty yards long, the light is intensifying.' Now, you let the radio go silent. You and your partner drive the scout car into the back of a large U-Haul truck. You head west. You assume new lives in Arizona. Twenty-five years later to the day and moment, you back the scout car out of the U-Haul at the same spot in Detroit. Wearing the same uniforms, you key the radio mic and pick up where you left off. 'My god, did anyone else see that? It was amazing. My body is humming. We need a supervisor immediately.' Dispatch had no idea who you are, and neither does the supervisor who shows. They find a twenty-five-year-old scout car and officers wearing uniforms to match. The problem is, they have old bodies and gray hair. Nice. I've been abducted by aliens and held for twenty-five years. The department owes me twenty-five years of back pay and my pension. Can you imagine the media stories? Best part is, it's time to retire and to start collecting that money."

"Do it now!" he hollers.

For a moment, I pondered that. What a great plan. But high-speed chases and hold-up men jolt me back to the present. That's what I want, and more of it. I tune him out, and scan the street in front of me. Yeah, I'm sure this is what I want.

TIME TO MOVE ON

It was about this time, one of my sergeants suggested I move on. She had worked at a number of different units and told me it kept the job fresh. I wanted to learn more, so I was willing to take the next step.

I was a little apprehensive, as I would be leaving the comfort and safety of 86-S. I finally was familiar with the precinct and the job. Learning the streets of a precinct or district was tough. In the beginning, I had to walk around with a map in my pocket all the time. Location and direction mean life for a police officer. If you chase someone and catch him, it could result in an incident-free arrest, a street fight or a shooting. You better be prepared for all three, and you damn better be sure you know where you are at if you need help. There is nothing more sickening for a police officer to hear a fellow officer screaming for help into the radio and you can't find them.

So I would be leaving all of the comforts behind and starting new. I asked the sergeant how I would get started. She said I had to complete a transfer request and have the officer in charge of my unit sign it and send it through department channels. The unit I was requesting would do an investigation and either approve or reject my request. If approved, I would go onto a transfer list for that unit. With my time on the job, I would be quite low on the list.

The other option was blue slip units. This avoided the transfer list and you could move right away. I have no idea if this was setup for friends of friends, but it sure seemed like it. All I had to do was fill out a slip and the boss of the unit I was requesting could approve it. I would be gone the next day. She told me there was a spot at Vice, and that they needed a white male officer. I'm white and male, so I've got that going for me. If I were black and male, I'd be fighting fires right now. It's funny how the race thing keeps coming up. I had watched Miami Vice on TV, and it was very cool. But this being Detroit, I was well aware that I wouldn't be wearing a suit, or driving a sports car. I knew locking up prostitutes all day wasn't my cup of tea, but I needed a change. I figured I would give it a try, and the worst-case scenario is that if it didn't work out, I would end up in the precinct.

I sent my blue slip in. She knew the sergeant at Vice, and the next day I was down interviewing. I felt it went well, and I was transferred within a week.

2ND COMMAND - VICE

CODE NAME BUBBLE

The first day at Vice was very interesting. It was like going from a convent to a motorcycle gang. I first met the entire crew.

Including me, there were seven officers who worked the street and one sergeant. This sergeant is the one I had mentioned earlier who eventually would be appointed up through the ranks to assistant chief. There was one female who did administrative work and who occasionally worked the street. She seemed bitchy right off the bat, which is consistent with inside personnel. She also was sleeping with one of the married guys on the crew. There were two other floater guys, who I saw every now and then.

I thought the one guy was awesome. He looked like a street vice cop — one of those types you look at and would never guess he was a cop. He was quiet, and had the thousand-yard stare. I learned on my first day that this was not going to be Miami Vice — this was going to be Detroit Vice. Our basic duties were to arrest prostitutes, check topless bars and raid Blind Pigs, which are after-hours drinking establishments.

Okay, the topless bar thing sounded great, but I wasn't sure about the rest. But I wanted to broaden my horizons, and this was it. As always, I thought, give it your very best and go from there.

The first task for the day was a code name. It was explained to me that when you communicated on the radio you did not want to use an officer's real name. Instructions from the sergeant were that I needed to come up with one in 60 minutes. If I couldn't come up with one, they would give me one. It had to be short so you could say it quickly on the radio. I was pretty sure I didn't want them to give me one, so I started thinking, "Everyone wants a cool sounding name — Dragon, Thor, Thumper, Eagle, Spider, Viper, Crusher, Stomper, etc." I kind of already had a street name, but only was proud of it because the street gave it to me.

To understand the name, you have to understand the story. I had worked a bunch of street narcotics as a young officer in the Cass Corridor. Now, everyone knew about narcotics work. Some officers would "Put dope" on people to make a case. An example of this would be you see a guy on the corner selling. He is going back and forth to cars as they pull up. He has been there an hour. You know he is selling, but you really are not close enough to see a transaction. You roll up on him and find a white Styrofoam cup on the ground with ten packs of heroin. Although the suspect did not have narcotics on him, some officers might say he did. I never worked with anyone like this, but people had reputations.

My partner and I learned that if you could get in a spot, say a vacant building, or garage, and watch with binoculars, you could catch them handling the narcotics. Most guys on the street never would have dope on them. It always was in a stash somewhere — a crumpled up potato chip bag, under the cap of a fence post, mail box, or inside a car tire. This way, when the cops rolled by, if they stopped and searched you, they had nothing. If they wanted to put dope on you, they had to find it. So a customer drives up, you take their order and money, walk over to your stash take out the desired amount and give it to the customer. This is all done in seconds.

Some would be a three-man operation, featuring an order taker, money taker and narcotic handler. I knew a guy was selling one day, but had no idea where he was keeping it. He always would have his back to us. We got plain tired and went to investigate him. We stretched him on the car and searched him for weapons. We had placed his keys a small knife and the box of Lemon heads candy he was eating on the car. He was nervous, and we knew something wasn't right, but we couldn't find a thing. It finally clicked for me, and I looked in the Lemon Head box. Underneath the lemon heads were eight rocks of crack cocaine. It was another lesson learned, and there was no need for me to get upset. I thought, "He is doing his job, I'm doing mine."

The bottom line is that I always would tell the bad guys that I eventually would get them. I would get them, and get them the right way. I arrested quite a few people I had issued that warning to. We always talked about it on the way to jail. I gained quite a bit of respect on the street for it.

One day, my regular partner and I serviced a rape run in the north end of the precinct. When we arrived, the person reporting the offense is a prostitute from the corridor. We are in a well-kept apartment, and it seemed odd to see her in this setting. She told me her child had gotten a cab ride to her apartment and had been fondled by the cabbie. As she was talking to me she would say, "You know, Bubblegum, that's how it is on these streets." "Can you help me, Bubblegum?" After about the fifth Bubblegum, I had to stop her and ask who Bubblegum was. She said, "That be you." I was confused, and asked why that is me. She said it was my street name — the criminal element in the corridor gave it to me about a year ago.

Now I was flattered the streets had given me a name, but Bubblegum? I asked her why, and she explained that the way I handled myself on the street was respected. I treated everyone fairly and never talked down to anyone. My reputation of letting people go and assuring them I would catch them later had created a corridor legend. I was like bubblegum on someone's shoe. Once I got on it, they couldn't get me off. She explained I always got my guy, no matter how long it took. Wow, it made me feel good, but really, Bubblegum?

I gave it some thought, and realized I was more proud of the name Bubblegum, than some of the ribbons I had received. So I informed the vice sergeant of my choice. If the streets were going to nickname me, I had to respect that. He looked at me a little weird. He OK'd it, but knew it most likely would be shortened to Bubble. It has been Bubble ever since.

So I have a new code name, and two new partners for my first day at vice. We went out to lunch, came back and were done for the day. That was it. No work, no nothing. I felt we were off to a bad start. Most of the time, I never even took a lunch. I was hoping the second day would be better.

Officer Bruce Williams
Detroit Police Department, Michigan
End of Watch: Wednesday, December 5, 1990

Officer Bruce Williams was shot and killed when he was robbed as he was pumping gas. When he attempted to take action, he was shot and killed. The suspect was convicted and sentenced to life in prison without parole.

Officer Williams previously served with the United States Army, and he is survived by his wife and two children.

JOHN OPERATIONS

Day two was a bit more exciting. We would be conducting a prostitution/John operation. I later would learn it was not an operation but the thing we would do almost daily. "Operation" made it sound important. I now know why I was recruited for the unit. I looked like a John. And why did I look like a John? It's because I'm white.

This is how it was laid out to me: I would be in an undercover vehicle, and I would prowl around looking for prostitutes. When I saw one, I would pull over to see if I could get a case (a case being her offering sex for money). Fifty dollars for "Around the World" is street slang for everything. If she gave me a case, I would tap the brakes on my undercover car (U/C), and a takedown crew in a marked unit would pull up and arrest her. She would be loaded up into a police van that would be trailing me.

When we had six or seven girls, we would go to headquarters to process the girls. Yep, you guessed it — we had to deal with female detention and the lazy crew. They really hated vice because we always had six or seven girls, which made for lots of work.

On the street, the majority of the time, the girls would just jump right in the car instead of talking to you outside of it. I never liked that. Now, as you drove, you would try to get a case. They would slide up right next to you and want to get busy right away. There was lots of dirty talk, and how they knew you had a big "Donkey." If they tried to touch me, I would lift their hand and tell them, "Let me pull over, I don't want to wreck." Most of these girls were street people and narcotics users. They smelled and were high most of the time. It's nothing like you see in the movies or on TV. The quicker they could do the deed, the quicker they could re-up their drugs. I had experience with prostitutes in the corridor, as I had worked a prostitute beat once. It gave me a little street insight into this trade. There was one girl called "Stinky." Her legs were rotting from heroin use and you couldn't get within ten feet of her without gagging. Both of her legs had ballooned to three times their normal size, and the skin looked like a Chinese checkerboard from the injection points. She worked sitting on the curb. I asked the girls how she got business, and they said the Johns liked the skankiness.

I once had two girls working the corners about a block away from each other. One was in the street the other on the corner. I stopped to talk to the girl in the street. She was pissed and began yelling about "Tina." She was upset about Tina's service fee. I asked why that was a problem. She said it's because "that bitch is charging $2.50 for a blow job." Obviously, Tina was the Walmart of the corridor and must have been dealing in volume. The girl I was talking to was giving a bargain basement price herself for a blow job — five dollars cash money. The standard across the city was between ten and twenty dollars. I informed the upset prostitute that competition always is good, but I agreed that the $2.50 price was a bit low. She informed me Tina was a, "snake in the grass, skeezer bitch ho," and she would love to cut her. Knowing I had not yet acquired the knowledge to intelligently solve this problem, I told her to stay out of the street and drove off.

I knew I couldn't stop the girls from working. If you arrested them, they would spend the night in jail, appear in court the next morning, and plead not guilty. They would be given a court date and released. They would walk out of court, get about three blocks away, and start working again. If they got picked up, they would complete the service and have the John drop them off at the corner they got arrested on. It's the oldest profession in the world. Police aren't going to stop it. But, on occasion, I tried to. I felt that if a girl was standing on the same corner every day, it was a total disregard for my legal authority. I would let the world know I wasn't going to stand for it. Every time, I saw her, I would lock her up. After a couple of weeks of arrests, I raised the white flag. She had to do it every day. I didn't. I was such a rookie back then.

SHE'S NOT WHAT SHE SEEMS

One day, I'm rolling down Michigan Avenue dressed in my best suburbanite John outfit. I see a girl on the corner and pull over. She jumps right in and snuggles up to me. Yuck. She makes the offer, and wants to do it while I'm driving. She is a bigger, muscular girl and I start fighting her a bit as she is trying to pull down my pants. I now am banging the brakes like a son-of-a-gun and pull over as the trail car activates its overhead lights and hits the siren.

I jump out like a scalded cat as the team pulls her out. They inform me they are letting her go, and I'm upset and want to know why. Well, it's because "she" is a "he," and they can't have a male riding in the van with the female prisoners. Now, working in the corridor, I had learned to always look at the feet and the Adam's apple. It is a dead giveaway for a guy dressed like, or trying to become, a girl. This guy had it all together — no Adam's apple and little feet. So it was my first case where the guy/girl gets a get-out-of-jail free card because of his gender. Great, I knew I was in the wrong unit.

I jump back in my U/C and proceed down Michigan. I spot another girl. Slowing down, I give her the once over (not wanting to waste my time by picking up another guy). I stop and she jumps in. I get the case, and tap the brakes. As the marked unit pulls behind us, she jumps out. I have her by the back of the neck and drag her through the driver's side and out onto the street. Mind you, I'm a little upset about the previous case, and this one is not going to get away. I push her onto the hood of the car and tell her to quit resisting. I must admit it was a little profanity-laced and aggressive.

The crew then ran up to assist me, and started yelling, "Let her go, let her go."

Now, why would I do some stupid shit like that? Then, they actually grabbed me and pulled me back. I started fighting them, asking them what the hell they are doing. They tell me that I don't understand, and that she is "shitting herself."

"What?" I asked.

"Get back, she is shitting herself," they hollered.

I'm still trying to decipher all this when I get my first whiff and almost throw up. This prostitute has just filled her drawers with pudding. On command, mind you. Who can do that? I already know what is going to happen next. We are going to let her go, because we can't put poopy pants in the van with the other girls. They would tear her up.

At this point, I'm pretty depressed. I was a different type of cop. They let her go because she shit herself. I would have locked her up every time she did it. Let her sit in her own feces for a day and see how she felt about it. I bet she would have stopped. Now she went wherever, changed, and then was back on the street.

DUSTY LEE DAWN

I had thought I gained some knowledge about prostitution from working the corridor, but Vice would be another chapter in my street textbook. The wear and tear on street girls was incredible. They would be all scarred up, many with gunshot wounds. I knew a girl who worked the streets after having one eye shot out. Missing teeth either because of drug use or having them knocked out were common.

We locked up a girl once named Dusty Lee Dawn. I'm not kidding — that was her name. She had a fresh six-inch vertical wound on her forehead. It had been stitched the day before as the result of a John beating her with a pipe. We were processing her and four other girls when she began sobbing. I didn't give it much thought until the other two girls kept saying, "Just tell him."

I had checked her Adam's apple and feet, so I knew I hadn't been fooled. I pulled one of the other girls aside and asked what the issue was. She told me Dusty was a juvenile (sixteen years old) but this girl looked forty, if not a day. A check proved she was a juvenile. The street aged you quick.

BLIND PIGS

As the weekend approached, I was going to have the opportunity to do a different type of vice work. Break from the "Hoes," as they say on the street. It was our first raid, and I was pretty hyped. I would be dressing up in full tactical gear — which is probably what every policeman wants to do at least once in his career. We would be targeting Blind Pigs. These after-hour joints could be run out of residential houses or commercial buildings. It all depends on the size of your crowd.

Now, you need a search warrant to enter and investigate illegal activity in most places. To cover this at vice, we would first send in someone undercover, with no ID and no weapon. Some of these places really were jumping, and could have several hundred people in them. Once the undercover man was inside, they would be looking for certain things. There's the houseman, who is the guy controlling the whole operation. He usually is seen picking up money from everyone. Then there's the doorman, who was at the front door checking for weapons and identification. He usually was armed. Then there's the guy running all the gambling, which usually included a dice game and cards. Lastly, there's the bartender and female entertainment. Once they all were identified, the undercover man would notify the crew, and they would prepare to raid the place.

Everyone was briefed as to the layout and location of suspects, and the crew had specific jobs. I was running the ram (to force the front door). This weighed about fifty pounds and had two handles on it. It looked like a cannon barrel.

I had a shotgun man behind me. His job was to clear the entrance once I breeched the door. Then the rest of the crew would enter. Once we entered, everyone would be ordered to the ground and the location would be cleared and secured. At this point, all the identified suspects would be arrested and all the patrons issued tickets and released. It sounds pretty simple, but it never was.

First off, you were dressed in that raid gear. This consisted of your regular clothes covered with a police-inscribed raid jump suit. I was the first guy through the door, so I also wore my regular bulletproof vest. Over all of this, I wore a flak vest, my tactical raid belt, weapon and ammo. We all wore black Nomex facemasks, which hide your identity to all the suspects and patrons, as you may be the undercover operative who has to go in the next location.

Needless to say, if you raided in the summer, you got sweaty. On several occasions, the crew got lost running to the designated location and I had to lug that ram several blocks. Your adrenaline always was thumping but it could disappear quickly when you were frustrated. It always was scary going through the front door, as you had no idea what was behind it.

The maximum manpower we ever had was probably ten officers. That's ten people to control two hundred. As you can guess, this was an obvious safety issue. Once we hit the front door, everyone ran as if the building was on fire. I have seen women in evening gowns jump out of second story windows. I always thought this was ridiculous, as most of the people received a loiter ticket in place of illegal occupation tickets, and they may get a fine of one hundred bucks.

The people running the place had the best deal from the legal system. They would be charged with a misdemeanor and could get up to a five hundred dollar fine. Most of the time, it was two hundred bucks. All the liquor and gambling equipment was confiscated.

So if you run a blind pig, the first thing you do is not to let anyone in that you don't know. If the police don't see it, they can't raid it. Now, more than likely, the police will know something is going on. When you have fifty to sixty cars parked in a residential area at 4:30 a.m., you know something is going on. It's up to the police to figure out how to get in.

The best nights of operation are Friday and Saturday. You charge ten to twenty bucks a head to get in, and beer and mixed drinks are five dollars and up. There is gambling, but the house takes a cut of all money wagered. You can make two thousand to five thousand dollars a night. Now if you do get caught, you may face a two hundred to five hundred dollar fine. I think most of us can do the math — it's a great moneymaker.

This was the regular routine at vice: Prostitutes and raids. I was getting bored quickly. I knew going in that this really was not going to be for me, but routine in police work can get dangerous fast. I reminded myself daily to not to get complacent.

EXTRA TICKETS!

We did handle several other types of cases, but it was not the norm. We ran a ticket scalping operation that made me chuckle. It wasn't a difficult detail, as all you had to do was walk through the crowd. There were plenty of people selling tickets, which is illegal. Everyone has seen this at a concert or sporting event. Someone stands there and yells, "Extra tickets!"

We would walk up to them, ask how much, and once we settled on a price, we would confiscate the tickets and issue them an ordinance violation. We were working a Rod Stewart concert one day, and had just pulled in our first catch of the day. Mind you, our equipment was covered and our radios turned down before we approached a potential seller. Once the deal was done, and we reveled our identity, we lifted our shirts displaying guns, cuffs and radios.

My partner and I now were standing there with our badges displayed around our necks and our radios chattering. We were writing this guy a ticket on a clipboard when another guy walked by yelling for people who need tickets. I motioned him over, and he quickly snaked his way through the crowd. He is now is standing in front of my partner and I, as well as the guy we are issuing a ticket. I ask him how much, and he tells me one hundred dollars apiece. I tell him that is way too much, and ask if he can come down.

"No way," he says, and starts haggling over the price, stating these tickets are a bargain at that price.

The guy we are writing the ticket to begins laughing, but he is trying to muffle it. He is just like us, and wants to see how far this will go.

It goes on for several minutes when I finally point my finger at the guy's face, which he looks at. He follows the tip of my finger as I slowly point down and around to the badge around my neck. He stops and then begins to laugh himself. All four of us are now standing in the middle of this huge crowd laughing our asses off. I probably would have given him a break, but since we wrote the first guy, we had to write him. They both paid the fine, but got a lifetime story out of it.

THIS ISN'T SUNDAY SCHOOL

Another type of vice operation was liquor license enforcement. A major liquor license violation was party stores selling to underage kids. Now, in a city where they shoot three to five people a day, this doesn't seem important, but believe it or not, these little things matter.

So Detroit Vice is assigned the task. Our boss asked us if we knew of any juveniles willing to work undercover in this capacity. Off the top of my head, I didn't know one. That night, I went home and told my wife about it. She immediately suggested a 16-year-old kid from her church. I warned her this could be dangerous, and said he would need to get a waiver signed by his parents. She was sure they would go along with any department requirements.

Okay, I wasn't sure about a 16-year-old churchgoing, white suburbanite heading into a jungle. Then again, I thought, what 16-year-old would not want to work with the Detroit Police on some undercover operation. I spoke with his parents on the phone, and they exactly were as my wife described — willing to help to make the world better. Wasn't religion grand?

I pick him up the night of the operation and explain things to him. He is what I envisioned, complete with a proper suburban haircut and wearing khakis and a polo. He is going to look as out of place as an elephant in the artic. I explain to him what he will be doing. We want him to go into a liquor store, pick up some beer and carry it to the counter. He needs to have his money in his hand, and hopefully they will give him a price at which time he should just hand over the cash. I tell him that if they ask for ID, just walk out. If he can purchase it, just bring the beer out to the car.

I assure him that one of our officers will be in the store with him at all times, and he doesn't need to worry. If a purchase is made, we'd re-enter the store and issue a ticket to the clerk or owner.

This went pretty smooth, and he made several buys. He was nervous at first, but after several attempts, he gained confidence. After the fourth one, you would have thought he just locked up Al Capone.

Now, the boss chirped on the radio that he wanted everyone to meet up on Eight Mile for a change in plans. When the crew arrived, he pulled me aside and asked what I thought about getting the kid into Hot Tamales.

I immediately tried to picture this innocent, church going kid going to Hot Tamales, which is a notorious topless bar. It does not employ your twenty-year-old, plastic surgery correct dancers. These are your seasoned ghetto, thirty-five-year-old saggy girls. There are lots of drugs and illegal activity there. As such, my answer to the boss was, "no way," because I'm responsible for this kid. How am I going to explain to his parents that we took their kid out to buy liquor, with the sole purpose to better the world, and we then took it upon ourselves to introduce him to the world of Ghetto Boobs. There was no way, no how.

Then the little devil figure appears on my shoulder. What sixteen-year-old would not want to go into a topless bar? It wouldn't matter who was dancing. They were woman and had no tops on. Not only would he be going in, he would be working as an undercover operative with the Detroit Police Department. I flipped back in time, to being a sixteen-year-old. This one incident, this moment in time, would stay with him the rest of his life. It would be a story he would tell until the day he left this world. I told the boss okay, I would ask him.

Deep down, I already knew the answer. After listening to my explanation of the operation, he hesitated for a moment and then agreed. He told me if it would help the department, then he was willing to try. Riggghhht —helping the department.

So in we go. I knew we wouldn't be in there long because he looked all of sixteen, but those few minutes were wonderful. Ever see the part in Willy Wonka and the Chocolate Factory when the kids first enter the candy room? He had that look. He missed nothing, as mature jiggling breasts danced by him. We hadn't even taken a seat and were tossed. They requested his ID and I went with the old, "It's his birthday and the ID is in the car," line.

Our waitress looked at me with her hand on her hip, boobs resting on her tray. She glanced at the kid, and right back at me. Her eyes said it all: "O'hhh hell no, you all got to go."

I would have been better off trying to convince her that I was Harry Houdini. I grabbed his arm, and had to tug a second time, as he was locked on the tray/boobs thing just inches from his face. We walked out, and I don't know if it was the light from the neon sign, but the kid had this glow about him. His speech was slow and low. It was almost sing-songy.

The boss thanked the kid for the attempt and shut the operation down for the night. I drove the kid home. It was silent, with no talk about what had just happened. When I pulled up to the door, I told him it would be completely up to him if he wanted to tell his parents. He stepped out of the car with a curl in his smile. He looked at me all kind of grownup, and just said, "If you ever need help again, make sure you call me."

My wife never was confronted at church, so I guessed our few magical moments at Tamales would forever be our secret.

OTE: IT SEEMS SIMPLE ENOUGH

We also ran a kind of reverse prostitution thing. It was called an OTE operation. OTE was an acronym for offer to engage the services of another for an act of prostitution. We had two girls who worked the unit, and we would set them out on a corner, where they would pose as prostitutes. They simply would walk up and down the street, and the rest of the crew would watch them. If a car pulled over, the female officer would talk to the occupants attempting to get a case. When this was established, our girl would pull on her hair for a signal, and we would swoop in and lock everyone up.

This seemed simple enough, but it actually was a very dangerous operation because it would take a few seconds to get to the girl if she was in trouble. A few seconds would be all the time needed if they pulled her into a car and drove off. We had a few sticky situations out there, but we never had a policewoman hurt.

Understand these operations were run in specific areas. The OTE operation and the John operation were both run where prostitution was rampant. You could get the girls off the corner for a couple of hours, but you couldn't stop the customers from showing up.

Most of the prostitution is on the outer hub of the city. Johns from the suburbs do not want to drive too far inside the city for sex. They realize the deeper into the city they drive, the more dangerous it becomes.

About this time, the city began a forfeiture program for these cases. If a john was arrested or issued a violation, his car would be forfeited. This came with a very heavy fine to get your car back. This additional cost really didn't slow anything down; it just created more bitching and crying when the Johns were arrested. Usually, they were driving the wife's car, so the crying was easy to understand. They might be able to hide a court date from their better half, but the registered owner had to pick up the forfeited vehicle.

POLICING THE PERIMETER

The last significant thing I did at vice was working a Malice Green detail. I had talked about this earlier, and there still were plenty of protests and demands for justice over his death.

Malice Green had died in front of a crack house, after he was beaten by Detroit police officers. It actually was an old storefront with a house attached in the rear. You would walk along the east side of the storefront, and enter the house in the rear to buy drugs. The old storefront was made of concrete blocks that ran right up from the sidewalk to the second story. A local artist had painted a five-foot by five-foot picture of the deceased on this urban canvas, and it almost had a holy look to it.

Several churches held rallies there protesting police brutality, and several black civil rights leaders flew in and spoke at this location.

Working in a somewhat undercover capacity, I was to mingle among the crowd with my black female partner. We were to keep an eye out for violent behavior and any weapons violations.

Putting a white officer in the midst of a simmering black crowd did not seem like a good idea. I decided my observations would be made from the perimeter, with accessible escape routes available. I was a bit surprised that the incident did not cause a riot. The mayor and chief of police accused the officers of murdering Malice Green. The whole incident stayed in the media for years. The trial of the officers was long and wrought with racial tension.

Neighborhood people would place flowers and, believe it or not, beer or narcotics at the site. To this day, the picture still is there. The Green family won a multi-million dollar lawsuit from the city. The family all ended up suing each other for the money. The officers were convicted and sent to prison.

Police Officer Richard Michael Leskie
Detroit Police Department, Michigan
End of Watch: Monday, July 1, 1991

Officer Leskie was shot in the back and killed while pursuing a burglary suspect. Officer Leskie had chased the suspect into the basement of the building. As Officer Leskie descended the basement stairs, the suspect, who was hiding under the stairs with a 16-gauge shotgun, fired, striking Officer Leskie in the back.

Officer Leskie is survived by his wife, two children and an aunt.

THE HAMSTER WHEEL

I had worked vice for just over a year and was pretty burnt out with the whole thing. You were on a hamster wheel daily, locking up the same girls and guys.

"Legalize it," was my thought. Create a red light district that could be monitored. The most valuable lesson I learned working vice was that no matter how many people you arrested, you were not going to stop the world's oldest profession. I had that mindset going into this unit, and locking up all those guys and gals didn't do a thing to change my mind. It was time to go.

I began looking for a new command, but the department saved me the trouble. They shut the entire vice unit down. I really couldn't understand this. It wasn't my cup of tea, but someone had to work it. Some of the areas we worked were residential areas. How would you like to come home and see girls walking down the middle of your street? Or servicing

Johns in front of you house? I watched a girl once get out of a John's car, and walk into a quarter car wash stall. She picked up the wand, which had a slow stream of water flowing from it, hiked her skirt and washed out that Kitty. Down went the skirt and she was freshened up for her next customer. This car wash was right across from several houses.

I guess you get my point. It's bad enough for adults to see this behavior, but what about kids?

A DIFFERENT KIND OF HOME COMING

Word had come down to the supervisors that they were going to shut the unit down, so the bosses gathered us together. We were allowed to make choices on where we would like to go. I requested the Thirteenth Precinct, as this was the place where I started. New Center was inside the precinct boundaries. I knew some of the personnel, and wouldn't have to walk around with a map all the time. It would be a coming home of sorts.

Later in my career, I realized this was just a "make you feel good gesture." They had no intention of sending you anywhere but where they needed manpower. The department worked in a numbers world. I was a number and I was sent to the Third Precinct. So much for my request — I still was learning.

This was not the only change in my life at this time. We had been house shopping ever since they attempted to gun down my neighbor in his front yard. We based our city search on two things: Safety and schools. This was something Detroit sorely was lacking. Choosing what was considered one of the safest cities in the country was a no-brainer. We located an affordable house in Livonia and soon moved in.

The peace of mind I had just purchased was unbelievable. When I was at work, there was no concern of someone breaking into my house and assaulting my wife. I slept soundly at night knowing that when I woke in the morning, I would not find my car up on milk crates. My wife could push the kids in the stroller with absolutely no fear of being hit by a stray bullet.

Bubbling with confidence and a newfound sense of security for my family, I headed to number 3.

3RD COMMAND - THIRD PRECINCT

BUILD A FORT AND FILL IT WITH SOLDIERS

Great. This was the Malice Green Precinct. They still were receiving death threats. It was kind of strange talking to officers about this precinct. The non-workers desired it. The workers hated it. The lazy officers had a built-in excuse for not working: Why would they work if they were going to be accused of murder? It was a valid point, but the job still had to be done.

I watched the trial and the testimony of the officers involved in the Malice Green death. I never try and second-guess an officer, unless I was there, but their testimony was not the best. The autopsy photos were pretty damning evidence, as he had multiple severe lacerations to his head. It was obvious Green had been repeatedly hit.

Over my career, the department would be involved in a number of controversial incidents. The working officers would come back doing the same job, and the non-workers would use it as fuel. That was the atmosphere I stepped into in the Third Precinct.

This precinct also had a large industrial area covering the southern portion. More industry meant less police runs. It was a good spot for the lazy.

One of the most unique spots in this precinct was Fort Wayne. This is where the city had started. First thing: Build a fort. Second thing: Fill it full of soldiers. Make it safe for people, and they will come. It was kind of what this whole police department thing was all about.

I knew going in that I was going to finally be exposed to full-blown precinct life. I had heard horror stories and prepped myself. The first day,

167

I was assigned to midnights. I checked my uniform and polished my boots. I expected big things from myself and was hoping for a good partner.

I already knew no one wanted to work with the new guy. Controversy always swirled around specialized unit officers. It was just the nature of the beast. The thought was, if you worked for a specialized unit, you were either an ass kisser, or you knew someone. To get booted out of one of these units, you had to be a real zero. After changing in the locker room, I headed out into the unknown.

SLUMBER PARTIES

Roll call was held in the upstairs gym. I walked in early, and no one was there. Officers eventually filtered in, and what I saw was embarrassing. Almost all of them had a raggedy look to them. It was as if they had no concern for their appearance, as they wore wrinkled uniforms and dirty boots.

As we were told to fall in, an officer stepped through the door with a sleeping bag and a tiny portable TV. He placed it at his feet, while the supervisor conducted roll call. I looked around and no one seemed concerned that this officer was pretty much saying, "As soon as I get out of here, I'm going to watch TV and fall asleep."

There was no way I was working with that guy, and my first day was going to go down in Third Precinct history if they paired me up with him. Luckily, I got a brand new out-of-the-box rookie. This was a good draw, as I knew I could teach him something. He had not been tainted by precinct life and was, as usual, afraid of his own shadow. The best thing about him was that he spoke Spanish. The Third Precinct had the largest Hispanic community in the city. He might make a good interpreter, and maybe could teach me a bit of the language.

They completed roll call, and everyone would go down to the garage to receive radios. As I stood in line, I noticed the officer assigning the equipment was a bit over-the-top with his laughing and cutting up. He was in plain clothes, and apparently was working restricted duty. Restricted duty is when you are injured or have some other issue that will not allow you to suit up and work the street. As I got closer to him, he appeared high.

Now I don't care where I'm working, I was not going to tolerate any officer who was high or drunk.

After I received my radio, I pulled my supervisor aside and informed him of the officer's status. He informed me he knew about the situation, and it was okay. He was on restricted duty, and they would take his gun away when he showed up for work.

Took his gun away when he arrived? What about the ride to work?

It was a sad story that he explained. He had been in a car accident on duty and was injured. He became addicted to pain killers, and the department was trying to help him. Having him come to work was not helping him, as far as I was concerned. It endangered all of us.

My out-of-the box rookie really was confused. It's okay to come to work high? I stressed to him that this was wrong, and assured him I would take it up the chain of command. I did, but it didn't matter.

THE ROOKIE AND I

The first day at the Third Precinct was going to be a doozey. My shift was a mixed bag of officers. Some were young, and some very old. I never could understand the guys with twenty years on the job pushing a scout car. It was a thankless job of abuse and repeated police runs. I figured get promoted or try to go to a different command. The streets could wear you out in a hurry.

At this point, I had no idea who the workers were, so I was going to try to pair up with the rookie as much as I could. This did not prove difficult, as no one wanted to work with rookies. First, they were a threat to expose whatever you were doing wrong. Plus, they didn't know very much, so you had to watch them all the time. They were dangerous to work with because of their lack of experience.

The only plus was I could see was that it was going to be easy to lead this shift in felony arrests. I didn't see a ton of gung ho, go get 'em attitudes. I had experience and a fresh set of rookie legs to run down bad guys. Let's do this.

WHEN THERE'S NO ROOM FOR THE EASY ROUTE

I can honestly say I never went to work worrying about being killed. After a close call, you would get a chill, log it in your memory bank and just simply press on.

I always looked back and compared it to war, and wars were fought with young men. They were aggressive, fit and carried the attitude that they would live forever. I looked at police work the same way. We lost officers, but I never thought it would be me.

I was concerned at my new command, as your platoon was your

protection your backup. My new family was somewhat lacking. Every day, I knew I would have to be on my toes. Toss in a rookie partner, and this was going to be a little extra dangerous.

How many times have I said that police work is all about experience? Now I had some. When I first started, many officers avoided runs they knew nothing about. I volunteered for them. You had to have a desire to learn. Oh, I looked like an idiot plenty of times, but I was fortunate to survive my mistakes and better prepare myself for the street. The academy trained you to pass a state test, but it did not come close to equipping you with the tools you needed for the street.

At my first command, I attempted to be a sponge soaking up as much as I could. It helped. Now I was going to have an opportunity to give some of that back.

That first day left a bad taste in my mouth. Don't get me wrong; there were workers out there with me. It's just that there weren't many. The majority of officers always wanted to take the easiest route. There was no room for the easiest route. You had a job to do, so just do it.

An example of this was evident on one of my first runs. We volunteered to back up a unit on a domestic violence complaint. When I arrived, the husband and wife were arguing and screaming at each other. The first unit stood by and allowed them to carry on with this behavior. As the backup unit, I didn't intervene. This was their run and they would handle it. They let the couple continue to scream and yell for about ten minutes.

She claimed he threatened to kill her, and he was making the same accusation against her. As we walked off the front porch, I asked the first unit why they let it go on for so long. They informed me that they responded to the same run at least twice a week. The husband and wife were harmless.

We didn't have time to be responding to the same runs over and over but okay, I guess that was Third Precinct business. Several hours, later the same run came out and the initial unit volunteered to service it. We again responded to back them up. It was the same yelling, same accusations.

Now, the primary unit might not have minded servicing this run twice a week, but I did mind backing them up. I didn't have a problem backing anyone up, but backing them up for the same run over and over was ridiculous. This time around, I would intervene. I was going to bring this to a halt.

I informed the husband and wife that if I had to come back, I would lock them both up and send their kids to protective services. I explained there was no valid reason for us to play mediator for their domestic squabbles. I told them to get a divorce or get along. As we stepped out the door, I reminded them I was brand new to the precinct, and to mind what I had said. I was an officer of my word, and would arrest them the next time I showed up.

One hour before the end of the shift, you guessed it. It was the same address, same run. Again, the initial unit volunteered, and we responded for backup. As I entered the location, they were sitting across from each other screaming and yelling. The officers were attempting to calm them both down when I walked up to the husband and ordered him to stand. I placed handcuffs on him and turned him over to my partner. The husband was confused and stopped talking. I quickly turned to the wife and ordered her to stand. I placed my second set of cuffs on her and began escorting her out. I don't know who was more stunned. The couple I arrested or the officers standing there with their mouths open.

The couple began yelling at me, and I asked them in a calm voice if they remembered our last conversation, and what I was going to do if I had to return. They responded, "arrest us."

I turned and asked the officers the same question, and they responded, "arrest them."

The couple quieted down and the other officers remained silent. I explained I was not going to be responding to their home twice a week to listen to them argue. We, as a police department, have more serious matters to attend to, I said.

I told the couple I would monitor the radio every day, listening for their address, and I would be the first to respond and arrest them every single time. The couple went quietly and, I was hoping, I had taught the responding officers something.

For the rest of my stay in the Third Precinct, that run never came up again.

WOULD YOU LIKE BOLOGNA OR BOLOGNA?

My first trip into the cellblock at the third precinct was an experience. It was like entering a dungeon. There was very poor lighting, the odor of urine and sweat, and plenty of moaning and yelling. The only thing it was missing was the "rack."

Now, the person who handled your prisoners was called the doorman. Prisoners called them "Turn keys." He or she was a police officer who volunteered for this job. They did not work the street or wore their uniform (only pants and shirt, and no badge or belt). I always considered this a "slug position." Who in the hell would want to work in this environment?

Working officers always wanted to get in and out with their arrests. If you brought someone in, you were at the mercy of the doorman. His speed would dictate when you returned to the street. It always seemed they would slow down when the prisoner count went up. Not only did the precinct have to accept its own prisoners, but it also processed arrests brought in by other units working within their boundaries. This included narcotics, tactical services, traffic enforcement, etc.

The doorman would bitch to the command officer if these units brought in too many prisoners. The command officer would make a notification to dispatch that their cellblock was filled and to reroute arrests to other precincts. The precinct and doorman were trying to make a point: You are creating all this work for us, and we are not going to put up with it. Now, I always admired these other units because they would complain, but they would take their prisoners to other locations. The first chance these units would have to work that precinct again, they actually would shut the cellblock down with arrests. They would bring in the skankiest, stinkiest prisoners they could find. They would do it one right after another, so within a couple of hours, the precinct was full.

The Third Precinct had a reputation for this. I know I belonged to the Third Precinct family, but I still cheered for the other guy whenever they shut the cellblock down.

Now, the dungeon-like atmosphere was complete as prisoners were not supplied a blanket or pillow. They either slept on the floor or a concrete riser. Prisoners did not have to deal with choices from the food menu. Everyone got the same: Bologna sandwiches and a Styrofoam cup of water. They received one of each for breakfast, lunch and dinner. Now, I knew they were prisoners, but I felt this was extreme. Some of the better doormen would put mustard on sandwiches. On the holidays, the prisoners might get garlic bologna.

This whole cellblock, prisoner processing was new to me, and I was learning. Previously, I just brought in an arrest and bitched about the doorman being slow. The whole overall process and particulars would be a complete chapter in my department education.

Prisoners also learned. They learned how to play the system. They could claim illness or need of prescription medication, and be sent to the hospital. This was a real pain, as a car had to be called out of service to transport the prisoner. If they really played it up, they got to ride in an ambulance (and the City of Detroit would be handling all the bills). So, they'd get a nice warm bed, hospital food and female nurses, which sure beat a bologna sandwich and a cement bed.

This always was a police run I never wanted. You would pick up the arrestee at the precinct along with his property and paperwork. Once at the hospital, you would need to find the police detail stationed there. Everyone wanted this hospital police detail job. It's quiet, as you only have to process a few prisoners and get to walk around the hospital talking to nurses.

Conveying a prisoner to the hospital involved another department policy that made no sense. You could drop off the prisoner at the hospital, but his or her property would have to go downtown to be held at the First Precinct. You know what that means: Better have a partner, or they would tow your scout car. Once the prisoner was treated and released from the hospital, you picked them up, ran downtown to retrieve their property, and returned all of it to the precinct. If they needed a prescription, you would run to the pharmacy and get it filled. You can see why working officers hated this type of run.

Still, plenty of prisoners with valid illnesses and disease went untreated. There were several incidents where prisoners died in police custody. The problem was they had been dead for hours. One prisoner was discovered with several bologna sandwiches resting on his cold body. Doormen were required to check on the prisoners every hour. This meant waking them and getting a verbal conformation that they were okay. The doorman wanted to keep everything quiet once it settled down, so he would be hesitant to wake anyone. This would allow the doorman to catch some sleep in the early morning hours.

I was really learning about precinct life. Again, none of this was taught in the academy.

MANNING THE DOOR (AND INK PAD)

I had about six years on when I went to the Third Precinct. One day, the supervisor informed me I was going to be the doorman. I told him I never had worked prisoner processing, at which time he immediately accused me of lying. I informed him I wasn't lying, and that I know it was difficult for him to understand, but in six years, I had never worked the door. After convincing him that I was being truthful, I agreed to tackle the job. Patience was going to be needed today, by all arresting officers. Six years, and I still was learning.

Mind you, this was back in the old days, when we still rolled prints with ink. The prisoner would stand behind you and you would grasp his hand. You would press his first finger in ink and then roll it on the print card. It was a bit of a skill, and you had to roll it just right so that the print was readable. You would repeat the process for each finger and thumb. You also did four fingers together and a palm print. If he was a felony prisoner, you had to do four cards total. My first prisoner was a fiasco. The room looked like a kiddie class doing finger painting. There was ink everywhere — ink on me, ink on the prisoner and ink on the wall.

After my seventh attempt on the same finger, the prisoner stopped me. He must have been getting tired, or hungry for a bologna sandwich. He asked if he could help. He repositioned my stance from behind, placed his hand in mine folding his fingers under mine. He let me press his index finger into the ink, and then said, "Let me roll it, you just watch."

I had my hand over his as he rolled the first one. Perfect — it looked like the FBI had done it.

"You try the next one," he told me.

Using the same technique, I rolled the second finger. It was not bad, and I improved with each digit.

Needless to say, that prisoner got mustard and an extra sandwich that night. I think the precinct got frustrated with me, and this would be my last time as doorman.

FIND YOUR HOLE

One of the most talked about thing on midnights at the precinct was the "hole" or "your hole." This was your midnight hiding spot. You goal was to get to the "hole." Many officers knew how to work the system. A hard working crew could service ten to twenty runs a night. This would vary depending on what type of runs you serviced. A dead body could tie you up for six hours. A homicide or serious arrest could do the same.

A lazy crew would pick and choose what type of runs they would take by milking whatever they were on. A missing person run could be drug out until they heard an accident run. They could clear and respond to the accident and then wait for a prisoner transport run. The object was to get a run you could milk for an hour or so. You then would head to your hole.

This would be a vacant warehouse, park or even the precinct parking lot. You would slide in, catch some sleep, and forget about the radio. I never understood how someone wearing a loaded gun could just go to sleep.

But, by managing your night like this, you might service five to six runs and get some sleep. It always was the same officers answering up for the most serious runs. If you were on midnights, you just hoped enough officers were awake. I always feared the sleeping bag guy snuggled up, with his TV answering the run. Picturing me in the middle of a blazing gun battle crying for help and him responding was not a comforting thought.

The midnight mentality lessons continued for me. You and your partner usually switched off driving every day. According to the department, you were to switch every four hours. Plenty of people wanted to be the jump person on midnights so they could sleep while the driver drove.

Two of my co-workers were driving down the main drag in Number Three, and on one particular night, the jump person was fast asleep. The driver, apparently lulled by her partner's snoring, also nodded off. They traveled but a short distance when the scout car jumped the curb and sheared off a fire hydrant. A geyser of water shot two stories into the air as the car came to rest against a cement retaining wall. Lucky, neither officer was seriously injured.

This type of story would spread like wildfire through the city. It made me embarrassed to admit I worked that precinct. It was a good story though, and cops needed good stories.

My rookie partner would be wide-eyed as he listened to the stories told by more senior officers. It was good to see that enthusiasm, and it reminded me of my early days. Time had drug me into some of those wild tales, and I wore it proudly. I never would quit learning, but my partner was just starting his education.

Police Officer Norman E. Spruiel
Detroit Police Department, Michigan
End of Watch: Sunday, October 3, 1993
Officer Norman Spruiel succumbed to gunshot wounds sustained three weeks earlier while working an undercover murder case. He was conducting surveillance with his partner while attempting to locate two suspects who murdered and then mutilated two young men. As the officers were finishing up their surveillance for the night, they drove a few blocks away to compare notes. Officer Spruiel was standing outside his unmarked patrol car when he was shot twice in the back by a man unrelated to the murder investigation. The subject claimed he did not know the two were police officers, and thought they were preparing to rob his brother's body shop.

The suspect was convicted of Officer Spruiel's murder and sentenced to eighty-five years in prison.

LOOK DOWN BEFORE YOU JUMP

One of my young charge's first foot chases came on a stop for a suspect carrying a concealed weapon. When you are new, you constantly are looking for lawbreakers. The problem is, you just don't know where to look. Most rookies think it will pop up right in front of you — all you have to do is make an arrest. With some seasoning, you come to realize that it is a rare occurrence when an incident takes place right in front of you.

You have to train yourself to be an eagle, not a frog just sitting around and hoping something comes within striking distance. I was teaching him, but he had a tendency to only look thirty feet in front of the car, and that was the end of his range.

He was looking his best this day. His uniform was only weeks old and military pressed. I taught him that appearance matters. People on the street respected that, and I required his uniform to always be in order. He was looking extra sharp on this particular day. As we rolled northbound on Junction Avenue, I saw two guys on the corner a block and a half away. The one guy had pulled a handgun from his waistband and was showing it to the second guy. This guy glances back, spies us and puts the gun back in his waistband. He then does an about face, and starts walking west on a side street.

My partner sees none of this because he is concentrating on running the license plate on a car directly in front of him. So, I spell it out for him. Remember, he is a novice. I have to keep him calm and lay it out step by step. As soon as I said that guy up there has a gun, his adrenaline skyrocketed.

"See the guy wearing the black T-shirt, and grey shorts, who just turned west bound from the corner?" I ask him.

"Yes," he says.

I tell him he has a handgun in his waistband, right side. He looks at me, and I can almost hear his heart thumping.

"Make sure you watch his hands," I tell him. "I am going to pull up behind him on your side, but we will be a distance back from him. He is either going to pull the gun or run. Use your door for cover. Pull your weapon and open your door with your left hand. You'll be ready if he starts shooting."

We now are about thirty feet behind the guy. I can hear the tension in my partner's voice as he machine guns me with questions. But there was no time for answers because this was going to happen right now. The suspect knows we are there, and is giving us the usual criminal glance back (he is trying to look at us without turning his head).

I stop the car and open my door, and my partner does the same. The bad guy is off like a rocket as my rookie starts jumping out. I grab him and pull him back in, yelling at him, "you always chase him as far as you can in the car!"

The suspect already has made the corner of the alley as we attempt to close the gap. This is his best opportunity to ditch the gun. If he is smart, he will toss it in the trash, someone's yard, or under a car. The best spot is on the roof of a garage. Most cops don't check there, and you can return later and get the gun.

We now have chased this guy for about a block, and my partner's first lesson is in progress but going way too fast for him to process. I'm closing on the suspect, as I glance at my rookie. His eyes are as big as saucers, and he is holding on to the dashboard for dear life. The suspect heads across a vacant lot, and he is quickly closing on a six-foot fence. I can see there is a small open spot in the fence, probably just big enough for him to squeeze through. I tell my rookie to get ready, as he is going to have to chase the suspect on foot. I have that pang of anxiety, knowing this kid could get killed.

I yell extra loud, "Be careful!"

The sprinting felon is through the hole in the fence, as I skid sideways through the lot. The car comes to a stop, and the passenger door flies open. The young officer takes one giant step before he goes ass over apple cart into a big mud puddle. He tries to get up to continue the pursuit and slips again. I holler at him to stop. He looks up from his pig waller and I can't help myself. I burst into laughter. He was completely covered in mud. The goo is dripping from his nose.

But he still is excited and concerned about the suspect. He wants to continue the pursuit. I take time to calm him down, and explain to him that he has his whole career to catch that guy. He now begins to settle down and assesses his appearance. I thought he was going to start to cry. He is a mess and, I don't think that mud missed a single spot on his blue uniform.

I take him back to the station, making sure no one sees him as I sneak him in the garage. His pride is damaged enough, and to let the whole precinct see him would be unforgivable. He slips into the locker room and changes.

He needs cheering up, and I tell him about the first time I chased someone and fell. There was no mud, but I didn't see the four-foot ball of wire in the alley, and I went down hard. It took ten minutes to untangle me. I asked him what he learned, and he just stared at me. Enough said, and I'm quite sure he will look down the next time he jumps from the car to chase someone. He was learning.

GET MY BAGS, BOY

One of our Crazies got my rookie good one night. We responded to a police run at about 4 a.m. at Aurora hospital on a disturbance. I talked to the female security guard, and she said there was a guy in the lobby who had been walking around outside with his "thang" out. He now was seated inside, and she directed us to him. We turned the corner to see your standard homeless guy. He had on multiple coats, possessed several ghetto suitcases (garbage bags) and had a box containing a number of returnable bottles.

The tell-tale sign of people living on the street is the shoes. He had on classic "Old Chuck Taylor All-stars." Apparently, they were once white, but were now a muddy black. The left one only had the sole, and it was worn like a sandal, as two wraps of duct taped secured it to the foot. It was a common shoe repair technique that I had seen before. The other shoe was complete, but very tattered. His right baby toe completely was exposed through one of the holes. It was a very poor looking toe, reminiscent of the sweaty knife/picking-my-feet guy in the corridor.

It was apparent to us that the pony was back in the barn, so we could talk to him. The first question I posed was what was he doing at the hospital. He said he was there to meet the head doctor in order to purchase the hospital. I informed him of the 4 a.m. hour, but he was sure the meeting had been set for this time.

Trying to keep him calm, I continued to go along with his story. Our intentions were to get him to peacefully go to the Crisis Center. Nobody wants to fist-fight a guy who bathes once a year and poops in a field.

The next question I posed was what a hospital goes for these days. Without missing a beat, he stated a million dollars. I had him there, because I knew he didn't have a cent to his name, let alone a million bucks. This was my angle to get him to go with me. It was kind of the street way of saying you need help.

"So you have a million dollars?" I asked.

Without hesitation, he reaches behind the row of chairs he was sitting in. He pulls out a six-foot by two-foot "Price is Right" type check. You guessed it. It was filled out to cash for a million dollars. It was one of the only times on the job that I started laughing out loud. We informed him we would cancel the meeting with the doctor and reschedule it for a later date. The man and his possessions (check included) made a quiet trip to the Crisis Center.

He got to my rookie before it was over. After I checked the "Hospital Buyer'" in at triage, we started walking toward the doors to enter the Crisis Center. In a calm tone, he ordered my partner to, "Get my bags, boy."

Like a true rookie, he picked up the bags and walked about four or five steps before he realized what he was doing. I've never seen anyone throw something down so hard. This was the second time I got to laugh out loud.

I stressed to my rookie that experience will come, and as it does, these types of incidents will be few and far between.

MR. KNOW-IT-ALL EATS CROW

I have watched a number of interviews with U.S. soldiers — World War II to the present. They all talk about the importance of experience. If you can but survive the first few days of combat, then you become smarter. Those lessons never taught in boot camp have to be learned with bullets whizzing overhead. I previously said that a little luck is a necessity. Police work is the same way. If you can survive those first few close calls, you definitely learn a lesson. All of this was piling up on my young charge. Experience, experience.

One of his most important lessons was on a traffic stop. You are taught at the academy to keep all persons inside their vehicle. This means if you make a traffic stop and the driver or passenger exit the vehicle, you should order them back inside their car. On this particular day, I was driving and he was the jump man. Yes, I previously broke the unwritten rule and let my rookie drive. I found it much easier to learn the precinct when you are driving and so did he.

We pull a vehicle over for a minor traffic offense, and can see only one occupant in the car. Something else I was not taught was to watch the brake lights. Make sure the brake lights are off, and the car is out of gear — it saves you from running back to your scout car if the bad guy speeds off. So, I let my rookie know the brake lights are off and we exit the scout.

The driver jumps from the vehicle and turns toward us. I already have my gun on him, and order his arms up. I instruct him to walk back toward me and place his hands on his own trunk. He complies, and as we approach him, he shouts he doesn't have a license. I immediately put cuffs on him. Not that I need to make a traffic lockup, but this guy's behavior is screaming that something is wrong.

My rookie is now Mr. Know-It-All and wants to tell me about making the guy get back in the car. He rattles on about "the academy this" and "the academy that."

I don't say a word, and follow him as he escorts the prisoner to the car. I tell him I am going to check the vehicle, and he sits in the scout with the prisoner. He tells me he didn't feel comfortable with me not ordering the guy back in the car. I still don't say anything, and walk up to check the vehicle. The driver's door still is open, and as I look in, I can see a large framed loaded .357 Magnum sticking up between the driver's side seat and the console. It was time to do a little teaching.

I walk back to the scout and ask the rookie what area of the car we are supposed to search. He responds with the right answer: The immediate wingspan of the arrested. I then ask him to check the vehicle and he will understand why I don't order guys back into a vehicle that they want out of. I watch him walk up to the car, peer in and immediately stiffen up. He walks to the scout, much paler than when he left. He sits and looks at me. His first question is how did I know. My answer: Experience. Most criminals want out of the car for a reason. It may be stolen, or there is something in it they do not want to be connected too. Mr. Know-It-All now is Mr. Apology.

I wasn't upset, but explained to him that most of this job does not come out of a book. You learn it as you go. The more you work, the more you learn. He was starting to buy what I was selling.

STRAITJACKETS AND PAPER APPETITES

One lesson I wanted to cover again with my rookie was the Crisis Center. I had gone over the procedure with our "check guy" when we committed him. The giggling and laughing can turn deadly in an instance with someone who is mentally unbalanced or on medication.

I told him of my first trip to the Crisis Center with Georgia Ann Spiller. She was the lady whose imaginary kids were in the tree. When we told her we didn't see any kids in the tree, she then responded by assaulting my partner. When the senior officers picked us up that day, they just drove us to the Crisis Center. We figured out that Georgia was crazy, but we had no idea what the process was to deposit her at the Crisis Center. We never even heard of a Crisis Center in the academy. We escorted her into the hospital and played it by ear. We told the nurse we had found a "crazy lady," and she directed us to the Crisis Center section of the hospital, and buzzed us in.

Your first step into that place was one you wouldn't forget. Back in those days, they still could put you in a straitjacket. There always were two or three people in straitjackets, and several would be singing rock tunes while the others sang county western songs. There always was someone sitting with their gown over their head exposing their genitals.

Someone would be kicking paper, and others would be eating it. And there always were two or three who would want to touch you.

The staff constantly was yelling at the patients. I would learn most of them were regulars and were well known by the staff. I'm sure they recognized us as rookies, so they handed us a form on a clipboard and requested we fill it out. This paperwork explains why this patient should receive treatment. Basically, the officer has to identify one of several symptoms, including whether they are a danger to the patient themselves or to others, or whether they have an inability to care for themselves. Once the officer completes the paperwork, they are free to go. A doctor, who determines the treatment the patient will receive, then will see the patient. Ninety percent of the time, they prescribe some type of medication or give an order to continue the medication the patient was on. Once treated, the patient is released back out onto the street. This process will take about three days.

So it is like jumping on the hamster wheel with the mental cases. Take them in and they get back out, take them in and they get back out again. Some officers get frustrated and just want to wash their hands of the whole deal. A different tactic that will creep in is instead of conveying them to the Crisis Center, the officers just drive them into another district and drop them off. It works like this. You get a mental run. You show up and it is Georgia Spiller, the same girl you've conveyed a hundred times. You load her into your car and drive to another district. You put her out on the street and tell her not to cause any trouble. By the time she works her way back home or into your district, your shift is over. I never could figure out why some officers did this. It was a known fact that some officers worked harder at not working than if they just did the job. I know I've said that before — it just seems to be an ongoing theme. Eliminate your problem by making it someone else's. As I was learning, so were the slugs.

CLIFF NOTES OF CUCKOO FOR COCOA PUFFS

I always have made every attempt to maintain a professional manner, no matter how funny the situation was. As I've explained, sometimes you can't help yourself. Every now and then, one of these commitment forms would land you in court. Someone would contend that this person should not be under psychiatric care. So I received an appearance notice for court at the city county building. This was my first trip to the commitment court and I had done my homework. It was pretty much like regular court, as far as testimony is concerned, but there's no chance for a jury because the judge made the ruling.

I take a seat in the front row and wait. The judge takes the bench and a signal is made to bring in the patients. Picture the Crisis Center but in a more formal setting. They wheel in several people on dollies and some have straitjackets on. Others come in mooing, singing and passing gas. They want to touch everything. My first thought was that they should have a much better setup for this. How about a holding room and bringing out one patient at a time? It wouldn't be as disruptive.

There were several cases before mine, and the patient was allowed to take the stand if he or she wished. I wondered who came up with that idea. Maybe it was the patients. No one testified until the third case. Then a patient took the stand and was seated in the box about three feet from the judge.

Several questions were asked and the patient calmly answered them. The judge then asked why he felt he no longer needed psychiatric care. The patient stood up turned his back to the judge, bent over pointing his finger at his ample rear. He shouted in a booming voice, "I have a TV in my ass."

"Excuse me," the judge responded.

"I have a TV in my ass," the patient hollered even louder. He then began jumping around yelling, "I have a TV in my ass, I have a TV in my ass."

I made an unsuccessful attempt to hold in my laughter. The entire courtroom was laughing. I'm sure this was the response the patient was looking for and it got all of us but one. I could see the judge's expression never changed. He was stone-faced. He waited for the patient to calm down and then told him he was excused. I guessed it wasn't the worst behavior that judge had ever experienced in his courtroom.

I dumped all of this acquired Crisis Center knowledge on my partner. The cliff notes of "Cuckoo For Coco Puffs."

REQUESTING A 2400

Probably, the biggest eye-opening experience for my young partner about the realities of precinct life was the day he almost got one of shift sergeants killed.

We were not working together this day because he had been assigned to the desk. I was in the locker room changing for on-duty roll call. He came upstairs and asked me about several calls he had received. Someone was looking for one of the special operations officers, a female, and kept calling over and over. This wasn't a police matter but a personal one. I told him to just take a message for her and to end it.

He went back to his post confident the problem was solved. About fifteen minutes later, I could hear loud yelling coming from the lobby. I ran down the stairs, prepared to find some unhappy citizen in cuffs. By the time I made it down, the commotion was over. My rookie looked like he had been punched in the stomach. I asked him what happened.

He said he had gone back to his desk assignment when he received another call for the same officer. He took my advice and told the person he would take a message and have her call back. There was no need for them to tie up the front desk police line.

Within minutes, the female officer appeared at the front desk and began chewing out the rookie. She was very upset that he had told this person that she would call him back. If she received a phone call, she wanted the rookie officer to get up and find her no matter what was going on. It was a profanity-laced barrage and, even in Detroit, it was quite disruptive.

The shift sergeant came out of his office and asked her to quiet down. His rank apparently meant nothing, as she continued to rant and rave. He then asked her to step into the police garage, which is directly attached to the front desk area. It was a good supervisor move because this would take her out of the citizen-filled lobby. But this request seemed to upset her even more.

She refused to calm down, and the sergeant requested a 2400. This is a call for the big boss who over sees the entire city on the night shift. Several officers now were in the garage. They also were trying to calm her down. She was informed that the 2400 was on the way, and that they should wait in the supervisor's office. The sergeant turned and walked back into the lobby. The female officer was several feet behind him, and two officers were following her.

What she did next stunned everyone. She pulled her service weapon and placed it in the small of the sergeant's back. No one knew what her intentions were but, luckily for the sergeant, the two following officers tackled her immediately. After a brief struggle, she was disarmed.

Now, I'm sure the citizens in the lobby had no idea they were going to get a story they could tell for the rest of their lives. What did they think of the Detroit Police Department and its officers? Remember, she not only represents our department but everyone in law enforcement.

The officer was conveyed to the psychiatric ward at Ankra hospital. The poor sergeant now was in the garage smoking cigarettes as fast as he could light them. He was visibly shaken. When I asked if he was okay, he looked incredulous. He wondered how in the hell could he survive this job for twenty-seven years, and then get shot in the back by a police officer. He retired several weeks later. Imagine my rookie. He felt responsible for the whole thing. If she shot the sergeant, he probably would have quit. Again, I was embarrassed to be part of this department.

THE SMELL OF THE STREETS

The tutoring of young officers is an everyday all-day thing. It took him weeks to get over the incident at the precinct station. I was six years removed from my first day experiences, and wanted to ensure he didn't make the same mistakes I did. I would give him scenarios and ask him to give me solutions. If his answers were wrong, we would correct them. It didn't take long to know which rookie would make a good cop and which one wouldn't. My guy had the right stuff, and his enthusiasm told me he was well worth the time I spent instructing him.

One of his next lessons dealt with a tough repulsive situation. In police work, there are a number of odors you have to deal with. The most common are urine and body odor. Mix this together with human feces, bad tobacco and the cheapest wine you can steal, and you create quite a perfume.

One of my senior partners and I had once been on a run where we had chased a suspect into a vacant abandoned house. My partner went in and came out dragging the suspect by the collar. He was mad as a hornet and I asked him what was wrong.

"I stepped in "bum shit," he said.

He lifted his boot, displaying a caked shoe sole. I began laughing and asked him how he knew it was "bum shit." He said it smelled of bum sweat and cheap wine.

I had learned my smell lessons in the Cass corridor, where you never get the smell of urine and wine out of your nose. There, the homeless do not have a restroom readily available, at least not the type we are accustomed too. I caught a guy defecating in a vacant lot on my beat one day. I still was an inexperienced officer and was pretty upset about the whole thing. *How can someone just pull their pants down and crap in a field with people walking by?* The guy said he had to go. I asked him what he was going to wipe with, and he showed me a McDonalds bag. I couldn't find an ordinance offense for defecating, but figured who could crap without peeing, so I wrote him the urinating ordinance.

Most homeless people would at least go inside a vacant building. In Detroit, there were plenty of them. So, when you entered one, you had to be careful or you could step in bum shit.

The toilets and bathtubs in the abandoned buildings of the corridor always were filled to the rim with feces. The tub was used because you could sit on the edge and dump without worrying about falling in. Another good spot was a corner of a room where you could brace yourself. I schooled my rookie to be aware of these areas.

Again, none of this was covered in the academy. If you stepped in bum shit, it was a lesson you wouldn't forget.

By far, the worst smell was a dead body. If it was mid summer, and the body had been there a couple of days, there is no smell on the face of this earth you can compare it to. The body bloats and turns black. It swells to three or four times its original size. Fluids will run or bubble from all of the open orifices. This death odor will linger on you for days. It seems to cling to your body and get into your skin. It seemed no amount of soap could wash it out. You usually learn about these police odors the hard way. I learned to plug my nose. There's no shame in that, and it is better than puking at a crime scene.

One day, my rookie and I had a run on the service drive of one of our freeways. We pulled up to a two-story house, and it was obvious to me it was going to stink. The grass had not been cut in months, maybe years. It was trampled down from the sidewalk to the back porch creating a goat-type path. There was trash everywhere in the yard. The building was turn-of-the-century old with wood clapboard siding. It looked like it had never been painted. Now, here is the main clue to identifying the odor thing. The inside of the windows were coated with fly crap. The outsides were dirty enough, but the fly crap was a dead give away.

We were servicing a call for a woman who fell getting out of the tub. Every officer hopes that when they service a naked woman run, they are going to find some runway model in all her glory. It usually is a woman who looks like an overweight caveman. Due to the appearance of the house, I was leaning toward caveman.

As we approach the back door, I turn and tell my rookie partner, "This is going to stink. You may want to hold your nose."

Like most young officers, he informs me he can take it. I warn him again, and tell him I'm not kidding. This really is going to stink. He is having none of it, and tells me to go ahead. I knock on the door several times, and see a set of eyes peer over the bottom of the window. I know the person inside is either a midget or is in a wheelchair. Either one is going to be scary. I can hear the eighty-two locks being unchained. I already have grabbed my nose, and the door opens. I have no idea why, but these stinker houses are like those vacuum-sealed tubs. Once they opened that door, the air rushed in and came roaring back out.

I stepped inside and struggled to get by the guy who opened the door. He is sitting in a wheel chair. My young trainee takes one step over the threshold and loses it. He begins puking all over the back porch. He continues throwing up as he stumbles down the broken stairs and through the thick brush back to the collapsed garage.

I now am alone as I enter the house. This never is a good idea, but I have no choice. Several people are moving or crawling about in the other room. The door opener points a fingerless hand in the direction of the bathroom. I can see a body on the floor and figure the quicker I am in, the quicker I am out. The smell is seeping through my uniform, as I dart through the kitchen, which resembles a city dump. The only thing missing is the seagulls.

I enter the bathroom and find a seventy-year-old woman on the floor. I have no idea what she was doing in the bathroom because she is dry and fully clothed. The floor is slippery because of who knows what. The time has come for me to take my fingers off of my nose. I am going to need both hands to get her up. I take a deep breath and release. The odor was horrific. Now, all I want to do is get her up and get out. I grab her under the arms and lift. She is small and I can move her easily, until I try to set her on the toilet. She is wearing old granny hose that go over her calves. One is caught in the splintered wood floor. Now, I have to hold her with one arm and try to free her with the other.

The door opener now is in the bathroom with his wheelchair wanting to help. Whatever was on the floor now is being whipped into the air by his wheels. I order him out, and rip the old ladies stockings with a massive pull. I plop her on the toilet and inform the residents that if she is sick, they need EMS. I bolt out the door and with a leap miss all of the stairs. The polluted Detroit air is a relief as I take a huge breath. Panic sets in, as I can't find my partner. I run to the side of the house, finding him slumped over the trunk of the scout car.

If you remember that scene in the movie ET where they find him in the river pale and depleted, then you will have an idea of how my partner looked that day. We get into our scout car, and I asked him what he learned. He hollers out in a loud voice, "Listen to my partner and always plug your nose."

Police Officer Benjamin Louis Short
Detroit Police Department, Michigan
End of Watch: Friday, March 25, 1994

Officer Short was shot and killed when he intervened in a bar fight while off duty. Officer Short intervened in the fight after observing one of the fighters produce a handgun.

THIS GUY IS LOCO

I must admit, I did learn something from him. My rookie could jabber Spanish with the best of them, so I started picking up words here and there. I figured if I was going to stay in this precinct, I better pick up some of the lingo.

This precinct was situated right on the southern edge of the city. It bordered the river with Canada. Old Fort Wayne was located there, and you could tour it on the weekends. This area is home to the biggest Hispanic community in the state.

Now, the easiest thing for a criminal or illegal alien to do was to act like they didn't understand any English. This is pretty frustrating when you are trying to conduct an investigation. It was amazing that they suddenly could speak more English once you pulled your handcuffs out.

I requested my young partner give me daily lessons. I learned basic words at first, then usable phrases. "Put your hands here. Put your hands up," that type of thing.

About a month into my Spanish lessons, I end up working with an old timer, Arturo Sanchez. We called him Arturo the Burro. He was right from old Mexico. For lunch, he would take you to the mom and pop Mexican restaurant for brain tacos. They were 15 cents apiece. He didn't like to work, but had plenty of stories and was a great guy. It always made for an entertaining eight hours.

I told him about my Spanish lessons, and he tells me to try some of it on him. Using my best accent, I give him a sample. He looks at me with a puzzled look and asks if a Bulgarian is teaching me Spanish. I tell him my rookie is my teacher. He laughs, and tells me I should have come to him first. He explains that what my rookie is teaching is book Spanish. It is a whole different ballgame on the street.

While he is telling me this, I realized why most of the people we dealt with on the street looked confused when the rookie was talking. To me, it always sounded good, but it must have been gibberish to others. So the Burro gives me a little street language to teach the rookie. Next time we worked together, I try it on him. Now he looks at me puzzled. I don't think he understood a word, and I came to the realization that he probably wasn't communicating with anyone on the street. Now I was the student again.

I finally melted down one day dealing with the language barrier. We had a run on a man causing a disturbance or more specifically, a crazy guy. When we get there, we find a Hispanic male who is about fifty years old. He is screaming in Spanish and the "Burro" is using his soft street language to try and calm him down. After five minutes of this guy ranting and raving, I lose it. However, I can't get in the game, because I don't have all the tools. But screw it. I turn to the guy, and with a hard glare, I start to rattle off every Spanish word I knew. I was loud and continuous. I shouted, "street, book, pen, police, meat, put your hand up, shoes, paper, road, put your hands here, food, door, window, kiss, eyes and feet."

He immediately stops yelling, and now is giving me the eye, unsure of what I am all about. He now starts talking to the "Burro" in a very low subdued voice. The only word he spoke that I understood was "loco." He doesn't say another word and walks off. I was quite proud of myself.

BAD APPLES SEEK GRATUITIES

I've talked of slugs and workers, but I probably should give you a little background on precinct personnel. They are the meat and potatoes of the department. They are the guys and gals in the trenches, fighting this war. You need their make-up to more thoroughly understand the whole precinct environment. I was one of them, and so was my rookie.

Like all of the precincts and units in the city, there were good workers assigned to the Third Precinct. They were the minority, but they were out there doing it. You always hoped they would be the ones who came running when you needed help. Kind of like the cavalry coming, you didn't want the muleskinners and cooks showing up with the chuck wagon. You wanted the warriors.

I said it before, the more you worked at your trade, the better officer you became. You always were hoping those workers showed up.

I discussed briefly about assignments at my first command. How you would dread being assigned with certain officers. Within minutes of being in a scout car with someone, you could tell whether you were going to do any work that day. I've had people want to go eat right off the ramp, even though they hadn't serviced a single police run (and all precincts usually were backed up with priority one runs). When I got promoted and went to the Eleventh Precinct, we started each day with an average of twenty to thirty priority one runs in the hole. These are shooting, robberies and B&E's.

Some officers would want to pay their bills or even go shopping. This wasn't going to happen if you worked with me. So it worked in reverse. If you were a worker, you wanted to be paired with a worker. If you were a slug, you hated the workers and wanted to be paired with a slug. Looking at our daily detail and assignment sheet caused a lot of anxiety. I know of plenty of officers who called in sick because of their assigned partner.

As you've noticed, I've talked about these types of officers at previous commands. I've also talked about assignment issues. Every command I worked at had the same problems.

Worker or not, even the ins and outs of your lunch break had to be learned. By contract, you would get a thirty-minute code, which is the fancy police term for lunch. If it was busy, your code request would be denied. Even the workers needed to learn to play the game. If it took thirty minutes to handle a multiple car accident, you wouldn't clear or make yourself available for an hour so you could get lunch. Gratuities and lunch went hand in hand.

Many places offered gratuities to officers. These included discounts, like half off or even the whole thing free. We were taught in the academy not to take gratuities. I always had my money in my hand when it was time to pay the bill. If they refused to take it, I tipped my waitress the entire price of the meal. The city was paying me, and I did appreciate the recognition, but I was taught to always pay my way.

Other officers had it down to a science: They knew which places to go to so they could maximize their gratuity dollar. Several officers were caught off duty, dressing up in their uniforms and going to get free food for their family. They would claim they were picking it up for inside personnel at the precinct. The sickening part is they kept their jobs after being caught. You would figure they should be fired because these few rotten apples reflected on the reputations of the good cops. These bad cops perpetuate the image of cops and donuts.

Detroit has one donut shop in the whole city. Can you imagine the perception of an officer eating a donut while 1,200 people a year are being shot in their city? After my first few years, I learned it was easier to just pick something up and eat at the base, and I never ate a Detroit donut.

LESSONS FROM THE THIRD PRECINCT

One day, I was working with a guy with eight years on the job. Several blocks up, I see a canary yellow Mercedes Benz cross our street going west bound. There's no way this car belongs down here. My partner doesn't see it, and as we pass the street it went down, I can see it parked in front of a vacant lot.

About mid-block, I tell my partner to pull over. The driver of the Mercedes gets out and walks toward us. He now has walked a half block and turns north. Remember our other lesson: Don't put someone back in a car that he wants out of. This is similar because you don't park a stolen ride in front of your own house. And you don't park the get-away car in front of the place you are going to hit. Stolen ride already has clicked in my head.

We stop him and start questioning him. He doesn't know what we saw, and spins his tale. None of it makes sense, and since he has several outstanding traffic warrants, we arrest him. We go back to the Benz, run the license plate, and discover it was taken in a carjacking. Our arrestee matched the description to a tee.

All of this is experience. You have to want to gain that experience. If you don't, you'll drive around like a rookie your whole career. This not only is dangerous for that officer, but for everyone whom works with him.

Even working alone, you can acquire knowledge on the simplest of runs. I was working a one-man car and had a run to the Ambassador Bridge. There was an elderly man who was disoriented. I found him in a parked vehicle, near the bridge ramp. I asked him a few questions, and he seemed sketchy about the answers. I called for EMS to check his physical state. He was okay, but a bit confused mentally. I checked his wallet and found a North Dakota driver's license. The plate on the car also was from North Dakota. I conveyed him to the precinct leaving his car.

I called information in North Dakota and matched his name to a city. There was a registered phone number, which I called. I identified myself and could hear a concerned and hesitant voice asking if I had found him. My response was that he was fine. I sensed her concern and wanted to give her that instant relief that he was okay. Not the "I found him."

There would be that short pause as she wondered if he was dead or not. These are the people skills you gain through experience. I discovered I was speaking to his daughter, and she explained that he had Alzheimer's. He had left the house to go to the store, and had been missing for twenty hours. They were sure they would find him dead. He could not explain to me how he got to the bridge or what route he took, and he had no idea why he drove to Michigan. You never can lose the human side of police work. You have to realize that everyone you deal with is someone's parent or child. You have to have compassion. I wish I could have been there when they were reunited.

AN UNUSUAL VIEWING

While working this precinct, I serviced one of my favorite runs. It was on a dead body. I know that doesn't sound right, but the deceased was in her nineties and had lived a long life. I was working with the sleeping bag/TV guy, so being tied up for several hours would be relief for the both of us. He didn't have to chase bad guys, and I didn't have to drag him everywhere.

We responded to an upper flat in the Wayne State area. Three females, who all were over seventy years old, greeted me at the door. They all were dressed to the nines with evening dresses and matching shoes. They allowed my partner and I in, and I asked about the nature of the run. They said they did not call, but a dead body was in the house. Expecting the worse, they escorted me to a small bedroom. Laying on the bed, dressed in a beautiful lace dress, was a ninety-year-old deceased female, surrounded by flowers and lace pillows. It was quite beautiful, and she looked almost angelic. I looked back at the other old ladies and it clicked. Apparently, she had passed in the night, and they were laying her out for viewing.

I walked from the bedroom and noticed all the wooden folding chairs, and several hors d'oeuvre trays. I had to give the gals an A for effort, but this practice was discontinued years ago. I remember my mom telling me how my grandmother was laid out in the living room for viewing. Staying in touch with that, I handled them carefully. I explained that for health reasons, this was not allowed anymore, and after some tears and a few white lies, I convinced them she needed to go to a funeral home.

Now, if you have a natural death, and age and health issues are apparent, Homicide will release the body to a funeral home. This avoids having to involve the Wayne County Medical Examiner and going through a long wait.

I had to make several phone calls in an attempt to contact the last surviving family member. It ended up an international call to England. I finally got family and doctor approval and called Homicide. They gave me the okay and I called the funeral home for the ladies. We had to stand by until the body was removed, and were told it would be about twenty minutes.

I was relieved, as the ladies really loved their friend and the funeral home would handle the body with some care. About ten minutes later, dispatch calls asking for me to contact Homicide. I call and apparently the overseas thing wasn't going to work. Yikes. The morgue was going to have to pick up the body. The morgue has a tough job, and the crews can be a bit callous at times. I had no idea what I was going to tell the ladies, and figured I would explain it when the truck showed up.

We heard a knock on the door, and it was time for me to face the inevitable. I began explaining the situation, and those poor old hens began clucking like no tomorrow. I now was a liar and a bad guy. I had to assist getting the morgue crew by the ladies as they had locked them up with the evil eye.

I was going to ask the Morgue crew if they could show a little bit of care, and I stopped talking…as the look in their eyes told me the deceased was going to be handled like any other Wayne county resident. She was loaded on to a stretcher and covered with a sheet. Okay, this was going to be unpleasant and I did feel like a liar and bad guy.

As we turned into the hallway, we had a straight shot to the front door. I don't know why I was surprised, but standing at the door was all three ladies. Their backs were pressed against it and their arms intertwined. You are not taking her they shouted. The morgue guys looked back at me with that "This is the police part" look, and I stepped in front of them. I told the ladies they would have to move, and we were indeed taking their friend. They all stiffened and pulled together closing their ranks. I'm pretty sure this situation is not in any law enforcement book. I know it wasn't in ours. I had to physically pull the three of them out of the way, so the morgue could get out.

These are the non-violent cases that can stick in an officer's head. The job had to be done. It wasn't pleasant and they weren't happy, but you handled it the best way you could. Even though they were crying when you left, you have to learn from it and move on. That's the tough police persona, but we also have hearts. And mine ached a little.

CIRCUMVENTING DIVINE INTERVENTION

This job never stops teaching, and above anything else, you have to pay attention. No matter how many police runs, no matter how many years on the job, this one thing never changes. One puzzle I really didn't know how to figure out was a stabbing in the Third Precinct.

We arrived at our run location, finding a vehicle with blood on the driver's seat. There was no victim, but a large butcher knife was visible on the floorboard. It also had blood evidence on it. A secondary unit arrived to back us up, at which time I spoke to several witnesses. I was told, a man had been stabbed in the chest by his girlfriend. According to the witness, he was seated in his car, and she was talking to him through the window. They began arguing, when she pulled the knife and plunged it to the handle into his chest. This was no pocketknife. It was the Halloween/slasher-movie type of knife. With the amount of blood at the scene and the size of the knife, I was sure it wasn't looking good for the victim.

Procedure dictated we would stay with the vehicle for evidence and the secondary unit would respond to the hospital for the victim's medical condition. If he wasn't going to make it, we had to call homicide section. They then would take over the investigation. If the victim was going to survive, it would be handled by precinct detectives.

Sometimes lazy police can be helpful. The secondary unit did not want to go to the hospital. They would hold the scene while we checked on the victim's condition. This worked for me. If he didn't make it, I could convey his clothing directly to homicide and do my report there. It's much better than waiting for the evidence techs, which could take hours.

Here is an example how I forgot there was an actual human being possibly fighting for his life involved. I'm concerned about what is the easiest route for Officer Haig. Doing it over and over every day sometimes allows you to lapse into a detached routine. In a few minutes, I would be jolted back to reality and that struggle for life. We arrived at a small hospital, which probably was not the best spot for this victim. A trauma one facility would have been much better, but this hospital was less than a half-mile from the scene.

As usual, we arrive finding the emergency room in chaos. There are five family members fighting the security personnel. There is plenty of yelling and crying. We quickly help security settle the family down. I ask for the attending physician, expecting the worst kind of news. He walks from the back, and I ask the patient's condition. He says he can't give me one. I ask, "Why? Is he dead?"

No, he is alive, but he can be dead, I'm told.

Okay, I tell him I didn't prepare for a quiz today, and then ask for a straight answer. It is imperative I get a condition, as I have a unit holding a possible homicide scene.

He calmly tells me he understands, but he still can't give me a condition. Again, I ask why. He asks if I ever have heard of Jehovah Witnesses. Sure I have — they are those bible thumpers who hand those cards out at you door. He tells me those are the ones. He asks me if I know anything more about them. I reply, "Should I?"

"Today you should," he said. "They are the reason I can't give you a condition."

"Why?" I ask.

He explains that Jehovah Witnesses do not believe in any type of medical treatment. If God doesn't save you, nothing else should. He tells me the patient is alive, but if he doesn't get treatment immediately, he will die. The family and the patient all are Jehovah witnesses.

I'm back to not caring about the victim and worrying about me. What if he hangs on for ten hours? I'm stuck at the hospital with a unit guarding the scene on the street. This is Detroit — we are way too busy to be waiting around for divine intervention. I look over my shoulder and the family is huddled in a circle, holding bibles. Every few seconds, one of them will glance up to the ceiling, apparently hoping to see a sign.

I look back at the doctor, and he smiles at me. "We see it all the time," he chimes.

Now what the hell am I supposed to do? I ask him if there is anything that can be done. He takes me in the back, and explains that they already started working on him. This was before they found out he was a Jehovah Witness. This is kind of a loophole, as they can stabilize him and probably save his life. The doctor believes whatever they started, they can finish. He points me to the room of my victim and I enter with a new rookie partner, fresh out of her box.

We can hear yelling, and a struggle as we approach the doors. We burst in, finding a scene from a horror movie. Three people are attempting to restrain our victim. He is about 300 pounds and still is bleeding from his chest wound. Blood coats the floor and is sprayed on the walls and medical instruments. I grab a pair of latex gloves and rush to assist the medical personnel.

My new rookie is frozen at the doors. I immediately slip on the blood but catch myself at the gurney. With my help, the patient is quickly restrained. We all now are breathing heavily and slipping about on the blood-soaked floor. It was no easy task, restraining this guy. The doctor asks me to come to the other side to help him. Thinking he needs assistance to buckle down the other arm, I skate to his side of the victim. He hands me a clear plastic tube about three feet long. It is about as thick as my baby finger. I thought he must want me to suction up some of the blood on the floor before we all fall. He tells me to hand him the tube, when he asks for it. He pulls up the victim's gown and with his first two fingers begins feeling along the rib cage. Apparently finding what he needs, I watch as he switches his left hand to the spot and picks up a scalpel.

Apparently he didn't notice that I was wearing a blue uniform, badge and gun. I figure I better lean over and remind him I'm a police officer. He nods and tells me to just hand him the tube when he asks for it. I watch as he makes an incision almost the size of a dime, then places his finger in it. He asks for the tube and jabs it through the hole. As I am now assisting in this medical procedure, I figure I better give my opinion. I tell the doctor that I think he has lost enough blood, and putting a tube into him to drain more would not be in our best interest. He shoots an evil look at me, and yells that his lung is collapsed and he's trying to re-inflate it. I correct him, and tell him that we are trying to re-inflate it. My department first aid training included abrasions, not lung inflations, so I would appreciate it if he cut me a little slack, and if he continues to jabber that we may lose our patient.

It soon was evident that our work had been successful, as our patient now had quit struggling and his lung was back to normal. I ask the doc what all the fighting was about. The patient was screaming he was a Jehovah Witness, and if it is God's will, blah, blah, blah. He didn't want medical treatment, and was fighting with all his might to prevent it.

Everyone now was calm, but I still was back to the same question. What was his condition? According to my new medical partner, he was going to die without further medical intervention. Not wanting to lose my first patient, I asked if there was anything we could do.

The doctor replied yes, and he already had started the process. The victim was somewhat stable and had been sedated. The trick was to send him to a bigger hospital. The hospital receiving him would say they couldn't talk to the patient to honor his request. So the smaller hospital would load him up and send him off to be someone else's problem. After he was transported, they would inform the family. It was a great idea, albeit it was a bit shady.

I promised my newly acquired medical associate that I would follow up with our patient, but I concluded a condition of stable would be best applicable at this point in his treatment. My esteemed colleague agreed.

The funniest part about the whole thing was my rookie still was frozen at the swinging doors. Her color had turned paler and her mouth was open. I snapped my fingers several times in front of her face, and said, "Let's roll."

In a zombie-like state, she walked to the car. I knew her mind was trying to figure out what had just happened, but for some reason, it just wasn't computing. She kept looking over at me like I just threw a bag of kittens in the river. I had cleaned my boots at the hospital and was fairly certain I didn't have any blood on me. The whole thing must have appeared ghoulish in her eyes. We didn't talk much the rest of the shift, and she never looked at me the same way.

SOME THINGS TO GET OFF YOUR CHEST

I got to experience what I like to call the ribbon push at the Third Precinct. This is where you put yourself in position to receive a meritorious write-up. A unit responds to a bank robbery, the suspect comes out the front door and fires a shot at the officers. They run him down and catch him. The "Ribbon push" officer recovers the suspect's gun, knowing full well that anyone associated with this arrest will likely get decorated. There's no risk to the "push" officer. No one was shooting at him, and he didn't have to chase anyone. He was involved though, and he can tell the story like it was his own. It's amazing how many officers do this.

We had responded to a shots fired run in the projects. We all were out on foot and heard several gunshots go off. One of the officers began yelling he was shot. We ran over, finding him on the ground, yelling, "I'm hit, I'm hit."

In a panic, we quickly checked him, finding no wounds or injuries. He said he had been hit in the foot. We checked his boots finding a fresh scratch mark on the outer edge of his sole. Amazingly, we found a spent round on the ground.

Apparently, the shot had been fired from some distance and had ricocheted off of the concrete striking the side of his boot. We all began laughing. I had been shot at before, and you know when someone is shooting at you. The whizzing of the rounds is a great indicator to take cover. Detroit has random shots fired every day, and this seemed one of those cases.

The officer was having none of it, and felt someone was trying to kill him. He recovered the spent bullet and rushed back to the station to make the report. He photographed his boot and placed the picture and round on evidence. I couldn't understand the big deal. Even if the bullet hit him, it probably did not have enough force to penetrate his clothing. Several days later, I discovered what all his fussing was about. He was in the sergeant's office requesting a meritorious write-up. He wanted to receive a wound bar as he had been shot in the line of duty. I felt that, at best, he had a good beer-drinking story. It showed me to what lengths officers would go to get decorated.

We all wanted ribbons in the beginning. It was a pride thing. I wanted to be better than the rest. Not just better, but the very best. I looked at senior officers with envy as they walked by with ten or fifteen ribbons on their chest. Even after I received my first ribbon, I didn't think it was warranted. I was just doing my job as a police officer. I felt something above and beyond the call of duty or some extraordinary police work would have to be done to receive a ribbon.

The department guidelines for a meritorious write-up required them to address each action with the same scrutiny. Unfortunately, they didn't. Here is how it worked: A supervisor would submit the write-up and it would be sent through the chain of command. As it worked its way to the chief's office, it needed to be endorsed so the appropriate award could be given. The officer could receive either a commendation or a citation. The citation would include a ribbon and possible medal. If you did receive an award, you would get paperwork with it. There were a number of boxes for endorsements, and you could see who bumped your award down or up. In the ribbon world, it would prove valuable to have friends in high places.

The B&E ribbon actually was not the first one I received. I learned some valuable lessons with my first one. One day, the supervisors made a big to do, and at roll call, read a meritorious write-up concerning New Center Patrol (my unit). The chief had approved a unit citation for us. It told of all the great work we had done (which I didn't think was much), and how we should be recognized for it. Apparently, it made it through all of the command officers' endorsements, and the chief approved it. We all received a red ribbon. I thought what about the do-nothing slugs — the ones who ran from any type of work or danger? They were going to get the same ribbon that I did?

I asked some senior officers about that, and they said don't get too upset, and to just wait until I'm working with a slug and risk my life making some unbelievable arrest. Even if my partner that day had never gotten out of the car, they get the same award as me. Remember the run sheet incident? I signed it so we are both responsible, no matter who wrote it out. This also applies in the award world.

Well, one ribbon looked pretty lame by itself, but after I was awarded the second one, I started wearing them, and I wore them with pride. It did make me wonder how command officers and senior officers had so many ribbons. They must be true heroes and the hardest chargers out there. That's what I wanted to be. This was all shattered when I received my first perfect attendance ribbon. I had to check as I thought this was a joke. I didn't want to wear it so people could make fun of me. All I could think was, "I received an award for me showing up to work?" Maybe I could get one for picking up my paycheck.

Let me explain a little more about the awards. The ribbons were for very specific types of actions. If you got the same ribbon again and again, you could wear a metal oak leaf on it. This would signify you received the award multiple times. If you received the ribbon five times, a gold leaf was attached. Now, I have my perfect attendance ribbon with clusters. I guess I was proud of it. You know how the kids in school looked at those perfect attendance kids? They thought they were dorks. I didn't think so, but I wouldn't want to be thrown in the dork category for showing up every day. I now was starting to understand the system. I soon received my first no crash ribbon. It's awarded if you didn't wreck a scout car for a whole year. Soon, I had that with clusters. Who was coming up with this shit? Then it went back to the promotional system for me. If you never really worked the street, how could you obtain ribbons? I received the Pope detail ribbon for following the pope around for two days. I received the Super Bowl ribbon for working the Super Bowl. I also received the major league all-star game ribbon, the Rosa Parks ribbon, and it went on and on. I realized most of the officers with the bowl of fruit cocktail on their chest were not heroes but clowns.

I have to admit that I had a meltdown the last time I received some ribbons. There is, at the minimum, supposed to be some type of presentation, whether it is at roll call or at a formal ceremony. They read your meritorious write-up to the whole platoon, and then present your award. At this time, I was working a specialized plain-clothes unit. I was sitting in the squad room when someone came in and asked if I was Officer Haig. I said yes, and they handed me a wrinkled brown lunch bag. I dumped the contents onto the desk, finding five different departmental ribbons. A ripped piece of paper had a scribbled explanation for each one. The young officer across from me sat in awe.

"Man, you must be something to get all those ribbons," he said.

I started laughing and said, "Kid, don't ever be impressed by time, rank or ribbons."

I asked him how he liked the way the department presented them to me. He felt it wasn't the best, but didn't want to diminish my important occasion by being critical.

I was pissed. I was wearing a skullcap and placed my no crash ribbons with clusters on the front of it. I'm sure this shocked the young officer, but I was not overly concerned. He had been placed in this highly specialized unit with two years on the job. His family knew the chief. I had to run to headquarters and never took the ribbon off. I entered the elevator, with one of the command officers. She looked over at me, and I pointed up to my hat. As she looked up, I said, "No crash ribbon with clusters. Nice."

She was so befuddled she had no response and stormed off the elevator. It may have been insubordinate, but it made me feel much better.

Don't get me wrong — I have been awarded plenty of decorations I am proud of. I just wish the department would take that same pride. I eventually quit wearing my ribbons. I figured the next time anyone would see them would be at my funeral.

WATCH OUT FOR THE LEFT HAND

Training was another part of the department we had to learn about. Training was few and far between when I first got on the job. At that time, it was all about numbers. Your command would have to send a certain number of officers, and that was all they were concerned about. Not the training, just filling that numbers slot to appease the department.

I was out of the academy for about four months when my command sent me back for first-aid training. I was first-aid qualified and it was good for a year. I asked my supervisor about this, and was told just to report and don't ask any stupid questions. My first day back in the academy, I found my instructor would be Cabbage Patch, my old academy sergeant. As soon as she walked in the room, she looked at me and asked what the hell I was doing there. I gave her the standard, "I have no idea, they just sent me" answer. I guess the academy was part of the numbers game, as she knew I was qualified but didn't send me back.

Many officers would volunteer for the training just so they wouldn't have to work the streets. They'd sleep on their desk or read the paper. It was a good break for them.

While I was at the Third Precinct, I was sent to the academy for defensive tactics training. I arrived finding a female officer I worked with at New Center instructing the class. This put her in a bad spot, as she knew I knew what type of cop she was. She most certainly wasn't the get-out-on-the-street-and-get-busy type. She actually was one of the officers who hid behind the dirt mound and ticketed all the GM employees. I'm sure she didn't want me to spread her reputation around so she treated me extra nice. That's not to say that anyone needed my help to find out what kind of officer she was. We would all see it during her first defensive tactic move.

She asked for a volunteer and male officer stepped up. She was going to show us all how to block a punch. She held up her fists in a defensive stance. She instructed him to get in a fighting stance, and he did. Right away, I noticed there was something peculiar about this male officer. She continued to talk and apparently didn't notice. She then instructed him to throw her a stiff punch. He was hesitant, but she yelled, "Hit me!"

He did as instructed, and knocked her flat on her ass. She looked puzzled as she dabbed the blood from her lip. What was peculiar about the officer is he was left-handed and had set up in a southpaw stance.

She assumed he was going to throw a right, and as he began moving, her left arm went up in a blocking motion. The problem was there was nothing to block, as his left shot right to the button unimpeded. That set the tone for the rest of the class, as most of us would rely on what we already knew.

What the hell could she teach us, when she got the crapped knocked out of her in a controlled environment, by a person she set in front of her and told to throw a punch?

The kicker for this was that about three weeks later, they needed another body to go to training. Guess who they sent? It was the same training, same instructor and same results. I had a very easy week.

Police Officer Jerry Foster Philpot, II
Detroit Police Department, Michigan
End of Watch: Thursday, May 25, 1995

Officer Jerry Philpot was shot and killed by suspected gang gunfire. One suspect was killed and three others were taken into custody. The shooter was sentenced to life in prison.

Officer Philpot is survived by his wife, child, parents, sister and brother.

HAND ON THE TRIGGER

While at this command, I came awfully close to shooting someone. In a city like Detroit you have your gun out and pointed on a daily basis, but actually shooting someone is rare.

On this particular day, we saw a guy speeding down the service drive. We were just going to pull him over, and tell him to slow down. As we lit him up (lights and siren), he accelerated and continued down the service drive at a high rate of speed. Our adrenaline immediately shot up, rushing through the multitude of scenarios that would soon face us. Was he a fugitive felon? Had he just killed someone, or robbed a bank?

We notified dispatch, at which time, he crossed the expressway, and flipped back east bound on the opposite service drive. He pulled over as our scout rushed up behind him. He jumped from the driver's side and ran to the rear of his vehicle.

We had both exited guns drawn and were yelling for him to put his hands up. He completely ignored us, and our orders became more frantic. He opened the trunk and reached inside. We now both were screaming at him, just knowing we had let this go too far. Fully expecting to be sprayed with an assault rifle, the suspect swung around with a large video camera. He began ranting of the injustice we had thrust upon him, and he wanted documentation of this outrageous act.

He had no idea how close he came to being shot. We were both simply relieved we hadn't killed him. He had a wife and two small kids in the car. She calmed him down, and I explained why we stopped him, and then sent him on his way. I don't even know if he had a driver's license. This is just an example of how you can be talking about putting training wheels on your kid's bike one minute and fighting for your life the next.

It took us both a couple of minutes to settle down. But we got more experience.

IT WASN'T HIS TIME

I also came across my second surviving headshot victim while still in this precinct. The run was "possible man shot." When we arrived, we found our victim in front of a local Coney Island. The cooks were administering first aid, and had his head wrapped in several towels. The towels were completely soaked in blood, and I thought we might have a stabbing victim, due to the amount of blood. The victim was conscious and explained what had happened.

He said he was walking down the street, when he heard a popping noise. It then felt like someone had hit him in the back of the head with a baseball bat. I told the Coney Island guy/emergency medical technician to remove the towel so I could inspect the wound. I now had a lung inflation procedure on my resume and quite possibly could be capable of saving this man's life.

I shrunk right back to being a police officer, as his hair was so matted and bloody, I really couldn't tell what happened to him. I knew this much: He had a wound in the back and a wound in the front of his head. My partner picked up his baseball cap and inspected it. He located in the front fold of the cap a spent bullet. It was somewhat flattened, and was about the size of a nickel.

Apparently, someone had shot at him, or he was just shot randomly. This must have been from some distance. The round struck the plastic strap on the back of his cap, penetrated his skin, and hit his skull. It had lost its velocity, failing to penetrate the skull, and ran under the skin just above his ear. It traveled above his right eye, and exited his forehead, coming to rest in the fold of his cap.

This gave ground to the old adage, if it's your time to go, it's your time to go. Apparently it wasn't his time.

JUST LIKE ANY OTHER LOONEY TUNE

One of my last incidents at the Third Precinct really was a good send-off for me. Remember my first day, with the officer handing out radios? The officer who was high? Be careful what you wish for. I was working a one-man car, and the shift supervisor called me into the station. He informed dispatch I would be out of service, meaning I would not receive any runs. Strange, I thought. Maybe I was getting off early. I reported to the base, and the supervisor pulled me aside. I could see Officer Sanchez seated in the sergeant's office. I was informed that I would be driving Officer Sanchez to Lincoln Hospital.

I had enough time on the job to know what Lincoln was about. It was the psychiatric hospital for the police. Okay, I said, and will you be going with us? The supervisor hands over the paperwork, which basically amounted to a commitment, and says I will be going alone. Really! You want me to drive this crazy, high police officer to the hospital and then tell him I am committing him to a mental institution? Who was making the decisions for this department? It sure wasn't a police officer.

I loaded Sanchez and his paperwork into the car, treating him like any other Looney Tune. We didn't speak a word the entire ride. I walked him through the emergency room doors, and he finally asked what we were doing at the hospital. I told him a doctor wanted to talk to him. I stood by as they triaged him. He was sitting on a gurney in a hospital gown as I left. I could see him through the shatterproof glass of the mental ward.

He smiled and waved as I walked out.

HASTA LA VISTA

My time at this command was winding down, and I knew it. I could hear the voice of my first sergeant saying, "Move around, it will keep it fresh."

I knew I didn't want to stay in Number 3, but wasn't really sure where I wanted to go. I was learning that the workers did get some rewards. The harder you worked, the more opportunities you had to move. Sure, there was the cronyism thing going on, but the command officers needed the workers to make them look good.

So, someone was going to make the decision for me. My old lieutenant from Vice called and said they needed a senior guy at Housing Section. This was a brand new unit, like the one I went to out of the academy. All rookies were assigned to patrol the housing projects. Federal monies funded this unit, though the officers would have been better utilized in the precincts. But, I thought, what the heck? I put in the paper work, it was approved, and I was gone from #3.

Adios, muchachos.

4TH COMMAND - HOUSING SUPPORT

CHEAP RENT

Everyone had a certain impression of the projects, as did I. Two of them were inside the corridor, and I had serviced several calls there. It was pretty run down, and there weren't a lot of people. These were huge complexes were set up by the government to provide housing for the less fortunate.

Our mission was to patrol nothing but the projects. Almost all the officers were rookies, and like myself at New Center, they were chomping at the bit to get out and do some real work. They could hear the chatter on the radio, but were confined to their imaginary project borders.

I was there to be some type of stabilizing influence. I was to teach them the job, but at a slower pace. It wasn't going to be the greatest gig in the world, but no one showed up to roll call with a sleeping bag and a TV.

The first offer I got after arriving was discount housing. You could stay in the housing project of your choice, family included, for one dollar a month. I thought this was a rookie rumor going around, so I pulled one of the sergeants aside, and asked him if this was true. Indeed it was, and they had plenty of apartments available. I laughed, but probably would have given it some serious thought if I were younger. You'd need one hundred fifty dollars' worth of locks on the door, and have to drive a Hooptee (raggedy ghetto ride) that was stripped down, with no radio and cheap tires. Throw in another couple hundred worth of roach spray and you could almost make it homey. It would be a great way to pile up some cash. At this juncture in my life, I gave it an emphatic no.

There was a second offer floating around the department at the time, which I most certainly would have taken advantage of if I was younger. The civil unrest in Kosovo now had involved UN forces. The department would allow you to separate and go Kosovo, assisting in law enforcement. The government would pay you for one year at the rate of one hundred thousand dollars, tax-free. Detroit was like a war zone anyway, what would be the difference? I had just started my family at the time, and had to turn it down. But it would have been quite the experience.

I knew the best part about the new unit would be the young officers. That enthusiasm always inspired me. The majority was eager to learn, and had not been tainted by the politics of the department. I knew I would like this part about my new job assignment. At times, though, I would have to curb their enthusiasm.

PEDAL TO THE METAL

One of the first lessons you learn on the job is to not chase a chase. As a young officer, you always rushed in headlong trying to get into the action. Someone would call out a chase, and you would head right to their location, hoping to get in on it. By the time you got there, they already may be at the same spot you started from. Just like a game trail, the trick was to determine where they were headed or what exit ramp they would get off at. Lay in wait at this location, and the game eventually would come to you.

One of the rookie units had made a traffic stop right near one of the expressways. They requested my scout to meet them, and I figured they had something they just couldn't figure out. We responded, and I was letting my rookie drive. Like I said earlier, the biggest drawback is that rookies had a tendency to drive a little bit too fast. He was one of those guys, as he got up to 50 on the side street. I told him to slow down, and informed him we have to get there in one piece to help them.

He throttled it back a bit, but not by much. We were about a block away, when the bad guys apparently made the decision for the other unit. The suspects had grown tired of waiting and took off at high speed. The rookies called out a priority and jumped onto the expressway in hot pursuit. These are tough calls as your first impulse is to chase them (which we all do). You have no idea what they are wanted for.

Maybe it's just traffic warrants or the driver has no license. Maybe they're just afraid of the police. Now their actions and yours are endangering innocent lives. It's something rookies don't really think about. I know I didn't when I was new. I just wanted to catch the bad guys. So the rookies are chasing the bad guys for who knows what and are on the expressway, heading out of the city. I let dispatch know we are about a half mile behind them trying to catch up. Surprisingly, no one calls the chase off and we continue through several jurisdictions.

My rookie driver now is cruising at more than a hundred miles an hour and increasing speed. I tell him to slow down, and he just looks at me like I have three heads. He bears down on the wheel and increases speed. The telling him to slow down was in a calm and clear voice. I now scream at him, "Slow the fuck down, before I drag your rookie ass from behind the wheel and throw you out of the fucking car."

This has an immediate effect, and he slows considerably. He is doing about 80, and much more frightened of me than cracking up. I repeat in a slow calm voice, we have to get there in one piece to help them.

Like every young officer, he has full blown tunnel vision. The first unit now has reversed its course and is heading southbound on the expressway. We are still heading northbound. In a minute, we should see them fly by going in the other direction. If the rookie had been paying attention, the proper action would be to get off and wait topside on the service drive at the next southbound ramp. You don't want to get on the expressway before them, as they may exit behind you. If you get on right after them, they already may be getting off at the next ramp. Patience always pays off. The funniest part about my young guy is the police helicopter had just picked up the suspect vehicle and had lit it up with their spotlight. In the middle of the night, this is very easy to follow. I watched as they turned on their light, called out the vehicle direction, and turned southbound.

My driver still is staring intently north with the gas pedal mashed, when I tap him on the shoulder. I point out his window, as the helicopter thunders by, illuminating all three southbound lanes and the suspect vehicle. These are the times I really enjoy working with young people. The look on his face is, "Am I really the stupidest cop in the world? How could I miss that?"

We flipped directions, the bad guys were caught, and a lesson was learned. I explained to him that I went through the same thing when I was a rookie. I did things that were so stupid it was wonder I was alive. You can't learn these lessons in a book. We survived it and went home. The lecture seemed to soothe his ruffled feathers a bit, and he turned out to be a pretty good cop.

As for the end result of a police chase gone wrong, I always tried to take time to drive the rookies to the city vehicle repair facility to see all the wrecked police vehicles are kept there. I felt the visual thing had a bigger impact on them. Some later admitted that it did.

STANDING IN THE RAIN

Some young officers are just destined to be poor decision makers. For many, the badge and gun have permanently changed them. They feel it gives them special powers and privileges.

One time, I was assisting a unit on a traffic stop, and it was raining cats and dogs. The suspect vehicle was pulled to the curb, their unit behind it and my unit behind theirs. I walked up to the scout to find out what was going on. The one officer informed me that one of the people in the car was wanted on a misdemeanor warrant. What should they do?

I asked if it was for misdemeanor traffic warrants, and they said yes. This was quite the minor charge in Detroit. They apparently had a problem with the offender, as they had let him go before and told him not to drive. Today, they had been waiting for him to get off work and they saw him driving after they warned him. The problem was, the guy had his wife and kids in the car. Remember, it is pouring rain. These are the kind of defining decision-making moments for young officers. It kind of tells you what route their careers are going to take.

I never would advise an officer to not arrest someone or to not write a ticket. I always ask them what the arrest or ticket will accomplish. Mind you, this is only for misdemeanor arrests that you can make this kind a decision on. For felonies, everyone goes. I locked up a guy on a felony warrant once. He was in the kitchen, wearing an apron and basting the Thanksgiving turkey. His charge was assault with intent to commit murder. Holiday or not, he had to make the trip. We still have a job to do.

But in this case, would it be better to pick a different day to arrest this guy? I gave the crew the choice, and they made it. They emptied the car of all occupants. They arrested the offender in front of the family. They made that family stand in the rain as they searched the car. The wife and children were soaked. After the search, they told them they were free to go. Go as in walk because the vehicle would be impounded. The look on the faces of the family told the whole story. The officers had made a point with the offender that they were not to be trifled with. What they failed to recognize was the everlasting impression they made on the wife and those kids. I brought it to their attention back at the station, and it didn't seem to faze them. Police authority had changed them.

They were not alone because there were plenty of officers on the job with the same issues. The problem was that I also was law enforcement.

That is what those kids, wife and suspect will see the rest of their lives. It won't be the individual behind the badge, but the uniform those two officers were wearing that night. I wore that same uniform, as does every officer they ever would come into contact with. It's a delicate balance to maintain and, you guessed it, not a subject taught in the academy.

TAKE COVER AT MIDNIGHT

While at Housing I also learned the difference between Detroit New Years and Housing New Years gunfire. Now, many people do not know this, but on New Years Eve, the majority of officers return to the station, about fifteen minutes before midnight. This is to take shelter from all of the gunfire in the city as the residents ring in the New Year. I have lived in the city all my life, and have heard plenty of gunshots. This New Years was going to be a different experience.

Our base was positioned about a half a block from the Jefferson projects. When the clock struck midnight, the celebrating began. It felt like a war zone. I couldn't even begin to determine how many rounds were fired. There were automatics, large caliber, small caliber, single shots and shotguns all going off. Rounds were ricocheting off of the vacant buildings. I truly took cover behind the concrete walls. This went on for several minutes and I sat amazed, wondering how my city had come to this. Once the gunfire died down, we headed back out.

Sergeant Earl Lavelle White
Detroit Police Department, Michigan
End of Watch: Saturday, August 26, 1995

Sergeant White and Officer Lindora Smith were killed when their patrol car collided with another patrol car during a pursuit. The two officers had attempted to stop the vehicle for reckless driving at 0240 hours. In addition to Sergeant White and Officer Smith, a Police Explorer who was on a ride along was killed in the accident. The officer in the second patrol car was injured.

> **Police Officer Lindora Renee Smith**
> **Detroit Police Department, Michigan**
> **End of Watch:** Saturday, August 26, 1995
>
> Officer Lindora Smith and Sergeant Earl White were killed when
> their patrol car collided with another patrol car during a pursuit. The
> two officers had attempted to stop the vehicle for reckless driving at
> 0240 hours. In addition to Sergeant White and Officer Smith, a
> Police Explorer who was on a ride along was killed in the accident.
> The officer in the second patrol car was injured.
>
> Officer Smith is survived by her parents and brother.

BOB DYLAN HAS NOTHING TO DO WITH IT

Racism was evident in the department, although officers never
wanted to talk about. My first visible, out-in-public incident happened
while I was at this command. A number of officers were sitting in the
squad room talking about the OJ Simpson verdict. It just amazed me how
they found him innocent. Any officer who reviewed the evidence should
feel the same way. The only answer to all of this incriminating evidence
was that it was planted by the police.

That meant white officers had to specifically be targeting OJ
Simpson. Once the bodies were found, the white officers would have to
formulate this elaborate plan to frame OJ Simpson. All of this would
have to be done on the streets with the media and other officers around.
Now, here is a little known fact that many people do not know: Anyone
in law enforcement caught doing this would face the death penalty. Yes,
the death penalty. Was this worth chancing your life on? Let's frame OJ
Simpson and see if we can get away with it?

In the squad room, I was going on about OJ's guilt, when a black
officer who I didn't know walked up to me, and yells, "You wouldn't be
saying that if it was Bob Dylan."

I went ballistic.

"You don't even know me. You know nothing about me or how I
think," I told him. "If I looked at the same evidence, I wouldn't care if it
was the president of the United States, I would find him guilty."

Color for me had nothing to do with it, but for him, it had everything
to do with it. He could see he picked the wrong guy and walked away. I

calmed myself down and wondered how that guy got on the job.

Twenty minutes later, he walked up to me, stuck out his hand, and said, "Come on, dog, we was just talking."

I said we weren't talking, that he was yelling. I told him I knew exactly what type of person he was and wished him good luck with his career. He eventually got promoted, and is an instructor in the academy.

As my career continued, I was becoming more tainted. I was acquiring that thousand-yard stare and bitterness to the hiring process and promotional system.

BRASS ON THE STREETS

This command also was my first opportunity to really see a command officer operate on the streets. Two rookies received a run on an attempted suicide. I volunteered to back them up, as these types of runs could turn nasty quickly. The call was to the low Rise projects.

Upon our arrival, I could see one officer talking to someone in the trash-strewn front yard. I walked up to him a little pissed, and asked him where his partner was. Wherever he was, this officer should be with him. He told me the guy trying to kill himself was inside, and his partner was trying to talk him out of it. Then I really got pissed. I said, "Come with me, you need to be with your partner."

We walked through a roach-covered hallway that smelled of a combination of grease and urine. I could see into the rear bedroom, and could tell the officer was talking to someone. I had pulled my gun when we entered the apartment, and peered around the corner into the bedroom. I could see a male who was about twenty-three years old, and clothed only in his boxers. He was sitting on a toilet that did not belong in the room. The room had a mattress on the floor, with food and clothing tossed about in no order. The male was holding a large butcher knife and was touching his stomach with the tip. He was threatening to end it all.

From the moment you exit your car, you assess everything. You are running scenarios through your head at an unbelievable pace. This is where experience comes into play. The first order of business was to get the officer out of the room. I motioned for him to walk to me, and he did. I whispered to him that he needed to have an avenue of escape in case things went bad. He should have positioned himself in the doorway instead of deep in the room. But he was a young officer, and was relived I was there. He had no idea how to talk a guy out of killing himself, and to be honest, neither did I. There was no training for that in the academy.

I started talking to him, asking simple questions while maintaining a soft and quiet demeanor. He somewhat opened up, and explained he couldn't support his family. I asked about how they would be able to go without him, and we talked for about ten minutes. Just as he was ready to turn over the knife, a commander and his driver walked by me into the room. I was shocked. The commander walked right up the guy standing less than a foot from him. My first thought was how much trouble I would get in if I shot the commander. If the guy with knife jumped up and started stabbing him, I figured I would just start firing.

I was only six feet away, and figured a commander that dumb needed to be removed from the equation. His conversation with the guy was pathetic, at best. The commander and his driver eventually stepped out. I couldn't believe the danger they had placed everyone in. He did have a chest full of ribbons though. Maybe you got one for talking to a suicidal person. It took a few minutes but I got our guy settled back down and we continued our talk. We soon came to an agreement. I promised not to take him to the Crisis Center and he promised to give me the knife.

Once I had the knife, he immediately realized I lied. We tackled him, and placed him in cuffs. En route to the Crisis Center, all I kept thinking was I should have that commander and his driver in the backseat. They really needed some psychiatric evaluation.

We arrived at the hospital and went through triage. Once our paperwork was completed, we were buzzed into the circus. It was packed, and we had to help get our guy strapped to the gurney. He kept repeating over and over, "you lied, you lied, Officer Haig, you lied."

A woman wrapped in a straitjacket was seated at the end of her gurney, sitting cross-legged near our guy's head. She leaned forward, coming within inches of his face, and said in a firm voice, "Welcome to the real world."

I chuckled a bit, and crazy or not, she sure had that shit right.

A BATON BEATING

I did receive some additional training when I was at Housing Support. The department was going to start issuing the PR-24 baton. The first unit to receive them would be Tactical Services, which Housing Section was under. Most everyone can recognize the PR-24. A black baton with a T-handle, it's most famous for the beating of Rodney King.

I arrived at the base for my two days of training. My instructor was a K-9 officer and obviously was ex-military. He had the whole marine haircut demeanor thing going on, and was loud all the time. I was hoping to see Oscar (my favorite K-9), and was disappointed when I couldn't find him. There only was one other officer who would be participating in the training.

When I met him, I thought someone was pulling a joke on me. I have no problem with race, gender or size as long as you are capable of doing the job, but this guy had all kind of issues. He was about 5'5" and maybe one hundred pounds. He was one of the smallest guys I had ever seen. His biggest issue was he was Vietnamese. It wasn't his ethnicity, but his speech, as he could barely speak English. When this guy was talking, I couldn't understand him because his accent was so severe that everything came out garbled. If he could enunciate a word properly, he would talk so fast that all the words just ran together like a song.

I couldn't believe it. Who hired this guy? You could not understand him, not even a little bit. After my first attempt to communicate, I resigned myself to nods and smiles and a whole bunch of "uh huhs."

We started training, and would switch off holding a large training bag. This looped through your arm, and was similar to the type a football player would use for a drill. It was kind of like a shield to protect yourself. I would start with the baton. My counterpart seemed barely capable of holding up the bag, let alone hitting it. I attempted to go at about half speed, fearing I would hurt him. Sgt. Stars and Stripes was not going to play that. He began screaming at me to beat the bag as if my life depended on it.

Okay, I can follow orders, and threw a beating on the bag and my training partner. I actually beat him across the room, and right to the ground. He started yelling something in his machine gun delivery and I sensed this might mean stop. He stood up and looked at the instructor and I, and smiled. I'm thinking, "This is great."

This is not a job where you train to take a beating. It was obvious he couldn't take it, and we now were going to see if he could give it. It was his turn to use the baton, and we switched positions.

He began going to work with the sergeant screaming in his ear. It was ridiculous. He was so small and the bag so large that he couldn't generate any power. It was like he was hitting it with a large ostrich feather. No matter how hard the instructor yelled at him, he just couldn't put any umph into it. This went on for two days. We completed our training and in typical department fashion, they passed both of us. This guy didn't need baton training — he needed a weight program and speech therapy.

He couldn't defend himself or talk his way out of anything. He should have been fired, along with the officers who hired him.

A BRIDGE THAT CAN BE SACRIFICED

My stay at Housing Support came to an end one night when I was patrolling the low-rise projects in my old precinct. I bumped into two guys I had worked with at vice. They were cruising in an undercover vehicle, and I stopped to talk to them. We engaged in the typical police small talk, and they asked if I was interested in going to the Special Assignment Task Force, which was the new unit they were working for.

They gave me a lengthy explanation on what they were doing, but it boiled down to being a glorified vice unit, which really wasn't my cup of tea the first time around. But they were really shopping for a white guy and needed me. Yeah, they needed me all right. They needed me because I worked. I was willing to listen, and I agreed to call "Slim," who was the sergeant I worked for at Vice.

Slim spun a yarn about undercover work, secret identities and all kinds of cloak and dagger shenanigans. I was hesitant, but housing was going to shut down soon, as the federal money was running out. That meant I'd be back to the precinct. I agreed, and was told not to report to Housing the next day, just report to SATF. I informed Slim this might not be a good idea, and my bosses probably would get a case of the ass. For the non-police, this meant getting your panties in a super serious knot. He said it would be covered, and I was to call him tomorrow for my base location and a reporting time.

The department worked that way sometimes, and although you never like to burn a bridge, I felt housing was one I could give up.

5ᵀᴴ COMMAND - SATS

NOT YOUR TYPICAL WAITING ROOM

The following morning, I'm up early and ready to start my new adventure. Deep down, I knew it wasn't me, but change was good. I dropped a dime to Slim, and was told to meet him on the east side. I showed up in a parking lot where Slim gave me a hug.

He introduced me to my new lieutenant, whose street name was Fire Wood. This is followed by introductions to the rest of the crew. Three males and one female officer already had worked with at Vice, and another male and female officer had come right out of the academy. It was obvious they were connected. They had no street experience, but were just given a spot because of people they know. You don't even have to be a cop to imagine how dangerous this was.

I ask why we met at this location, and the boss tells me they have been working a prostitution operation for the past week. Spot (one of the officers) was inside a surveillance truck in the parking lot of the apartment building keeping an eye on things.

When I ask what is the operation, I'm told they really don't know — just that there is an apartment where guys go in and get service.

Wow, they have been working this a week and that is all they have. I asked if they knew the apartment number and they didn't. They know the apartment is at the end of the hall on the first floor. I go back and sit in my car, depressed. Fire Wood and Slim are conferring for some time, and Wood walks up and asks if I think I can get in. In where, the apartment?

"Yes," he replies.

I tell him I'm willing to try anything, but that is pretty weak. I have no idea what or who to ask for. I have no references, and they expect me to knock on the door and get in. Anyone with any street experience knows that you're going to need some information to gain access to this type of operation. This isn't like locking up prostitutes on the street: These old gals obviously had some experience with this type of thing.

Wood tells me they really need to get in there, and asks whether I'd be willing to try. I thought in for penny, in for a pound, as the old saying goes. I volunteered to join this bunch, so I might as well jump right into the deep end. I give up my gun and badge, in case I'm frisked going in. This always left a pit in my stomach. If it breaks bad, you will be fighting for your life.

You immediately begin thinking of your back up. I know some of these guys, and they aren't exactly the A-team. And they're being followed by rookie officers. I'm really beating myself up now. Boy oh boy, have I turned into a whiner. I'm here for a few minutes, and already want out.

The plan is this: If I can get in the door, they leave me in for five minutes and then they come and get me. I have five minutes to see enough or ask enough to get some type of criminal case.

There's nothing like that kind pressure on your first day. Now, just to get in the apartment building, you have to get buzzed in. I don't want to spook anyone and do the buzz-all-the-apartment trick, so I kind of hang in the parking lot and time the door. I'll just enter behind when someone else unlocks the door.

It works and I follow an older female in, catching the door for her. I look to my left and at the end of the hallway is a door facing me. I sure hope this is the one, or someone is in for a surprise. I walk down the hallway, with about a half a plan in my head. Most of this stuff you make up as you go. The first step is evaluating your first contact. Who is going to answer the door? Would it be a prostitute offering her services, the house lady running the joint or security?

I knock and the door is cracked open. The chain is on and I appear to have the house lady. She's older, is wearing lots of makeup and is acting flirty. I click into nervous suburban John mode. She doesn't even get to speak, and I tell her that I only have twenty minutes for lunch, and ask if she can she squeeze me in. I glance over my shoulder acting as if I don't want to get caught in the hall. She starts to say something and I cut her off. I plead please, and explain that I hit the four-digit lottery yesterday, and hid it from my wife. I have to get back to work and the clock is ticking, I would just like to … Before I finish, she unchains the door and lets me in.

She asks to see the money and I pull a large wad from my pocket. She tells me to have a seat, which I do. The front of the apartment looks like the waiting room of a doctor's office, but with a twist. The house lady sits at a desk with phone, calculator and some type of record book. A small light, pens and pencils complete the picture. I sit on a small couch and have another customer seated across from me. The reading materials strewn across the table are not People or Highlights magazines. All are pornographic, and are being perused by the other customer. I scan the rest of the apartment, and a scantily clad-female exits a room and walks out into the hall, closing the door behind her. Hmmmm, someone would notice this, so they must have another room, and it can't be far.

The house lady asks if I have any preference on the girl and how much time. I told her no preference and I'm going with the minimum time. There now is a knock on the door, and my fellow customer and I stand up. I'm hoping it is my crew, and watch as the house lady cracks the door. I have seen no weapons, but have no idea who or what is in the rest of the apartment. Unlike street prostitution, where you can get a blowjob for five bucks, this is usually one hundred dollars and up. So this place will have some money. Having money means you have to protect it, and protecting it means men and weapons. I really wish I had my gun.

I can hear the guys identify themselves and, luckily, she opens the door. The crew quickly clears the apartment, finding no other persons, but they do recover a sawed-off shotgun. There was a third customer being serviced by another gal in one of the bedrooms. I let the crew know about the girl who left, and they find her one door down with another customer.

It turns out our lady was running a pretty neat two-apartment operation. I would guess it was a minimum of one thousand dollars a day, but probably could be as high as two or three thousand on a good day. The rooms were well kept with a box of sex toys, and closets had several uniforms and costumes in them. The logbook had a ton of incriminating evidence in it, including appointments and dollar amounts. I looked like some type of super undercover operative with the crew, and scored a ton of brownie points with the bosses.

As I was walking out of the apartment, all I kept thinking about was why they had been sitting on this for a week. As I approached the exit, I discovered the urgency with this case. In walked the chief of police and several of his cronies just minutes after the arrest. They were followed by several camera men and news crews.

Here's another thing about police work: Always go with that gut feeling. I knew right there and then that I should have gone with mine. I had made a bad choice.

GENERAL HOSPITAL MEETS DAYS OF OUR LIVES

My new unit was based out of the old Southwest General Hospital. We would work out of ten offices located in the basement. It was obvious old Wood had Inspectoritis, as we called it. The next step up from lieutenant is inspector. This is an appointed position, so as a lieutenant, you need your unit to do great things and put up great numbers.

I like to refer to it as suckling at the promotional tit. All these lieutenants are like little piglets, trying to climb over each other to latch on. There's lots of squealing and fussing, and "Look at me! Look at me!" The only people who suffer are the officers under that command. They are driven for the greater good of the lieutenant and no one else.

My first day at the base was filled with controversy and tension. A female rookie officer was sleeping with a married police officer in the unit. The problem was this guy had slept with two other girls who used to work Vice, and one of them now worked in this unit. Supervision knew about it, so apparently it was okay. There was nothing against it in the general orders, so it also was okay with the department.

Now, the rookie officer was bitching to her new man, telling him his ex was treating her bad. He took this to Slim the sergeant, who felt this caused a negative vibe for the unit. REALLY!!!! He felt we should all have a sit down in the conference room and work it out. I felt like blowing my brains out.

A rookie officer, who didn't know shit from Shinola, had caused all this by sleeping with a married officer, and basically was dictating how it would be handled. I really liked the senior officer — she was a good person and a hard worker. After the meeting, she left crying. How about booting the adulterer and the rookie? They both were useless anyway. This was all off to a great start.

THE BIRTH OF TONY ANDOLINI

I had been promised some things when they first recruited me for this unit. I would be working undercover for months, I was told. Hardy har har — I knew this was a line of crap but it was intriguing. It never happened, but I did have an opportunity to acquire a secret identity.

I was told to go to Lansing to complete paperwork and pick up my new undercover identity. Maybe this could improve, and the yarn spun by Slim to get me over here would come true. I have covered picking a code name, so you know how I felt about that. I would give this new identity name deep consideration. I'm Italian on my mother's side and a huge Godfather fan. The last name was a lock, as I chose Andolini. Remember the scene from the second one, when little Vito is at Ellis Island? They read his name, Vito Andolini from Corleone. The processor then says Vito Corleone and writes it down. I was taking the godfather's real name. It made me feel very ethnic, and I had that dark Italian look anyway. I couldn't go with Vito for the first name because it was too cheesy and I might bump into a godfather fan while undercover. I chose Anthony, and it would be chopped to Tony Andolini. It had a good ring to it.

I lived at 1650 (my badge number) Teal (my favorite duck to shoot). I made it so everything would be easy to remember under stress. I had a special wallet with my special license but never got to use it.

The undercover thing collapsed under the weight of Inspectoritis. They would need numbers and Special Assignment Task Force turned into Vice. The officer banging all the females would be appointed crew chief of the inspection crew. He and two others would do all the monitoring of the topless and nude bars in the city. It was a tough detail. Oh, they would have to do some regular liquor inspections, but they would concentrate on the topless variety. Boy, this was sounding familiar.

Bubble gum would be appointed crew chief of the illustrious OTE crew. I would get all the rookies, including two females and a male, along with several other "friends of friends" officers. There was not a whole lot of street experience in this bunch.

Police Officer Patrick Michael Prohm
Detroit Police Department, Michigan
End of Watch: Tuesday, January 9, 1996

Officer Patrick Prohm was shot and killed after attempting to arrest a subject during a felony stop for a stolen vehicle at 0035 hours. The suspect exited the vehicle and shot once at Officer Prohm, striking him in the head. He was pronounced dead at the scene. Other officers on the scene returned fire and arrested the shooter, thinking no shots hit him. The shooter died from a bullet wound to the chest after arriving at the detention area. The wound was not noticed because of the large, puffy jacket he was wearing. The shooter also was a suspect in a multiple shooting the night before in Kalamazoo.

Officer Prohm had been employed with the Detroit Police Department for more than two years. He is survived by his three children, parents, six siblings, nieces and nephews.

BRING IN THE NUMBERS, BOYS

As I explained earlier, OTE is the acronym for offer to engage (offer to engage the services of another for the act of prostitution). What this meant was an everyday decoy operation. My crew would put one of the female officers out on the street, posing as a prostitute. She would be covered by two "eyes," which were officers in undercover cars, positioned fairly close to her. They would be able to quickly react if she was in any danger. There would be a "take down crew," which would be two officers dressed in raid gear and driving a marked scout car. Once the female officer got the case, she would signal the eye, who would then call the takedown unit in. They would swoop in and arrest the suspect.

The female officer would have to get an offer of sex for money — something like, "I have twenty dollars, can I get a blow job?"

The bottom line for this whole operation at the time was money: Forfeiture money. Once we arrested the suspect, we would drive him several blocks away to a staging area. If he had no warrants or even if he did (for misdemeanors) and he had valid identification, we would issue him a ticket and release him.

As he was being issued a ticket, several officers would be filling garbage bags with all the property out of the car. We really didn't want him; we wanted the car. He would be forfeiting it, and would need to come up with six hundred dollars to get it back.

So, we had a little assembly line going and as the guy stepped out of the police car with his ticket, he would be handed several garbage bags and sent on his way. I liked the guys who had strollers in their cars, as we could really load those up. It also seemed a little more humane, allowing them to push their property instead of carrying it. I really had no sympathy for these guys. As you can see, the cash register was k'chinging for the city every time we got a case.

Numbers and money were just the prescription for Inspectoritis.

Wood wanted six to eight cars a day. The problem was that he apparently lacked basic police knowledge. He constantly would be calling wanting to know what the numbers were. How many you got? If he was told one or two, he would pout. Come on, Bubble, you have to produce. I lost it with him one night and told him the obvious: I can't make them stop. The girls are not allowed to dress provocatively, so we can't bait the hook any more than we have. Some days were just slow. We worked in all kinds of weather, rain or snow. This always affected the pace. He already should know these things.

The other crew was nice and warm having a little alcohol and watching tits and ass, and I was being driven like a pack mule. Man, did my gut ache.

BUT IT'S NOT MY CAR ...

The funniest thing about forfeiting the cars was this: The only person who could get the car back was the registered owner. The majority of the time, the guy would be driving his wife's car. Worse yet, on occasion it would be his mothers. As I was the crew chief, I had to explain to these sex searchers the process of recovering their cars. Once it sunk in, they panicked. I had many a man drop to his knees grabbing me around the legs and crying, "No, no, I can't."

I had to drag a guy half way across a parking lot before he let me go. One threatened to jump off of the freeway overpass, if I took his car. I informed him, he was free to go, and he could do as he pleased. He failed to take the plunge and pushed his stroller full of personal belongings toward home.

I could only imagine the stories they told their wives or girlfriends. They would just have to give up the whole story or turn into a mailbox watcher (hoping to head off any court notification with their name on it).

I had an eight-month pregnant wife call me once concerning the loss of her car. This was only three hours after we had issued her husband a ticket and sent him on his way. It is three in the morning, and I am trying to explain to her what happened. She is having none of it, and told me her husband fully explained to her that we mistreated him. He told her he was stopped for a traffic offense. The officers had roughed him up, and confiscated their car. Because the officers were such asses, they were going to charge to get the car back and that she would have to pick it up.

I explained to her that the picking up the car part was true, but the rest had been twisted a bit by her loving husband. I explained he had attempted to pick up a female officer posing as a prostitute. He had offered money for sex, and had been issued a miscellaneous ordinance and released. She was a little shocked and thanked me. Now I wish I had their relationship, because 10 minutes later, she called back and told me I was lying. She confronted her husband, who denied everything. So it must be the police lying, and she called me back to chew me out.

I remained calm, as I had been through this before. I asked if her husband worked days, and if she was a stay-at-home wife. She said yes on both counts. I told her all she had to do was check the mail. He would be receiving a court notice within fourteen days. She could attend the court proceedings, listen to the testimony of the arresting officers as well as the female officer decoying as a prostitute. I think after the first phone call she knew the truth but was in denial. I could hear her beginning to cry on the other end. All I could tell her was that I was sorry this whole thing had happened.

Deep down, I was pissed. You want to fool around on your girl, that's your choice, but doing it with a prostitute, and then taking everything that goes with that home to your bedroom or household is unforgivable.

THE UNFORGIVEABLE

As I sat there and thought about that poor woman, two incidents flashed in my memory. Both were from the Third precinct. We had a girl who worked the Fort Street corridor. She was documented to have contracted AIDS. She knew it, and we knew it. Now there are laws in place that state if you are aware you are HIV positive and knowingly have sex with someone, you can be charged with a crime should they contract the virus.

Remember, you have to prove the intent in court. If one of her Johns ever contracted the virus and wished to pursue charges, all she would have to say is that she told him she had AIDS. She would say he wanted it anyway. There's no way to prove what anyone said out on the street, and it's tough for him to fight that.

One day, we caught this girl in the alley, behind a burnt out apartment building. She was bent over some boxes, pants around her ankles. She was being penetrated from the rear, by some white suburban guy wearing a sweater. I wish I would have had a camera. He is trying to get off standing in this filth with an HIV positive prostitute. They immediately stop upon seeing us. I asked him only one question: Are you married?

"Yes," he said.

I told the prostitute to tell him. She looked at me, and I screamed at her tell him. She did. I demanded his license, and quickly wrote his name and address. I told him "three days."

"Three days for what?" he asked.

I told him he had three days to tell his wife. If he didn't tell her, on the fourth day, I would show up in uniform and tell her myself.

I hoped the threat would make him confess to her.

The second incident only was several blocks from the first. Now, most Johns would prefer to do it right in the car, leaving less exposure on the street. It's safer that way. You find a blacked-out vehicle, with no lights on, parked in an area it doesn't belong at three in the morning, and you can be pretty sure someone is getting busy.

On this night, we located a minivan parked just off of Fort Street. As we pulled up behind it, and lit it up, two heads appeared. We pulled them both from the car. One was a white male who was about thirty-five years old, 5'6," 140 pounds and very nerdy looking. The other was one of our local girls. I checked the van, and located a carrot on the seat. Not your ordinary carrot, but one the size of a small pumpkin. It had to be six inches around at the base, but was very stubby, and about six inches long. I had to ask, and she confirmed its use as a sex toy. I was about to ask who received and who gave, when I saw a small picture taped to the dash with several flowers around it. It was our guy with, apparently, his wife and three small girls. His daughters. This made me livid. I asked if they knew, and he said no. I couldn't even collect the words to start yelling at him.

Knowing a lecture would do no good, I told him to at least have the decency to take the picture down. He then could enjoy his vegetables in private.

MY FAVORITE JUAN

During an OTE operation, once the female officer had signaled to the crew she had a case, she would walk off and be picked up by an undercover car. The next time the John saw the decoy was in court.

My favorite John was a Hispanic male who spoke very little English. Our female officer gets a case on him and he is quickly conveyed to the staging area and goes through the process. We wrote him a ticket, bagged his property and sent him on his way. We get a couple of more cases, and I put her on the corner for one more.

An orange Camaro pulls up, and she soon twirls her hair signaling a case. The takedown unit does its job, and carts the whole thing back to the staging area. I swoop down and pick up the decoy. She is laughing as she gets in my car. I ask what is so funny, and she says we just locked that guy up. Just locked him up when? She says about an hour ago. I ask if she is sure, and she says yes, he asked for the same thing. I head to the staging area, and sure as shooting, it is the same guy. We sent him on his way about an hour ago.

Now we have two of his cars. I make a command decision and we arrest him for the second go around. I just couldn't stand to lock him up a third time.

MANAGING THE LAZY

Some days, the OTE operation was good, and others were bad. For Detroit, my work ethic must have been a little warped, because I never understood why the crews wanted to eat as soon as they got on duty. Work needed to be done, let's get after it. The explanation from the officers was that they might not get another opportunity.

Now at SATF, half the time we were leaving early anyway. Boy, did I hate lazy. I had to chew the rookies out once, and they got full force Bubble on this one. They chose to dine with the other crew on a regular basis. They liked to go with the other crew because the female rookie was sleeping with one of them. I didn't mind the company they kept, they just didn't adhere to designated times when they were with this crew. If I instructed the crew to meet at 7 p.m., they would stroll in at 7:10. So there would be a whole team waiting on two rookies.

Now on this particular day, they were about twenty minutes late. I was beside myself. As soon as they showed up, I cut into them. I probably had let it build up a little too much, but I was pissed.

The shocking thing was that they didn't think they were doing anything wrong. They began defending themselves, wondering what the big deal was. "What's the rush? We still need to get the same amount of cases no matter what time we show," they said.

When I got on the job, if you even thought of talking back to a senior officer, you probably would get your ass beat. I knew the reasons for their behavior. They never worked in a precinct. Someone pulled some strings for them because they knew someone, and they went right to a specialized unit. Not only did they jump completely over the experience end of the precinct, but also the respect. They felt they were owed something. If you sent them to a precinct, you might weed them out. In this case, they would be led along by the hand and receive every special consideration they could get. There was no training, just privileges. What a great way to build officers, and trust me, there were plenty of them.

When we closed the operation for the night, and I returned to the base, the boss wanted to see me. He wanted to know what happened out there, and felt we should all sit down and talk about it. I asked him if he was crazy. Talk about what? Why two diaper-wearing rookies couldn't show up on time to conduct an operation? What, were their feelings hurt because they got yelled at?

I told him I was sitting down and talking with no one. He appointed me crew chief and I was running my crew. If he was ordering me to sit down and hold those rookies hands, I told him to transfer me. Now here is the tricky part for him. He needs to keep me, because I'm a good cop and doing the lion's share of the work. He still needs to pacify the rookies and smooth over any waves with the higher ups that know them.

Personally, I could care less how he handled it. I didn't sit down, and I didn't get transferred. I kind of wish I would have. This was the start of my dark times.

Initially I tried to help the rookies, but it got to the point where I just gave up. We were running an OTE operation and the female rookie was working as a decoy. She called a case, and the takedown crew moved in and did its job. I was watching as they took two suspects out of a vehicle, at which time they requested I make their scene. I pull up, wondering what the issue could be. According to the rookie officer, once the takedown crew pulled up, the driver had dropped something out of the window. She pointed to the ground and I could see about twenty rocks of crack cocaine.

Okay, I asked, what was the problem? Hmmmm, nobody on my entire crew knew how to handle a dope case? Amazing.

I tell one of the officers to scoop up the evidence and place it in an evidence envelope. He hands it to me and I examine several of the rocks. Looks like crack, and unlike my TV counter parts, I don't taste it, smile and go, "Crack Cocaine." I crumble one of the rocks and it does not have the consistency it should. It is way too hard. I learned from years in the corridor that plenty of guys are out there selling fake crack cocaine. Simple enough. You target only suburban buyers so they don't come back and shoot you. As the buyer usually wants out of there in a hurry, the rock itself is normally not inspected after the purchase. Money is exchanged for dope, and the buyer screeches out.

Two of the best on fooling the eager dope fiend are soap (the white bar type) or bread. With the soap, you just crumble off whatever size rocks you are selling, bag 'em up, and go to handling your business. The bread is better, but a little more time consuming. You form it into your appropriate size rocks and zap it in the microwave to give it the hardness you need. It's the same drill from there — just bag it and sell it. I pull the guy aside and ask him what it is. He claims it's not his. I tell him to relax, and I'm not charging him, as I know it's fake. Mind you, he can be charged with selling fake narcotics, but he just dropped it, and I already have thoughts about training my young charges. He is hesitant, but reveals the fake dope is broken up Lemonheads. It doesn't look bad, and I give him an A for effort. I now explain to my crew what they are going to do. I tell them the dope is fake and broken up Lemonheads. I tell them I am giving them a training exercise. I need the rookies to head back to the base with the fake dope and put it in evidence. They need to complete a report, and call the narcotics section and tell them exactly what happened.

The key thing is that they saw the suspect drop the evidence. I tell them narcotics will either give you a case, or you'll no case it. If they no case it, you process the evidence at your base and submit your report. If they case it, which they should, taking into consideration the circumstances, they will have to convey the evidence to narcotics section. There, they will fill out some papers, and an officer there will do a preliminary test on the evidence, and confirm whether it's narcotics. This is a preliminary test and only a small amount of the evidence is used. The rest will be placed in a lock seal folder and sent to the lab for more thorough testing. No way is this case going any further than the preliminary test, but this type of case and report are one of the mainstays of police work. Even if you don't work dope, you will stumble across it on a regular basis. It was time for them to start learning about being the "Real Police."

Off they go, with very simple and complete instructions. After an hour, I shut the operation down and we head back to the base. There, I find my rookies still working on their paperwork. I ask one of them why they aren't down at narcotics. She explains she called them, and told them the dope wasn't real but Lemonheads. This immediately tells me they are afraid to do any police work. They don't want to learn, and they don't have to. I chew them both out for not doing what they were told. This is strictly all for them to learn — there was no other reason. But it doesn't faze them.

My anger is tempered by the ridiculousness of the whole thing. I pick up her evidence tag, which reads 28 pieces of suspected Lemonheads. I ask her if she has a lab that will confirm the authenticity of the candy, and throw the tag back to her. I had to walk out of the room, as I began laughing. Suspected Lemonheads indeed. This was the future of the department.

UNAUTHORIZED CHOIR PRACTICE

After several months of stress and cat fighting, SATF is going to have choir practice. I felt this was a great idea, and a few drinks might loosen people up. They may be more open, and willing to talk about issues. These types of things always help to eliminate the bad blood.

This evening, we go to the very back of a large lot bordering the railroad tracks. We want to be sure to be out of everyone's line of sight. You know that police perception thing. It is very early in the morning when we setup. This way, we are not bothering anyone, and they aren't bothering us.

I'm sitting on the hood of my car enjoying my third beer, listening to the stories, when almost the entire crew stiffens up. We have ten people out there, and they begin throwing their drinks over the fence. I ask what the hell they are doing, and they point to the rear of the building about a hundred yards away. A car had pulled around the corner, and they were whispering, "It's Wood. It's Wood."

I told them great, give him a drink. He needs one.

They were terrified. Wood pulls up wearing a large frown. "Shut this down, and I need to talk to everyone tomorrow," he trumpets.

I continue to drink my beer and tell him sure thing. He pulls off, and the rest of the crew looks like five-year-old kids who just got caught stealing cookies. They slink to their cars, whispering how much trouble they are in.

This explained the whole makeup of the unit and why it acted the way it did. I knew I could go anywhere and work with anybody. I knew police work, but I didn't know command officers who would protect me. I earned my bones on the street, not because I knew someone.

We sat down with Wood the next day, and he explained how horrible it would look for the chief and blah, blah, blah. He was right to a degree, but he really didn't truly understand police officers and that bond. The bond between the officers who knew the job and risked their lives every day. They risked it alone and together. They banded together to make a difference. I would be willing to take on anything with these types of officers. Hell, I wouldn't even get on a merry-go round with my crew.

This whole thing was a circus, and Wood was running it. That was our first and only choir practice.

A MASSAGE FROM HELL

My biggest concern was the inexperience of the crew. We were raiding blind pigs and I was manning the ram. I was the first guy through the door, and had a bunch of non-workers and rookies behind me. It was difficult enough to get up enough ass to go through a door where armed men may be waiting, but to have a backup crew like I did almost was bordering on suicidal. I was scared, and I let everyone know it. It peaked one night while I stood on a porch in the Tenth Precinct. I looked back at the crew and told them that if they start shooting, to get the fuck out of the way because I'm not going in. It was at this point I knew it was time to move on.

Before I left, I did have the opportunity to do a few interesting things. Some were good and some were horrible, and some would mark me for life. Being white allowed me the opportunity to look more suburban than some of my coworkers. This would work heavily in my favor in certain situations.

Many of the operations we conducted were off of complaints that went to the chief's office. We received one concerning a massage parlor up on Grand River. Some type of illegal activity was going on, and it had to be addressed. Slim asked if I would be willing to go in and investigate. I couldn't believe it, they needed the suburban looking guy for something fun. There probably were naked woman in there, so I readily volunteered. I asked what we knew about the place, and he said, "nothing."

It's funny how "nothing" really concerned me most of the time. A massage and naked woman seemed to change that concern. I admit I was curious and took the one hundred dollars in secret service money. These were marked bills that the team could recover from the location or arrested persons. They would be needed as evidence to prove payment for services.

I entered the location, minus my badge and gun. I was wearing a pager that was a one-way radio and it would be my safety net. I could alert the crew if things got sketchy inside. Once I entered, I was greeted by an older Asian female. She had a strong accent that I could barely understand, and asked if I wanted a massage. I told her yes, and was informed it was fifty dollars for a half hour. I paid the money and was led down a hallway with a series of small rooms.

The set up was similar to a doctor's office. I was directed to the last room, and the older female entered with me. Crap, I was going to get the great granny of erotic massages. She told me to take all of my clothes off. Yikes. Nobody said anything about taking clothes off. Time to improvise. Like every vice operation, we always were trying to get a case. It was decision time. If I didn't take my clothes off, I would be under suspicion and most likely tossed. But one thing was for sure: I wasn't going to get naked. What if they had a camera on the room? First, with my clothes off, I wasn't really the Adonis type. Maybe more King Kong Bundy. Second, what if the experience itself caused some sort of physical reaction (the physical reaction occurring somewhere above my upper thighs and somewhere below my belly button).

Okay. I went into super undercover operative mode. I'm sure the crew outside was cracking up, as the old bird's request had gone through the one-way radio. I began undressing, as she stood like one of the guards in front of Buckingham palace and watched. I had turned my back to her, and when I got down to my tighty whities, she handed me a towel. I pulled the old, fingers in the back of the undies and gave her the moon shot, and she left the room. As she was leaving, she instructed me to lay face down on the table. I pulled my underwear back up and jumped on the table covering my important parts with the towel.

After several minutes, a young Asian female entered. She appeared to be of age, and very average in looks and build. I wondered if the price was higher for the more attractive girls. She looked at me and said something along the lines of, "Mow ta guuww yeng tow." I had no idea what the hell that meant, so I just remained prone. She began massaging my shoulders, then jumped on the table and began walking on my back. She was no hundred-pounder, and I immediately thought of asking for my money back.

Her weight emptied my lungs and she heard me grunt. Hearing this she then gave me the, "Yung how tay mec goo," response. I was hoping she wasn't asking if that felt good. There was no need at this point to worry about that physical reaction thing. Being stomped was keeping those urges at bay.

I could truly say she did a fine job of balancing. She would lightly touch the ceiling as she walked the length of me. Oh, there was leg and arm rubbing eventually, but nothing bordering on the illegal. After awhile, the old granny came in, pointed a finger and "Ying yang yowed" us. I assumed this meant our time was up. I had observed nothing illegal, so I asked the girl if there was anything extra. I can't ask for a specific act, but thought maybe she would take the bait. In plain English, no accent she said, "Like what?"

I gave her my little kitten purrr, and replied, "You know what."

I told her I had plenty of money. She studied me quickly, and gave me the, "We don't do that type of thing here."

That was the right answer, but her hesitation and the actions I observed told a different story. I redressed and exited the location. I met with the Slim and informed him, that I didn't get a case, but I told him of my suspicions, and he said we would make a plan to get back inside.

Many of these operations are hesitant to give a person they do not know any type of play. It may take several visits and payments to gain their confidence. It wasn't that bad, and I agreed to give it a whirl in a couple of weeks.

> **Police Officer Shawn Phillip Bandy**
> **Detroit Police Department, Michigan**
> **End of Watch:** Sunday, December 6, 1998
>
> Officer Shawn Bandy succumbed to gunshot wounds the day after being shot in the head twice by automatic gunfire. Officer Bandy and two other officers were attempting to stop a van wanted in connection with an abduction that occurred earlier in the day. As they were attempting to stop the vehicle, a suspect in the back opened fire on the cruisers, striking all three officers. Officer Bandy was the passenger of the first marked cruiser when he was struck in the head by two rounds. The driver of the second unmarked vehicle was struck in the head by one round, and his partner was injured by flying glass. Four of the suspects were convicted of first-degree murder and sentenced to life in prison. The fifth suspect was sentenced to five to fifteen years.
>
> Officer Bandy had served with the agency for four years. He is survived by his daughter, parents and brothers.

THE WORLD FAMOUS CHERRY

They also recruited me to go into the Dizzy Duck. This was a full nude bar. Being a full nude bar, they were not allowed to serve alcohol. That was the basis of the complaint, that they were serving alcohol. Now, I didn't hesitate on this one — completely nude woman, dancing? This would be great.

Off with the gun and badge, I picked up my money and headed in. Awesome. I get a break from OTE and maybe just maybe this was a reward for all the hard work and effort I had put forth. The cover charge was twenty-five dollars. As soon as I entered the door, I knew I had made a mistake. I entered and walked down a long dark hallway. I could hear music and headed toward the light. I remembered they tell you to never walk toward the light. I should have heeded that advice. I entered the main room, and it immediately reminded me of some of the basements I had been in. The carpet was red and heavily stained, and to my right was a bucket still collecting water from the ceiling. The whole place had the smell of stale alcohol and mold.

There were six tables, none of which matched, and they were scattered about in no order. They all had mismatched chairs. A bar was positioned along one wall, with no liquor visible. An unattractive female who apparently was my server asked what I would like to drink. I asked for a beer, but she informed me they only served pop due to license restrictions. I ordered a Coke, and it quickly arrived in a plastic cup.

At this point, a DJ attempted to inspire applause from me and the only other patron in the place. He was loudly introducing the world famous Cherry. Ignoring my surroundings, I perked up trying to get a glimpse of the World Famous Cherry. She had pulled back the curtain, exposing a plump, short leg.

I immediately reached for my missing gun as Cherry stepped out onto the stage. Expecting a Victoria Secret model, I got my lunch lady from fourth grade. She was awful looking. She was about forty years old and 160 pounds. She was not completely nude, and was wearing some kind of girdle around her midsection. I assumed this was to either contain her spare tire, or to hide some type of hideous scars. I couldn't tell if she was wearing an atrocious wig or just had really bad hair. Either way, it was dirty and thinning in the rear. Her melons had traveled south years ago, and now covered the front of the girdle. I won't go into the appearance of her nether region.

When the music started to play, she started to move. With her first swing around the pole, I gagged a bit and became light headed. The waitress now was at my side, and I flat out told her I'm going to need something stronger than pop. I would prefer a double shot of bourbon, but a beer would fit the bill for now. She didn't hesitate, and returned with a warm beer. It cost ten dollars. I gladly paid, signaled the crew over my pager and stood by for their arrival. I had no problem from restraining myself from looking at the stage.

Once the crew arrived, I pointed to all the persons involved and fled the location. Outside, I desperately searched for the boss, wanting to beat the feathers out of him. I eventually calmed down, and realized my expectations may have been a bit high. After all, this was Detroit. What was I thinking? I should have known better.

THE RED HEAD

One of my other unusual cases was an example of how certain businesses can operate under law enforcement's noses without raising suspicion. We had another chief's complaint concerning a private club on Oakland Avenue. They wanted to try and get me inside into what was described as a bath house/dinner club. I was a little hesitant, as I didn't like to sit in a hot tub with men, let alone the old roman bath orgy thing. They assured me this was a high-class place, and I would not be required to participate in anything like that. I still was having bad dreams of a naked and girdled world-famous Cherry. So yeah, I was hesitant.

But I manned up and agreed to give it a try. The location was in the precinct I first started in, and I didn't even know it was there. It was positioned on the west side of the street, and appeared to have been an old storefront. The entire front except for the door had been cement blocked in. The building was two stories and had been painted a dull grey. The door was solid steel and opened to the street. There were no windows or other doors visible. There was a small parking lot on the north end of the building that had a high fence surrounding it, covered with concertina wire. It was full of vehicles and I was shocked I had never even noticed this place before. I always thought it was just an abandoned building.

Since we had no intelligence on the place, I would just straight up knock on the door. I was surprised when it simply opened and buzzed shut after I entered. I now was standing in a small foyer with a large window of bulletproof glass directly in front of me. A man was seated behind the glass, and asked if he could help me. I played it on the fly, and just asked for dinner. He told me he was sorry, but he couldn't allow me in. I thought I had struck out, and told him okay. He stopped me, and said, "Come back on Thursday."

I asked why Thursday. He handed me a flyer, and Thursday was listed as single's night. Unbeknownst to me, I had showed up on couple's night. As I was asking about the hours on Thursday, I'm sure what happened next was planned. Stepping in behind the man was a beautiful young woman. She had long curly red hair with a gorgeous figure, and was wrapped in a white cotton towel. Her hair was wet, and she flung it back like Rita Hayworth. She now smiled at me and winked. The man informed me that Donna also would be here on Thursday. I wanted to start jumping like one of the springy dogs, and told him I most definitely would be back on Thursday.

I hustled out to the car, and began rattling all kinds of stories to the boss, including a huge prostitution thing going on, possibly kilos of cocaine going in and high-end stolen cars being retagged in the back. It's quite possible this may be the resting place of Jimmy Hoffa, and I had read an FBI brief that DB Cooper may have lived on Oakland in the 60s. I let him know that Thursday would be the most probable day these activities would take place, and I would restructure my schedule to make myself available.

To this day, I have no idea if it was my visible enthusiasm or that we just couldn't make time, but we never went back. The worst part is that every time I drift off thinking of Donna and that towel, the world famous Cherry and a paper plate full of tater tots keeps showing up.

RUSSIAN ROULETTE

We also continued the routine of raiding on the weekends. At most of them, I still maintained the same fears of working with the inexperienced crew against large numbers of people. One weekend, we hit an after-hours place in one of our western precincts. Topless dancing was the main complaint on this one. A guy could open up his house, and charge a set cover price to enter. Once inside, you could buy drinks and watch topless dancers. On average, there would be about five girls performing. After the dancing was done, the majority of the girls would then provide sexual services.

So we would try and get an undercover guy in and then hit the place. As usual, this place had way too many people for our small crew. Our undercover gets in, and sees enough for a case. He makes a quick call to the boss and we hit the joint. The entry goes off without a hitch and we secure the premises. We now have about forty guys in the front room in the kneeling position. They are in four rows of ten, all facing the wall. It is much easier to control them this way. Now we have to search them and to do this, I will start with the row closest to the wall. I am in full raid gear, so this is going to be tight. I don't want to go into this crowd armed, as they could easily overpower me and take my gun. So I unholster and hand my weapon to one of the crew.

Now, two officers are supposed to be covering me. I begin searching, and the first row goes without incident. As I begin the second row, I notice a guy in the third row reaching for his waist. I look at my cover officers who are talking and turn back to the suspect. The suspect now has a large framed .45 cal pistol pulled from his waistband and is raising it. This is all happening in a split second. I am instinctively reaching for my gun, which is not in its holster. My right hand rises from the empty holster and my fingers close to a fist. I am already swinging and catch him right on the chin. The impact causes him to drop the gun as I dive on top of him. My cover officers now jump into action to assist me. One scrambles and recovers the loaded pistol.

The suspect is not seriously hurt, and pleads with me to not beat him. Why would I beat him? I have no idea what his intentions were and he already is arrested. I ask him what he was doing, and he said he just wanted to drop the gun, so he wouldn't be charged. I believed him. I looked at my cover officers, and tell them thanks, because a couple more seconds and I could have been dead.

Sometimes you know when the situation is dangerous, sometimes you don't. The times you do, you better be on red alert. If you know trouble is there, you better contain it. Inexperience was written all over this. I spoke to the bosses again about my fears, and they promised me they would address it.

I began to dread raid night. I felt it was like Russian roulette.

HIDDEN THONG, CROUCHING DRAGON

I did get to conduct an operation in a real strip joint. The only reason for my involvement was the owner knew all of the other Vice officers. So, in I go and try to get a case. They gave me a couple bucks for the cover charge and drinks. I take a spot at the end of the bar, looking back at the front entrance. I can scan the whole place from my position.

Plenty of men don't know this, but lap dancing is illegal. This is where a dancer straddles and grinds on top of a customer. It's the easiest case to catch, and the guys are charged with acts of simulated sex.

So, here I am in the bar, and after about twenty minutes, a guy approaches a dancer. After a brief conversation, they head down to my end of the bar. He positions himself on a bar stool, and she backs up into him, spreads her legs and begins gyrating on him. This goes on for several minutes, at which time I call the crew in. They are both issued tickets and released. We acquire the owner's license number and complete a liquor write up to the Liquor Control Commission (LCC). They could lose their license for the violations. This helps monitor the business, and hopefully keeps it clean. All of this is pretty standard stuff, and we accomplished what we went in there for.

Well, the court date eventually arrives and they both show. The problem is they disagree on guilt. He pleads guilty, and the dancer pleads not guilty. She fights it, probably solely for the fact that if found not guilty, it may help the bar win the LCC case. Her criminal case is rescheduled, and we end up in LCC court. I told you that I love trapping attorneys, and I get a chance with this one. He sets up the big poster board with the diagram of the bar. Seating positions, stage, everything. It looked really good and I can see where he has placed the defendant and I on the diagram. I already know which direction he is heading, and he is going to claim I didn't see what I saw due to our positions. I really enjoy this as he rambles on and she testifies. I take the stand, and he is preparing to thunder that all-important question. "Officer Haig, you have already testified you couldn't see the color of her G-string. You also testified that she was grinding on Mr. Simms. How could you possibly see both from your position? It seems to be able to see one that you would have to see the other."

I say that "her G-string was kind of tucked up in there. But I did have a clear view of the large red, yellow and black dragon tattoo, running the length of her inner thigh to her ankle. Oh, sorry that would be on her right inner thigh."

He began deflating as he looked at her with steely eyes. I knew he would be scolding her about information he should have known before the case was called. He knew nothing about the tattoo. A mistake, and one that I am sure he wouldn't make again. In this line of work, it seems we always learn the hard way.

THE HOUSE DOESN'T ALWAYS WIN

It was amazing how lazy the other crew was, and what they got away with. They once sent the male rookie out to check an east side bar for a gambling complaint. This kid couldn't find a parking complaint, let alone a gambling one. Why in the world would you send a rookie out on the street by himself? It was because senior officers on that crew had been shaped the same way — they were given privileged assignments and no experience.

I told him I would go with him, just for the protection factor. If he got killed, I couldn't live with myself. On the way, he tells me about the complaint. They have a poker machine in the bar, and apparently have been paying out on the prizes or accumulated winnings, which is a no-no in our state. We make the location, sit down and order lunch.

As soon as we entered, I saw an older male playing the machine positioned at the end of the bar. The kid didn't even notice. After about twenty minutes, I watch the older male jump from his stool with his arms raised. He motions for the female bar tender, who walks to his end. She spins the machine around and gives him a high five. They then both walk to the center of the bar, and she pulls a cash box from underneath and counts out several hundred dollars. She fans them out and places them on the bar. There's nothing like trying to hide your illegal poker machine payout.

Now, the poor kid had been rambling about something or other, and in true rookie fashion, he forgot why he was there. I told him we had a case, and puzzled, he follows me down the bar. I pull my badge and identify myself first to the barmaid, and then our winner. I have them both at the bar, and order him to remove the money from his right front pants pocket. He starts whining.

"Come on officer, I've got about six hundred dollars in that machine," he said.

I inform them that they shouldn't have been so blatant about winning or the payout. She is pissed, as she knows what goes with it. An LCC write-up, and I confiscate the cash box and the poker machine. She also knew she was going to have to make a tough call to her boss.

The winner, or I guess I should say loser, did have my sympathy. I like to gamble and winning isn't easy, and six hundred dollars is a lot of frog skins. When I saw him in court, at least he could laugh about it. He asked if I knew a good gambling counselor. I told him most gambling losses have a story, and this would be a good one.

WHEN YOU KNOW YOU'RE IN THE WRONG

Eventually, all my bitching forced the bosses to attempt some sort of training. They picked my crew to train, which was well needed. Maybe there would be some progress. When they explained what they were going to do, I couldn't believe it. When we place a female officer out to decoy, she is covered by two sets of eyes: One on her side of the street, and one on the opposite. These eyes are not very close because they would spook the Johns. I never wanted to be more than fifty yards away, as you have to react quickly if something goes bad. The reality of it is, if they wanted to assault or abduct her, it could take us as long as ten seconds to get to her. She had a very dangerous position. You never wanted to decoy more than one girl, as it was difficult enough to watch one, let alone two. Two girls out made an already dangerous situation deadly.

The training they had set up was this. Slim pulled me into the office, and told me he wanted two different people on the eye for today's operation. He wanted to see how the officers were going to react. He was going to drive up to our decoy, tell her to get in and drive off. I couldn't believe his idea of training. If the officers didn't recognize his car, they could panic. They could shoot at the vehicle or run into it in an attempt to stop it. I expressed my concerns but he assured me it would be okay. I knew it wouldn't be.

I began thinking that this wasn't the training that I had in mind, and why were we using the decoys? Then it struck me. One of the girls must have complained to him. My rookie was afraid of her own shadow and I could understand why. She had no street experience at all. My priority on the street always was safety first. We had her covered, but there always was a risk. Apparently, she wasn't ready for this type or work. I resigned myself to the simple fact that her rookie complaints had superseded mine and training would be at her direction. She really must know someone. We headed to the street and set up. Although I wasn't the eye, I was positioned so I could see the whole operation.

After about twenty minutes, Slim called me to let me know he was going to pick up the decoy. I saw his car heading north and then quickly pull to the curb. After about a minute of conversation, she got in and he drove off. The eyes were calling it textbook over the radio, including giving a full description of the car and occupant. When she entered and he pulled off, one of the eyes recognized Slim's car and informed the crew not to pursue because the sergeant had picked up the decoy.

After several minutes, Slim came over the radio, told me to shut the operation down and report to the base. When we arrived at the base, he was livid. We were in the conference room, and excluding me, he wanted to know why no one reacted to him driving off with her. The officer who called it out said he recognized his car. That pissed him off even more. Slim gave the standard law enforcement response: "Oh you saw a grey Camaro. How many of those are out there? Could have been a different car from mine."

Now, I found great joy in the officer's response. He said, "No, I saw the plate."

Honestly, I have no idea how he did that and who knows, he may have been lying.

"My plate," Slim hollered. "Okay what is it?"

Without hesitation, he rattled off Slim's plate. I wanted to jump up and cheer. This sent Slim into a tirade. He was yelling about everything. You know how you get caught in the wrong, and try to explain it? He should have just surrendered, but couldn't. I realized the bottom line was that he was questioning my handling of the OTE operation.

That was tough to take, as safety always was my number one priority. Man oh man was I in the wrong unit, and now I really knew it.

This all became crystal clear for me when we were running an operation on the east side. Several blacked out police cruisers pulled up in our staging area. The chief and a number of his cronies exited. You would have thought they were giving away bags of money, as my entire crew rushed up to him. He hugged everyone and I held fast with what I was doing and threw him a "Hello, chief."

The crew bounced around him for several minutes and he re-hugged everyone and left. What a bunch of ass kissers. This was how our department operated. You could be the hardest working officer in the world, but if you didn't know someone, you could end up working a scout car your whole career.

CHIEF RETALIATION

A little about our chief and what he was about helps explain the behavior of some of my crew. An officer from Tactical Services Section jeopardized his career when he took a stand against the chief. TSS is a kind of a strike force unit, and responds city-wide to major incidents. They had been deployed on a barricaded gunman on the east side. Everything was in place and secure, and the bad guy had an infant he was holding hostage. After hours of negotiations, Tactical Services officers talked him into giving up the child.

The officers carried the infant about a block from the scene through the alleys. They were just getting ready to exit when the chief took the baby from them. He now turned the corner into the bright lights of every reporter in Detroit. He had been just waiting for the officers to show up with the baby. Our leader exited the alley cuddling the child and smiling to the press.

You can imagine how that was going to play to the media. At that moment the chief, lost the respect of every officer at that scene. Not choosing to escort the officers and recognizing them for their heroic efforts, told his whole story. The Tactical Services officer drew and submitted a lengthy diagram with captions detailing the whole incident. It was published in the union paper, so that every officer under his command was aware. It was typical of our command structure, and probably helped him acquire the office he now held. These types of incidents really took the wind out of the department sails.

I've compared officers to soldiers several times. Picture this: The marines on Iwo Jima take Suribachi, plant the flag and secure the island. Then, their commanding general walks past the dismembered and bullet-ridden bodies of their comrades, summits the hill, pulls out his own flag and plants it. He does this right in front of his troops. What do you think would have happened?

My crew actually had the pleasure of working with someone from the chief's office. A female officer had somehow upset the chief with her behavior. We discovered she was related to the chief, and he had secured her a nice desk job downtown. Whatever she had done, it must have been severe. She was assigned to my crew as punishment and would be working as a decoy. She was a nice enough girl, but knew absolutely nothing about the streets.

Now I have a rookie and the punished gal on my team. Everyone, including the bosses, were afraid of her because of her connections. I could have cared less. I was not one of the "Huggers."

Several days after she arrived, we were working in my old precinct, when I put her out on decoy. It started to rain, and she stepped into a doorway. I pulled up, to pick her up and she told me to take her back to the base.

"For what?" I asked.

She told me this was bullshit and she was done with this. Wow, I thought I was the crew chief. I called Slim, and he told me to bring her to the base. We stopped the entire operation because she wanted to go in. I dropped her off, headed back and completed the night's work.

When we got back to the base she was gone, and I mean gone for good. Apparently, she made a phone call, made everything right and returned to her cushy office job. Years later, she was arrested at the precinct (her chief connection long gone) for stealing money out of the precinct flower fund.

FOR A GOOD TIME, CALL ...

I did have a second opportunity to take my clothes off while working this command. There was an ad in the local paper for an escort service. Apparently, a complaint had been forwarded to the chief's office concerning their activities. Volunteer Bubble Gum at your service, whether I liked it or not.

We reviewed the ad and it offered escort service and nothing much else. No one had ever worked this type of thing before, so I simply called the number to set up my date.

They asked me specifics on what type of girl I would prefer —

blonde, brunette, big boobs, tall, etc. I went middle of the road all the way around, and was told to call the following day. It was pretty straight forward up to this point. The next morning, I made the call and was told to go to a restaurant up on Telegraph and to use the payphone there. This was interesting, as it was kind of turning cloak and dagger now. I did as instructed, and was told my girl was willing and waiting. The price was one hundred dollars an hour. I said that was fine, and was instructed to a motel less than a half a mile away. I was to knock on the door at Room 102, and my eager girl would be waiting. I must admit that in the back of my mind, all I could picture was the world famous Cherry standing there in her girdle.

Clearing that horrible picture from my head, I focused the plan, which was this: No badge or gun, and I had the standard fifteen minutes inside before the crew was coming in. I figured I should be able to get a case in fifteen minutes. My safety again, would rest with the one-way pager. I knocked on the door, and was greeted by a white female who was about twenty-five years old.

She was a good-looking girl and had a nice figure. She invited me in, and closed the door behind me. This is the part I always hated. I had no idea what or who was waiting for me in there. I had a very specific case that stuck in my mind every time I went in a place like this. I only had a year or two on the job, when three officers were killed in Inkster. Two uniformed officers had responded to a motel to lock up a sixty-year-old female on a bad check warrant.

When they arrived, she invited them in, at which time her two sons appeared from a back room armed with assault rifles. Neither officer had time to react. They were both bound and told to call their supervisor. A sergeant answered the request, and upon his arrival, he was allowed into the room. He also was bound and all three were gagged. After about an hour, dispatch could not raise the officers on the air and additional units responded to the motel. The female refused them admittance and a barricaded gunman was declared. SWAT teams and other agencies responded.

After several hours, all three suspects surrendered. Inside they found all three officers bound and riddled with bullets. I'm sure they had time to think about their fate, before they were executed. It was a simple bad check arrest. That is the danger of police work.

So I carry that thought inside with me as I enter the room. She wanted to get busy and asked if I had the money. I peel off my hundred dollars of secret service funds and hand it over. I asked her what that cash would buy me, and she said a massage and dancing. I looked shocked. Time to start acting. That is it? For a hundred dollars? She informs me that is all the escort service provides.

I complain that is awfully pricey, and say I better get my money back. She hesitates a moment, then asks what I was looking for.

"You know what," I responded, and added that I had extra money and was willing to pay, but she would have to make it spectacular.

Now without hesitation, she asked if I had a condom. Of course I did — it came with my stage prop kit. She requested fifty more dollars, which I paid quickly. Now, I still don't know if anyone is in the room, and this took all of about 10 minutes. I now have five minutes to kill and this is where it gets dicey. She tells me to take my clothes off. Yikes, again with the taking the clothes off thing. I've already told you how I felt about that. I inform her I'm paying, so I want her to undress and then undress me. I thought that was pretty smart. I could drag this out forever and also get a show.

The problem is that this runs a red flag up for her. Obviously, my acting skills are more daytime soap than academy award. She is getting uneasy and asks if I am a cop. I tell her no, and flip it back at her.

"Are you?" I nervously ask. Then I tell her I want to go, and ask to get my money back.

"Okay, okay," she says. "Let's take them off together."

I'm running out of options, and am forced to agree. In preparation for the operation, I really didn't consider my clothing a big deal. Remember experience? This is how you get it. I have on a T-shirt, shorts, undies, socks and gym shoes. I look across from me and she looks like a clothing warehouse. Off with my shirt, and she unties, the kerchief around her neck. I'm really talking now, and struggle as if my arms are tangled in the shirt. She unbuttons her top, which actually is a vest, and takes it off. I take my shoes off, unlacing them very slowly. No flat tire removal, and I take great care in pulling each bunny ear individually. What is happening? Did the earth quit revolving, stopping time? She unbuttons her next shirt and removes it. Underneath, she has another body hugging shirt. I am now wrestling with my socks. I take each one off, taking care to turn them right side out, and then neatly folding each one. She starts unlacing her shirt, and I'm down to the shorts. No belt, damn it. I'm really thinking that it is way past time and wondering if the crew just left. She still is working on her top, and has a bra underneath it.

Mom always told me to wear clean underwear in case I was in an accident. I am most certainly in one now, and drop my shorts. I am standing in the room in my underwear, holding my shorts in front of me, when the crew hits the door. When they enter, I look naked and she looks fully clothed. They start cracking up as I scramble to redress.

Luckily, we didn't tape these types of operations, or I would be in serious trouble. No one else was in the room, and we locked her up.

One chief's complaint was closed and one lesson was learned. I never worked another escort service case again, but was fully prepared to lecture on the layered clothing look being an absolute must for undercover operatives.

Police Officer Richard Daniel Scalf
Detroit Police Department, Michigan
End of Watch: Friday, February 5, 1999

Officer Richard Scalf was shot and killed while attempting to arrest a suspect in a prostitution sting. The suspect was the passenger in a truck who had propositioned a female officer posing as a prostitute. The female officer signaled the five backup officers, who then attempted to stop the suspect's truck. When the truck stopped, the passenger fled and was chased by Officer Scalf and another officer. The suspect suddenly turned and opened fire striking one of the officers in head, critically wounding him. Officer Scalf took a defensive position next to a truck and exchanged fire with the suspect. One of the suspect's rounds struck Officer Scalf in the hand, severing a finger. As he reached down to retrieve his service weapon, another round struck him in the left shoulder, through a gap in his vest. Other officers on the scene returned fire, killing the suspect. Officer Scalf succumbed to his wounds while being transported to a local hospital.

Officer Scalf had served with the agency for three years. He is survived by his parents, two brothers, nephew and two nieces.

PUTTING ON THE RITZ

We were having many issues with the unit, including constant infighting. It was an ongoing law enforcement soap opera. Slim decided we needed a night of bonding and requested everyone come to work in their best dress-up clothes. Maybe this was a good idea. Choir practice didn't work, but maybe a more formal environment might help. We met at the base and then drove to the restaurant located downtown. Dinner was pleasant, but it still was filled with tension. The dissention between the crews and the cat fighting between the girls just wouldn't go away. I couldn't wait to get out of there.

We had been there for several hours and I think everyone was having the same thought. Let's call it a day after dinner. That may have been the plan, but Wood called and wanted us to hit the street to get cases. Man that Inspectoritis really can change you. Now, we were all pissed. We had to go out and lock up prostitutes all dressed up.

I wanted this over as quickly as possible, and volunteered to John. I tore into the corridor, knowing I could get a case within minutes. I spotted a girl wearing a short one-piece dress and pulled over. She jumped in and within seconds I had my case. I signaled the take down and they pulled up behind us. She glanced over her shoulder and decided today was not a good day to go to jail. She already had her door open and was leaning out.

"Oh no you don't," I said, and grabbed the back of her dress as she attempted to bolt.

You know how when you are having a bad day, it just seems to keep going from bad to worse? I had no idea what I was thinking, as she ran right out of the dress. We now have a completely naked girl running eastbound through a vacant lot. If my well-dressed white ass gets out and chases her, I run a high risk of being shot.

Luckily, someone from the crew cut her off and we had one in custody. I returned her clothing, which fortunately had not been torn to shreds.

After this, I started plotting and making phone calls. Whatever it took, I wanted out.

POLICE-EATING SNAKES AND DEADLY FROGS

It also was at this command where I learned a little something about my own kind. The whole trustworthy, fearless, heroic public perception of the police easily can be shattered. There simply are some things the public just shouldn't know, including a raid we conducted on the east side. It was an after-hours joint and we made entry without any issues. We were clearing the location, when one of the officers came running out of a small office screaming, "Snake, Snake!"

He ran behind a wall and peered back, then yelled, "Don't go in there. There is a giant snake!"

This officer was the workout type — super buff and always wearing tight shirts. He looked quite imposing in his tactical gear and facemask. Now, watching this guy flee for his life from a giant snake scared the heck out of me.

Shotgun ready, I crept toward the doorway. There was light in the room, but it was dim. My heart was thumping as I started through the door. If the giant snake lunged at me, I was unsure if I could react in time. I pictured myself in giant coils, having the road apples squeezed out of me. Once inside the room, I could see an aquarium, with a small python in it. It was about two feet long and was lying quietly. I immediately realized this must be the offspring of the deadly giant snake, and swept the room back and forth with the shotgun. Nothing. The room was small, and I jerked the shotgun overhead thinking I had not checked the ceiling. Nothing.

I asked Jammer (the officer) to come and point out the giant snake. He said he wasn't coming in there. I told him it was okay— I was armed with a shotgun and would cover him. I needed to locate that snake. Jammer cautiously stepped toward the room, and looked in. He pointed to the aquarium and began yelling, "There he is, there he is," and ran to the other room.

Now, I had worked with this guy for a while, and he feared no man or situation. I honestly believe if he was forced to stand next to the aquarium that he would faint. I walked out to him, and gave him a comforting hug. I told him Bubble would protect him, and shut the door. The poor guy had the jumps the rest of the night. As we processed prisoners and evidence, he kept glancing to that door. My thought of snake coils and road apples must have been nothing compared to the reptile horrors running through his mind.

I also had worked with a bodybuilding officer who informed me he was terrified of frogs. I began laughing, and told him I had never seen a scary looking frog, and felt most of them were quite cute. No way, he said, insisting they are very scary. He said someone threw one on him one time, and he thought he would just die. One of those big jumping legs got caught in his T-shirt collar and began kicking. He started running, which caused the frog to accelerate his kicking. The faster the officer ran, the more frantic the frog became.

Apparently, he thought amphibians are capable of kicking out your carotid arteries. He shivered as he told the story, and kept glancing around, as if a herd of deadly frogs were stalking him at that very moment. Like the snake officer, he also needed a comforting hug.

RAVING LUNATICS

Every couple of years, I would stumble across some type of police work I had never heard of. I felt I was a thorough, dedicated and street-smart cop, but every now and then, something new would pop up. My first rave party was exactly that, and I would experience it at this command. I had heard of them, but really didn't know what they were.

One evening at SATF, we were going to raid a rave. Let me give you the groundwork for one so you can better understand it. A person (or persons) secures a large vacant warehouse or building. They contract with several bands and hire a staff. They then advertise the party and distribute flyers. The charge is twenty-five dollars per person. Once you are admitted inside, you can purchase juice and pop at a very inflated price. Nitrous Oxide also is available for a fee. You pay for a shot of it, and it gets you high.

These are just a few of the things provided by the agent who arranges the party. Usually, a number of illegal drugs are available and are sold by persons attending the party. Most of the locations where the parties are held are right in the middle of the city. Almost all of the people attending are white suburbanites. The number of people attending easily can surpass five hundred.

One of the jump-off spots was a bar in the downtown area. What you would do is, find a guy selling tickets at this location. Once you paid, you had to wait several minutes until a bus picked you up. These were rented by the agent from the airport, and would carry about thirty-five people. This probably is one of the main reasons I never even knew a Rave was going on. No vehicles were parked at the warehouse.

So we have the bar located, and we send a male and female in to buy tickets. Once they are loaded onto one of the buses, we began following them. The driver of the bus made a number of turns to determine if he was being watched. In police terminology, he was "Cleaning" (meaning he was getting rid of any police tails). He eventually made it to a warehouse district. A male who was wearing all black met the bus at a locked gate. He opened the gate, and the bus drove deep into the complex and disappeared.

We had two undercover officers now inside. The plan was to wait for the next bus and then hit the location. Buying the tickets, the transportation and being let in were violations, but we needed the whole ball of wax. After about twenty minutes, the next bus arrived. It was about 3 a.m. We had extra officers with us, as we already knew the numbers were going to be pretty big.

Well, in typical fashion, once the bus entered, we tried to close in before the gate shut. As I said, this was a warehouse district, so sitting unnoticed was fairly difficult and had to be done at a distance. By the time we made the gate, the man in black locked it and ran toward the rave entrance. We all stood there looking at each other.

Eventually, someone showed up with some bolt cutters and we gained entry. As usual, I was the first one through the door, and immediately jumped back out yelling "Fire."

I came from a family of firefighters, and a thick smoke was hanging at about shoulder height. I looked in again, and under that smoke, were hundreds of legs. I entered with my whole crew behind me, and amazed at what I saw. There were hundreds and hundreds of people standing in this smoke. Some were dancing, some were talking and some were doing, well, the "nasty." Our entrance didn't seem to upset anyone. I'm sure the man in black warned everyone, but they must have paid him little attention.

It took about forty minutes, but we finally gained control of the building and everyone inside realized what was going. We opened a number of windows to let the marijuana smoke out. Remember that random drug test I had to take? I would fill out a report later, documenting my contact with the drug and its smoke. I had to cover myself, and so did the rest of the officers.

There were more than six hundred people inside with two bands and two bars. At twenty-five dollars a head, you can do the math — it was a real moneymaker. We were there for about five hours writing tickets. The agent was arrested and his money was confiscated. Everyone else received a ticket for loiter in a place of illegal occupation.

These tickets kept me going to court for years. We had a number of people from out-of-state and Canada who had driven in specifically for the party. I guess it was quite common to go to another state to attend. I could now check a Rave Party off of my police experience list.

BIKINIS OR LUNCH

There is a certain area in the city that is frequented by working transvestites. Working this command brought me in close contact with the He-Shes, as we called them. Their area is very seedy. There are a number of homosexual bars, and the boys-slash-girls work this area with no concern for the police. It is not unusual to see four or five guys out working within a hundred feet of each other. Unlike our regular working girls, they wear the short skirts, tight tops and high heels. They don't get much pressure from the marked units, as they are fighters. Most prostitutes will go along quietly, but not this bunch. They are runners and fistfight at the drop of a hat. Most officers don't even want to be bothered and will drive right past them. We are up in the area one night, working a — you guessed it — chief's complaint. We are in an

244

undercover vehicle, and park in a lot right on the main drag (no pun intended).

After about ten minutes, my partner and I observe a black transvestite walk from the side street. This in itself was not unusual, but his attire was. He is dressed in a bright orange bikini and high platform shoes. Now this guy/gal is all of 6'1," and cut like a gymnast. He is very dark-skinned, and the bikini is tiny and barely covering his cooter mints. He begins to walk up and down the street, and my partner keeps asking me, "Are you seeing this?"

"Yes, I'm seeing this," I reply.

Since we are up in this area for a reason, my partner decides to roll up to him. Thank goodness our beach baby is on my partner's side of the car. They begin talking, at which time our suspect stands up and starts walking away. I really can't hear what they are saying, but I can see my partner is frustrated — and pissed. He doesn't like the whole guy-wanting-to-be-a-girl thing, and it makes him uncomfortable. Like I'm not? He asks the suspect why he is leaving, and the guy's response sets my partner off. The suspect shouts, "You all are making me nervous!"

We are making him nervous? My partner looks at me and says, "We are making him nervous? This motherfucker is wearing a bright orange bikini, and we're making him nervous?"

My partner's reaction is like the starting gun at a track meet. Our suspect kicks off his platforms and starts those size thirteens a churning. He is off like a gazelle, heading westbound across Woodward. He's long-legged and running like the wind. All we see is dark skin wrapped in an orange blur, and it's quite a striking sight — almost beautiful. My partner screeches out of the lot and fishtails after him. He is swearing to himself, as I tap him on the shoulder. I ask him, "And when you catch him, you are going to do what?"

I think he immediately pictured himself rolling around on the ground with a transvestite wearing a bikini. He slowed down and looked at me with the, "I can't believe it" look.

I suggested lunch as an alternative, and he quickly agreed. That was enough of bikinis for one night.

AN INDECEPT PROPOSAL AND REVISITED REMORSE

I previously told you that, at times, I felt bad about tricking someone. This happened to me when we had to service a complaint about a bar staying open after hours. This particular location just plain continued to serve customers after the other bars closed. There was no attempt to hide it, and it puzzled me because it was a very popular location. They had a good business, why jeopardize it? I was finding greed motivated all kinds of crimes.

As most of the patrons are white, I am volunteered to go in. Immediately, I feel this is the wrong place, as the only people in the location are myself and two others. It's not exactly a hopping joint, but just the same, I take a seat at the bar and order a beer.

The female bartender starts to small talk, and I begin to weave my story. I tell her I'm staying at a downtown hotel, as I am part of a big roofing crew in from out of state. Blah, blah, blah, and this goes on until bar shut-down time. Once we hit the witching hour, I notice no one is cleaning up, and we are not given the famous last call notice. At about fifteen minutes after, I ask for another beer. She doesn't hesitate, and asks me if I'm wondering why she is serving me. I tell her that as long as she keeps bringing them, I'm not going to question it.

After about twenty minutes more, I realize why there was a complaint. The bar now quickly starts filling up. Within fifteen minutes, it is packed. Most of the patrons are bar and wait staff from other locations that, according to state laws, have closed at the appropriate time.

Now this guy had a gold mine going, because the price of drinks doubled after hours. My backup crew has watched the steady flow of customers, and there is no need to notify them that I have a case.

The entire team now enters the location, announcing their presence. All the patrons are issued tickets and sent on their way. I am required to issue the barmaid her ticket. She was steamed like a clam. The ticket didn't bother her as much as the story I told. She just kept repeating it wasn't right, it just wasn't right.

"You didn't have to go through all of that. I really believed you," she told me.

Soon several tears dropped on the bar and she began crying. I felt horrible, finished the ticket and walked outside.

This unit really wasn't me, and you may be noticing a trend in my new assignments: "Sketchy" would be a good description.

SHACKLED TO THE NEXT ASSIGNMENT

For my excellent bar work, I was awarded my next undercover assignment. It would take place in the homosexual world. A chief's complaint had come in concerning a bar called Shackles. The complaint only listed illegal activities. At this point, I have no idea this is a gay bar, but I should have thought something was up. Who names a bar Shackles?

As procedure goes, we now needed to get someone inside to scout it out. Slim calls me in the office to discuss the complaint. He asks if I will try to get in a bar for him. Of course I can, as anything beats the OTE operation. He looks down and hesitates. Then he looks up and tells me it is a homosexual bar. I scream absolutely not. Nothing against that community, but it is definitely not my world. Slim begins pleading. "No, no, no," is my reply.

How about a slide day, he suggests. A slide day is eight hours off with pay. You are on the books, but not really on them if you get my drift. Mmmmm, all I have to do is go in and scout it out? No touchy no feely? No interaction at all? Ten minutes inside is all he needs me for?

He explains he doesn't like it either, he just wants to close out the complaint. I agree to do it. I already know nobody else in the unit would do it and that's why he came to me. It's great being dependable, as you can see it will get you all kinds of things. Our master plan is the same as always: Badge and gun off, and Bubble in. If I don't come out in ten minutes, they will assume I turned to the dark side.

We really don't have any intelligence at all on this joint, so we pull up and watch for a few minutes. The front door and windows have ghetto bars. These are the steel prison type bars you see used for security. All the windows are blacked out so no one can see in or out. My tummy begins to turns. Some clubs or bars have a password or require references, and since we have no idea what this place might want, I am just going to have to walk up and knock. I exit the car and receive several "be careful" snickers followed by, "watch your back, Bubble."

I walk up and pound loudly on the front door. It creaks opens and the rush of a hopping bar pours out. Music, smoke, men's voices, and stale liquor flood onto Michigan Avenue. A white male, who is about 5'6" and 130 pounds, asks if he can help me. He is wearing a leather captain's hat, leather Daisy Duke shorts. He has two leather straps crossing his chest, and gives me the slow eye roll from my head to my toes.

I think of just bolting on the spot. I would just tell Slim they refused me entry. I quickly realize this isn't going to work and we would just have to keep coming back over and over. He now has one hip up and one down, with his finger on his lower lip. "Can I help you?" he yells. I stutter that I'm just looking for a good time.

My mind is protesting, and I can't believe I really just said that. I'm looking for a good time. My worst fears now are realized as he unlocks the grate. I step in, and he slams the bars and door shut behind me. He asks if I want to buy a chance for the door prize. I probably should have just said no, but like an idiot, I ask what it is. I'm waiting for him to say a

"Bubblegum Choo train," when he replies that it's a six-pack of beer. I buy a chance for five bucks, hoping this helps with my cover.

My head now is spinning and my stomach feels like a bingo tumbler. The bar is dimly lit, with disco lights swirling about. The clientele is far ranging, including whites, blacks and Hispanics of all ages. Some of the patrons are well dressed, wearing suits or shirt and tie. Some are in shorts or blue jeans with pullover shirts. Several men are slowly dancing together, and others are softly caressing and kissing at their tables. The music playing on the jukebox is the rap song, "I don't want no short dicked man."

I'm getting one slide day for this? I realize I should have held out for more. My first thought is to get my back against a wall, more specifically, my backside. I know this is going to be obvious, so I decide to pick a stool at the bar with open spots on both sides of me. It gives me a little buffer zone, if you know what I mean.

The bartender walks up to me, and he is a giant sized version of the door guy. He's wearing the same outfit, but is about 6'3" and 260 pounds. I make a quick mental note reminding myself that if things get dicey, to not yell anything including the word gay. There is no way I want to rile up the bartender.

Besides the passionate kissing and some aggressive fondling, I don't see anything illegal. I do notice quite a bit of activity in the back near the restrooms. I could see the sign for restrooms on the wall: One for men, the other for woman. I was trying to figure this one out, as there were no women. Do they just use both? I could see patrons filtering in and out of both, but the number coming out didn't always match the number going in. I made another mental note to not go anywhere near the bathrooms. I was going to stick to the plan and do as I was instructed. In ten minutes, we'll close out the complaint and I'll be outside. There's no sense in risking losing some ass over eight hours slide time.

I stay safely on my stool and watch the clock. I am avoiding eye contact and staring straight ahead, when a guy takes a stool two down from me. Because I have on my trusty one-way pager, the crew is outside monitoring and I could just flat out yell for help if things got out of hand. The pager is capable of picking up any conversation within ten feet of me. Now, a second guy walks up to the gentleman who just took the seat to my left. He aggressively grabs him, kisses him full on the mouth and hollers, "Ewwh, didn't I suck your dick good last night?"

I sit there stunned. I now realize within a nanosecond that disgusting dirty statement just went out over my wire. All the crew can hear is the conversation, as they can't see seating positions or people. THEY THINK HE'S TALKING TO ME! I start with a cough, cough "It wasn't me" into the pager. I repeat this several times. Hack, hack, hack, "it wasn't me."

In panic and disgust, I throw a dollar on the bar, and tell Captain Courageous that I really have to run. I head toward the door and I'm in luck as Baby Captain Courageous is letting someone in. I almost topple everyone in the doorway as I jump from the first stair. I take a huge breathe of fresh air, and thank the Lord I am out.

Sitting on the corner is my take down crew. All the doors are open on the vehicle, and one crewmember is on the ground. They are laughing so hard some of them are crying. One guy keeps repeating, "They've turned Bubble. They've turned him to the dark side."

I open my mouth to start to explain, but know it is no use. I give them several minutes and when the gasping and crying settle down, I get in the car. We headed back to the base in silence. Every couple of minutes, a muffled giggle could be heard.

Yes, I did get my slide day, but it certainly wasn't worth it.

Police Officer Shynelle Marie Mason
Detroit Police Department, Michigan

Officer Mason was shot to death during a confrontation with three men. She was off duty with several female friends when the men began a conversation. When the women refused to participate, the men started arguing with them. Officer Mason identified herself as a police officer, and one of the suspects pulled out a gun and shot her. The bullet entered Officer Mason's side and pierced her heart. She died en route to Sinai-Grace Hospital. The suspect fled the scene, but was identified and arrested early the next morning and charged with murder. Officer Mason previously had arrested the man for carrying a concealed weapon, and it was determined that he murdered her in retaliation for the arrest. The other accomplices also were charged in connection with this case. The suspect was convicted of first-degree murder and sentenced to life in prison July 6, 2001.

Officer Mason had been with the Detroit Police Department for two years.

AN OFFICER BUT NOT A GENTLEMAN

While at this command, I also experienced some uniformed officer's actions that stuck with me the rest of my career. One day, we were running our decoy operation up on Michigan Avenue. Once we were in position, we would call for a zone clearance. A zone clearance means dispatch would notify all marked units that they should avoid the area. About two blocks away from where we were set up was a topless bar. Previously, when we had worked at this location, there was a marked unit parked in the rear of this topless bar. Once dispatch broadcast our operation, the scout car disappeared. I have no idea what they were doing that day, but I know it wasn't police work.

On this particular day, after we got our first case, a marked unit pulled to the rear of the bar. After ten minutes and a re-notification to dispatch, the car still was there. We had a supervisor with us, and he shut the operation down. Taking myself and the two officers in raid gear, we made it to the bar to see what the issue was. As we entered the bar, I could see two officers in full uniform. One was standing at the end of the bar, the other was seated on a stool, with a dancer on his lap. ARE YOU KIDDING ME? Who were these clowns? The officer at the end of the bar immediately tossed what was in his glass.

We walked directly up to the officer on the stool, and he looked at us like he didn't want to be bothered. I was furious, and my boss almost lost it. He told the officer to standup. His response "Why?"

"Standup, I need to have a word with you in the back," my sergeant said.

The officer, upset we had interrupted him, stood up. My sergeant grabbed him by the arm to guide him to the back. The officer violently pulled away and said, "Don't touch me."

I couldn't believe what I was seeing, and this officer had no idea who he was trying to play with. My sergeant was about fifty years old, but he was an ex-Navy Seal with two tours in Vietnam. He never talked about it, unless he was full of liquor, but I thought I was going to witness one of his war stories right in front of me. Everyone calmed down a bit and we all went to a backroom out of site of the patrons and staff.

The officer then informed us that he had every right to be there. He was on his requested code. A code 9330 was lunch and would have to be approved by the dispatcher. My sergeant asked who approved him eating in a topless bar, and he said it was his precinct commander. Now, the way the general orders read, you can take a code in any licensed liquor establishment. Yes, this was a licensed liquor establishment but why as a police officer would you even think of going into a topless bar in uniform? Not only are you in a topless bar, but in one we called for clearance on through dispatch. These guys apparently forgot about the saying, you don't only represent yourself but all of law enforcement. Who hired these guys?

Both officers agreed to clear from their code and left, but it was obvious this was not going to be the end of it. My sergeant contacted the commander of the precinct to confirm the officer's story. The commander informed him not only was it okay for them to take a code at the topless bar, but he was going to pursue a complaint against my sergeant for grabbing his officer's arm. Holy shit, forget about the officers, the big question now is: Who appointed this guy to his position as commander? He is condoning his officers taking their codes at a topless bar. If I were the chief, he immediately would have been demoted for being an idiot. He should have been fired. No one was disciplined, and the commander held his position until he retired.

This is how my department slowly deteriorated. Why should any officer do it right? Our Code of Ethics? What a crock. The rules and code only applied to some. No matter how hard you tried to do it right, someone always was doing it wrong and getting away with it.

Can you imagine conducting a roll call, and telling the officers to not let anyone tell you that you can't take a code at the titty bar? It's amazing. The officer in question eventually was fired. He came under federal investigation as a number of people came forward accusing him of robbing them. You can see why things were changing for me.

I always preached experience, experience, experience. While at this command, I didn't realize the issues that experience itself could cause me.

NOONERS AT THE COUNTY BUILDING

Apparently, the chief's office had a stack of complaints generated by the gay community. Getting in Shackles would open the floodgates for SATF. The complaints began pouring in and needed to be addressed immediately. Let's go to the most experienced guy in the department — the one who has the most experience in this type of thing. I was going to have to learn to be careful with experience.

First one up was the City County Building. City County Building? What could be going on there? Homosexual activity in the restrooms was what was listed in the complaint. Okay, I guess that is possible. My first concern was going to be the Bubble solo mission again. I wasn't going for the one-slide-day flim flam. It was going to have to be the whole crew or nothing for me. So we all sat down and the entire crew was briefed on the operation.

Again, I could hear muffled giggles, and "Bubble this" and "Bubble that" being whispered. They were looking to me for leadership on this one. I was getting queasy already. Apparently, there were two restrooms in the basement, and if you went down there at lunchtime, you could get a little treat. There was no other information as far as the illegal activity, just that it was taking place in the bathrooms.

So, we were all paired up with a partner, and sent into the bowels of the City County Building. I figured when we went down there we might find one or two guys doing some dirt. I really didn't expect to see what I saw. Once you made the basement floor, it was like a beehive of homosexuals. A number of guys were loitering on the stairways at both ends, and it was obvious something was going on.

They gave me that creepy head to toe once over. I had seen this look before, and didn't like it one bit. When I made it to the basement proper, there were guys everywhere, just loitering. Like Shackles, some were dressed up and some were in jeans.

My partner and I took a position at the far end of the hall where we could view the entrance to both restrooms. Guys were going in and out of the restroom at a very steady pace. Some would stay in, others would be in for a second or two and come right back out. Something was going on in there, and we were supposed to find out.

I asked my partner if he wanted to go in first. He immediately started talking about me being experienced in this type of thing, and that I should go first. I would carry that "experienced in that type of thing" label for the rest of my career. The problem was he was right — I did have experience and, like it or not, that still was important. So I figured why not, the sooner this was over, the better. Let's knock this out and go home. Then my conscious self reminded me what happened last time at Shackles. This thought slowed my walk, and I now was a bit jumpy.

Once I entered the restroom, I could easily see what was going on. There were six stalls, and two of these stalls had four sets of feet in them. The feet were pointing toward each other and very close. Get the picture? The four urinals were open with no dividers, and they were all occupied. The guys were all standing further than normal from the urinals. The three remaining stall doors were cracked open, with a set of peering eyes in each.

I quickly deduced the City County Building Rendezvous protocol. Go into the john. Step up to a urinal and unzip. Step back, so your junk is visible. The occupied stalls crack open. If the occupant of that stall likes what he sees, he motions you over and in you go for some afternoon delight. I'm guessing the most desired stall would be the handicapper. There was plenty of room, and bars to stabilize yourself.

I exit and inform my partner of my observations, and bring him up to speed on the layout. To get a case, we are going to need some type of offer for sex. I tell him this obviously is going to involve one of us going up to a urinal and ... okay, I'm pretty sure that is not going to happen. No pony out of the barn for me, and he quickly agrees that he wants his pony to stay in the barn. My new plan is to walk up to the urinal, fumble with my zipper, look over my shoulder and give him the Bubble doe eyes. I really hadn't figured what I was going to do if I got motioned over because there was no way I was going into the stall with anyone. What if he locked the door on me? My partner agrees with the plan and, as usual, we will play it by ear if we get motioned over.

This walking in and out of the john and up to the urinals went on for about 40 minutes. Homosexuals, urine and poop did not make a good combo for me. I was frustrated and after exiting the john once again, I told my partner that this was bullshit. He looked at me, and said, "I don't know about you, Bubble, but I'm feeling uncomfortable."

I wanted to sock him in the mouth.

"You're feeling uncomfortable," I yell at him. "I'm the one walking in and out of these love dens."

I get steaming mad and I tell him, "I'm going in and getting a case. If I have to initiate it, so be it."

There was a stall that had been occupied about fifteen minutes and it only had one set of feet. I quietly enter the adjoining stall next to it, jump up on the toilet and peer over. He looks up like a cat about to bolt. I straight up ask him, "Can I come in there with you?" As the last word exits my mouth, I can see his pants down around his ankles, and realize he is actually taking a shit. Whoops. He thunders, "You better get the fuck on!"

As he scrambles to pull up his drawers. I'm already doing the Bambi on ice trying to get out of there. I skid around the corner and tell my partner we have to go as I jog toward the stairway. He doesn't even question me and follows. Once outside, we gulp fresh air, and I start laughing. I have just scarred that guy for life. Everyone's most dreaded public restroom fear had just come true and I caused it.

You know when you're sitting there and someone comes in, you do the fake cough or the flush as an "I am in here" warning? You always are afraid someone will try to get in your stall, so you hold the door. Can you imagine a 6'0," 260-pound guy climbing over the top, and requesting to get in there with you? How would you ever be able to take a public crap again?

Fortunately for us, one of the other guys got a case and we arrested two people. I never thought anything like this would be going on at the City County Building, but the two arrested enlightened us. It has been one of the hottest spots for more than forty years. The older of the two informed us it started around World War II. People come in from all over the state. I didn't want to, but I had to log this under the new experience category. You most certainly couldn't learn that in a book.

RAINBOW OPERATIVES

We completed several other operations within the gay community, and although I never got comfortable with it, it did get a bit easier. They sent me in a higher-class bar called the Tool Box (which is great name, but if I owned one, it would be called Nuts and Bolts). My escort was the young male rookie. He was blonde with a ponytail and had a feminine look to him. He was terrified. I must admit I puffed with pride as we strolled in and everyone put an eye on us. They all were very jealous. I showcased him for about twenty minutes and as we left, I slipped my arm around his shoulder. The poor kid was weak kneed by the time we got out of there.

Being a successful Rainbow operative always was taken into consideration when the bosses got a new chief's complaint.

I guess I reached my pinnacle when they wanted to get me in the biggest homosexual club of them all. It was called CCT, and was located up on Eight Mile. We had very little intelligence on the location, but we knew they didn't just let anybody in there. I actually had to drive to Ohio with the crew and sign up for a membership in a club down there. This was to establish a reference, if needed. It was a hundred bucks for the membership, and after Tony Andolini supplied his driver's license, I was a card-carrying member of the club in Ohio.

When they handed me my membership card, they also gave me a towel and buzzed the door for me. Yuck a towel? I glanced at my watch and said, "Ohh my goodness, look at the time. I'll have to take a rain check on that one."

I never did get in CCTs, but when we scouted it, someone from the club had law enforcement connections, because several of our license plates had been run. All the plates on our cars were suppressed, so when someone tried to run them through the law enforcement intelligence network, they would be flagged. It was nice to have connections, I guess.

Believe it or not, Shackles came up again. Slim wanted to see me one day, and as I entered his office, he asked me to shut the door. This might be it, I thought, maybe I'm transferred. The second word out of his mouth is "Shackles," and I'm out of my chair.

"Calm down," he says.

"No, no, no," I'm telling him.

"Just listen," he says. "They need a case out of there and they are not going to let this one go until we get one. You've been in there, you know what it's about."

Experience, experience, experience.

"Do this for me," he pleads.

"No," I respond. "I wouldn't do it for my mother."

He tells me he needs me, and wants to know what it will take. I tell him, "Nothing, I just won't do it."

"How about some slide time?" he asks.

Rigggghhht, No thanks — I fell in that trap before, mister. He now goes for the throat and offers three slide days. That gets me thinking, and he knows it. He starts buttering the bread and reminds me that duck season is coming up. Attach those three slide days to some court time and I could have a whole week off. He knows how to hit a duck hunter, and I buy what he is selling. I hope I don't regret it.

We brief with the crew, which only was interrupted by the occasional muffled snicker. We gear up and head to the scene of my last disaster. I really need to get the image of that kiss and the "Oooh, didn't I suck your..." out of my head, and stay focused.

Once we arrive, it is the same routine to get in. Entry didn't present a problem, but as I step through the door, I rush through my mental notes from last time. Number one was don't rile the bartender. Number two, and I remember this specifically, was don't go near the restrooms in the back. Well, I was going to have to break that one and I can see that there is a long hallway heading to the back of the bar. It is dimly lit and several guys are congregated around the entrance. The restrooms branch off about mid hallway.

After one beer, I build up enough courage and head back. As I turn the first corner, I come nose to nose with a guy wearing a black latex vinyl S&M mask with a zipper mouth. I'm scared of everything anyway, and I about jump out of my skin. My eyes adjust and can see he is quite bizarre looking. He's a regular guy, wearing a plaid shirt and Dockers, and sipping a beer through his S&M zipper. I decide to cautiously proceed, as I almost lost my road apples on that one.

There are several guys standing in the hallway, and as I approach, I can see they are positioned near an opening in the wall. It looked like this opening used to be a service window of some type. Now what? As I move closer, I can see both men in the hallway are jumping and cooing,

"Oww, that hurts. Oww, that hurts."

I can hear a snapping noise, and when I come into full view of the window, a guy is standing there cracking a small whip. He is gently striking both guys in the hallway. Trying to avoid getting hit by the whip, I hustle pass the threesome. I now am looking straight down the bathroom hallway. There are two restrooms and the one posted "women" is completely dark. The second has a light on, and casts a spooky glow into the hall. I can hear noise coming from the women's restroom as I pass, but dare not look.

As I reach the end of the corridor, I now can look directly into the men's room. There is a small hallway leading into the john itself, with two guys standing between me and the restroom entrance. I back my caboose into the corner and begin sipping my beer. Confident with my back end protected, I now have a full view into the restroom. I can see that the two guys now are cuddling, but there's nothing illegal about that. I jump as Baby Captain Courageous from the first trip asks if I need a drink. How in the hell did he sneak up on me? I tell him I am fine, and he saunters off.

I now have a young male who is about twenty-two years old walk past me and give me the head to toe eyeball roll. I have grown to hate that look. He enters the John and just stands there, looking at me. I'm looking everywhere but at him.

After a few seconds, he walks right up to me, and is way closer than I feel comfortable with. He stares into my eyes, then breaks into the batman dance. You know the one, where you criss-cross your arms scissoring them across your partner? Starting at the head, then seductively working your way down to the ankles. I'm frozen. I don't know if it is fear, surprise or what. After his second trip up my body, something clicks for him. I'm not giving the "I want to play" sign or something, and he looks at me with disgust and stomps off.

I am standing there, shell-shocked. I can't believe that just happened. I am shaking as I try to sip my beer. I need to recover and recover fast. Now, an older male walks by, and you guessed it, I get the once up and once down look. He enters the john, and walks into the stall. After several minutes, he walks out with his pants down. He kneels on the floor and starts to box his clown. I am now rubber-legged as he motions for me to come in with him.

My head almost spins off my shoulders, as I motion "no" repeatedly. Again, I'm not giving the right signal (thank god I never discovered what that was), and he zips up. He now approaches me. I am tensed up and ready. If he grabs me, I know I will go on autopilot and will probably just start swinging and screaming. As he comes into the light, I can see he has on pink nail polish and makeup. He asks if I'm waiting on someone.

"Ohh, yeah," I tell him, "actually several people."

He then asks if I have to pee. I tense up again.

"No, I don't have to pee," I thunder.

Why in the hell would he ask me some dumb shit like that?

"That's okay," he says. "When you have to pee, let me know, I want to be your toilet."

As he walks away, I start gagging. I'm light headed and begin clicking my pager. The crew is inside within seconds. I point out the offenders, knowing that "boxing your clown" in a public restroom was some type of violation.

The crew escorted the suspect outside and began writing him a ticket. I was standing the length of the parking lot away from him, but got to witness the crew getting a little bit of what I experienced. Every time they asked this guy a question, he would get very close to the officer before answering. We were trained not to let anyone in our space, so this caused the officers to take a step back.

By the time they finished the ticket, the suspect had forced them all the way across the parking lot, and the whole group of them was now standing next to me. One of the officers even had some of the suspect's sprinkle makeup on his sleeve. I certainly gave them all the business on that one.

For me, the case would not quietly go away. An MLLC write-up was submitted, and after several weeks, I received a subpoena to appear at a hearing concerning the case. I arrived at the appropriate time, finding my "toilet" seated at the defense table. He waved at me as I entered. Yuck.

The hearing proceeded without incident, until my testimony. After a number of questions were asked and answered, I knew what was next. The commissioner asked, "Officer, what was Mr. Smith doing as he knelt on the bathroom floor?"

"Masturbating," I responded.

There, I said it, and the depraved scene flashed back to me at that very moment. My mind visualized him motioning me into the john. Double Yuck.

I almost didn't hear the commissioner's next question. It was a doozey.

"Officer, you know what masturbation is, correct?"

"Yes," I responded.

Now, I have no idea if he was just flat out clowning with me or not, but he said, "For the record could you describe the act you witnessed?"

The court recorder, a female, was seated right next to me and she started to giggle. You must understand in court when you are asked a question, you have to answer it. No head nodding or twisting. No ducking or blocking. You have to verbally give a clear explanation so it can go into the written record. Great, I started describing his erect penis and him stroking it. For some unknown reason, I was acting this out in the witness chair. Italians have a tendency to talk with their hands, but this was a bit ridiculous as my hand was going up and down on some imaginary ... Oh, just forget it. I glance over at the lady court reporter as she is struggling to not laugh.

The commissioner curtly says, "Officer, that is enough."

I realized what this whole picture must have looked like and gave my whole body a quick shake, like a dog shaking water off. It didn't work and the whole gayness thing still was on my mind. I was dismissed from the stand, and Shackles was found guilty of the violations. Their license was suspended, and I slunk out of the room, feeling soiled.

The duck season was a bust because I seemed to miss every flight of ducks that corkscrewed in. My brother told me it would be okay, I just needed to concentrate.

The Shackles thing was haunting me. I was going to confess to him, and I just started to when I caught myself. Explaining what I had experienced could possibly crush his image of his big brother and ruin his trip. For several years, I kept that story to myself. Choir practice pulled it out of me one night, and that is the type of story that becomes department legend.

ARE YOU CHOKING?

Inexperience would surface a number of times in this unit, even with the senior officers. In one of our operations, I was sent into Jerry's bar in the corridor. There were reports of prostitution, which wasn't surprising. Of course there were — this was the corridor. I was volunteered again, but informed my boss it may not work. I had spent quite a number of years in the corridor, so I knew many of the regulars. They wanted to stay with a white guy, and they weren't going to send in the rookie with the ponytail, so I really didn't have a choice.

At least for this gig, I was allowed to keep my gun and badge, which was comforting. So in I go and take a seat at the end of the bar. It doesn't look promising, as I'm the only guy in the place. About ten minutes had passed when a heavy-set black female entered and plopped herself on a stool. She is at the bar, positioned almost in the middle. Within minutes, an older white male entered and took the stool next to her. Okay, here we go.

I watch them as they talk for a moment, and then he hands her some money, and she hands him back a coin envelope. This is all done underneath the bar edge out of the bartender's line of sight. The male now leaves and I throw three dollars on the bar and follow him out. I'm pretty sure she didn't just give him her phone number. I watch as he enters a brand new red Corvette and pulls out of the lot. I get into my undercover vehicle, grab the radio from under the seat and follow him south onto Third. I inform the crew, "I'm following a red Corvette, and the driver just copped dope from a heavy-set black female, wearing a gold dress and gold sandals. She is in Jerry's, seated at the bar. I need a marked scout car to pull the Corvette over, and someone to go to Jerry's to arrest her."

Even if she doesn't have any dope on her, we have a felony case because she just sold it to our suspect. It takes a minute or two for our marked scout car to pull the Corvette over. I can see our suspect toss the dope into his mouth, hoping to swallow it. No dope, no case. We are not the type of department that is going to obtain a search warrant to pump someone's stomach. I grab him with a Bengal Tiger death grip around the neck.

"Spit it out," I yell. "Spit it out!"

The other officers have no idea what I'm doing, and they step back. After several gags, he coughs up two rocks of crack cocaine. Now the officers understand what is going on, and I put the cocaine into a small evidence envelope. I jump back in my car to get on the radio to see if they caught the female in Jerry's. I'm thinking about the officers from my crew who made the traffic stop. It is almost impossible to work the streets and never see a guy swallow dope when attempting to make an arrest. It was glaring the inexperience my crew had.

I pull up to Jerry's and no one is there. I ask the rest of the crew for their location. They are en route. How in the hell did I beat them here? I walk through the bar by myself and find no one. I look at the bartender and he has that, "I don't know" look.

"Where is she?" I ask, and he doesn't respond.

His failure to respond tells me she is in here somewhere. I push open the ladies room door and can see one stall, and one set of golden sandals with feet in them. I tell her to come out, and she claims she is busy. I yank open the door, and she is trying to hide a brown lunch bag in the trash. I cuff her and retrieve the bag. It is about half full of powder, and rock cocaine.

Nice job, Bubble — You witnessed the crime, chased down both suspects and cuffed them both. I might as well do the paperwork, process the evidence and finish it with court testimony to convict both suspects. It is great having a bunch of ass-kissing inexperienced crewmembers.

It confirms my suspicions that there are two police departments working in Detroit. One I call the working class officers, and the other I call the kissing-ass officers. As I've said before, this is a very dangerous combination.

There was a plus with this case, as I had an opportunity to joust with the defense attorney. The main issue would concern the swallowing and recovery of the narcotics. On the day of the trial, I am questioned by the prosecutor and then turned over to the defense attorney for cross-examination. I'm ready, as is the defense attorney who, as usual, begins strutting. The prosecution had asked about the recovery, and I had testified that I witnessed him place the crack cocaine in his mouth, at which time he began choking, and I attempted to help him. This was the truth. Well, maybe minus a word or two about my intentions, but it was the truth. The defense attorney starts building his case for that all-important Coup de gras question.

"Officer, do you know if my client has any type of medical condition?"

"No."

"Bronchitis, emphysema?"

"No, I am unaware of any medical problem."

The defense attorney has pulled the trap spring back and triggers the release.

"Officer, if you are unaware of any medical condition my client might have, then how in the heck did you know he was choking?"

Now, delivery on the stand is everything. You don't want to hesitate, and you don't want to act surprised.

I looked directly at him, and in a loud voice said, "You mean besides the gasping for air, the gurgling obstructed sounds, the tears from his eyes, the red face and the coughing?"

I actually could see him deflate as he shuffled to his seat. He meekly said, "No further questions," and sat down.

I gave a quick smile to the defense attorney as I walked out. It's good to have that experience, which fuels confidence. It wasn't learned by reading a book, but through years of testimony. In the beginning, I had stumbled many times. I always flashed back to years ago. The, "Officer, where is the knife?" Experience always kept me humble. Confident, but humble.

All of these lessons helped me develop solid investigative skills. I couldn't stand the, "not knowing." Lack of information can get officers killed. The whole not knowing aspect bothered me. If I didn't know, I wanted to learn. Where was the knife? I had no clue on the day that question was posed. You can bet that finding out where that knife was number one on my list.

Police Officer Neil Keith Wells
Detroit Police Department, Michigan
End of Watch: Wednesday, April 4, 2001

Officer Neil Wells was shot and killed while he and other officers were investigating a complaint of drug dealing in a partially vacant apartment building. Officer Wells was in plain clothes and wore a vest. As he searched the building, he encountered one of the suspects and was shot twice, once in the chest and once in the side, with an AK-47 rifle. At least one of the rounds bypassed his vest. Three suspects were apprehended at the scene shortly after the shooting. It was learned the shooter had been released early from prison after using a false name. He was apprehended after murdering Officer Wells, and sentenced to sixty-two to ninety-two years for the murder.

Officer Wells was a member of a unit that policed high-crime areas. He had been employed with the Detroit Police Department for fourteen years, and is survived by a teenage son and a teenage daughter.

RESISTING TEMPTATION

Not only did the team lack experience, the unit lacked solid intelligence skills. I came to work one day and was told they wanted me to infiltrate a high-end card game. Okay, where was it? They had the address, but nothing else. What do you mean nothing else? Who is developing this stuff? Just try it, they tell me — knock on the door they might let you in.

I make the location, which is at the back of a business establishment. There is a thick steel security door, which opens out. All the cars in back are luxury vehicles, and I'm dressed in a suit, which is a good thing. I knock on the door, and an eye-level slot on the door slides open. The guy on the other side looks just like me — big and Italian.

He asks, "What?"

"Looking for the game," I respond.

He laughs and slides the slot shut, and I can hear loud laughing inside. I walk back to my car, with my thoughts racing. First, I'm thankful I didn't get in. It removes the risk of Antonio Andolini ending up with an ice pick in his eye. Second, who comes up with this kind of plan? It was no plan, no intelligence. The stress of work is starting to spill over into my everyday life.

My last operation probably pushed me over the edge. I got a call at home, and was told to dress up for work. We were going to be doing a joint operation with several agencies. The action would include county and federal jurisdictions.

I show up at the base, and find out we will be working with thirty officers. A county guy is going to brief me. They are targeting a specific a person who sets up high-end parties. This operation will be taking place at a local bar on the southwest side of Detroit. It is a mob kind of thing, big money with expensive girls. I will be taking the male rookie in with me and the county guy hands me two tickets worth seventy-five dollars apiece. He says get in, observe as much illegal activity as we can, spot the target, and signal the crew. That's it, he says.

"Okay, mind if I ask a question? Where did you get the tickets?"

"That's none of your concern," he tells me.

I tell him, it is my concern because that probably is going to be the first question they ask me. I explain to him that I'm guessing there only are about a hundred tickets. My tickets have a number on them, so I am assuming someone is keeping track. They probably have a checklist for each number as that ticket enters the location. As I am the undercover operative with no gun, I would like to know where the hell the tickets came from. He now admits to me he really doesn't know. Great. This guy would fit in perfect with SATF.

I brief the rookie, who looks completely lost. We load up in the undercover car and head to the bar. I give it a drive-by to check the activity, and can see it is packed. Now bless their souls, I love the feds, but some of them really don't know what is going on. I notice a general assignment car parked right across the street from the front entrance. Two white guys in suits are trying to blend in. Trust me, they are not blending.

This bar is in southwest Detroit in the neighborhood where I grew up. I'm hoping I don't bump into anyone I know. Although I've never been in the place before, there is a first time for everything. We walk through the front door, and immediately see a long table with about ten people sitting at it. I recognize three of them as police officers. One of them I used to work with. He jumps up and yells, "Hey Bob."

He looks me up and down, and sees I'm dressed for a night out. His mind spins and it must click what unit I am working with. His face loses color and the hug he was going to give me now turns into flight out the door. Some cops are pretty perceptive. I'm concerned my cover is blown even before I got started. I quickly glance around the room. Nobody seems to have noticed, and the first floor appears to be just a regular bar.

There's no way the cars outside match the number of people I see inside. I notice a large stairway at the end of the bar, which doubles back. Dragging my rookie, I head for it. I can see we are going in the right direction, as we pass by several well-dressed people. On the stairway, there is a small crowd. They are being stopped at the top of the stairs, as two big guys in suits are checking everyone coming in.

Everyone has to present their tickets, which are checked off of a board before you are allowed in. It makes sense that if you were throwing an illegal private party and gave out X-amount of tickets, that you would know which ones were missing, if by chance you lost some of them. Does that thought sound familiar?

We get to the top of the stairs, and I present our tickets. I've already told my rookie to remain silent. The guy with the broken nose and no neck checks the list, and looks at the other no-neck guy. Both give me the fish eye. I tell him my name is Tony. They must not be the brightest bulbs on the tree because they let us in. I figure out right away that we are on the clock, because someone eventually is going to come to their senses and question who we are and how we got the tickets.

I'm doing a super quick scan trying to pick up anything illegal. I can almost hear my rookie's knees clacking. I spot the target of the operation, and he's dressed in a black tuxedo. The feds are trying to pull an Al Capone on him and prosecute him for tax evasion. I scan the room, and we appear to be in the liquor serving area. This is attached to a bigger banquet type area. I know I have to work my way over to the bigger room where the action is.

As I drag my rookie, I get a tap on my shoulder. Another guy in a suit asks if he can have a word with me. I say sure, and he asks us to step downstairs. I realize my plane now is on fire, and I better grab a parachute. We walk downstairs and he asks us to have a seat at a round table in the back. He pulls our tickets from his pocket and asks where we got them. I go into speed undercover mode. I tell him I was at a topless bar on Eight Mile Road and ended up drinking with a guy named Frank. He was wearing a high-end suit, and looked like he had money. After a couple of hours, we are both drunk and he tells me about this great party next week. He says there's going to be plenty of fine woman and drinks. He says he bought tickets for it, but has to fly to L.A. and will miss the whole thing. I tell him that's too bad because it sounds like a good time. He tells me he can get me in, and if I have one hundred fifty dollars for the tickets. I know the bartender and give him the look and point to Frank. The bartender gives me thumbs up, and I buy the tickets. So here we are. I brought my boy, for his birthday. He just turned twenty-four years old. We are old southwest siders and ...

The guy now cuts me off. He looks at my rookie and asks, "Does he talk?"

"Of course he does," I say.

My rookie gives a dull, "Yeah."

The guy starts explaining to me that the tickets were stolen. I jump up and ask whether he's accusing me of stealing those tickets. If I did, why wouldn't I just try and sell them? Why would I show up? He apologizes to me and says we can't go back in because the tickets were stolen. I'm going crazy, and get real loud.

"So, I'm out one hundred fifty bucks, and our whole night is shot?!" I shout.

He continues to apologize, and asks me to sit back down. He then asks how can he make it right.

"Let me back in," I say.

He tells me that is not going to happen. He pulls out a large money roll and starts peeling off twenties. He lays out one hundred dollars and asks if that will do it.

"Absolutely not. I paid one hundred fifty dollars," I say.

He peels off the rest and says, "Here, take the money."

I told him our night is ruined.

"We drove all the way up from down river," I added.

He peels off an additional fifty dollars and tells me that should more than cover the inconvenience. I scoop it up and tell him okay. I knew it was a done deal anyway, and he wasn't letting us back in.

Previously, I've recovered large amounts of money in narcotic raids. The thought never crossed my mind about taking any of it. Now in this case, I felt I had put on an academy award performance, equal to any of the great thespians. I really was thinking of just pocketing the money. It was fed money to begin with.

It is scary how temptation can challenge a police officer. We left the location and met the supervisors for debriefing. The whole crew is there and I turn over the two hundred bucks and tell the story.

Keeping the money was just not what I was about. It never was.

THE BEGINNING OF THE END

We then hit the place and they arrested a bunch of people, including several of the girls. Once we head back to the base, one of these girls ends up missing. Apparently, one of the county guys let her go. He actually took the cuffs off of her and let her go. It caused a huge investigation, and made me think that my department wasn't the only one infested with problem officers.

After this incident, I finally got up enough ass to sit down with Wood. I told him I couldn't do this anymore. It had become so dangerous, I was afraid to come to work. I told him that I had busted my hump for him, and the only thing I expected was to be transferred to a precinct of my choice.

Wood told me that going to the precinct of my choice would be a one-for-one trade. I would be replacing the person Wood picked to come into his unit. Whoever they took, I would have to go to that precinct. It amazed me how dense he was. I told him I was not one of his rookies. He worked under an inspector who reports directly to the chief. He could get this transfer thing done. He said he would try, but I already knew the outcome and hoped for the best.

I had the next five days off and felt like a weight had been lifted off my shoulders. I requested one of my old precincts and kept my fingers crossed. Two days later, I got a call from our clerk. I always liked her, and she just wanted to give me a heads up that I had been transferred to the 10th Precinct. Number 10? Their reputation wasn't the best, and they were known as a dumping ground for misfit officers.

She told me I never was going to go to the precinct I requested. Wood wanted a guy from the east side and he was all set to go to SATF. The day before the transfer, the guy beats up his girlfriend. The transfer is nixed, and Wood's second choice comes out of Number 10. That's how this thing works. I was going to Number 10.

No worries — it was just good to be free of all the ass kissing and danger.

6ᵀᴴ COMMAND - TENTH PRECINCT

GOODBYE AND HELLO

On my last day off, the unit called and wanted me to come in. Slim liked me and convinced me that if I came in, we would work for about four hours and then celebrate my release. He knew I was unhappy and really wasn't cut out for this type of police work. The pace was way too slow, and he knew the ass kissing was killing me. I was going to miss some of the people on the team, and others not at all.

So we sit around doing paperwork at the base for the first few hours, then pick up a couple of cases of beer. We found a secluded spot about two blocks from the base and conducted choir practice. The whole unit showed. Nine hours later we still were there, and someone had called the police on us twice.

There were tears and hugs as we parted. We probably shouldn't have been driving, but we all made it home. I did take some good memories with me, as well as some valuable experiences. This unit was my first full dose of the department politics. I knew about the politics, everyone did, but experiencing it first hand was something completely different.

My first day at the 10th Precinct, I was wearing a black mark. Rumors were running rampant, and I could hear the whispers, "How does a guy from a specialized unit end up in #10?" No one wants a new dog in the pack.

"Was he a spy for the chief's office?" They would have laughed if they knew I requested a transfer. Officers would give their right arm to get out of the precinct. I was out, but now was coming back. I knew I was facing all of this when I stepped through those doors, but it really didn't faze me. Cops know cops, and it doesn't take long to recognize the workers. Everything would sort itself out over time.

I really don't know how to express precinct life, let alone Number Ten. Number Three was precinct life, but it was at a much slower and secluded pace. Ten was the real deal. You would have good bosses and bad bosses. There would be good cops and bad ones, and senior officers and rookies. It's a jambalaya of police officers. The one constant thing anywhere is a line drawn between the workers and non-workers. The workers do it because they like it. The non-workers are here for the pay (and to explain to the workers why they shouldn't work so hard).

The first thing I noticed when I walked through the doors for the afternoon shift was the inspector. She was female, and stood in the middle of the lobby with her arms crossed. She looked like a person surveying her kingdom. The first thought that came to my mind was Benito Mussolini, El Duce. You may have seen those old World War II photos of him, jaw jutting out, just oozing arrogance. That was her. We would butt heads on a regular basis my whole time at Number 10. Somehow, I knew it from that very first glance.

I was fortunate, and ended up on a pretty good shift. There were plenty of young officers who were enthusiastic and willing to learn — which were my kind of people. It seems that at every precinct, each shift is comprised of the same type of cops: Senior people who did nothing. Mind you, they were experienced but avoided work. They were content to work patrol their whole career. They would sometimes back you up if they weren't doing anything else like eating, shopping, paying bills, etc. If you were in trouble, they always showed (it just might take them a little longer, but they showed).

You had your over-the-top senior officers. They worked, but they did so on their own agenda and by their own rules. These officers were dangerous because they could make quite an impression on younger officers. They come in with confiscated guns and dope and appeared like heroes to the younger officers. The problem is that some of those confiscations may have been questionable. You hope the rookies are not drawn to this dark side. Then there are the workers. They always are there, no matter what. They do it by the book, and are willing to volunteer for any run or to back anyone up. They are doing the job, and doing it right. I felt it took about five years of working the street to get me there. This is where the camaraderie comes in on the job. The group of workers grows tight.

Then there are the wide-eyed and confused rookies who always will be in their own category. It is the unspoken job of the experienced officers to keep them alive until they get seasoned enough to fly on their own. Then you have the quiet police officers, the ones who do the job at a steady pace. They don't have great arrests or great numbers, but they are there every day doing it.

Lastly, there was the administrative staff: The people who volunteered to work inside. You're supposed to be a police officer, why would you work inside? That tells you what type of officers they were. Unfortunately, we always were at their mercy, as everything had to be processed through the front desk. So, you worked as quickly as they worked, which could be pretty frustrating sometimes. While there were some good staff people, it wasn't the norm.

I must admit it really felt good to be back on the street doing police work. I knew there would be a whole lot more bad than good when it was done, but it's where I belonged.

My first day at #10, they put me in a one-man car. I no sooner got off the ramp when I made a felony arrest on a warrant. I knew what category of officer I belonged in, and this would start me down that road of acceptance.

My second day at the precinct, I was seated in the squad room, when I saw an old guy walk by. If I had to guess, I would say he was about 80 years old. He was kind of dressed like a policeman, and I stood up to get a better look at him. He was hunched over as he slow rolled by the door. He was wearing a faded blue short-sleeved shirt and a badge but had no nametag. He had on blue police pants, but they didn't match the shirt. He had on a gun belt, with a gun in the holster. The holster once was black but it now was so worn that you could see the brown leather. His cartridge holder had three different types of rusty rounds in it. He had on black boots, which were dirty and worn like the gun belt.

I had to ask a guy in the squad room who he was. I was told he was the oldest guy on the job. Okay, has anyone in our command structure noticed this guy walking around? First off, he represents the entire department, and he looks like a homeless bagman. Second, he is armed. If you don't want him to retire, put him somewhere where he doesn't have to deal with the public. You certainly don't let him drive around in a marked police unit.

Luckily, he wasn't assigned to our precinct. Usually, the new guy has to work with one of the unwanted members. I would have gone home if he were my new partner. I never did see that guy again, and often wondered what happened to him.

Police Officer Michael T. Scanlon
Detroit Police Department, Michigan
End of Watch: Tuesday, February 12, 2002
Officer Michael Scanlon was stabbed to death after making a traffic stop in Redford Township at about 2150 hours.

Officer Scanlon was working a traffic detail in the Eighth Precinct when he observed the driver of a vehicle make an illegal turn onto Six Mile. He followed the vehicle into Redford Township, where he initiated a traffic stop on Beech Daly Road. After the vehicle stopped, he removed the driver from the vehicle and began to frisk him. While searching the suspect, the suspect attempted to flee and was tackled by Officer Scanlon. During the ensuing struggle, the suspect stabbed Officer Scanlon in the neck and back nine times. While trying to defend himself, Officer Scanlon shot the suspect in the chest, seriously wounding him. The round also struck Officer Scanlon in the arm. The suspect then stole Officer Scanlon's patrol car and service weapon and drove himself to the hospital, where he was taken into custody. Another person in the suspect's vehicle also fled the scene. The suspect was convicted of murder in September 2002 and sentenced to life in prison.

Officer Scanlon had been employed with the Detroit Police Department for seven years. He is survived by his wife, two young children, brother and sister.

YOU MIGHT NEED A NEW LINE OF WORK

While at Number 10, I didn't work patrol very long but I did have some fun doing it. One day, we received a run on a dead baby in the basement of a vacant house. I was working with a female partner, and when we pulled up in front of the location, she got a little fidgety. I asked her what was wrong, and she said she couldn't see that. I asked, "See what?"

"A dead baby," she said.

"You stay on this job and you are going to see more than a dead baby," I told her.

She told me she just couldn't stand to see that, and wasn't getting out of the car. I told her at the minimum, she was getting out of the car to back me up.

"I'll go in the basement, but you will be on the porch to protect me," I added.

I noted to myself that she couldn't protect herself let alone anyone else. I'm pissed as I walk down the stairs, knowing I don't want to see a dead baby either, but we have a job to do.

I have my gun out and go into creeper mode. The basement smells musty, but there's no death smell. As I look into the first room, I can see a small head and hair. Shit, there is a dead baby. This is where many people fail to recognize what an officer deals with every day. Can you imagine your emotions on finding a dead baby?

As I peer around the corner, I see another head, and the pasty white body of the first baby. Oh my god, there are multiple dead babies. I now step into the doorway, and I see a room full of dead babies. I'm estimating fifty bodies. I flip to police mode, and my first thought is that I'm going to be here forever doing paper work. I know I'm trying to block out the death of an infant, as there is nothing more tragic in police work.

Then I realize they are baby dolls. There are no clothes or shoes, just a room full of baby dolls. What if they were real babies?

I begin to think of the mental case who gathered all these dolls and how long it took. He probably pushed around a grocery cart, filling it whenever he could.

Relieved, now I'm going to give my partner the business. She asks if there is a dead baby down there, and I tell her there actually are a bunch of them. She gags and almost vomits. I tell her they have been down there for some time, and it's not pretty. She starts to tear up and gags again.

Satisfied that I have gotten my point across, I inform her there is no need to worry, as they are baby dolls and not real babies. I remind her of other job opportunities she can look for, as I really don't think this is her line of work. She has dried her tears, tidied herself up and looks at me.

"Why would I?" she asks.

I never worked with her again.

IT'S NOT LEG OF LAMB

On occasion, we would get runs on suspected human remains. One day, I had with me an out-of-the-box brand new rookie, and we were dispatched to investigate a "possible human remains" in a vacant field just off of Grand River. A look of apprehension was all over my partner's face. I had been a rookie before, and I knew what was running through his head. We arrived at the scene and began walking through a field, searching for who knows what. I knew his mind was racing at this point, fully expecting to find a mangled or decomposing body. I'm pretty sure he wasn't ready for that, and you actually could feel how nervous he was.

Experience told me that unless you get a couple of police calls to the same location, you probably wouldn't find a body. We might find something, but not a body. He walked gingerly glancing back and forth, and I marched with a purpose. The quicker we found it, the quicker we were out of there. I soon discovered the reason for the call. Lying on top of a clump of matted weeds was a large leg bone with scraps of meat attached.

"Got it," I yelled to my partner, and motioned him over.

Like I said before, you never know what you are going to do the first time you are confronted with this type of situation. He is expecting something horrible, just as I had years ago. He doesn't want to throw up or, even worse, faint. There's nothing worse than a passed-out police officer.

He peeks over the tall grass, and yells, "Oh my god, someone's leg!"

I am trying to stifle my giggles as I ask, "Someone's leg? Who's, a giant's or maybe even a brontosaurus?"

The girth and length of the bone almost is a dead giveaway for a cow leg. The knee joint is huge. He starts wringing his hands and repeating, "That's someone's leg right there."

I have to grab him to stop his pacing.

"Look," I tell him. "You've seen a skeleton, does that look anything like a leg bone?"

"It might," he says.

I tell him to compare it to his own leg. He looks at it and realizes the bone, by itself, almost is bigger than his own leg. His face now floods with relief. He is happy again, and life is good.

All of these reactions tell you a little something about the officer. He has potential, and can even laugh at himself a little bit. Lesson one on a run on suspected human remains has been learned. Twenty minutes ago, he didn't know it, but now he does. My final conclusion is that he is a good kid and willing to learn. It looks like he is heading down the road to that good officer category.

THIS AIN'T HAIR SPRAY

I've said this once, I've said it a thousand times: I'm always paranoid about being shot by one of my coworkers. That first trip to the range planted that seed. Being thrust into a new bunch of officers always is harrowing. You keep a close eye on everyone. You learn to watch the bad guys first and the police second. Many a day I've had a gun pointed at me by coworkers. Not deliberately mind you, they just weren't paying attention or weren't caring.

So when the department graduated up to a secondary weapon, it created a second paranoia for me. Pepper spray was not as deadly, but it certainly was dangerous.

There also was a chance we were going to get tasers. We had a nasty incident in the 1970s where the cellblock officers were using cattle prods to control the prisoners. There was a rumor running around that we didn't get the tasers because of the misuse of those cattle prods. Detroit had a dark past that current officers constantly would be paying for.

So pepper spray was going to have to do. I have been on the job twenty-five years and have never deployed pepper spray. I looked at it this way: Imagine a lion attacking you. If you pepper-spray him, he is not going to stop and start sneezing and rub his eyes. He really is going to hurry his process of killing you. It's the same thing with bad guys. Some officers thought it was a save-all and used it all the time. I just never thought it was that effective. Use that mouth of yours and talk to people the right way. That always was my secondary.

I was working with a new guy and had an opportunity to experience pepper spray first hand. He wasn't a fresh out-of-the-box rookie, but close to it. We had a domestic violence run, and had the husband up against the front porch wall. He and the wife had been arguing and it turned a bit violent. He wasn't completely complying with our orders, but he wasn't fighting either. This is where talking to a suspect becomes so critical. I am telling the husband to relax, when the new guy pulls his pepper spray.

"Stop resisting or you are going to be pepper sprayed," he yells.

I start telling my partner to hold on one second, but he deploys the pepper spray. He is holding it less than a foot from the suspect's face, and delivers a three-second burst. Just like the academy teaches, he has warned the suspect and delivers the proper burst. The problem was he missed the suspect and sends the stream directly into my left eye.

Now I become the blinded lion, and start swiping at my partner. He does an excellent job of avoiding my swings, and is apologizing in speed mode.

The only good thing about this whole fiasco is the suspect quits resisting, and attempts to assist me. He repeatedly asks if I'm okay, and hollers for his wife to bring water. He is very compassionate, and even turns around so I can cuff him.

I quickly convey him and my weepy eye back to the precinct, as my partner keeps repeating, "I'm sorry, sir. I'm sorry, sir."

"Forget it — I will recover. But," I say, "just remember if you ever deploy pepper spray around me again, I'll kill you."

This incident worked out okay, but others can have deadly consequences. I have talked about officers screaming over the radio for help. It always is a stomach-turning feeling and no matter who is doing the screaming, everyone responds to help.

Two of our female officers were working together and they were both zeros. They avoided action like the plague and to hear them even come on the radio was a rarity. On this particular day, they come over the air, screaming for help. We can hear them struggling, but can't clearly understand either of them. We request their location and dispatch gives us the address that they responded to for a disturbance.

We pull up to the location within minutes. It is a large apartment building, and we can see the first officer sitting on the steps with her head hanging between her legs. Our adrenaline meter just went from high to redline. Your experience tells you to scan everything as you run up. Look at cars, people, windows — everything.

She is by herself and crying. We have no idea if she is injured or where her partner is. My heart sinks, fearing the worse. As I tilt her head back, I can smell the pepper spray. I ask if she is all right, and I want to know where her partner is.

"I'm fine," she states. "My partner is in the lobby."

We hit the door, which like any Detroit apartment building, is locked. I hit every buzzer and someone lets us in. We rush to the lobby and find her partner on the ground, trading blow for blow with another female. We dive in, drag them apart and quickly cuff the woman. It looked like we had missed the first couple rounds of a great fight. There were torn clothes, pulled hair and police equipment everywhere. And there was plenty of cussing and yelling. We finally settle the officer down and get the story.

Management of the apartment building had called because they wanted a female intruder out of the lobby. She had snuck in because it was very cold outside. When the officers arrived, they told her she had to leave, at which time she refused because she was freezing to death outside.

This is where a police run can and will go bad if not handled properly. If I'm there, I tell her we will find her a warming center to take her to and make sure she gets a meal. Our tag-team gals tell her that she better get her ass moving or she is going to get locked up. Disrespect is the number one motivator of fights on the street. The suspect tells the officers they can go ahead and try to lock her up, and the fight was on. One officer tries to spray the girl, misses and sprays her partner. The sprayed officer wants some relief, runs out of the building and locks herself out, leaving her partner to duke it out with one very pissed off lady. This minor run now had turned deadly in seconds. Our transient lady now had to make the trip to the cellblock for fighting with the officers. Poor judgment ruined everyone's day, including mine.

I guess I'll go ahead and admit I did deploy my pepper spray once. It probably contributed to my hate of it. I was in the squad room completing a report, and making a phone notification. There were several rookies in the room cutting up but keeping a watchful eye on me. Rookies always are scared of senior people, no matter what type of officer you are. I notice the smell of pepper spray and start yelling at them.

"What did I tell you guys about using that pepper spray? Now someone has a leaking canister because of all the grab-assing," I say.

The curious thing was that pepper spray makes a distinct sound when it is deployed, and as I hadn't heard that, I assumed someone just had a faulty can. Rookies always fiddle with their equipment, and would shake the pepper spray for some unknown reason. The room was soon filled, and within minutes, we all were scratching and crying.

Just as I was preparing to evacuate, I reached down to check my spray and discovered I was leaning it against the counter just enough for it to seep out. It's good to be experienced, as I yelled at the rookies for being a bunch of idiots and that they should have listened to me about pepper spray deployment.

As I wipe my face dry, I tell them that if I find out which one of them had a leaking can, I'll kill them. They scurry away in fear whispering to each other. I smile, knowing I was there once myself — scurrying from the thundering of a senior officer.

AVOIDS BECOMING SWISS CHEESE

You have to be careful with rookies sometimes. One of the things you learn on the street is to yell to your partner. This may sound simple, but for a police officer, it is a decision you have to make in a split second. If I yell, the bad guys will hear me. Should I get on the radio? What should I do? I learned to yell and yell loud. Say you are chasing a guy on foot, he jumps several fences and is heading in your partner's direction. The first impulse as a young officer is to get on the radio, and give the suspect's direction. This is exactly how you are trained. By the time you do all this, he probably has run right by your partner, or worse, attacked him. You know danger is heading your partner's way, warn them and warn them loud.

This almost backfired on me once. We were servicing a shots fired run, and were out on foot. The scene was a residential area with no streetlights. I was with an experienced partner, but we had a whole gaggle of rookies show up looking for the excitement. They have spread out like ants sniffing for action. They have no idea what to do with it if they find it, but you have to love their enthusiasm. I don't want to get shot, so I make mental notes of where the rookies are searching.

I now am positioned about three or four doors down from the bulk of them, when a full-sized van comes roaring west bound with no lights on. It screeches to a halt, one house east of me, and I now have my gun out and leveled at the van. The side passenger door opens, and a body either falls out or is pushed from the vehicle. The door slams, and the van now accelerates west bound. The rookies have seen the van, but not the body.

"He dumped a body out," I scream, realizing in an instant that this is not enough information for the rookies.

I am looking at them and they have all drawn their guns. The van almost is to them, and I want to look away. I know if any of them squeezes the trigger, they all will open up. This van is going to turn into Swiss cheese in a hurry. Fortunately, all of them make the right decision, and no one fires.

I run to the body, discovering a lady trying to stand. It is obvious she has been beaten, and her ankle is broken. I tell her I will order EMS, and she refuses. I ask her what happened, and she tells me she was drinking with her boyfriend and got in a fight. This was before domestic violence laws were in effect, and she doesn't want to press charges. She informs me most of the time she whoops his ass, but he got the drop on her today.

"I gots this one, officer," she yells back to me as she limps down the street. "Don't you worry, I gots this one."

Neither one of them had any idea how close they had been to getting shot.

"I'M GOING TO JAIL" MOMENTS

The precinct was feeling me out, and I was doing the same thing to the precinct. The first couple of weeks, I got to work alone several times. This is good and bad. The good is that you are by yourself and can prowl. The bad is they give you all the crap runs, including missing persons, accidents and parking complaints. Well, I had one of my "I'm going to jail moments" while servicing an accident run by myself. All working officers will have these "going to jail" moments more than once.

On this day, I am dispatched to an accident run on Joy Road west of Dexter. I pull up, and see two parked cars at the curb, with a full-sized van in between them. The problem is that the van is backing into the car behind him, then smashing into the car in front of him. He is doing this as fast as he can operate the gearshift. I can see the driver is elderly, about sixty-five years old.

There is a woman in the parked car behind him, and through her open window, she yells to me that he is trying to leave the scene and she has him pinned in. The vehicles are so close, he can't pull out, so he continues to smash forward then back. I walk right up to the van, and he doesn't even know I am there. He has a blank look on his face and just continues crashing.

To me, it is obvious he is high or drunk. I start pounding on the window, and he looks at me with that same blank stare, and continues working the gearshift. I am starting to get upset, and really bang the window. This only seems to encourage his actions.

Quite a large crowd now is on scene. They are shouting, but I have them tuned out, and concentrate on the task at hand. I entertain the idea of breaking out the window, but fear I might injure the old-timer.

Suddenly, he puts the car in park, and unlocks the door. Now, that wasn't so hard, but I'm pissed and yank the door open and pull him out. I now am yelling, and have spun him around to cuff him. He still is maintaining that blank look, and I can smell no alcohol on him. Once I secured the cuffs, he crumples to the ground. I now notice his eyes completely are dilated, at which time someone from the crowd screams, "The officer is killing him."

What? Killing him? I look around, and now the entire the crowd is screaming. I am hearing every other word, and it is not good. "Kill," "officer," "him," "motherfucker," "that's how the police do."

I get on the radio to call for assistance and request an EMS. The crowd is getting louder and begins to closes in. I'm actually starting to think that I am killing this guy. I already have taken the cuffs off of him, and this does little to help. He is completely unresponsive, and his eyes are fixed, staring upward. I yell back to the crowd that I'm not killing him. It is not my best yell, and is fraught with fear.

Have I killed this poor guy, and I'm going to prison for the rest of my life?

Backup finally arrives, and I feel a little bit safer. EMS also is at the scene and loads the guy into the back of their unit. I nervously pace outside, and open the side door to inquire about the patient. I'm told it doesn't look good. Doesn't look good? Is he kidding? EMS can see I'm upset, and tells me they are going to try two of the ghetto miracle cures. Narcan is one. Give this to someone who has overdosed, and they wake up fighting. It probably saves them, but they want to fight because you have just ruined their high. The other is Dextrose 50. This is for diabetics with low blood sugar. They start with the D-50, and it truly is a miracle because he comes right back to life.

All of those images of me in a state-issued orange jumpsuit disappear. I'm overjoyed, as the only thing I'm stuck with is an accident report. I hate those reports, but will do it gladly.

I walk around the EMS unit and inform the crowd that the man is going to be fine. I have the patient wave to the crowd to confirm his wellbeing. A loud cheer goes up. Traffic, adjacent to the EMS, still is at a standstill with all the gawkers who are cheering. A guy on a motorcycle now rear-ends the car next to the EMS, which causes him to cartwheel in the air thirty feet, clearing the car he has hit. He lands violently on the hood of an SUV, shattering the windshield.

This just wasn't my day, as the crowd started up again.

"Did you see that? The officer caused that guy on the motorcycle to wreck."

POTS & PANS, NAKEDNESS AND LOUD MUSIC

Every police run helps you hone your skills. Experience will teach you not to become complacent because of the nature of the run. They all are different, so be prepared for it. I always felt police runs, and how they are handled, are big parts of supervision. It is the meat and potatoes of police work. This is where you learn the basics. If you never work the street, you never will know. Pay attention, as each one will teach its own lesson.

One day, we serviced a police run, where a woman was throwing pots and pans at the neighborhood kids.

That's exactly how it was dispatched. Remember I talked about running scenarios through your head when responding to a run? You can imagine what I was thinking. We turn the corner onto our listed street, and can tell the address is going to be about mid-block. We already are scanning far ahead, and as we approach, I can see the front yard is full of pots and pans. Not a couple, but like fifty were scattered all over. We park one house down, and can see about ten little kids running from the scene.

The address is a two-family flat, and I can see the reason for our run.

A female who is about thirty years old sits in a kitchen chair completely naked. She is on the second floor porch with a pot in one hand and a boom box blaring in the other. I ask if she could please turn down the radio. I'm using a very calm voice, knowing at this point she holds all the cards. She turns down the music, and I ask her to come down and talk to us.

"Wait!" I yell to her, knowing I almost missed something, and ask her to first put on some clothes.

This doesn't need a lot of reading into. She obviously is loony, and the trick is to get her outside so we can talk. She complies and bounces down the stairs. As she bursts through the front door, she still is arranging the large floral moo moo she has put on. Now I can get a bit firmer and ask her what the heck she thinks she is doing. She tells me the kids aggravate her, so she started throwing pots at them to keep them off her lawn. Okay, I can almost see that. After all, this is Detroit. I give her the don't-kill-the-kid-with-a-pot lecture, the no-loud-music lecture, and the no-being-naked-in-public lecture.

She seems to be cooperating, but every time she speaks, she raises her hands. This allows the moo moo to ride all the way up to her chest. This not only exposes her kitty, but a horrible jagged scar that runs diagonally across her large midsection. You could rest a softball in her belly button. I guess you get the picture.

I now want to cut the conversation right there so she will stop raising her hands. I honestly couldn't take one more look. She assures us she will stop with the music, the pan throwing and the nakedness. With moo moo flowing, she heads back up to her perch. I hated to send her back in the house, and knew we were taking a chance.

It was a bad choice, as I can hear her stomp up the stairs, and she soon appears on the upper porch. She looks directly at me, and pulls off the moo moo. She reaches over, turns the boom box up all the way and plops herself into a chair. Everything jiggled for a moment and then came to rest.

Now I start kicking the pots and pans around. Long story short, we finally get a hold of the landlord and a passkey to allow us in the house. We carefully made our way to the second floor, finding her now waiting for us. She was naked on the couch and had armed herself with a hatchet. A very awkward brawl ensued, and the only thing we lost was some dignity.

She ended up getting a free ride to the Crisis Center, and we learned a lesson. Next time why take a chance? She should have made the trip the first time she came downstairs.

Police Officer Scott T. Stewart
Detroit Police Department, Michigan
End of Watch: Sunday, August 11, 2002
Officer Scott Stewart was shot and killed as he placed a suspect under arrest for illegally possessing a handgun. Officer Stewart and his partner were called to the 11200 block of Corbette regarding a group of men gambling on the sidewalk. When they arrived, Officer Stewart discovered one man was carrying a concealed handgun. As Officer Stewart was cuffing the suspect, another man approached Officer Stewart from behind and fired one shot at his head. Officer Stewart was rushed to St. John's Hospital, where he died several hours later from his wound. The suspect fled the scene, but turned himself in the following day. The man was convicted of first-degree murder and sentenced to life in prison, with no possibility of parole.

Officer Stewart was assigned to the Ninth Precinct, and had been employed with the Detroit Police Department for five years. He is survived by his fiancée, who also is a Detroit Police Officer, and his parents, and two sisters.

BAD IMPRESSIONS

I have talked about having a special place for rookies. You could tell right away if they had heart. The department made every effort not to pair up rookies in a scout car. I never have seen two out-of-the-box rookies together, but have seen a rookie paired up with someone having only a year on the job. It was the same difference, as far as I was concerned. It took me five years to feel comfortable on the job. You can see the danger. The point is, I always try to make their runs.

One of our younger scout car crews received a possible dead body run. I pulled up to find the primary unit (young officers) on scene with an EMS unit that was treating the victim. It was a horrible scene. There was a female, who was about twenty-five years old, completely nude and badly beaten. Her nipples had been sliced off, and a broken broom handle jutted from her vagina. It was easy to see the young guys were shaken. Hell, even the old guys were shaken. I asked the officers if they had made their notifications. They told me they had. It seemed obvious there was some type of sexual assault, and I informed them that sex crimes should be notified. They left for several minutes and when they returned, they told me sex crimes did not need to be notified. I asked who told them that?

"The guy at sex crimes," they answered.

I dialed sex crimes, asking for the officer who gave that advice. I asked him if he fielded the call, and he said yes. He explained that if she died, homicide would handle it. I told him I knew procedure but felt they would be interested in this type of crime.

"Why?" he responded.

"Because her nipples have been cut off and she has a broom handle jammed up her crotch!" I screamed into the phone.

I'm not the brightest bulb on the tree, but that seemed to be some type of sexual thing. He began back peddling, but I knew I was fighting a losing battle. The obvious explanation was he just didn't care, or was too lazy to write anything down.

This was very common for my department. It didn't matter if you couldn't do your job. When I was a young officer, I found this shocking. After a while, you just become accustomed to it.

I had been around the block, but the rookies hadn't. What impression did it leave on them? What kind of example were these do-nothings making on our new officers? Like it or not, young officers looked up to the specialized units. They thought they were detectives or heroes. They must have had something going on to attain those detective type positions. I told the guys they did everything right, and to not be influenced by an uncaring or lazy officer.

TRAINING DAY

Rookies were at the complete mercy of the department. Whoever they stuck you with, that was your partner. The majority of officers didn't want to take the time or risk of working with young officers. While I was at the 10th Precinct, the department instituted a training program, where a senior officer would be paired with a rookie.

The senior would be responsible for the rookie's training. Daily paperwork critiquing the rookie would be completed and filed. I really didn't like the way it was slapped together, but at least they were trying. Anyone could put in for the position of training officer, and many did, as it was a minimal pay raise of about sixty dollars per month. It didn't matter if you were a good or bad officer, you would be appointed to the training officer position by the commander of the precinct. There was no formal training — it just was made by the decision of several command officers. "El Duce" and my lieutenant decided I would make a good training officer. I figured what the heck, I liked working with rookies, so I might as well get paid for it. I didn't like "EL Duce," and she didn't like me. She certainly liked to act like the police, and felt her rank gave her a corner on the knowledge market.

I'm called into her office one day for my big interview. I'm asked several questions before she pushes herself from the desk, folds her arms behind her head, and says, "Okay, I tell you, you can't have the job. What are you going to tell me to change my mind?"

I guess she was expecting me to beg.

I answer, "Nothing."

She sits straight up and yells, "Nothing."

I look her straight in the eye, and tell her my reputation speaks for itself.

"I'm more than qualified for the job and have volunteered to do so," I said. "If that's not enough, apparently the department doesn't want me training people. Any more questions?"

Then I walk out.

I started as a training officer the next day, though it really pissed her off.

The program itself was just like the academy. There's lots of paperwork and no way you could flunk the program. The rookie would rotate through phases, having a new training officer at each phase. If you flunked every phase, you would be recycled and sent through the whole process once again. It always cracked me up that the department worked harder at keeping bad officers than it did trying to get rid of them.

So now I'm a training officer pulling down big bucks. Trust me, sixty dollars is big bucks in my department.

Once I was assigned a rookie, I would sit them in the car and give them my standard speech. The very first thing I told them was to never be impressed by time, rank or ribbons because they don't mean a damn thing. The second thing that I tell them is that if I see them on this job in five years, I will shoot them myself. I probably say that because I didn't heed that sage advice when I was a rookie. The third thing I tell rookies is that, unlike other senior officers, I will let them drive the car. All rookies want to drive fast and hear that siren whine.

Remember, I tell them, there never is a stupid question. But there can be a stupid result if you don't ask the question. Finally, I tell them, pay attention and the things I teach you will keep you alive.

THERE'S A TIME TO STAY AND A TIME TO RUN

The very first thing I teach rookies is to never hold up a gun or evidence of a crime at the scene of the incident. For example, you make a traffic stop, and there are four guys in the car. You get them all out and pat them down. You tell the rookie to search the car. He finds a gun, and naturally holds it up for the world to see. The result is like firing a starter's gun at a track meet. All the suspects are going to be flying in different directions.

So to avoid this jailbreak, just come back and let your partner know there's a gun or start cuffing people. You eventually will come up with a signal of some type, such as a word or hand gesture. It makes life a whole lot easier. It is a priority that you always watch your suspects no matter what. Hmmmm, where and how did I learn that? I learned it on the street.

We conducted a traffic stop once, and both the driver and female passenger were wanted on misdemeanor warrants. We got them out, and searched them at the back of the vehicle. There were no weapons, so I was going to see how the rookie played it. It was kind of like a mother cheetah knocking the crap out of a small gazelle and not killing it but using it as a training tool. The gazelle can't hurt the cubs, and she watches. Both suspects have their hands on the trunk, and we both walk back to the car. That's the first no-no. I'm not going to fault him for that. He still has that rookie shine on him, and because I did it, he may think it is okay.

He starts running the names in the computer. I'm watching the suspects, and the male is getting fidgety. I crack my door so I can get out in a hurry, just in case we missed a gun. I suspected he is wanted for something more serious, and suddenly he takes off running.

He jumps a fence and runs east across the expressway. I watch him as he starts to climb the opposite embankment. I tap my rookie and point. He looks in the direction I am pointing, then glances back to me puzzled. The suspect now has disappeared into the shadows. After about a minute of looking down, the rookie asks, "Should I be chasing him?"

"Not this time," I tell him, and give him a quick lesson about watching his suspects. One of us should have been with both suspects while the other ran name checks.

I told him not to feel bad, and that he has twenty-five more years to catch that guy. The computer proved he only was wanted for a probation violation, which eased some of his pain.

I never liked anyone to get away, and put our suspect in the wanted section of a logbook I kept. We caught him two days later.

Young officers are easily impressed (I know I was when I first came on the job). I was working with a new trainee, and had just finished my training speech. I was telling him to look several blocks ahead instead of right in front of him because it is important to have an expanded observation field. Experience soon will help identify where threats or dangerous situations may be lurking.

Two blocks a head, a black Jeep Cherokee came out of an alley. It was evident that it was being driven by someone who wasn't the owner. The driver was speeding and being very reckless. I bring it to my rookie's attention, and tell him this is what we are looking for, and that the Cherokee most likely is stolen.

I can almost hear the adrenaline rush through him. I close in on the vehicle and get the license plate. I tell him to pick up the radio and say exactly what I tell him to say. He does as instructed in a very excited voice. Dispatch informs us the car is stolen, and as I relay instructions to my partner, the Jeep floors it. He is pulling away, but I have to drive with a bit more caution and control. He now has about sixty yards on me, and turns into an apartment complex. He soon runs out of road and bounds over the curb up onto the grass. This slows him down, and I close in on him quickly. I come to the end of the road, just in time to see him smash into a fence.

Four suspects bail out of the Jeep and scatter in all directions. I slide through the lot sideways and come to a stop.

My rookie now is leaning forward at the edge of his seat. He is looking at the action with a fixed stare, and his hands are gripping the dashboard of the scout car. His eyes are as big as saucers, and he looks at me. There is a slight delay, as I wait for his reaction.

"This is the part where you run," I tell him in a calm voice.

He scrambles out and, luckily, we caught two of the four. My rookie couldn't calm down the remainder of the shift. His family was going to get one helluva story tonight.

EVERYONE HAS BAD DAYS

Police officers can have bad days, but so can criminals. Every now and then, I felt sorry for some of them. We received a run of "citizens holding one." This meant some neighborhood people had caught a person doing wrong and had taken action.

We made it to the location and found a large crowd and three cars positioned around a fire hydrant. Our suspect was being pinned against this hydrant by four burly guys. He had been beaten, with scratches bumps and bruises all over his head and chest. His white T-shirt is blood-stained and shredded, and he is missing one shoe and sock.

He starts screaming for our help when we exit the car. The guys holding him are armed with rakes and shovels. A number of people in the crowd carried sticks and boards. It reminded me of that scene in the Frankenstein movie where the town chases the monster into the windmill. I stand him up and cuff him, and place him in the scout car. He is blubbering his gratitude and thanks me repeatedly. Keep in mind we have no idea what is going on, but we are guessing this is our suspect for something. Cuffing him and putting him in our car is at least protecting him until we can find out what is going on.

The crowd directs us to our victim. She is a heavy-set female who is about thirty years old. Our suspect is about seventeen years old and weighs all of 140 pounds. I speak with the victim, who tells me she exited the store with her groceries, and was loading them into her car when our bad guy spots her as an easy mark and snatches her purse. I can see the store is about two blocks away. I'm sure our bad guy wasn't expecting her reaction when she kicked off her sandals and started chasing him. He probably had carefully picked this older, heavy-set gal to avoid any type of confrontation. She begins yelling for help when they enter an alley.

She tells me several citizens assisted her in catching the suspect and someone found her purse in the alley. She said the citizens then held the thief in a peaceful manner while awaiting the arrival of the police department. Our poor suspect is so shook up, he admits to everything. He agrees with our victim's story right up to the point where they enter the alley.

He said several guys caught him as he attempted to exit the alley. As the men hold the suspect, the lady catches up and starts kicking him. They all want to know where the purse is and the suspect claims he doesn't know. That was the wrong answer, as they drag him back into the alley.

He now is pistol whipped by the gang, and eventually points out the yard where he threw the purse. Fearing they were going to kill him, he breaks away and starts running, but the crowd recaptures him at the fire hydrant. He tells me he was holding onto it for dear life as they continued to assault him. He feared they would drag him back into the alley for more pistol whipping.

I never saw a guy so happy to go to jail. He just kept repeating, "It just isn't my day."

HALT, POLICE!

I worked with a number of rookies at this command. Some were good, and some bad. Through them, I relived the beginning of my career, and it made me wonder how I survived those first ten years.

One day, I am partnered up with a young kid with a ton of potential. He is both attentive and eager. We receive a report of men stripping a car in an alley.

"Do not drive directly to the run location," I tell him. "Take a peek down the alley entrance about a block away, and you can see if someone is there. If so, then you can make a plan. Keep an eye for lookouts as you cruise, they can be positioned anywhere."

We follow this procedure and can see two cars in the middle of the alley. We have made these observations from the east alley entrance, and I tell him we are going to the west alley entrance and park. Once we get there, we will get out on foot and see if we can sneak up on them.

I park the scout car, and tell him to wait. I am going to walk up to the alley to see how far we are from the vehicles. I can't see because of the brush and step into the ally, staying concealed on one side. I'm only about thirty yards away from the cars and can see a guy jump the fence and enter the alley. He is a good fifty yards east, but walking my way. I was stuck in my spot now because he might see me if I exit the alley.

I know my rookie probably is nervous, and I shouldn't have left him. I look back and my assessment of the young man was correct. I knew this kid had potential. He is behind me about ten yards and concealed in the brush. I give him thumbs up and pull my gun. Our suspect probably is going to walk within ten feet of me, and he is going to get the crap scared out of him when I grab him. I start giggling as he approaches. He is almost on top of me, and as he reaches my position, someone screams, "Halt, police!"

Now I almost crap myself, and just about drop my gun. I look back and my rookie is in the middle of the alley, in combat stance, again yelling, "Halt, police!"

He is doing it with such authority that I almost feel like I had done something wrong. Now, the "halt, police" thing usually never works. Luckily, in this case it did. Just like in the old west, our guy reaches for the sky.

I walk up to him and cuff him. We walk him back to the scout car, and place him in the back. I now pull the scout up to the two stolen cars, which are partially stripped.

I know my rookie is excited, and we sit quietly for a couple of minutes as I order tow trucks. I want to give him time to gather himself. I finally look at him and ask, "What do we have?"

"What do you mean what do we have?" he replies.

"Why is this guy locked up?" I ask.

I can see the wheels in his brain start turning as he ponders my question. I don't want to see him embarrassed or fumble around for an answer, so I try and help him a little. I tell him I have no idea what he saw on his side of the car. Maybe the suspect opened the door, tried to pull a tire off, or picked up some property from inside the vehicle. I exit the scout car and let him know that I am going to inventory the two cars. I tell him to think about what we got. I've pretty much laid the groundwork for him, now he has to figure it out.

After several minutes I come back to the scout car, and ask the same question. He looks directly at me and says, "Nothing."

He knew he had his bad guy, but never saw him do anything to connect him to either stolen ride.

So we simply had a guy walking down the alley, passing two stolen cars. I didn't have to lecture him because he already knew the answer. Next time, let the suspect do something illegal before doing the "halt, police" thing.

He turned out to be a pretty good cop, and I didn't have to shoot him because he left the department after five years.

THE BLANKS IN THE BELT OF LAW ENFORCEMENT

I continued training rookies at the precinct, but experienced several incidents that truly explained why my new home was considered an island of misfits. Remember, you didn't have to be a good cop to get promoted. The main requirement was to be able to master the exam, which required a lot of studying. I detested inexperienced or uncaring sergeants. They could demoralize an entire shift by just walking into the room with an air of self-importance. They were blank cartridges in the gun belt of law enforcement.

The most detested were those who were promoted because of political influence. Our promotional system really sucked at times. We had plenty of charter promotions.

I had been working at the precinct for several months, and was standing at the front desk completing some paperwork. The front desk is about twenty-five-feet long and slightly elevated from the lobby floor. The desk sergeant sits in the middle, flanked by a clerk and a reports officer. He or she is in charge of all desk activity. On this day, the lobby was full, and there were several officers working on reports. I watch two guys walk in and address the sergeant. It appeared that one of their relatives had been arrested. Both of these guys are drunk. The sergeant tells them about the bonding process, and tries to explain how to get the arrested person out.

One of these guys starts to raise his voice. As a police officer, you can tell when someone is posturing and it is obvious this loudmouth is doing just that. The guy is looking around as he begins to curse, "fuck this, and just let my boy out."

The sergeant tries to calm him down, and he gets worse. Everyone now is looking at him, and it's obvious the sergeant has let this go on way too long.

This guy now is running the precinct. Finally, the sergeant tells him he is going to be arrested if he doesn't leave.

"Fuck that, I don't have to leave," he says, and he goes on and on.

I am steaming, but don't interfere. The other guy finally drags the loudmouth out. I can see them outside, standing around arguing on the sidewalk. The loud mouth storms back in, walks up to the sergeant, and says, "Fuck you and fuck the police. I want to see my brother and I want to see him now."

I can't believe the desk sergeant is allowing this behavior. I finally explode into action. I run around the corner, grab the guy and push him almost into the sergeant's lap. I cuff him and he falls to the ground. I drag him the length of the floor, through the cellblock door, around the corner and into the processing area. This is directly behind where the sergeant is seated, and I yell to him, "I have one for disorderly conduct."

The guy on the ground is crying, and I tell him, "I'll make sure you see your brother. I'll hook you up with a cell right next to him."

He is apologizing like there is no tomorrow, but it was way too late for that.

Detroit is a war zone, and we are fighting a war. We are soldiers. This job is not about beating people and doing something just because you are the police. It is about respect and order. Allowing someone to act like a drunken idiot and disrupt the precinct lobby encourages every bad guy out there.

You have a uniform on and you represent everyone who wears that uniform. Act professional and you will be treated as a professional. Your job is to keep order. This sergeant had failed in that responsibility, and I'm sure most of the civilians there were appalled by what was going on. How did they perceive the police department? Are these really they guys I need when I'm in trouble? I was ashamed.

Don't get me wrong, there are some great sergeants out there, and several helped shape my career. But the bad ones stand out like crab grass in a beautiful field of waving golden wheat. Public opinion usually is focused on the crab grass.

Like weak defense attorneys, I did have fun with some of the clown sergeants. I once was at a shooting scene at a bar when a young sergeant showed up. Standard procedure dictates that if the victim of an assault dies, homicide will be notified, at which time they immediately will take over the case. If the victim is going to survive, no notification to homicide is necessary and the precinct will handle the case. If the victim is alive and transported by EMS, a crew will stand by at the scene, while another unit goes to the hospital for an attending doctor and condition report.

Okay, let me say that again, there's no need to notify homicide if it looks like the guy is going to live. All homicide needs to know is if the victim is dead or critical. The city averages 1,200 shootings a year, so you better know what you are doing at one of these scenes.

Now the sergeant walks through the scene, asking several questions. We have six officers in the bar. The sergeant picks me out and asks if I notified homicide. I tell her no need, as we have no condition yet. I have no idea why, but if a sergeant has way less time than you, they feel they have a need to boss you around. I respect any boss that deserves respect no matter how much time they have on the job, but don't start pressing my buttons if you just want to act like you know what you are doing. I'll press back hard. This sergeant insists that I must notify homicide. I tell her I will, once I have a condition.

She begins posturing and tells me to call them right now, and that she knows how to handle a shooting scene. Okay, she opened the door so I'll go through it. I ask for the phone behind the bar, setting it about three feet from her and everyone else. I dial homicide and they ask what I have. My end of the conversation is very loud. I tell them I have a guy with a gunshot wound. As usual, they ask for chart and condition. I tell them loudly that I don't have a chart and condition. The officer I am talking to asks why in the hell am I calling them. I tell him my sergeant ordered me to make this call. I stop and in a loud voice ask for the sergeant's last name and badge. I yell her information back into the phone. He asks if she is an idiot.

"Yes, sir," I say.

He asks if she is standing right next to me.

"Yes, sir," I say.

He wishes me good luck, and tells me to tell her she needs a doctor and condition before notification. I hang up the phone turn to her and everyone else and inform her that homicide told me to call back after I have a doctor and condition report, and that if I had any brains, I already should know that.

With no apology or acknowledgement of error, she spins around and quickly leaves the scene. She was a fine example of crab grass in the field of golden wheat. Experience always eliminates crab grass.

We did have one incident in #10 that summed up the decadence of the whole city. The feds were following a small private plane into city airport. It was loaded with bales of marijuana. The pilot either had engine trouble or decided to ditch it. He crash-landed in a field by a closed school. This is right in the heart of the city.

As the feds and our department pull up, the large crowd that has gathered scatters. The twelve bales being smuggled by the pilot now have been divided up by the would-be rescuers. The Feds ended up with nothing but residue and crumbs. The field was two blocks from the precinct. It gives you a feel for what we were up against and the environment we worked in.

Police Officer Matthew E. Bowens

Police Officer Jennifer Timathy-Ann Fettig
Detroit Police Department, Michigan
End of Watch: Monday, February 16, 2004
Officer Jennifer Fettig and Officer Matthew Bowens were shot and killed while making a traffic stop on Gilbert Avenue at 0200 hours. As the two officers were in their patrol car calling in the license plate information of the vehicle, the suspect exited his vehicle and opened fire with a .40 caliber handgun, striking Officer Fettig five times and Officer Bowens three times. The suspect then went out of view as Officer Bowens exited the patrol car, returned fire three times, and then went to help Officer Fettig as he called assistance. The suspect reappeared and shot Officer Bowens six more times before stealing his service weapon. Neither officer had an opportunity to return fire. The suspect fired a total of twenty-two rounds at the officers during the incident. The suspect fled in his pickup truck, but a portion of the shooting was recorded in the patrol car's camera. The suspect and his brother were arrested several hours later. The suspect was found guilty on four charges of first-degree murder and was sentenced to life in prison, where he died on October 15, 2010.

Both officers were transported to Henry Ford Hospital where Officer Bowens was pronounced dead. Officer Fettig was admitted in extremely critical condition and died from her wounds twelve hours later.

Officer Fettig had served with the Detroit Police Department for two and a half years, and was assigned to the Fourth Precinct. She is survived by her parents and sister.

Officer Bowens had served with the Detroit Police Department for three years, and was assigned to the Fourth Precinct. He is survived by his father and two brothers.

FROM THE COUNTRY TO THE CITY

Let me get back to my rookies and my favorite one of all of them. I am given a guy who came from Alpena. This is a small town in northern Michigan. He had hayseed all over him. He told me he had been trying to get hired for years and had driven all over the state applying at different departments. I had only talked to him for a few minutes, and was convinced this was the wrong department for him. This city was going to swallow him whole. He was eager, but was out of his depth culturally. I feared he never would get up to speed. His appearance and mannerism just magnified his mistakes.

One of our first runs together was an assault. We found a guy on the front steps of a porch with a broken leg. He had been beaten severely, and he was surrounded by a large crowd. I ordered an EMS unit for medical treatment because he was in pretty rough shape. Our guy really is moaning and groaning. I ask the crowd what happened, and several people told me the dope man beat him up because he couldn't pay his debt.

I understood that's the risk a dope addict takes. He knows the score. This is not a crime we will solve because he will not press charges for fear the dope man will kill him. He cries out that he needs help and he is dying. This ignites my rookie and he runs back to the scout car. He returns with our emergency first aid kit. This is a kit assigned to every car by the department. We carried them because of some complaint or lawsuit that had taken place several years ago. This thing wasn't going to be of much use, as I knew I had more medical supplies in my cabinet at home. The kit was about as big as a small tackle box, red in color and had a zip tie lock. If you broke the zip tie, you had to complete paperwork.

To this day, I never have seen anyone open one of these. If you did open the damn thing for any reason, you had to complete paperwork and replace the items used.

My rookie rushes back with his red kit, continually urged on by the crowd. Not upset, I ask him what he is doing. He says he wants to help this man. I tell him I am pretty sure there is nothing in that box for a broken leg. I also inform him that I took the same first aid training he did. Our man is going to need more help than we can supply. He looks at me puzzled as EMS pulls up. I point to them and say, "Medical personnel for medical emergencies."

I point to him and then to me, and say, "Law enforcement personnel for law enforcement emergencies."

He still looked puzzled as we walked back to the car. I'm shaking my head, and he's clutching the lifesaving red tackle box.

In small town USA, his actions would have been hailed as heroic. In Detroit, the whole situation is something we avoided.

My favorite incident with him was a few weeks after I was assigned as his training officer. To make it easier on the youngsters, I usually do all the questioning at incident scenes and let the rookies write it down. Once they get used to the routine, I switch and let them ask the questions, along with doing the writing. It allows them to be a little more focused. If they miss something, I can chime in asking the appropriate questions. We responded to a robbery at a local motel. Our victim begins to tell his story, stating he had rented a room, and then gone out for something to eat. When he returned, he discovered his door kicked in. He had lost about four thousand dollars' worth of NFL leather jackets. These were knock-offs and illegal counterfeits, but he didn't care. He was mad that he lost them. So he wants to make a report.

Well, my rookie does a pretty good job with the questioning and we find a witness. She appears to be drug dependent, and works as the maid. She claims she witnessed it all. She tells us a tan camper van and pulled into the lot.

"Okay stop right there," I interrupt. "A camper van?"

"Yep," she says. "You know, the van (on the) front end with a big camper on the back."

It's very unusual for this city, but okay. She says a guy and a girl get out and the guy only has one arm. If you do police work long enough, you run into plenty of kooks who just want to talk to the police. She is beginning to sound like one of them. She is adamant, and says the guy with one arm kicks the door in, and both he and the female load the camper up with the jackets. They then escape west bound on the boulevard in the described vehicle.

So, I summarize for her, "You see a tan camper van, driven by a black male missing his left arm. He gets out with a female, kicks the door in and they steal all the coats. They escape in the tan camper van."

"Exactly right," she says.

Riggghhht. Okay, we head back and generate a report. Two weeks later, we pass the motel and turn north on Linwood. My rookie is driving. We travel several blocks, when a tan camper van pulls from a side street directly in front of us. We are about three car lengths behind it, and I look at my rookie. He has a blank look and not a care in the world.

We go about ten blocks and I tell him, "Hey pull this guy over."

He does just that and the tan camper van pulls to the curb. I tell him to be careful with this one, and we both approach. As I reach the passenger side, I can see a black female. I look at the driver who, you guessed it, is

TEN LITTLE POLICE CHIEFS

missing his left arm. I look at my rookie, who is asking for license and registration. Okay, let's see how far this goes. We walk back to the scout car, and he begins running their names. I ask him if any of this looks familiar.

He glances around the scout car, and I want to thump him on the head. I point to the van and the puzzled look does not change. Tan camper van, guy with one arm, motel, steals NFL jackets, has a female with him. Now he doesn't know what to do. He scrambles out of the car, but doesn't know if we can arrest them. Do you have probable cause? Yes, you do, I tell him.

He has gone from not a care in the world to the adrenaline thumping danger of a criminal confrontation in seconds. I fear he might faint. I tell him we are going to walk up to the van, get them out and cuff them both. I'll cover him while this is being done. For his lack of recognition, I'm going to have some fun with him. Once the female is cuffed, I know he is going to have issues with the male. I had the same problem myself once. He clicks one cuff on the male, and realizes there is no other arm to cuff. He stands there with that same puzzled look, and asks me what to do. I can't take it, and cuff the guy around his belt and through his belt loop. It's not super secure, but it's the best we can do. My rookie is excited, and soon drifts back to the place he was before I saw the van.

I hope I can keep this one alive. It will be a daunting task.

LOSING OUR OWN

I had been at Number 10 for about four months, when I received some bad news. My old crew was raiding a blind pig on the west side when two officers were shot. One was the guy manning my old spot on the ram and the other was his sergeant. Both were hit by gunfire as they came though the doorway. Luckily, they were both wearing flak vests, which saved their lives. I made some calls to check on both of them, and they were physically going to be fine. A big part of police work is mental, and no one knows how you're going to bounce back from something like that. Your head has to be right to properly function as a police officer. I was happy the officers survived, but knew I was very lucky. That would have been me.

A second call concerning my old crew came several weeks later. They were running an OTE operation up on Chene Street. One of the officers was shot and killed by a suspect. I was just arriving for my shift at Number 10, when I heard the news. I immediately left for the hospital. When I arrived, I found Slim outside smoking. He had a haggard look. I gave him a hug, looked right in his eyes and said, "I told you."

I walked into the emergency waiting room and located the rest of my old crew. Hugs and tears where given. The officer killed was new to the unit and very young.

"Experience, experience, experience" echoed in the chambers of my mind. I never try and second-guess officers or the end results, especially if I wasn't there. I already had formed my opinion on this one, as I had worked with this crew. I knew almost everything these guys did was dangerous.

I learned they had put two girls out to decoy. The only reason this is done was to get more cases. Everyone knew the extra risk this created. These were officers working in a dangerous environment in effort to make Detroit a safer place to live. One of them paid with his life. I didn't know the fallen officer, but I was sick to my stomach. I might not have known him, but I knew the situation. Was there something I could have done to prevent it? Probably not. I hate to even admit this, but the soldier side of me felt relief. First the officer and sergeant shot at the raid, and now this. I know there are going to be casualties, and I was just glad it wasn't me.

When the department loses an officer, I think of my first police funeral. You cry just being there. There are hundreds of officers in full dress uniform standing at attention, as bagpipes play Amazing Grace. There's the order to present arms, and we all snap a salute and hold it. The honor guard cracks off the twenty-one guns, and helicopters thunder over just above our heads. One breaks away from the formation to signify the loss of an officer. Finally, the slow moaning of taps echoes through the cemetery. It always brings me visions of my family standing there weeping.

A BAD DAY TO GO TO COURT

I was depressed for the rest of the week, and several incidents contributed to my funk. First, my wife's car was stolen from the security lot at a local hospital. She is a critical care nurse and works the emergency room there. Several days later, I had a stolen car case in juvenile court. I had to drive my 1978 Olds 98 to court because we were down to one car. It was my aunt and uncle's old car, and I had just brought it up from Florida. It had no alarm and no car club. As a lifelong Detroit resident, I knew this was a risk.

Arriving at court, I found a parking spot just down from the front doors, which made me feel much better. I checked in and after about an hour, my case concluded. It was my kind of morning — in for an hour and paid for four and a half hours.

I soon would regret the 4.5-hour payday and my trip to court. As I exited the front doors, I could see the spot where I had parked my car. The spot still was there, but my car wasn't. The pile of auto glass near the curb told the whole story. It was recovered several days later, missing the tires and having a cracked steering column. I honestly blamed myself for the whole thing. I should have known better. It cost me six hundred dollars for new tires and rims, and from that point on, I started it with a screwdriver until I sold it. That's the city for you, always unforgiving.

DOJO SMOJO

Even though I was a training officer, I never stopped learning on the job. I was working midnights, and came upon a guy walking in the middle of the street. He was carrying a large black nylon duffle bag. It appeared as if there was a rifle in the bag. We stopped to investigate, and I asked him to step out of the street. I asked what was in the bag, and was told it was none of my business. Okay, I immediately labeled this guy uncooperative. I'm a pretty easy officer to get along with, but let's not get started like this because I can easily turn into a hard ass.

I ask several more questions, but gain no ground. I then tell him I'm going to search the bag. He doesn't like it, but complies. Inside, I find a full-length samurai sword. Now, what the heck would he be doing with something like that? Being the highly trained officer I was, I asked why he was walking down the middle of the street at three in the morning with a samurai sword.

"Why you fucking with me?" he responds.

I am the type of officer that takes great joy in taking you to jail if you ask for it. In fact, I will tell you up front that I am getting paid to take you to jail, which has a tendency to ruffle a suspect's feathers. If you're going to use that line, make sure the suspect is cuffed before you start feather ruffling. In this case, I have (at the minimum) a violation of the city knife ordinance, and the more probable charge is possession of a dangerous weapon. So off to jail he goes. I'm happy. No fighting, and I've proven my point.

Several months later, I get notification to go down to the union office to make statements. The suspect is suing me, the city and everyone else for false arrest. False arrest? He is walking down the middle of the street with a samurai sword. Well, it seems like the bad guy has done his homework and I hadn't. He claimed he was coming home from his Dojo martial arts meeting when the police started hassling him. Dojo Smojo, who cares? Apparently, I should have. If you are leaving a religious ceremony or martial arts facility where training takes place, it is okay to transport throwing stars, spears, samurai swords, etc. — even if you are walking in the street at 3 a.m.

I know Number 10 is weird, but I can guarantee you there are no Dojos within its borders. It made me think I was set-up. I asked my union rep how many times this guy has sued the city.

"Six total," he told me.

Now, I'm not saying if I was set-up or not, but this guy was prepared and I wasn't. I made a note to myself and let the rest of the guys know. This guy knew the system and knew it better than me. It was a lesson learned. As they say on the streets, keep that grass mowed so you can see them snakes out there. Next time, you can be sure I will be better prepared.

IT'S NO LAUGHING MATTER, RIGHT?

No matter how bad the job can get you down, every now and then you service a run that can put a smile on your face. We responded to a domestic violence disturbance in the south end of the precinct. We pulled up to a large apartment building, and soon located our victim on the second floor.

She was drunk and claimed her boyfriend had been beating her. Signs of a recent assault were visible on her face. There were several scratches, and she had a split lip. She told us her boyfriend still was in the apartment, and he was responsible for her injuries. We walked her downstairs and I wondered what condition he was in. She was being very loud and was wound up pretty good. Sometimes, a woman could give as good a punch as she received, and alcohol can balance the power scales. We knocked on the door and identified ourselves as we pushed the door open.

It was a small one-room apartment, and our suspect was sitting on the bed. He was drunk and missing both legs just below the knees. I know it wasn't professional but for some reason this tickled my funny bone. She called us because he was beating her? Why not just take a couple of steps back from him? There was no way he could catch her. I'm trying to hold back from breaking out laughing when they begin shouting at each other.

"Hand me my legs, and I'll whip her ass," he says.

I look in the corner and there are two black prosthetic legs. They both have white-striped sweat socks on and a pair of high top basketball shoes, and the laces tied. They both are upright and standing next to each other. I have no idea if it was a buildup of all the stupid things I have seen in my career, but I lost it. I burst into a roaring deep belly laugh. I had to excuse myself and go into the hall. I left my partner in the apartment with the door open so I could see him. The guy pulls himself off the bed. He is trying to get at her, and she is kicking him. I head back in, still laughing. The guy looks up at me and tells me this is no laughing matter, as he swipes at her ankle. This sets me off even more and now. I'm crying tears of laughter. We separate them and convince her to stay with a friend.

She is delivering a profanity-laced goodbye as we escort her from the apartment. He is giving it back as good as he is getting it, and his voice fades as we head down the hall. We leave her with the simple advice to take one step back if he attempts to attack her again.

I have the giggles on the way out, and they stay with me for the next few days. It was very unprofessional.

SIBLING RIVALRY AND A PITCH FORK

Servicing runs in this precinct would load my "Experience" handbook. We responded to a location where a sister had assaulted her brother. It was early morning and when we arrived, and an EMS unit already was on the scene. We found the fifty-year-old female in the front room, and she was drunk.

"Yeah, I fucked him up," she told us. "He should have listened."

I yell for the EMS, and find them in the kitchen treating the victim. The guy is drunk and naked, sitting on a kitchen chair. He has the most bizarre pattern of tiny holes all over him — and I mean they are all over him. They are bleeding, but not severely, and EMS is patching him up. He is not the least concerned that he is naked, and only can mumble because of his intoxication.

I can't wait to hear this story, so I return to our drunken victim, or suspect, as I really wasn't sure just exactly what she was yet. It seems the brother came home, and turned on the TV. The volume was too loud, and she asked him to turn it down. He refused, and after several requests, she took matters into her own hands. She armed herself with a pitchfork and gave him the works.

A pitchfork? You have to understand that inner city lingo has to be interpreted sometimes. I asked a female robbery victim once where the suspect was standing in relationship to her.

"Relationship? Hell, I don't even know the nigger," she replied.

I once came across a working girl I hadn't seen in sometime. I asked where she had been, and told her someone told me she was incarcerated.

"Incapacitated? No, she never had them surgeries," she said.

You can understand where I'm going with the whole lingo thing. So when the sister said pitchfork, I thought of anything but a real pitchfork, even if it would explain the strange wounds. I asked her where the weapon was and she told me she tossed it on the back porch. I found it on the back porch, and it indeed was a full-length, hay-tossing pitchfork, and it still was dripping with blood. This again was before domestic violence laws. The brother admitted his faults and didn't want to press charges.

I couldn't imagine walking around in front of my sister naked, or having her arm herself with a pitchfork and giving me the pincushion treatment. It was just another routine run in the 10th Precinct.

YOU BETTER LIKE IT

There are incidents that bring you back to the dangers of the job. They remove any complacency that can creep in. I was working with an experienced partner, when we observed a narcotic deal in front of a party store. It appeared to be a regular everyday sale: One pack of heroin for cash.

Both suspects bolted, and I jumped out to chase the dealer. I caught him a half a block away in the backyard of a vacant house. I had tackled him and he was face down. I ordered his hands back, and he failed to comply. He began bucking, and I flattened myself on top of him. This is where police work gets very dangerous. I had no idea if he was armed or not. No one knows where I am. He has decided he is not going to go to jail, at least not easily. I have a loaded weapon on my side, but can't shoot him. I have just entered into a fight for my life when moments earlier, I calmly was talking to my partner about a daddy/daughter dance I was going to attend.

We continue to struggle, but I still have him pinned to the ground. He is not complying and the longer this goes, the worse it gets for me. I pull my gun, place it to the back of his head, and remind him of our current situation. I tell him there is no one else around, and I will not hesitate to blow his head off. Luckily, he doesn't call my bluff and surrenders.

This type of incident can change an officer. It can irreparably shake his confidence or make him stronger. Some will want more of it, and others will never put themselves in that position again. Our brotherhood comes from those officers willing to take those risks. I was scared at that exact moment, but felt good because I had done my job.

Earnest Hemingway said it best. There is no hunting like the hunting of man. And those who have hunted armed men long enough and liked it never care for anything else thereafter.

Trust me, in Detroit you better like it, or you are in the wrong line of work.

SICK TIME AND CHOIR PRACTICE

Department sick time and its use were learned at this command. Officers worked on a twenty-eight day rotation, which included eight leave days. The more seniority you had, the better your days off. If you have no seniority, you will be getting Tuesdays and Thursdays to enjoy your off time.

I didn't know much about sick days, as I never had to use them. I had submitted my leave days for the upcoming rotation, but failed to get one of my requested days off. My wife was having outpatient surgery, so the day was a must. I talked to my sergeant, and he informed me they just couldn't do it. So not really having a choice, I called in sick.

The next day, I show up for work and get the stare from the desk personnel. They want to know what I'm doing coming into work? They inform me that I am scheduled to be off duty, I bring them up to speed and tell them they must be confused, as I was off yesterday. They pull up the detail roster and point out that it shows me listed as sick. I correct them again, and tell them I was sick yesterday. Right, they tell me, but don't you know you can take three sick days off before you need a written doctor's excuse? It's like a mini vacation. Everyone does it, and the department can't do a thing about it.

They tell me to go home before anyone sees me. I couldn't believe it. I tell them, no, I'm staying, and they begin whispering. Who is this new guy, not taking his full three days? They now are going to have to keep an eye on me.

The following day, I'm out on the ramp lecturing the shaved head rookies about sick time: Don't burn sick time just to burn it, as you actually may need it one day. It also gives a big return when you retire, as you are paid out for a portion of the unused time. Also, unless you know someone, it is very difficult to transfer into any specialized unit. They want someone dependable, and this is the first thing they will scrutinize when recruiting new officers.

At that very moment, one of the laziest guys in the precinct walks out.

"Don't listen to him," he tells the youngsters. "You guys can take twelve sick days a year and the city can't do a damn thing about it. That's one three-day weekend a month."

Not slowing down, he walks right out into the parking lot, gets in his car and drives off. I'm standing there with my mouth open. The problem is that he is one hundred percent right. Young officers really are restricted as to what days they get off. If they need a day, they will have to utilize their sick days. It's a slippery slope to step on. Young officers are trainable, and that can go either way. It ultimately is up to them to choose the path.

I had a lieutenant address everyone at roll call concerning sick time use. Every precinct has sick time issues. Apparently, he was going to give us an inspiring speech. He tells everyone they always should come to work.

"Don't burn your sick time for nothing," he said. "You need to use that shit for something important. A big game on TV, or even better, you may want to get busy with your woman. That's what it's there for, and that's when you use it."

No, I'm not kidding. We are all standing in formation stunned. Who hired this guy? He eventually rose to the rank of commander.

I must admit that I started to enjoy Number 10, and met some great police officers. On paydays, we would meet at a small bar on the west side for choir practice. It was story-telling time at its finest.

These gatherings always gave us an opportunity to blow off steam. Chases and do-nothing officers always were favorite topics. The sick time speech by the lieutenant was hot for about a month.

Keep in mind that you spend more time with your partners than you do your family, so inevitably you grow close. One of the officers who used to come to choir practice was killed in the line of duty. I still frequent the bar, but every time I stand on that first stair, I think of the last time I saw him. He was standing in the doorway saying goodbye. He had a smile on his face. He loved being a cop more than anyone I knew.

Several months later, he transferred to another precinct. He was shot with three other officers as they attempted to pull over a vehicle wanted for kidnapping. The suspects fired an assault rifle through the back window of the van they were using. The officers never knew what hit them.

SHOT IN THE ASS, AND YOU'RE TO BLAME

I talked about the danger at the police firing range. The range officers are experts in gun safety, and it still was a dangerous place. On the street, we were dealing with untrained people who were armed to the teeth. Knowing there are guns in a building is frightening. Knowing that the people who possess the guns may be drunk or high on drugs just adds to the stress. You always are in an alert mode. The racking of a handgun or shotgun is a signal to jump for cover whether you are on the street or in the precinct.

There have been a number of officers who have been shot by their own gun. When this happens on the street, it usually involves a suspect disarming the officer and then turning it against him. It is one of our worst fears.

You would think and officer shooting himself, or being shot by a coworker, would be completely preventable. I knew an officer who was leaving the department because he had been hired by another law enforcement agency. The week before he left, he recovered a handgun on the street. It was a small .25 automatic. He placed it in his rear pocket, at which time the gun discharged, and he shot himself in the ass. He hid his mistake from his new employer and got the job.

One day, an officer pulled his gun out in the squad room. He was going to inspect it and it went off. Well a gun doesn't go off if you don't pull the trigger. The round hit the wall and, fortunately, didn't ricochet. No one was hurt, but there was plenty of ringing ears and checking of underwear.

Several of these incidents and you become a very jumpy person. No one wants to get it on the street, but you really don't want to get it in the station house.

THE KITTENS HAVE TO FIGHT FOR SURVIVAL

Every now and then something in the war zone touches you. It wasn't often, but it happened to me one day while working #10. We responded to a family trouble run and were met at the door by a middle-aged female. The house was trashy and unkempt. She told us her brother, who is a crack head, forced his way in and was inside. She was very upset and wanted him out of her house. Two small boys, ages six and eight, stood next to her at the front door. Both of them were loudly crying. I asked what was wrong, and they told me their uncle had taken their Yugioh cards.

I asked the mother if this was right, and she agreed. She told me they couldn't afford them, but she had scraped together some money and they had four cards apiece. Yugioh cards were the craze at time and they were expensive. Did this clown steal them to sell them? I have to admit I've seen worse, but I made my best effort to console the boys.

You always try to leave work at work, but I had small children. I hated to see those little broken hearts. When I got home that night, I gathered my three kids together, and told them what had happened. I wanted them to appreciate what they had, and to realize the unfortunate lives others were forced to deal with.

They listened intently, then immediately gathered up their Yugioh cards. My daughter found a binder with cardholder pages, and the kids filled them up. There must have been about forty cards in the thing.

The following day, my partner and I went back to the same address. I was met by the mother and asked to see the boys. They came to the door, with that same frightened look. I told them I had something for them and handed over the binder.

They opened it, and asked if it was for them. I told them my kids put it together as a gift for both of them. They stood in the squalor of their home in their dirty clothes and looked at me. The joy in their faces was indescribable. Their smiles and glow almost made me tear up. I knew this wouldn't last. It was more than likely the uncle would come back and take them. They were too young to fight for themselves, and mom was doing the best she could.

When I looked at the mother she was crying. I don't usually allow it, but I gave her hug. I never brought the job home, but I carried her emotion with me that night. Her warmth and love rushed through me as I wrapped my arms around my kids. That mother was exactly like me. Trying to raise a family with all the love she could. The only difference was her environment. Policemen must never forget that.

It seemed the children always were the victims, and that would be a constant throughout my career. We once responded to a disturbance run to a house that had no front porch, and we had to pound on the door while standing in a patch of overgrown weeds.

There was no answer, so we checked the door, which was open. We could hear young voices and jumped the three feet into the front room. An eight-year-old girl met us, and wanted to know what we wanted. We asked to see her parents or parent. She informed us the mother had gone to the store. I asked who else was in the house, and she said her brothers and sisters. I told her to gather them up and bring them to the front room.

The house was a disaster zone. There was feces everywhere, and roaches so bold they didn't scurry in the light. She brought us a total of eight kids. She was the oldest, and she now had a one-year-old baby girl on her hip. She had no clothes and no diaper. The whole scene was disturbing. This was a shit hole, with a shit parent, yet the kids were smiling. They still were innocent and knew no other life. One seven-year-old boy was dressed in a suit. I should say a suit coat and pants. He had no shirt, no underwear, and no socks. I figured he probably had no other clothes.

He giggled and smiled, nervously placing one dirty foot over the other as we talked. The normal procedure for us was to notify protective services, which we did. While I was talking on the phone, the mother showed up.

She wasn't drunk, but was well on her way. The liquor bottle she had purchased was open, and in a brown bag. Since she had returned home, protective services told us to leave the kids with her and they would open a case file on the incident. This was common for us, but hard to understand. I'll never forget jumping out that door, and looking back. There were a bunch of smiling faces peering through the boarded-up window, and that young boy in the suit was waving to me. I only could imagine how they all would end up.

In their neighborhoods, gunfire was common. To see someone bleeding or dead was just a part of life in the inner city. Things like house fires, wild animals, a lack of recreation facilities, and unemployment were common. Transportation usually was some local guy who would take a few bucks to give you a ride. You had to walk through a metal detector to go to school. It was a jungle, and survival was an everyday task. It would be their way of life. As a police officer, it was part of mine.

When I was kid, I found several small kittens in a garage. When I went to pick one up, it attacked me. Its cries brought the mother from the attic, and she also tried to jump me. I fled the garage before I got clawed. This makes a good analogy. The children were the kittens: They would have to defend themselves and scratch and claw for everything they got. They would be lucky if mom was around to protect them. I hoped the best for all of them.

COOL IT, SON

Patrol duties were coming to an end for me and I was just getting ready for a move to the Special Operations Section. This is a plain-clothes assignment in an unmarked car. I was looking forward to the change. I still was working uniform patrol, when we responded to a shooting in the south end of the precinct. Another unit was the primary, and we had volunteered to back them up. We could hear them on the radio, and they confirmed they had a female victim who was shot in the chest.

We could hear the urgency in their voices over the radio, and we figured she must be critical. When we pulled up to the scene, one of the officers was walking off of the front porch. I asked him about the victim, and he pointed to the front porch. He told me he was going to ask for an estimated arrival time for the EMS because it didn't look good. She had a bullet wound in the center of her chest. I jumped up the five stairs to the deck of the porch. The victim was about thirty years old and was wearing a flower print dress. She was lying on her back with an upended kitchen chair next to her. Her eyes appeared dilated, and she was not moving or making a sound. It looked as if she had been sitting in the chair on the porch when someone lit her up.

I inspected her wound with my flashlight and it looked odd. A closer look revealed the blood spot on the center of her chest was not blood at all. It was paint. She had been paint balled. I hollered down to the officer to cancel EMS. Someone shot her with a paintball gun.

Her eyes fluttered and she turned her head toward me and said, "A what?"

"Yes, a paint ball," I said. "You are not shot."

"Oh hell no," she yelled. "Damn these scandalous motherfuckers around here."

She had risen from the dead, and now was setting her kitchen/lawn chair back up.

"These niggers always be playing," she said, picking up her forty-ounce beer that still was in the bag. "Look what these motherfuckers made me do. Done spilt my drank."

She plopped back down, and was no worse for the wear, with the loss of only a few drops of her beer.

From death to life within seconds, these close calls are a common thing in Detroit.

One of the last runs I serviced before I went to plain clothes was one of those typical what-not-to-do runs. I was working with my "Halt, police" rookie, and he was developing nicely. We were responding to a run nobody enjoyed, a dead body. This was at the peak of summer, and the heat was unbearable. Dead body runs were the worst, but add in a little summer heat, and chances are it would be ripe. We responded to the given address and found the body inside.

The deceased had passed several hours earlier, and was discovered by the live-in caretaker. It appeared his death was due to natural causes. It was going to be a trouble-free run, but we had to wait for the medical examiner. We ended up spending three hours in the house, with no air conditioning. The morgue removed the body, which allowed us some relief from the stifling house.

Our patrol car would bring us no relief, as it wasn't equipped with air conditioning. We roll down the windows and jump on the freeway for some quick and cool fresh air. We finally clear up and inform radio we now are available. Dispatch now informs us that he hates to do this, but he has to give us another dead body. I already am miserable, and start ranting and raving about every lazy officer on the job. We didn't have a good shift working that day, so chances of someone taking it off of our hands was not good. Working officers never would let another unit take two dead bodies in a row. Someone always would volunteer to take it off your hands.

I'm steamed like a clam when we make it to the house. We are soaked with sweat from waiting out the last one. We head in and find an old man dead at the kitchen table. He has a telephone receiver in his hand, and is wearing nothing but a diaper. The only plus was that he must have just died. The body still was fresh. Remember I talked about losing the human aspect of the job? Well, here it goes again. Department procedure demanded that we contact homicide from an outside phone line. We would have to borrow a phone from one of the deceased's neighbors. I leave "Halt, police" with the body, and go knock on several doors. I get no answer.

I storm back in a fit of rage, and look at my rookie, and tell him, "Don't ever do this." I'm starting to lose it and I know it. I then attempt to pry the receiver from the dead guy's hand. Rigor mortis had set in, and I struggle to get it free. The receiver has a long cord, and now my leg and the dead guy's arm are wrapped in it. I almost yank him out of the chair during the struggle and fail to free the phone.

I look at my rookie with sweat dripping down my nose. He looks at me like I'm some crazed animal. I guess my behavior was a little disconcerting for him. He takes a step back as I untangle myself. I tell him to stand by and head out the door to again try and locate a phone.

I finally am able to get someone to open a door and am invited in by a lady who is about seventy-five years old. She could see my distress and must have had sympathy for me as I pleaded to use her phone. She led me into a very well-kept home, with furniture that was all from the 1940s. She points to a phone, and pulls a chair up for me. I still am livid, and bang the numbers as I call. I am mad at the world and all the lazy police officers. My female waddles off, and I finally get a hold of someone at the notification and control center. As I'm talking on the phone, she returns and places a standing fan next to me and plugs it in.

"There you go, baby. You look hot," she says.

The fan begins to osculate and cools me down. I begin to recover, not only physically but mentally. She disappears for a few seconds more, then soon reappears carrying a glass pitcher filled with ice-cold lemonade. The moisture has beaded on the outside of the pitcher. She places a tall glass next to the phone and fills it.

"That should help cool you off baby," she said.

The warmth and sincerity in those eyes melted everything. I forgave the slugs, dispatch, and everybody else in the world. I completed my notifications and thanked her for her kindness.

When I stepped back next door, I even threw the deceased a "Sorry about that, guy." I also apologized to my rookie, who remained terrified of me for several days.

The whole thing renewed my faith in the world and, more specifically, the city. There are good people here — we just didn't have the opportunity to interact with them very often. That old lady reenergized my determination to make the city safe for people like her and those rag tag kids who don't seem to have a chance.

THE COMPLAINT BOX

Lawsuits and union issues would be an everyday occurrence in the precinct and, as with police work, I would have to learn about these matters through experience. The first thing you realize is no matter how good of a cop you are, you always are going to have complaints, and at some point, you are going to be sued. The samurai sword guy was a perfect example. Many officers believe if you work hard, you are going to get a lot of complaints. I worked hard and had very few. Don't use complaints as an excuse for the quality of your work. Most good officers are in the same boat as me. But no matter how hard you try, you'll get complaints. No one prepares you for this, and it is not taught in the academy. You must learn by experience.

This complaint education continued one day when we responded to a domestic violence run. A young man had pushed his girlfriend through a window. She had some minor scratches, but didn't want him to go to jail. The problem was that domestic violence laws now were in effect, and we had to arrest him. She was pleading for us not to take him, and he was arrogant as hell. We conveyed him, and completed the paperwork, like any routine arrest.

About nine months later, we were notified to report to the union office for statements. Not having any idea what for, we met the union official. We soon discovered it concerned that old domestic violence run. The arrestee claimed we hand cuffed him, threw him down a flight of stairs and then kicked him repeatedly while he was in the back of the scout car. It was amazing that he didn't have a mark on him when he was processed at the precinct. This is an example of why our department operated the way it did. We have a reputation of paying off lawsuits, right or wrong. It costs way too much money to defend us. This investigation should have ended a long time ago. People on the street know our policies, and they take full advantage of them.

At the Union Office, we were asked a number of questions. One was whether our victim had any marks on her neck. Honestly, it had been nine months, and I couldn't remember. I asked my partner, and he couldn't remember either. Not thinking anything of it, I responded that she might have had some scratches on her neck. Once our interviews were over, we went back to the precinct. Two months later, we received a letter from the union, saying we were cleared of all wrongdoing and the complaint was unfounded. I expected that outcome, but not what was at the bottom of the notification. It stated we were found guilty of lying because we had made statements that she had scratches on her neck, but had failed to list them on our original arrest reports. Mind you, this was nine months after the incident, and we had no report present at our interview to review. This lying notification would be placed in our internal affairs file. What a way to get started in the precinct: I'm a documented liar. The unfairness of the situation pissed off both of us.

Just like street experience, dealing with the department, complaints and the union, was something I was learning on the fly.

JUSTICE ROLLS ON

Even business owners had to learn street lessons, and I had sympathy for one who had been hit by someone he thought was handicapped.

The victim ran a pest control shop up on Davison. Like every good business owner in the city, his place resembled a pillbox, with razor wire on top and bulletproof glass below. This day, he meets us at the door and buzzes us in. He is upset, and tells his story.

He gets a knock at the door and sees a guy in a wheel chair. He leaves his pistol in the desk and checks the sidewalk as he prepares to unlock the door. Seeing no one but the guy in the wheelchair, he lets him in. He relocks the door, and waits on his chair-bound customer. The guy buys several gallons of roach killer and pays with cash. The owner assists him to the front door, and carries the pesticide out for him.

The suspect's truck (a Cadillac SUV) is parked right in front. The owner loads the property in the back, then assists the suspect into the front seat, folding up the wheel chair and placing it in the back seat. The suspect has been making idle chitchat about his expensive radio and how it operates, and he asks the victim to go to the passenger side so he can better show him the radio.

The victim complies, and as he is looking at the radio, he notices the suspect pointing a small handgun at his head. The victim, before assisting the suspect out of the store, had placed his pistol in his front pocket and about two grand in the other. The suspect doesn't know about the victim's pistol, but he knows about the cash. As the victim tells it, he can't believe he is being robbed by a guy in a wheelchair.

It is so typical of victims in this city. They blame themselves for not being more prepared. This victim thought he was prepared, as he has a gun in his pocket, but now he doesn't want to risk his life over two grand. He turns over the cash and the suspect escapes. The problem for the suspect is that expensive radio. While scanning the channels, a name and address came up, and the victim made note of it. An hour later, I was taking the suspect and his wheelchair to jail.

Unfortunately for our victim, the case never went to court. Our suspect made bond because they apparently didn't consider him a flight risk. While out, he got involved in a major drug deal that went bad. He was shot five times. Yes, he was sitting in the wheelchair at the time. He survived, but was such medical mess, the prosecutor never pursued the case.

PERSONEL FOLLIES

My day always would get off to a good start if "El Duce" was in the lobby. I'd walk through the doors, and there she would be standing with her arms folded and surveying her kingdom. She was the type of person you just knew you didn't want to be in a scout car with. It would make me smile. She was inspector over the entire precinct. It always was easy to recognize police officers who were never "the police."

Working this precinct, I also learned all the ins and outs of Detroit police personnel. It was amazing how many officers failed to cooperate with each other. If you needed something from another precinct, you better know someone over there. If not, you got the cold shoulder. If you called, they would put you on hold until you gave up. I watched desk people pick up a ringing phone and just hang it back up. It's very frustrating.

As discussed earlier, this also spilled into the street. Remember the girl violated with the broom handle? I had something similar with a homicide once. We backed up a unit and found a multiple shooting in a four family flat. As we entered the center hallway, you could see bullet holes as we walked our way up the stairway. The upper right flat door had at least twenty bullet holes in it. We entered, and found EMS personnel treating a guy with a leg wound. The second victim was on the floor in a pool of blood. He was lying on his back and had multiple gunshot wounds. The worst was a shot to the back of the head. The round had entered at the base of his head an exited above his right eye. His skull was now cone shaped at the exit wound. Blood poured from his nose, mouth and ears. He gurgled with each shallow breath.

The second EMS unit rushed to him, as I stood next to the victim. The tech now was kneeling at his side, and looked up at me. We both had that same look. We knew he wasn't going to make it, and if he did, half of his brain had been torn apart.

"I understand, just do what you can," I told the tech.

He began treating the wound, as the shallow breathing slowed. He reached for the victim's pulse, and held it until the breathing stopped.

I got the story of the shooting from the surviving victim. Someone they had a beef with had knocked on the front entrance door, which was downstairs.

The deceased, not knowing who it was, answered the door and found a masked suspect armed with an assault rifle. The victim ran up the stairs as the suspect opened up. That would explain the rounds walking up the wall. The victim struggled with the door and was hit multiple times and stumbled into the room. The second victim was hit as rounds went through the wall.

It was a horrible looking scene. The deceased now was lying atop a large pool of blood. His pants and shirt were soaked. There were two jagged holes, apparently exit wounds, in his chest. In addition to the massive head wound, his face was discolored and swollen.

As I went downstairs, his family arrived. Everyone was crying and wailing. The mother and father were there, and I directed them into a lower flat. Several officers assisted me as the family attempted to force their way upstairs. They pleaded with us to see their son. I knew that I would not want that scene to be my last memory of any of my boys. It's one they would never forget. I explained to the father about procedure. He explained he was a Vietnam vet, and had seen all kinds of atrocities. I'm sure he had, but nothing he saw involved his loved ones. There was no way I was going to let him see his boy massacred like that.

Two officers from Homicide arrived, and feeling like they had control, I walked to my scout car to prepare my report. I really didn't have a choice, as they now were in charge of the scene.

Within minutes, I heard terrible high-pitched screaming. I ran back into the residence to see the father collapse at the top of the stairs. Homicide had allowed him upstairs to identify the body. I couldn't believe it. I had no idea what their policy was, but it sure wasn't mine. Maybe it was a short cut, so the family didn't have to make the trip to the morgue. At least at the morgue, the victim would have been cleaned up.

As they carried the father back down, I asked what idiot let him upstairs.

"We did," both officers answered.

They were proud off it, and because this was a homicide scene they were in charge. I already could see that no matter what I said, it wouldn't have made a bit of difference. Like so many times in this department, I gave up the battle.

EMS revived the father, and would transport him with a probable heart attack. I think of that case often. I also think of those homicide officers, and wonder if the tragedy and heartache of the victim's family ever affected them. If it didn't, they were in the wrong line of work.

Police Officer Kenneth Lee Daniels
Detroit Police Department, Michigan
End of Watch: Wednesday, September 1, 2004

Officer Daniels was shot and killed while moonlighting at a local nightclub. He had broken up a fight and ejected several men from the club. Later in the evening, as he walked to his car, he was ambushed and shot by one of the men. The suspect was convicted of second-degree murder and felony firearms possession in March of 2005. He was sentenced to a minimum of forty-seven years in prison.

Officer Daniels had served with the agency for eight years, and was a member of the Tactical Services Section. He is survived by his wife and two sons.

A SURE WAY TO MAKE MONEY

One of my last incidents on uniformed patrol was a doozey. I was working with Tim Carter. This guy had quite the reputation on the job. He had been involved in several shootings and had the "heavy handed" label. An officer like Tim is very physical with suspects. I really liked the guy, and never saw him do anything that was over the top. On this particular day, we were slow rolling down a three-lane street, when a car zoomed by us. It was obvious he was doing well over the speed limit, and it took us some time to catch up to him. We paced him at 60 in a residential area.

Once we had him stopped, we approached the vehicle. I could hear the suspect raising his voice, and watched as Tim pulled him from the car. I immediately went to my partner's side, and could hear the suspect screaming profanities. I know Tim and I know me. This guy had no driver's license and if he would have acknowledged this and been polite, he would have been on his way.

I really could never understand these guys who had an attitude. We were holding the hammer and he was encouraging us to drop it on him. Because he wouldn't shut up, we obliged him. After he was cuffed, I led him back to the scout car, opened the rear door and told him to have a seat. He said he wouldn't fit, and continued cussing us out.

It was very frustrating for us, as this situation happens on a regular basis. A suspect claims he just won't fit in the police car. I leave the guy with Tim, go to the other side of the car, and open the rear door. Tim pushes him at the waist, and he has no choice but to sit on the rear seat. I am now in the car and I grab him by the shoulders and drag him in. It was amazing how he fit in perfectly. We then drove to the station, processed him and completed our paperwork. I handed my report to the desk boss for approval, at which time my desk boss proceeds to ask me about the suspect's injuries.

"Injuries?" I ask. "What injuries? "

The sergeant tells me he has a split lip. Tim nor I ever saw any type of injury, and we certainly didn't hit him. Was this self-inflicted? It wouldn't be the first time, what with the city's reputation for paying off lawsuits.

No matter, we knew what was coming and, six months later, we are called to the law department for a deposition. Tim was not a regular partner of mine, but he apparently had been through this process many times. He asks me if I need a legal pad and pen. I looked at him, and asked if he is joking. He looks at me sternly and replies no. He is carrying enough legal crap to look like a lawyer.

We then are called into a large conference room. Present are myself, Tim the city attorney, the suspect and his attorney, and a special request is made for the suspect's mom to sit in during the deposition. Our attorney allows it, and I honestly didn't have a problem with it.

Like any deposition, everyone has a turn for questions and answers. When the attorneys begin questioning the suspect, his answers are herky-jerky, almost staged. I'm puzzled by this, and so is everyone else.

After about the sixth question, my man Tim jumps up and solves the mystery. He points at the suspect's mother and yells, "She is giving him the answers!"

Holy crap, how does he know that? The city attorney actually vocalizes my thoughts. The mom is positioned behind everyone and nobody is watching her as the suspect is being questioned.

In her lap, she has index cards with answers on it that read, "they beat you," "they followed you," "they used their flashlights."

She is holding them up for her son to read. We never would have seen it, but Tim saw the reflection of the mother in the TV screen positioned at the far end of the table. He could see the mom flash the individual cards. Well, our attorney makes a big deal about it, and has the mother and her index cards removed from the room.

In the end after all the issues, the city paid them anyway. They got six thousand dollars.

We were outraged. After all of that hullabaloo, they paid the guy off even though he had sued the city on four previous occasions. Our attorney explained it was cheaper to pay them than to pay the legal fees. Yeah, yeah, yeah — we have heard that before, but it doesn't make it right. It simply didn't matter if our actions were right or wrong.

As you probably guessed, there was no class on that in the academy either.

CUJO WINS

It was about this time, I moved permanently to Special Operations and started working in plain clothes. I initially would be assigned to the 11 a.m. to 7 p.m. shift, which was perfect. You still could get paid for court and put in a full eight hours. I thought working patrol had given me a full education. I soon realized the learning had just begun. I was fortunate, and had three good officers as my new partners. They all were workers, and we made some great arrests. Like any good crew, we grew close and became family.

We tried to do a little narcotics work every day in the precinct. I usually would be the eye and call the case. Just a reminder, we would pick a spot, and I would conceal myself in a vacant building with a set of binoculars. I would watch a suspect sell dope, spot his stash, identify the buyer, and then call in the troops. It was easy pickings because we could work a number of locations every day. You could lock up the dope man, but you never could get rid of the customers. They would keep showing up, and a new seller would magically appear to fill the void.

This story goes back to the tough fearless officer image I tried to project. I was tough enough and felt I could hold my own on the street, but certain things gave me the creeps. We had a couple of bad guys out selling heroin on a very active corner. This was a good setup because there was a large vacant apartment building about fifty yards away. I would be able to get in undetected. I slipped in, and the place is huge, being five stories high. I begin working my way to one of the top floors and encounter the usual — human and animal feces, used narcotic paraphernalia and miscellaneous garbage. The trick is to avoid stepping in any of it.

As I worked my way up, I begin to encounter animal carcasses — cats and dogs, partially eaten or decayed. This is not unusual, but there seemed to be way too many of them. There were at least ten or twelve bodies. I know I have seen the homeless chasing animals for food, and I think maybe these animals were part of someone's diet. I got a strange feeling when I made the top floor. Trying to shake it off, I find a room with a good view. I focus my binoculars and find my suspects still are there. I know to barricade the door and get ready to watch. This allows me privacy from wandering hobos and animals.

My mind cannot get rid of the image of those skeletons, and I walk back to check the door one more time. I can see the length of the building through the hallway. At that exact moment, about twenty rooms down, a large dog steps into the hallway. He was big, about a hundred and twenty pounds, with long matted fur. It was dirty and imposing looking. He glances down the hall in my direction for just a split second, and then walks into the other room. I panic, thinking he has spotted me. I think "Cujo."

This must be the monster that has been consuming all the small animals. Could that have been blood around his muzzle? I wasn't sure. Now I have no idea where he is in the building. It's probably stalking his next victim. I radio the crew that I'm coming out. They want to know why, as we just set up. I now am hustling down the stairway, glancing over my shoulder at every opportunity. I tell them I have to potty. They tell me to just piss in any of the designated areas. Thinking on the fly, I change my urgent need from peeing to pooping. As I hit the last landing, I'm traveling at light speed. I jump from the building, fearing the blood-muzzled monster has chased me the whole way.

The crew pulls into the alley and I scramble into the car.

"You must really have to go," my partner says. "You look a bit pale."

They have no idea how close to a disaster it had been. If something had jumped out, I would have crapped my pants in a heartbeat. I kept that secret for a couple months, and then told the truth over a couple of beers.

Luckily, I never saw that dog again.

IDIOTS BABBLE, WISEMEN STAY QUIET

Other officers can tell right away if you are the real deal. Keep in mind that we have plenty of talkers on the job. They will talk about feats of heroism and great accomplishments. They will tell you of the great arrests they made. The only way this bragging can be confirmed is by their performance on the street. Good officers usually are not the talkers. A philosopher once said that the idiot babbles while the wise man remains silent. I've used this line more than once on my rookies.

One day, uniformed patrol had investigated a shooting where two suspects armed with a rifle had attempted to kill a guy. The victim was shot twice and would survive. A witness knew one of the suspects by his first name and where he lived. Patrol was trying to solve it, and a sergeant called the house asking for the named suspect. He answered the phone, but when they made it to the house, no one came to the door. They were sure he was in there, but would need a search warrant. They probably went about it a little ass-backwards, but they were trying.

They called us for advice. I explained the procedure, but told them I would go have a look at the house. We were sitting about a half a block away when I saw a man from the gas company pull up across the street. I watched him get out of his van and enter the suspect's house. He was carrying tools, so I hatched a plan. I told my partner to just play along. We pulled up to the suspect's house, and I began pounding on the door. No response. I pounded louder and began yelling, "Is the gasman in there?" I continued to pound, hollering about the gasman.

After a short time, I heard a voice ask, "Who is it?"

"Police. We are looking for the gas man," I said.

A woman opened the door, and I again asked if the gasman was inside. I wanted to know if he was wearing a badge or showed any identification. I informed the female that we had several cases where suspects were posing as the gasman to gain entry. She immediately opened the door and pointed to the basement yelling, "He's down there!"

The gasman, hearing all the noise, came to the top of the stairs with a frightened look on his face. I ordered him over to me, and he began saying he was innocent. He said he truly was a legitimate gasman on a service call. Mind you, he was in full uniform, and this being Detroit, he had about twenty identification cards around his neck. Just as I was reaching for him, our shooting suspect came out a side room to investigate the commotion. My hand went directly from the gasman to our suspect, and we had our bad guy in-custody. He was in cuffs and out the door before he could figure out what happened to him.

Everyone in the house now was confused, and they were shouting in protest. The poor gasman still was pleading his case and followed us out. I had to explain to him what had just happened and why. I had made the accusations to gain permission to enter the house. It would take a while for him to sort it out, and he was walking along the side of my car still professing his innocence as we drove off.

Our uniformed guys were impressed with the ploy, and thankful for our help.

LEAVE IT TO NARCOTICS

We had many close calls that reaffirmed the deadly reality of the job. There was an occasion where our other special ops car wanted some assistance with a narcotics location. It was an apartment on the third floor of a large complex. This really wasn't my cup of tea because I had been involved in raids before. You never knew what was behind the door. You better be geared up and prepared if you were going inside.

The crew we were helping was determined to take this drug spot down, so we agreed to help them. Apartment raids are pretty straight forward: Look like a drug addict, walk up and knock on the door. When they ask who it is, just tell them what you need. In this case, the guy inside will know we need two packs of heroin. He cracks the door, takes your money, and hands the drugs out through the opening. Our plan is to force the door when he hands out the drugs.

We had a guy on the crew who looked like a great drug addict. He never appreciated the drug-addict-looking-guy label, but it made the job easier. The three of us are positioned outside the door, and he knocks. He tells them he needs two, and once the door opens to hand out the drugs, we push. We immediately have a problem, as the door will not open all the way. We have the suspect pinned against the wall and the door. One of our officers is attempting to squeeze through the opening, and I hear a loud clunking sound that I have heard before. It is the type of sound a large-framed handgun makes when it is dropped. The officer now is inside the apartment and he pulls the suspect forward, allowing us to open the door and enter. While the other officers are clearing the location (checking rooms for other suspects), I find a stainless steel .44 magnum revolver behind the door.

It's one of those police moments every officer experiences. You are pissed that you did something you knew was wrong, but elated that you are alive. All that our suspect had to do was start pulling the trigger. He could have had several dead officers lying in the hallway. I walk in the other room with the gun, showing it to my partners. I told the other crew that is why I leave apartment and house raids for narcotic officers.

YOU FEEL LUCKY, KID?

The close calls reoccur in police work, whether you like it or not. It comes with the territory. Another unit was chasing a vehicle for armed robbery. We answered the call to assist them, and soon picked up the chase as they entered our precinct. After several minutes, the suspect vehicle headed down a one-way street.

Knowing it had no outlet, they would have to cut through the alley and double back. We paralleled them one street west. This street was one lane, with vehicles parked on both sides. We figured we would park mid-block, and they would have nowhere to go. The street was full of people, as it was a warm summer afternoon.

Sure enough, they doubled back through the alley and were headed north bound, straight at us. My partner and I opened our doors and were kneeling behind them, weapons pointed at the suspect vehicle as it sped toward us. This is the point where things can go wrong, and life and death decisions have to be made instantly.

The clock is ticking, and we have about a second or two. The suspect's vehicle never slowed down. I was sure he was going to ram us. It was a bad situation for us because we had parked cars on both sides of us. Them ramming into us was something we had not factored into our game plan. At the last moment, they swerved between two parked cars. There wasn't enough room, or at least we thought there wasn't, but they made it, banging the parked cars out of the way. They now were passing us on the front lawn, and I stood up to look over the parked car. As my head cleared the roof of the vehicle, I was looking at a suspect hanging out of the passenger side window. He was pointing a sawed-off shotgun at me. I was pointing my gun back, but it seemed so tiny in my hand.

I could see people and children running and screaming, and the car was by me in the blink of an eye. I have no idea why he didn't shoot. I'm guessing I didn't shoot because of my training. The car fishtailed its way down the street, sideswiping several cars. The bad guys eventually crashed, and all three were apprehended. The loaded sawed-off shotgun was recovered.

It took about an hour for my partner and I to calm down. We talked about the positioning of our car, and why neither of us fired. We both felt lucky, and by the end of the shift, we were back to our normal selves. We were talking about our kids and hunting season. I teamed up with this same guy on many occasions and really enjoyed working with him. He was young and willing to learn.

WHEN A LION BLOCKS YOUR PATH

One of my precinct pet peeves is people walking in the middle of the street. In Detroit, this also is quite common. The reason for it was so no animals or people could surprise you by jumping out from between the houses. My young partner knew how I felt about it, and if you were walking in the street, I was going to confront you about it. One evening, we were slow rolling though our precinct. We could see someone walking in the street up ahead of us.

My partner was driving and sped up because he knew I was going to give the guy the what-for. As we closed in on this person, we got a real good look at him. He was 6'5," and looked like 260 pounds of cut granite. He was a black male, with his hair dyed blonde, and he was wearing sweat pants with no shirt, and was drinking a forty-ounce beer. His body was covered in sweat, and it glistened. We recognized him as a professional football player who had been suspended from the league. He was not from our town, but had gotten himself into the news because he had been in a fight with security personnel in one of our downtown hotels. They attributed the reason for the incident to his bipolar disorder.

Now, I have no idea what my partner was thinking. I could see it on his face that he was excited and ready for some kind of show. I told him to drive around the guy. Yes, I said, drive around the guy. My partner was puzzled, but he listened to me.

"Do you know who that was?" he asked me.

I told him I did.

"But he is walking in the street," he said.

I told him I was aware of that, and he could walk in the street as much as he wanted as long as he wasn't causing a major problem. My partner started going on about me hating people walking in the street and I cut him off.

"If you were walking a path in the jungle, and you came across a sleeping lion blocking that path, what would you do?" I asked my partner. "Would you start poking him with a stick, and yell get out of the way you stupid lion, or would you quietly walk around him, allowing him to sleep undisturbed?"

He thought for a moment, and then smiled. This job is not about the confrontations, but how you handle them.

Did we ignore someone breaking the law? Yes. Was I afraid of this guy? You're damn skimpy I was. Should we have asked him to step out of the street? Yes. The end result was we watched him, and he quietly walked about a half a block and entered a house. There was no harm, and no confrontation. Did I lose some of that tough guy bravado with my young charge? Probably. He would learn as I did, sometimes you have to ignore that pride. It will help you survive.

Yes, I was learning more, and it never stopped. I previously have talked about animal confrontations and how to avoid them. I was with this same partner, when we received a breaking and entering run. All dispatch could give us was that it was a brown house on the corner of Heritage and Webb. We arrived at the location and discovered two brown houses.

You never should separate from your partner, but feeling we had a handle on the situation, we decided to split up and check both houses at the same time. He took the west corner house I took east. As we had parked a distance back from both locations, I had the opportunity to walk by the garage, and backyard of the house I would be checking. The most likely entry point would be the rear door, so I could take a good look at it as I approached.

Naturally, I scanned the yard for signs of Fido. There were no holes, bones, bowls or poop. The rear door appeared secure, and I would have to enter the yard from the side of the house, where a gate was positioned. The gate had no lock, and I gave it the last Fido check by shaking it. If there is a dog in the yard, the fence shaking usually brings him running.

I opened the gate and entered. I would have to walk along the sidewalk, which was located between the fence and the house. The gap between the fence and house probably was four-feet wide. My total distance to the back entrance would be about thirty feet. I had my flashlight in my left hand, leaving my right hand ready for a Quick Draw McGraw move, if needed. I reached the corner of the house and as I took my next step, a large pit bull took his next step around the corner. He had been traveling at the same leisurely pace as I had. We were both startled as our eyes locked. I have no idea if they can do this, but the startled look on that dogs face turned into a shit-eating grin.

I told you my job involves being thrust into dangerous situations with only seconds to make a decision. I could almost read that dog's mind as he assessed his situation. He knew that no matter what happened — fleeing or shooting — that he was going to get a chunk out of me. My startled look also turned into a smile, as I realized what he realized. I had to give him credit for that. I knew quick action was necessary and grabbed the fence. I was vaulting it when he locked on to the rear of my right thigh. My right hand and foot were now on the fence, with Killer dangling from my ass. My left hand was free, and I swung my flashlight as hard as I could, catching him square on the head. To my surprise, he lost his grip. I was half way over, and this gave me an opportunity to swing my left leg over the top. I almost made it when he recovered and gave me a parting nip on the left calf. I was cursing and laughing at the same time.

I looked back in the yard, and he was sitting there just grinning. There was no fussing or barking. He must have been quite content with his work. My partner had heard the commotion and come a running. It's funny how police officers go from being dead serious to having a good time. He asked if I was okay.

"Yes," I said.

He asked what happened, and I said a dog bit me. I turned around and he could see my shredded pants and blood. He looked at the dog just sitting there grinning, and he began to laugh. I asked if I was bleeding, and he mumbled yes through his giggling laugh. I had no shame. I pulled my pants down right there in the street.

"You are going to need some medical attention," he laughed.

I hiked up my drawers, at which time the homeowner came out of the house.

"What the hell is going on?" she yelled.

I wasn't sure if it was my wounded pride or just simple embarrassment, but I yelled back, "We are trying to protect you from the B&E man."

She smiled that same smile the dog gave me at the corner of the house, and said, "I don't need protection. I have a dog."

WHAT THE COMMANDER DOESN'T KNOW ....

I also learned that precinct life is like Las Vegas. What happens there, stays there.

One evening, I was at home when I received a call at from one of the afternoon sergeants. This was unusual, and I feared that one of my partners had been hurt.

"Nothing of the sort," he explained, they just wanted me to work a case. He said they mistakenly released someone who needed to be located and arrested. They wanted the crew and I to start as early as we could. Our regular starting time was 11 a.m., but if they could clear it, we could all be in at 7.

The following morning, we were briefed, and I now understood their concern. They had two guys in the cellblock named James Smith. One was being held for traffic warrants, the other for multiple felonies. Someone had come to the front desk to bond out the traffic warrant Smith. They paid the two-hundred-dollar bond and told the sergeant they would be waiting in a car in front of the station. The sergeant told the doorman that James Smith had bonded out. The doorman went into the cellblock and hollered, "James Smith, you made bond."

Our felony-warrant Smith answers up and the doorman brings him forward. He signs for his property and is told a ride is waiting for him. They process and release this James Smith. He actually goes out front and opens the door of the waiting car.

"You better get the fuck out of my car," the female driver tells him, and he slams the door and walks south bound on Livernois.

She comes into the station asking where James Smith is. The sergeant informs her he just sent him out. She informs him that is not her James Smith. He now realizes his mistake and runs out the front door, just in time to see felony James Smith break into a full run. Several officers jump into scout cars, but Smith has vanished. At this point, the commander of the precinct has not been notified, and they are hoping special ops can get him back in-custody before anyone is the wiser.

It's scary but funny. Someone will lose their job if he does something bad. The only thing we have to work on is his two listed addresses. One is his girlfriend's apartment, and the other is his home address. We have two three-man cars working, and we split the addresses. My car goes to his last known address, and we find it vacant. We are heading to the girlfriend's place when the other car informs us via radio that he is not there.

I ask if the girlfriend was there, and they say yes, but she hasn't seen him. I tell them to meet us back at the girlfriend's apartment. These were pretty good officers, but they didn't have a lot of time on the job. We knocked on the girlfriend's door and she lets us in. She already is chirping that she doesn't know where he is. We ask if she minds if we search the place.

"Feel free," she says.

I notice several garbage bags full of men's clothes. There is mail on the counter in her name and Smith's. Some of her mail is from the social security department. I'm fairly certain she is lying, and tell her not to force our hands.

"I don't know where he is!" she yells.

I tell her to turn around, and I place handcuffs on her. She is stunned, and asks what she is being arrested for. I inform her it is for falsifying social security documents with the intent to mislead government officials, which is a federal offense. I told her I did my homework and contacted the office before we arrived. She has been misleading the government for years. She begins to cry. I tell her all we want is her boyfriend. We don't want her. We can overlook the federal case, and leave it up to the feds to find her. I say I'll even mislead them if she'll just give us the information we need. Is her boyfriend worth seven years in a federal penitentiary? She cracks and gives him up. He is in an apartment building in another precinct. She doesn't know the address or the apartment, but gives us a description of the building and the cross streets. I lecture her a bit more about the consequences of lying.

"Please let me go, I can't go to prison," she begged.

I un-cuff her and all of us meet out front to formulate a plan. Two of the officers are looking at me, when one tells me how much he admires me.

"How do you know so much? You must read all the time to stay current with state and federal laws," he says.

I ask him what he means.

"Falsifying social security documents," he replies. "Who knows shit like that?"

I told him that I didn't — I just made up the charge to get her to give him up. I wasn't really going to arrest her.

I love these police moments, he doesn't know whether to be pissed off or impressed. I went from super cop, to shifty scoundrel. I assure him he will get over it, and one day, he will have his own bag of tricks. I had come a long way from those rookie days.

We head to the given location and find the apartment building. Now we need to get lucky because we don't know what apartment he is in.

We locate the manager and ask if he had any new people come into the building in the last day or two. He says yes, and the new guy is staying with a life-long tenant named John. A quick review with the manager on physical description has our hopes up that felony Smith is staying with John. We ask the manager if he has a passkey, which he does, and he escorts us to the apartment. Once he opens the door, we find John sitting at the kitchen table eating cereal. He is about seventy years old. We ask in a whisper where Smith is, and he points to the bedroom. We enter the bedroom and find our suspect fast asleep. No blanket, he's lying face up and his hands are visible. I shake the bed, and our suspect's eyes flutter open. It takes him several seconds to adjust, and he shouts, "How the fuck did you find me?"

I smile at my hero-worshipping partner, look back at Smith, and tell him, "Excellent police work. That's how we found you."

Well, my whole crew now became heroes to the desk personnel from afternoons. A couple cases of beer and pop were waiting when we returned with our prize. We agreed to come back for choir practice to share our refreshments with the whole shift.

To this day, I don't know if the commander ever found out about the mistaken release of James Smith.

HEADING TOWARD A LONG VACATION

My first serious injury happened at Number 10. I had been in some minor fender benders and several fights, but just had bumps and bruises. This injury would be a bit more serious. My partner and I had lost a suspect in a stolen car chase several days earlier. This guy also was wanted for assault with intent to commit murder. He had a reputation for stealing cars, and usually had no problem driving them home.

On this day, we spotted him again. He was in a new stolen ride doing 70 miles per hour. We tried to catch up, as he screeched to a stop in front of his mom's house. He jumped from the vehicle and got inside the house, clanging shut the security bars. I immediately ran to the rear to cover the back, and I find no back door. There were second-story windows, but no first floor windows or doors. I yelled to my partner that I'm coming back up and there must be a side door on the east side. I found my partner standing at the corner, watching the front and side doors. We now could hear something at the rear of the house. I ran to the back just in time to see the suspect jump from the second story window, and he hit the ground running. Never underestimate what a suspect will do to escape.

I yelled for my partner, and the chase was on. As most chases go, this one was comical. I always taught my rookies that the bad guy is trying to get away a lot harder than you are trying to catch him. So right out of the gate, you are up against it. There was a light snow on the ground, and the first corner he comes to, he slips and falls. I smile at his misfortune. But he is up and running, and as I make the same corner, I experience the same results and go ass over apple cart. This happens several more times, him going down, him getting up, and me going down, me getting up.

I know this guy is dangerous, but can't help laughing as I go down for a fourth time. My partner has pulled up in the car, and jumps out.

"I got this," he yells, and takes off running.

He makes the other side of the street and slips and falls. I can hear him cursing as he recovers and continues the chase. The suspect now is running west between the houses. I take over our car and drive two blocks west, tuck in behind a parked car and wait. Sure as shooting, our suspect pops out between the houses, and attempts to hide between some bushes and a porch. He hasn't seen me, and I exit the car and begin creeping toward him. He either heard or sensed something, and he takes off again.

He now is running between the two houses, and I'm forty feet behind. At the end of the house, he makes a big right hand turn, runs into one yard, and then jumps from sight into the other yard. I slow down and approach the backyards cautiously. I peak around the corner, finding our suspect crawling and dragging himself across the yard. He seems to be struggling to breath.

My eyes are fixed on him, and I have my radio in my left hand and my gun in my right. Simple, I'll jump through the same bushes he did, because there is no fence between the yards. I'm still trotting and take the jump. Instantaneously, I know what happened to the suspect. Both my feet have tangled in wire, and I'm on the way down. And what is piled on the other side of the bushes? Broken concrete blocks. I attempt to twist sideways to avoid going face-first into that. I cannot brace myself, as I have both hands full.

Unfortunately, I land on a protruding jagged piece of concrete. It manages to fit perfectly between the side panels of my vest. I go down hard and can hear the whoosh of air as the wind is knocked out of me. I realize I am extremely vulnerable but have managed to hold onto my radio and gun. My first impulse was to yell for my partner, but the attempt was futile. Something was coming out, but it certainly wasn't words.

The only thing I had going for me was that the suspect was in the same shape. He had landed on the same pile of rocks, so back to the funny part. He has the wind knocked out of him, and is crawling like a crab to get away. I have the wind knocked out of me, and am crawling on my elbows and knees in pursuit. I catch him as he reaches the fence and I manage to cuff him.

We lay there recovering, and my partner eventually finds us. We transport our suspect to the station and start our paperwork. My side hurts but not unbearably. I then get a call from an informant on another suspect who we have been chasing for several weeks. He was wanted for multiple home invasions. The informant gives us his location, and we head over to try and nab him.

We locate the suspect and arrest him without incident. We head back to the station, and process our second prisoner. I sit down and begin to type our report.

At this point, my adrenaline dump must have been huge. It now feels like I have been shot. My side is throbbing. I try to stand up and can't. I call for my partner, who helps me stand. I feel better, but can't sit because of the pain.

We inform the boss that my partner is going to transport me to the clinic. He has a heck of a time getting me in the car, and fears I'm having a heart attack. He makes me laugh with the diagnosis, and I ask him when my heart moved above my waist on my right-hand side. It really hurt when I laughed. We make the clinic, and I'm already uneasy. There have been too many bad experiences.

I am standing, as this is my only comfortable position, and it's not that comfortable. They take a number of X-rays, and tell me I have three broken ribs. Well, it sure felt like something was broken. Department procedure dictated that the clinic determines and assigns you a duty status: Full duty, restricted duty or off until you are better. She fills out my status sheet and hands it to me. Restricted duty. I look at her and ask if she is kidding. I'm not a doctor, but I know this is going to be much worse tomorrow. I'm in unbelievable pain when I sit right now, and she wants me to go back to work. She will not change my status, and I return to the precinct handing over the form. I inform the boss that I don't care what the department doctor said, I'm going to my own doctor tomorrow, and I will not be in to work.

I cannot get into see my doctor until the following day, when El Duce has someone call me to chew me out. They want to know what the heck I'm trying to pull, and I need to report to medical section immediately. Medical section is not the clinic, and it's run out of a major hospital in the city. I guess she thought I was trying to get a duty disability or something. I report to medical as instructed, and they take several x-rays. I am standing in the examination room when the doctor comes in. She informs me I have broken ribs. I explain why I am there, and that my duty status is restricted. She looks shocked and asked who determined that. I told her it was on my slip. She looks at it and says, "No, no, no. You are going to be off a minimum of two months, maybe longer. You have three broken ribs. There is no treatment, they just need to heal."

I now have to deliver the doctor's report myself. My wife had to drive me to medical, and I instruct her to take me to the precinct. I struggle to get out of the car and drag myself in. I locate El Duce's stooge, and hand over my paperwork.

I inform him it was a good thing she sent me to the hospital and please let the inspector know I'll be off for the next several months, thanks to her concerns.

THINGS UNCOVERED FROM BEHIND THE DESK

I finally did come back to work on a restricted duty status and renewed my fight with El Duce. Because I was assigned to special operations, I was in the back doing paperwork and intelligence on current cases. She didn't like this, and wanted our lieutenant to assign me to the front desk to do reports. The front desk is rookie or slug work. That is the only way I could describe it. I was solving cases in the back, but that didn't matter. She wanted to show me who the boss was. So now I'm working at the desk, taking accident reports.

It's my third day on the desk and my crew brings in a stolen car arrest. I had just walked up to the desk sergeant to get a report signed, and I looked at their suspect. I immediately recognized him from a surveillance photo taken inside a bank that was robbed the previous week. It wasn't hard to make the recognition because he had a very distinct hat and haircut. I called one of my partners over and asked where they arrested him. He told me a bank parking lot. My partner now is making the connections, so I tell him to go get the bank surveillance photos I gave him last week.

He trots out to the car, retrieves the photos and returns. I'm standing in the same spot, looking directly across the desk at the suspect. I pick up the surveillance picture of him wearing that hat, hold it up and I pull my partner behind the picture. I love being a smart ass.

"It's the bank robber!" my partner yells.

"Exactly," I said. "You may want to add a second charge to go along with the stolen car."

I tell my partners to not worry about adding me to the report because I knew they eventually would have recognized him. I wanted them to get credit for it. I return to my spot at the desk and continue to take reports.

About ten minutes later, I watch as one of my partners opens the cellblock doors and lets the bank robber out with no cuffs. El Duce meets him and they walk back to her office. There are no cuffs and no escort. I'm livid. I grab my partner and ask what the hell she is doing. He tells me he is not happy either, but she is going to allow the suspect to talk to his father privately in her office. WHAT? PRIVATELY? I am beside myself. I felt she lacked basic police skills, but this was unreal.

After about thirty minutes, she walked him back un-cuffed through the precinct and turned him over to the doorman. Apparently, his father was a friend of an ex-mayor and that carried some sort of weight with her. Maybe he appointed her to her position, I have no idea. Her actions had implications. How do you explain that to a rookie officer or even an experienced one? I already knew there was a different set of rules and they only applied to the select few.

People like El Duce were nothing but a curse. Her type never was going to make the city safe. Hell, she was making the precinct dangerous. I eventually recovered and went back to my plain-clothes assignment.

WHO LET THE OGRE OUT?

They introduced a new officer to special operations. He was there to handle a specific job, but when we were short people, he would ride with us. He was a great guy, and funny — which always is a big plus in our line of work. This day, he is available, and we get a family trouble run.

We meet the fifty-year-old mother out front, and she tells us her thirty-year-old daughter assaulted her, and fearing for her safety, she fled the house. We asked the standard questions. Was she still in the house? She didn't know. Were there weapons in the house? No.

So, in we go with our victim. We identify ourselves as we enter, and receive no response. We begin checking each individual room when we come to an unusual door in the hallway. It had four large eyebolts running into the door casing. A large chain that crisscrosses the door in an X pattern secures the closed door. Someone has spray painted DANGER DO NOT OPEN on the door, which appears well worn and beaten.

Having some time on the job, we didn't give it a second thought. I figured it's a room for a dog or dogs. Our new guy just had to ask. Our victim tells us she keeps her husband locked in there. He can get out of control, so it's better to keep him under lock and key. Okay, many other departments would demand she open the door. We know better, as this is Detroit, and we stay the course. Who knows what is in there, and I'm getting that fruit loop vibe from her anyway.

We leave the new guy upstairs, and my partner and I begin searching the basement. We left him alone upstairs because we didn't want all our eggs in one basket.

After several minutes of searching, I now hear screaming and footsteps running across the floor. Realizing something is wrong, I run for the stairs. I arrive at the bottom just as the new guy arrives at the top. He has a concerned look on his face, looks at me, then looks to his left and screams, "Holy shit, he is loose!"

Our new guy then thunders down the stairs, running right past me. I've already drawn my gun and have it pointed at the top of the stairs.

I can hear him jabbering behind me, "She let him out. My God she let him out!"

I've told you before, I'm afraid of monsters, and now I'm on the verge of panic. I only can imagine what was locked in that room. I soon see the reason for his fear, as the husband rounds the corner. He is a black male, about sixty-five years old, 5'6," and weighs 165 pounds. He has salt and pepper hair, and that is about the only thing normal about him. His left eye is positioned high on his forehead, almost in the brow line. It is a bad eye and discolored. The right side of his mouth drooped open, exposing jagged and broken teeth. He is shuffling more than walking, and appears to be dragging one leg. It reminded me of the Mummy in a horror movie.

He is holding a claw hammer in his right hand, right above his right shoulder in a striking position, and he keeps repeating, "Kill, Kill, Kill," and swings the hammer to match each utterance. He clunks down the first stair and begins heading my way. All of us are now grouped together like The Three Stooges at the bottom of the stairs. We have our guns out, but know we are not going to shoot him. He gets half way down when we holster our weapons.

My partner now is positioned to the side of the stairway and I am right at the bottom with the new guy close behind me. As soon as he is within reach, we grab him. He has turned toward my partner, so I wrap my arms around his waist. My partner grabs the arm with the hammer.

His voice does not change, and he continues with the slow methodical "Kill, Kill, Kill." After several minutes, I become concerned because we cannot disarm him. The majority of the time, officers use only necessary force to get the job done. You really don't want to hurt anyone. At times, you have to. I rear back to punch our guy as hard as I can in the forearm. There is a nerve there, that if hit, will numb that arm. As I throw my power punch, our guy twists sideways. I now hit my partner, Drew, squarely on the shoulder.

Drew is all of a buck fifty, and the punch knocks him across the floor and into a pile of dirty clothes. Our Ogre is loose and resumes the "Kill, Kill, Kill." I'm fed up, and know this can turn deadly. I already may have killed my partner. I grab our guy and flip him to the ground. I stomp on his arm until he drops the hammer, then I grab it and toss it across the room.

I rush to my partner, and he says he's okay. I help him untangle from the pile of clothes he landed in. We turn around just in time to see our guy pull a jackknife from his right pocket. He unfolds the blade and in the same guttural voice again begins to mutter, "Kill, Kill, Kill."

We grab the new guy and head up the stairs, hitting only every other one. The front door is open and we escape through it. We skip the stairs and vault the banister, heading for the safety of our car.

Our victim is laughing as we run by, and yells, "I told you so. You shouldn't have let him out!"

We fish tail out of there as I hit the gas. I start yelling at the new guy, "What are you trying to do, get us killed?"

"Me? It was the Ogre trying to kill us," he said.

I'm still shook up and ask, "Is that what that was, and who let him out?"

My partner told me he was walking around smoking a cigarette, when the ogre came around the corner. The wife must have let him out, and the only way out for my partner was down the stairs. Okay, I can understand that, but I'm afraid of monsters too. Next time head, for the front door. You always need a survivor to tell the story.

TIME TO CALL A SITTER

I had about ten years on the job at this time, and was becoming pretty seasoned. Younger officers relied on me for help, and I eagerly supplied it. It was frustrating for them because they wanted to do the job, but they just didn't have the tools or experience yet. Ten years had flown by for me, and I still didn't know everything. I felt like I wasn't that far removed from my rookie status.

On one occasion, I was working with a young officer, and I was lecturing him on maintaining a log. This is a book of wanted suspects, intelligence bulletins, etc. You can't remember everything, and it's easier if you have it written down. He pointed at a house, and told me he knew a woman in there was wanted on a felony warrant for check fraud. Great, she is an example of someone who would go in your book.

Now, check fraud doesn't seem like a real big deal in the criminal world. But for younger officers, it is. Experienced officers know every case is a big deal. Did you forget about the three officers locking up the old lady for a bad check? They were bound and executed. I make sure I relate that story to my young charges.

He explains he investigated her once, and his car computer was slow. Her information did not come back for an hour, and he already had let her go when he discovered she had a felony warrant. He had tried knocking on the door and waiting for her to come out, but he had no success. At that moment, he pointed out her six-year-old son on the corner. I could see he had a black toy pistol in his hand. I told him to pull over and let me out. I walked up to the kid, and asked what he was doing with the gun. His response, of course, was that he was playing, which he was.

I asked where he lived, and he pointed two houses down. I asked if his mother was home, and he replied yes.

I told him let's go talk to her. We made it to the front porch with my young partner catching up. The little boy opened the front door, and stepped in, with me right behind. He yelled for his mom, who appeared from the kitchen.

The first thing she saw were the two police officers standing inside her house.

Apparently, this had been going on for some time with my young partner, and she had been ducking and dodging him. She obviously recognized him. Her first words were, "Is it okay if I call someone to watch my kids?"

She knew what we were there for and went without incident. It was a good lesson.

LIGHTS OUT, BOYS

Our poor precinct island of misfit toys had such a negative reputation that nothing shocked me. I'm pulling into the lot one day on midnights, and I notice all of the precinct lights are out. Being a highly trained observer, I noticed the Coney Island west of us had lights, and so did the bar south of us. Strange. I walk into the lobby and found the desk and report clerk working by candlelight. Did we have an electrical failure, or some type of damage to the system? No, I am told the city didn't pay its bill. The firehouse also has no lights. It's shocking, but true.

After 9/11, the city wised up and placed large generators at all emergency locations, including Fire, Police and EMS. The problem is that when the power fails, no one at our location can start or operate the generators. The city only had a couple of people trained to do it, and we never saw them. You think there would be a monthly test to check the condition or functioning of each unit. If the power went out, we had a generator, but no one could operate it or even tell us if it worked. This type of thing went along with our camera systems in the scout cars. It's a great idea to use them, but there's no money to update or maintain them. If they broke, well, they were broke.

It's always tough working under these constant conditions. Now candlelight?

DOG DAYS OF THE DEPARTMENT

Animal stories always were a constant, and things wouldn't be different at this command. I still can't determine if this one was tragic or funny.

Another precinct had requested two dog sticks from our precinct, as everyone was short of equipment. I was assigned to a three-man car, and my partners were a high-strung younger guy and a female. We were called on to deliver the dog sticks, which I agreed to do as long as I didn't have to operate them. It was about 10 p.m. when we arrived at the address, and it was easy to see we were in a higher-end neighborhood.

As we pull up, I can see what we referred to as "the auto," parked in the driveway. The auto is a large van used to transport prisoners to court. It was backed against the swinging gates that led to the backyard. I could see several officers next to the van, and one was lying on the roof.

Again, I have some time on the job, and I'm not shocked. Let's get out and find out what's going on. All three of us walk up the drive, finding a lieutenant and three officers outside the van. The fourth cop is on the roof dangling something down. At that moment, two large Rottweilers hit the gates barking. I can see the gates are secured with a pair of handcuffs. The fourth officer now has raised up his hands, and appears to be holding two pieces of baloney. It's a weird scene, and I ask the lieutenant what is going on. She asks me if I brought the dog sticks, and I tell her yes. She asks if any of us can operate them, and I tell her no. She tells me we are going to stick with plan A then. I guess we were part of plan B, and now are a relegated to a spectator role. Sometimes, this can be a very good thing.

It seems the two dogs trapped in the yard did not belong to the people living in the house, and they wanted them out. Animal control is not available at this hour, so it will be our job to catch them and take them to the pound. Per the lieutenant, this was how plan A was going to work. Six officers will be involved in the operation. Two will go to the far end of the yard and distract the dogs. One officer will un-cuff the gates and open them. Another officer will open the van doors, and the officer on the roof will entice the dogs into the van with the baloney.

I asked if she was kidding, and she gave me a dead serious look. I turned to my partners and said, "Do not shoot these dogs. Do not even put yourself in a position to shoot at those dogs."

Experience was screaming out, and it was obvious plan A had nothing to do with experience.

Both animals were healthy and well kept. They both wore collars, and obviously were not strays. And they looked like very expensive mutts. I suggested to the lieutenant that maybe the homeowners would allow the dogs to remain in the yard until animal control became available. No, she said, they wanted them out. I asked if she had asked that question.

"No, but I know what they want," she answered.

So I gave her both dog sticks and walked to the car.

My female partner came with me. My high-strung partner went into the yard on the east side of the location. I knew this was going to be ugly. The first two officers did their jobs distracting the dogs. This allowed the other two cops and the lieutenant to get into position. Our baloney dangler already was standing by. As soon as the officer began unlocking the cuffs, I could hear the first two officers yell, "Here they come!"

There was panic at the gate as the dogs rounded the corner. The officer charged with removing the cuffs from the gate could not open the cuffs. She scrambled back and drew her weapon. When the dogs hit the gate, the two officers and lieutenant opened up on them with their department-issued handguns. The first shot was a doozey, and it blasted the cuffs off the gate. I have no idea about the next ten or twelve shots. The dogs were hit several times, and I could hear rounds ricocheting off of the ground and into the garage. Both dogs ran back into the yard, where the other officers and my high-strung partner started blasting away. I couldn't count how many shots were fired, but it had to be close to thirty. Both dogs now were down and not moving. The screaming had stopped, and a pall of gun smoke drifted across the yard like a blue fog. My partner emerged from the east yard, still holding his smoking gun.

"What did I tell you?" I screamed.

"I had no choice," was his response, and he was dead wrong.

"How many times did you fire?" I asked.

"About nine," he said.

I just shook my head and walked up the driveway. All the officers still were shaking as I entered the yard. I yelled for the officers in the back not to shoot me as I was entering the yard. One dog was dead, and the other was yelping. I walked up to the lieutenant, and asked if she wanted to finish him off, and then I stormed back to my car.

I drove to the precinct so my partner could do the paperwork that we could have completely avoided. I sat outside, not wanting to talk to anyone. I see the Plan A lieutenant exit the precinct and walk toward me. She said my partner told her that I inspected weapons. I did, and it is required that someone qualified like myself inspected your weapon every ninety days. You carried an inspection card, which you needed to turn over anytime you fired your weapon. Today, she was going to need that card. Hers was not updated, and she wanted to know if I would just check her card and put last week on it. I told her of course I would, and signed it. I made sure I put tomorrow's date in the box. She never checked the date and walked off smiling.

It seemed like I had quite a few dog incidents at this precinct. I was walking around with my flap of my gown open during a department random drug test when a female officer came over the radio. She sounded very excited. They needed help, and she yelled that they were in a disaster zone. This upset me, as I had never seen a disaster zone in the city, and my gut feeling was that she was making a big deal out of something very small.

I filled my cup, got dressed, and we headed to her location. The sky was eerie when we left the clinic. It was cloudy and raining off and on. We only had been inside the clinic for a half hour, but everything outside had a weird glow. As we headed through our precinct, you could see a severe storm had moved through the area. Branches and trash everywhere, and power lines were down. I cursed myself for doubting her when we got to the location she had called from. It was a disaster area: Several houses were gone, and I mean gone. There were basement foundations, but no homes, furniture, trash or anything. Apparently, a tornado had touched down. It was a mess and a number of officers were recalled to help.

About four hours later, we were taking a break in the park where many of the victims had gathered. Suddenly, two dogs appeared, one being much larger than the other, and they started fighting. The larger dog had the smaller one pinned, and an officer behind me spoke to our boss.

"Sarge, you better let me shoot that dog, or he is going to kill the other one," he said.

The sergeant was standing next to me smoking a cigarette.

"Yes, you better shoot him. Go ahead," he said, despite the fact the park was packed with people.

I never moved and thought they were kidding, until I heard the crack of the gun. The larger dog yelped and released the smaller one. He slowly limped off into the alley. I stood there stunned. Who in the hell in their right mind thinks of shooting at a dog in this crowd? Worse yet, what kind of leader would approve of taking that kind of dangerous action?

Several minutes later, the owner of the larger dog showed up, with the animal on a leash. He had been shot through the side. He wanted to know why the police shot his dog. The sergeant explained the fight, at which time the owner explained that the smaller dog was his and they fight all the time. I walked off ashamed.

Police Officer Brian Eric Huff
Detroit Police Department, Michigan
End of Watch: Monday, May 3, 2010

Officer Brian Huff was shot and killed at about 3:30 a.m. after responding to a report of gunshots at a vacant home on Schoenherr Street. Several officers had surrounded the home, which was known to be a drug house, in response to the initial 911 call. When Officer Huff and the other officers who were positioned in the front of the home made entry, they immediately were met with gunfire. Officer Huff was fatally wounded, and four other officers suffered non-life threatening wounds. The suspect also was shot and wounded by the return gunfire. The suspect was sentenced to life in prison, without parole, on May 5, 2011.

Officer Huff had served with the Detroit Police Department for twelve years, and was assigned to the Eastern District. He is survived by his wife and ten-year-old son.

YOU'RE UNDER ARREST, OFFICER

My most memorable incident at #10 was not murder or some significant arrest. It was how the department treated its officers. My two partners and I were working a plainclothes car, when dispatch came over the radio with a call for a man armed with a gun.

They had given it to a marked unit and we answered the run as backup. We arrived at the given location, which was a street corner, and found the suspect just standing there. He matched the physical and clothing description given by radio. My partners placed the suspect on the scout car and searched him. I walked about ten feet down to the corner looking for a weapon he may have tossed. Unable to locate one, I returned to my partners.

At this time, the marked unit pulled up, and we informed them we hadn't found a weapon. They still wanted to check his name, so they placed him in the back of their car. We called dispatch to let them know we were available again and pulled off. We didn't go a block when we spotted and arrested a guy on a felony warrant. We transported him back to the base, processed him, and started our paperwork.

After twenty minutes, the desk lieutenant came back to our office and told us we couldn't leave the room. We thought he was kidding, and asked him why.

"You just can't," he replied.

Confused, I got up and walked to the door to ask him what this was all about, and he said, "I'm not kidding, you can't leave."

Okay, I took a seat. Luckily, a detective walked by and told us that someone was at the front desk claiming we robbed him. I was going to have to see this, and peeked around the corner. It was the sixteen-year-old kid we had just searched for a gun. Rob him? Rob him of what? He is sixteen.

The lieutenant finally came back and said the kid had six hundred dollars on him, and claimed that one of us took it. Okay, the first question would be which one? He didn't know. Second question, what is he doing with six hundred dollars? I trusted both my partners with my life, and I trusted them on the street. No one took anything from him. I know I hadn't, and both my partners were together, so if one of them took it, the other would have seen it. Never being through the process of being arrested by my own department, I was told to call my union representative. We were not allowed to leave the room until Internal Affairs arrived.

Our union rep arrived and told us to relax. Relax? I'm getting ready to be charged with armed robbery. I wasn't going to relax. He said this happened all the time. I was livid, and informed him that it doesn't happen to me all the time. We sat and stewed until Internal Affairs arrived. Then it got real interesting. They secured an office and led us in one at a time. We were given our Miranda rights and were searched. We were questioned about the incident, and then they searched our police car and lockers.

It was pretty clear we were under arrest — even a rookie could see that. This whole process took several hours. When they were done, they said they would let us know the results of the investigation and we could go back to work. Back to work! I'm going home, and don't know if I'll be back. A sixteen-year-old kid accuses us of something, you have no evidence of any sort, but you arrest us, search us, and then tell us to go back on the street. What would the precincts perception of us be? We went home disgusted.

The following day, I reported for my shift, and my partner was depressed. It was written all over his face and he told me he just didn't feel comfortable working. He decided that he was going home sick. I asked him why? He told me he was pissed off. So was I. I told him not to go, but he went to the front desk, feigned an illness, and left.

I wasn't going to stand for that. I walked up to the same lieutenant who had arrested us the previous day and told him I didn't think I could take the street today.

"Are you sick?" he asked, probably hoping I would say yes.

I told him I wasn't; I just didn't think I could take the street today.

His response was, "If you are sick, I'll send you home."

I repeated I wasn't sick. I told him, "I got locked up yesterday after servicing a police run."

He told me, "You didn't get locked up."

If I'm not free to go, and you give me my rights, I'm arrested. I told him I've been doing this for a long time, and that is what arrested is. I told him that I need him, El Duce, the commander or the chief to tell me how to properly do my job. I'm not going to run the risk of getting arrested for answering a gun run. This confused the crap out of him, and he asked again if I was sick. Absolutely not, I needed some answers.

He gets up and goes into another office and gets on the phone. He comes back about ten minutes later, and tells me they have someone I can talk to. I've been around awhile, and I already know what's coming. This is why my partner went home sick. They're sending me to the department shrink. I tell him, I'm not sick physically or mentally. He is now talking in a quiet tone like I'm going to go postal. The first order of business is to relieve me of my weapon. He tries to butter me up, informing me I can't take it into the hospital. I turn over my gun and am transported to the psych ward. Now, I'm the hold-up man and a nut case too.

I went in to talk to the doctor. She reviewed everything and tells me I am OK, no problems. But she cannot sign off and put me back to full duty until the head physiatrist talks to me. I won't be able to see him for two days, so they send me home.

Friday, I return to the clinic and have a full session with this guy. He clears me, and sends me back to full-duty status. Now I've been accused of robbing someone, the department thinks I'm a kook, and I'm out three sick days because they sent me to the hospital. I'm still at square one and have no answers.

The bottom line on the robbery investigation is that they never could get a hold of the kid. He lied about his name and address. Did he do it to cover a money loss? This is pretty common in our city. Was that dope money? You would think the lieutenant could have checked the authenticity of the information before he took three officers with impeccable reputations through a demeaning ordeal.

I went back to work, but I felt tarnished. Wouldn't it be great to have a department that would stick up for you?

WHERE DID THE (SICK) TIME GO?

I did have to fight to get my three sick days back. It was another valuable department lesson learned. If you are injured on the job, you have forty hours to file an injury report. No matter what happened to you — shot, car accident, slipped on a banana peel — you are on your own sick time until the department investigates it and deems it duty-related. Then, the sick time you lost would be placed in your sick bank. Your sick bank is important, because when you retired, your accumulated time is paid to you in cash. In some cases, it can be as high as $75,000. You get my point.

For this incident, I never claimed I was sick, the department did. I wanted to work, but they wouldn't let me. I had to file a grievance with the union, and after two years, the department wouldn't settle. So we had to go to arbitration. An arbitrator was flown in and paid. I was waiting in the hall when my union representative came up to me and asked if I would be willing to take half my time back. Not three days, but one and a half, and we wouldn't need an arbitrator. I wanted to punch the guy in the mouth. All of this and you want me to give the department back my time? The answer was no, and we went to arbitration.

Looking at all the facts, they sided with me. Three days went back in my bank. It wouldn't heal what I went through, but it soothed my angry mood a bit. I walked into the hall, when my union rep asked me to keep an eye on my bank, just to check if I got the time back. The union was embroiled in a class-action lawsuit with the department for not replacing sick time taken. So after all this, I probably was not going to get my time back anyway. Those old timers were right: I really should have left the department a long time ago.

After all this, I was wrung out. I still loved police work, but the department was bringing me down. The workers felt the same way that I did. There were raggedy police cars, no equipment and no manpower, but we still loved coming to work every day. Most definitely, it was a love-hate relationship.

After all that demeaning bullshit, I came back with a piss-poor attitude, but I came back. The funny part is that I had the same work ethic. It's strange how cops do that — even after the death of an officer. You deal with it, recover, and move on. I pouted for a bit, but soon returned to my old self. It was another lesson learned and another story to tell.

A female lieutenant, who now was in charge of special operations, told me an interesting story. She heard me grumbling about my sick time ordeal. She was going to enlighten me with her own sick time story.

When she was a young officer, she had been assigned as the front desk report clerk. She asked if she could run home for lunch, and the boss allowed her to go because she lived in the precinct. She drove her personal car, which is a no-no.

Before she is three words into her tale, I know it is going to be a train wreck. She arrived at home, eats lunch and as she is leaving out the front door, her cat runs out. He runs into the hedges next to the house and hides. She has to crawl into the bushes to get him. Once she has him, she walks onto the front porch, and he goes crazy. He slips from her hands and falls. She pins him on her leg, at which time kitty clamps down and bites her on the inner thigh. Kitty has a snapping turtle bite on her leg and won't let go. She finally pries him free, finding her pants torn, and she has a bleeding wound on her thigh. She tosses Tabby into the house and heads back to the precinct.

Once she gets back she reports the incident to her boss. Now, he is in a horrible spot. She is injured and wants an EMS unit. Is it duty-related? She is claiming it is because she was on-duty when it happened. This is a situation they don't teach you in supervisor school. He was trying to do her a favor and it bit him on the ass. No pun intended.

It all worked out for her and she got her time back. I was surprised she wasn't awarded a cat bite wound ribbon for it.

7ᵀᴴ COMMAND -
ARMED ROBBERY TASK FORCE

TIME FOR A MUCH-NEEDED CHANGE

It was about this time that I caught a break and was being recruited for a new unit. It would be called the Robbery Task Force. Usually, you had to be connected to be considered for this type of unit. I guess my reputation apparently impressed someone and they tossed my name in the hat. I was burnt out at Number Ten, and I knew it. It was time for a much-needed a change.

ZEROES FOR HIRE

Shortly thereafter, I was contacted to be interviewed for the Task Force. They must have liked what they heard about me and I was soon assigned to the team. Goodbye to precinct life. I knew I would miss many of the officers, and always would have the memory of El Duce surveying her troops. The new unit would be comprised of thirty officers. This would include sergeants, investigators and police officers. We met our new boss, who was an arrogant sort. I knew of him and didn't like him, but I wouldn't be dealing with him on a regular basis.

I recognized most of the personnel, and knew right away what this was about. About a half were real go-getter cops. The other half was, well, let's just say they were questionable (friends of connected friends). Our job was to be all about robberies — to aggressively investigate and pursue holdup men. Our new boss gave us the introduction speech, and told us some of us were going to be shot or killed working in this unit. It wasn't pretty inspiring, but it was the reality of this line of work. Police work was dangerous, and this was more dangerous. This unit would give me my PhD in police work. We were paired into four-man teams, with an investigator assigned to each.

I loved it. There already was competition, and no way was Bubble's team going to lose. Arrests came fast and furious, because we had plenty of time to investigate cases. It was like shooting fish in a barrel. We soon developed a reputation, and it was evident the gap between the workers and non-workers was huge. You easily could see who the experienced officers were and you could just as easily see the ones who were placed in the unit as a favor to some connected person.

The reason I bring it up is it was just like my first command. You didn't want to be paired up with a slug. One day, my regular partners were scheduled to be off, and I jumped in with another team for the day. We were going to concentrate on looking at an armed robbery suspect we already had identified.

The plan was to setup on his mom's house and wait. We got there early and parked about three blocks away. Surveillance always is tough, as it is boring the majority of the time. Only two things can happen while on surveillance. One is good, and that's catching the bad guy. The other is bad, and that's watching the bad guy get away after he does something horrible. You also have to be very careful. It is easy to get robbed or, even worse, shot. You have to have your head on a swivel.

After about an hour, low and behold, our suspect exits the house and walks down the street. We let him get about a block away and pull up to him. There's no need for talk, he knows who we are, and we cuff him quickly. One of our guys searches him, and we put him in the back seat. I sit in the backseat next to the suspect. We get to the precinct, and have to walk him through the garage to the cellblock door. He stops, looks at me, and asks if anyone is going to take this pistol off of him. My partner and I grab him, at which time a chrome semi-automatic .380 falls to the ground. There are several uniformed officers in the garage, and they must have been thinking, "What a bunch of idiots, walking a prisoner in here with a gun on him and jeopardizing everyone's lives."

I pick up the gun, which is loaded with 8 rounds. My partner walks the prisoner into the cellblock and I beeline for the idiot who searched this guy. I find him sitting, eating a bag of chips. Now, everyone knew this guy as a friend of a deputy chief. That's how he got to the unit. I told him what happened, and he didn't blink an eye.

"Everyone's okay," he said, "no harm done."

I catch myself before I go ballistic, and I know who to blame: Me. I've worked with enough people and know what the end result can be. He was a zero, and I knew it. I knew why he was down there, and I should have handled it accordingly. The shame is I knew plenty of qualified eager officers who would have killed for the opportunity to be a part of this unit. I knew they would never get a chance. That was the last time I ever got in a car with that guy.

Shortly after the unit started, our team got an addition. It was a guy with about two years on the job. It was evident he had no experience, and this was the last place he should be. His family had ties with the chief, so there you go. The city administration could care less about a good police department. It was all about advancement, position and making money. There were all kinds of people more qualified, but cronyism would prevail. This double set of standards was glaring.

We had a connected investigator handling a case, where out-of-state truckers were being robbed. It was a good gig for the criminals because most of these guys didn't want to come back to prosecute. Well, we catch the suspect and get several victims willing to come back. The investigator is going to meet them at a motel in the downriver area, and transport them to court. Some of our officers were allowed to take a department car home. He was one, and it was to be used for department matters only. The purpose of this take-home vehicle was to pick up victims or utilize it for any type of surveillance.

This particular morning, the victims are at the motel, but the investigator isn't. His son is a police officer and they live together. We contact the son and he hasn't seen his father since the previous day. The department car is missing. We now have to open an investigation to find our missing investigator. The court case will have to be adjourned, and we will probably lose our witnesses. They won't want to make a second trip back to testify. Well, tracking the investigator's debit card and phone, we discover he made a healthy withdraw and headed to the Casino across the river to do a little gambling and drinking. We eventually found him passed out and intoxicated at another residence.

So not only do we lose the prosecution of our hold-up men, but because he is connected, he faces no discipline at all. Driving a department car drunk is bad enough, but how about in another country? Obviously, he knew someone. Like I've repeated over and over, he represents everyone in the unit. He made us all look bad. He should have been immediately transferred, if not fired.

THE LADY IN THE FLINTSONES SLIPPERS

It wasn't all doom and gloom at my new command. At this point in my career, I had developed quite a reputation for attracting the craziest of the crazies. I was aware of it, and took precautions at every opportunity. We had gone to an address in an attempt to lock up a guy for homicide. There were ten of us, and we had entered the residence, finding the suspect gone.

As we were milling about waiting for orders, I was paging through the mail, which was on a table near the door. The other officers had gathered in the front room. I glanced up and saw a female who was about seventy years old enter the room. She was dressed in a housecoat and her hair was in rollers. She was moving very slowly and was weaving her way through the officers. It appeared she was heading toward me. I had no idea if she was looking down to watch were she was going, or if she just didn't want to make eye contact, but she didn't appear to be all there. As she came closer, everyone was now looking at her.

As she cleared the last officer, I now could see she had on Flintstone slippers. At the tip of each toe was a large plastic Fred Flintstone head. Now, I really was prepared as she stopped in front of me, and slowly looked up. When our eyes made contact, she unleashed a long looping roundhouse right. I already was in a defensive stance, and side stepped the punch. Mind you she was seventy, and pretty slow. The problem was that I stumbled back into the table, knocking the mail off and almost falling down. That was it: One swing and she already had turned around and was shuffling back. The guys were roaring. One of the guys was yelling, "Down goes Frazier, Down goes Frazier."

By this time, I was so accustomed to it, I didn't even try to explain that she missed. I let them laugh themselves down to a quiet snicker and we left. My reputation for attracting crazy people now was enhanced by the "Story of the Lady in the Flintstone slippers."

SIGN IN HERE

I got myself another time, while searching for an armed robbery suspect. He was a pretty violent guy. He dragged his last female victim down the street when she wouldn't let go of her purse. He was driving a car at the time.

We had identified the suspect, and my crew and I were going to attempt to arrest him. He was staying at a drug treatment center, which always caused issues. Any type of action at a treatment center is tricky because there is some confidentiality involved. They are not just going to let you in to arrest someone. A search warrant always is the best policy, but we were playing it on the fly. My plan was to talk to an employee to see if we could get our suspect out into the lobby. We certainly were not going to tell the treatment center we were there to arrest anyone.

I headed in, and the rest of my team was behind me, confident with our plan. We can see there is a waiting area, which is sealed off from the residents by a counter and a glass partition. Several people were seated in the lobby and a white male, who is about fifty years old, is standing at the counter. As we enter, he turns, and I can see he is holding a large clipboard and pen. He is wearing glasses and had on a white dress shirt with tie, Perfect: That's the guy we need to talk to.

He already is out from behind the glass, so we don't need a super story. I start talking to him, and tell him I am looking for Gary Champs. A family member of his is ill, and I was sent for notification. It was a good story, I thought, and the suspect should be concerned about a sick family member. The rest of my team, all three of them, are seated reading magazines. They are spread out, but are close enough to hear me talking. Mr. Clipboard, nods his head, and asks for the name again. I give it to him, and he nods his head several times. He continues to scribble on the paper, and the nodding seems to pick up speed. I now give him a better look, and realize that his white shirt is very dirty, and there is a mustard stain over the left chest area, and it runs over the tie. He has khakis on, and casual dress shoes, but one has no lace, and he isn't wearing socks. I begin to realize that I'm in trouble. The crew is not looking at me, and I think I can get out of this with no damage, if I just send Mr. Clipboard on his way. Before I can utter another word, a real employee of the center exits from behind the glass and starts scolding Charlie.

"You can't be out here, Charlie. You know that," she says.

She takes the away the clipboard, which actually is a sign-in sheet, and rips his scribble sheet from it, and places it back on the counter where it belongs. She escorts him into the back, and I can hear him singing, "Old McDonald had a Farm, EI-EI-OH."

I don't want to look back, because I can hear the crew snickering. They have seen everything. I'm already out the front door to try and compose myself. As soon as the crew clears the door, they burst into laughter. One actually goes to the ground because he can't control himself.

I knew my request not to tell the others was falling on deaf ears. The only thing that saved the day was when we re-entered, I got a legitimate employee, spun our web, and locked up the bad guy.

THE DRAGON

There are many incidents that can define a police officer's career. As young officers, you look up to everyone and everything. You can't help it. You simply don't know any better. Rookies are clean-shaven, their uniforms are neatly pressed and their boots have a mirror shine. Yet they secretly yearn to look like veteran officers. They don't want to be new out of the box, they want to appear worn and experienced even if they are not.

Watching a veteran officer walk by with a bunch of citations pinned to his uniform leaves an impression. The young officers have no idea what the ribbons are for or how they earned them. Those decorations and a confident stride are all that is needed to easily impress the newbees.

I was in that boat as a young officer, paddling along with the rest of them. It's probably why that to this day, I have a place in my heart for rookies.

As you gain experience and time on the job, you realize what is what, and who is who. When you have an opportunity to do something rookie officers will never forget, you better jump all over it. Who knows, the incident itself may turn into a department legend. A legend rookie officers would never forget.

While at this unit, I was filling in for the officer in charge, when just such an opportunity came up. One of my squads had tracked down a robbery suspect and arrested him on the east side.

This was routine for us, but the phone call that followed really upset me. The story started with the officer telling me how they first spotted the suspect. He was driving a pickup truck with a second suspect seated in the passenger seat. Once they had positively identified the main perpetrator, they affected a felony traffic stop.

Using caution, all four officers approached the suspect's vehicle with guns drawn. They ordered both suspects to raise their hands. They both complied. The problem was, when the passenger raised his hands, he was holding a four-foot alligator. This immediately triggered all kinds of police action. The main suspect was pulled from the vehicle, forced to the ground and cuffed. Now the two officers on the passenger side were yelling "dragon," "alligator," "Velociraptor," "Gila monster," and any other identification their racing minds could get to their mouths. They were jumping around, bound by duty to cover their partners, but terrified that they were going to be either bitten or incinerated by this fire-breathing beast.

The two officers cuffing the suspects were focused on their task. Their eyes were big as saucers as they heard their partner's descriptive yells. Their panic did not phase the alligator, which surveyed his kingdom from his lofted position with his mouth agape. Dragging the first suspect to the passenger side of the vehicle, the first two officers were now jumping around with the others, screaming, "Drop the alligator. Drop the damn alligator!"

Luckily, the second suspect lowered the alligator. With pleading voices, the officers instructed him to exit the truck, and leave the alligator. The second suspect complied and was quickly cuffed. With both men secured and the alligator locked in the truck, the officers could get back to being the police. Their nerves were a bit frayed, and there were repeated over-the-shoulder glances back at the truck, but they had gathered themselves enough to complete the investigation. They soon discovered they did indeed have their main suspect, but the passenger was not wanted for any offenses. The vehicle came back clean and properly registered. They were going to let the passenger and alligator go. The alligator seemed to be some type of violation, but they couldn't figure out what. Not wanting the passenger to carry the alligator down the street, they would release the truck to him. The interior of the truck would have to be searched before they could let it go.

Now the passenger was instructed to do exactly the opposite of what he was ordered. He was instructed to slowly open the door, and to pick up the alligator. All four department issued weapons were at the ready, as the officer jockeyed for positions. If someone would have yelled boo, the poor alligator and passenger would have never made it. The officers quickly searched the vehicle, now glancing over their shoulders away from the truck. No evidence or contraband was found, and the passenger was allowed to load up his reptile and he was released.

Great story, but here is the part I was upset about. Imagine what the rookie officers in the precinct and the citizens waiting in the lobby would have thought. Veteran plainclothes officers bring in a suspect wanted for multiple robberies. Not only that, but they also would have been pulling a roped dragon along with them.

Now that is truly the stuff of legends.

JUST WHAT TYPE OF OFFICER ARE YOU?

Our unit developed into a pretty good bunch, and we made some great arrests. An eye-opener for all of us happened one day when two of our guys attempted to locate a shooting suspect. This is routine action for officers. They were on their way to pick up some reports, when everything changed in seconds. Dispatch broadcast a shooting run that was about three blocks away. A marked unit already was at the scene, confirming the shooting, and gave out a description of the suspects. Our guys didn't know this suspect had just attempted to carjack an elderly victim. When he resisted, the suspect shot him in the head, then walked off. The victim had lost a large portion of his skull.

Good officers treat every incident the same way: As if it is the most dangerous situation you could come across, and these officers were good ones. They spotted the suspect as they rounded a corner. He was standing in front of a party store. They pulled up a few yards past him, and pulled their car up on the curb. They now were less than ten feet away, when the suspect pulled his gun.

Both officers were partially out of the car when the suspect started shooting. Both officers returned fire. The suspect fired eleven rounds, missing both officers, but making a mess of the police car. The officers hit the suspect six times. He survived and later stood trial and testified that he was taking the gun out to drop it, but the officers started shooting him. The elderly victim died.

This incident is true police work and displays the life and death risks taken every day. It's a close call they won't forget. It was a close call none of us would forget. Maybe the boss was right and some of us would die.

As I said, I didn't bump heads with our commander much. I knew he was connected downtown. He was one of those working fanatics, and it seemed like he never slept. I was a dedicated officer, but he was ridiculous.

One night, we had brought in four suspects for robbery, and I was in a back office, waiting to transport them. It was about 8 p.m., and I was seated with my feet up on the desk. He entered the adjacent office with a large cigar in his mouth. He looks at me, and comments about how hard I'm working. I begin stumbling through an explanation as he walks off. Great, I'm caught looking like a slug by the boss.

After transporting the prisoners, we continue working into the early morning hours. We make two more arrests and around 4:30 a.m., I'm back in the same office waiting to transport. My feet are up on the desk when you-know-who enters the office. Cigar in mouth, he just looks at me. I start to say something, when he holds up his hand and shakes his head no, turns and walks out. It was the one time he made me smile.

He really rubbed a bunch of us the wrong way when he held a meeting for the whole team. He started talking about a six-year-old girl who had been severely burned. He puts her picture up on an overhead screen. Her house had been firebombed with the intent of killing her drug-dealing father. She was the collateral damage. It was a very sad case, but this city was full of similar ones. He continued with the story, and then turns to the hook. They are looking to send the little girl to Disneyworld and are asking for donations.

If it was left there, I may have made a donation, but he kept going on and on about us not being the officers he thought we were if we didn't donate. I was furious. Apparently, he had no idea what type of officer some of us were. Is this what he was accustomed too? Donations and support for the higher-ups?

Needless to say, I didn't donate, and neither did many of the crew. Everyone knew being connected took a whole bunch of ass kissing. There were a number of people in our unit because they were ass-kissers. I didn't know the entire background on our boss, but being connected hung on him like cheap suit.

INTERROGATION 101

While working this unit, I learned the overall investigative end of handling a case. It's something I thought I knew, but really didn't. I always was striving to better myself, and this unit gave me that opportunity. I learned early to watch experienced officers and how they handled cases. It is typical of any type of police work, you take a little something from everyone, and eventually put your own mark on it. Interrogations were a big part of investigations, and I was determined to be the best at it. I had minimal background in this, and figured I would sit in with as many officers and investigators as I could. I wanted to get a feel for it, and learn the dos and don'ts.

The first time was an eye-opener. I sat in with our lost/drunk investigator. Remember to not be impressed by time, rank or ribbons? He had time, so I figured he knew something. We sit down with a suspect for multiple robberies. The investigator lights up a cigarette, leans across the table and says, "You're going to tell me what I need to know, or you are going to wind up in prison, getting fucked in the ass."

"Fuck you," the suspect responded, and that was the end of the interrogation.

Wow, I didn't have the background, but figured this wasn't the way it was done. I eventually developed my own style, and it worked.

My style allowed me to assist in several high-profile homicide cases. One day, we were sent to the Fourth Precinct to obtain information from a suspect who wanted to talk about a recent shooting. The information he had pertained to a case concerning the father of a local celebrity. We interviewed him, and he gave up five pages of information. He basically laid out the homicide and all the players involved. The information was solid, and we knew it. We returned to our base, and handed the paperwork over. Homicide was the lead in this case, and they would pick it up from there. Several days later, we were summoned to homicide to discuss the case with a lieutenant. We were told to wait in his office, and did as instructed. I could see paperwork on his desk that had the name of the suspect we had talked to. I picked it up, and it was the exact statement we had taken, but in the lieutenant's handwriting. It looked like he had made a duplicate of the information we had gathered and put his name on it.

I put it back on his desk and waited. When he entered the room and took his seat, I asked him about it. He knew he was had, and quickly placed the file in his desk drawer.

"Nothing," he said. "It was nothing."

These are the types of things that some officers do to attain the next rank. They do anything to make themselves look good in the chief's eyes — even if it means stealing the work of other officers. At this point, I had learned a lot about police work. I also was learning an awful lot about the politics of getting promoted, and it stunk to high heaven.

RACIAL WHAT??

The last incident at this unit was so typical of my department. The politically connected officers felt they were owed something, and expected everything to be handed to them without having to work for it. A new lieutenant, who was a white guy, had been assigned to be in charge of our unit.

Several officers from the various teams in our group were given take-home undercover cars, and I was one of them. I assumed it was because of the work I produced with my team. Never for a minute did I think it was because of my race. Well, two black officers felt there were too many white officers taking cars home. They demanded one, claiming the whole thing was racially motivated.

This poor lieutenant didn't have a racist bone in his body, and the two officers in question were the absolute laziest guys in the unit. We had labeled them the sergeant's lunch-chauffeur crew. They drove around with our lead sergeant and held his hand, I guess. I never saw them work their own cases the entire time the unit was in existence. We had been operating for about nine months, which made that almost impossible, unless they were being protected.

If I were the lieutenant, I would have called everyone in for a meeting. I would have told each crew to bring in all of their case information and the results. This would include the number of cases they opened and closed, prosecution results, and current cases they were working on. I would have stood each officer up, and let them tell the entire unit what work they had done. That would have solved the whole racial issue really quickly. God, I hated that. For them, it was not about your work ethic, but the color of your skin. My feeling always was to hire the best, keep the best and promote the best. It seems simple.

A NUMBERS GAME

My unit had a sister program, labeled the B&E Tasks Force. Combined, we had about fifty officers. Numbers always have been big in Detroit. Personnel numbers, arrest numbers — they all have to work. Our numbers were good, but fifty officers is a lot. Every new mayor and every new chief wants to let the public know they are going to put more officers on the street. It didn't matter what type — just more, particularly more in uniform. So when the new regime took over, everyone was ordered back into the street. It didn't matter how much good we were doing. It was kind of funny because at this point, I had been through this very same thing several times.

8ᵀᴴ COMMAND - HQSU

NO PARKING

I was spared uniform patrol, and was one of five officers folded into a new Headquarters Surveillance Unit. All the officers chosen from the robbery unit were workers. The problem was that we got the same amount of guys from the old HQSU, and the majority of them were not workers. This unit would be all about using undercover vehicles and doing surveillance work. The robbery guys had all done a little surveillance work before, but this was going to be a bit different. We went into an accelerated training program, and after several weeks of instruction, I felt pretty confident.

We were going to be at the beck and call of the department, and they would decide what cases we worked. After several months, I realized surveillance wasn't for me. I just wasn't patient. I would get bored quickly, wanting to make something happen. This was the absolute last thing you wanted from a surveillance officer. Patience was critical. I really wasn't happy with the targets the department was supplying, so I kind of invented a position for myself. I would be the surveillance intelligence officer. I would develop patterns and suspects for the unit to follow. I had become pretty good at this type of thing while working with the Task Force. Good intelligence led to great arrests. It worked out for me, and I could keep the crew on the hottest cases going.

The only problem I had was to be stuck in the office with a female sergeant who was connected. The majority of her day was spent shopping or paying bills. A big incident for her was when she dropped her keys down the elevator shaft — yep, that little crack at the bottom of the elevator. I could avoid her the majority of the day, which was good for me.

I felt one of the officers was going to actually kill her one day. Everyone knew she was useless, and she made no attempt to hide it. Our base was very close to downtown and parking was an issue. We all received a number of parking tickets on our personal and undercover vehicles that we parked around the building. It was her job to take care of these tickets because there was no other available parking. The police department and parking enforcement just couldn't get together on this issue.

Well, one day, my partner and I had just left court, and I was going to walk back to the base five blocks away. He told me he would give me a ride. I told him no, as I always remembered Mrs. Pickens telling me that my big ass needed to walk anyway. But he insisted, and I was walking in the direction of his car anyway, so I figured I would pacify him. As we approached the vehicle, I could see there were going to be issues. He had a parking boot locked on his right front tire. I know it wasn't right, but I started laughing, and told him it looked like I was going to have to walk anyway. We both knew what had happened, our lady Sergeant never took care of the tickets.

We called parking enforcement, which has nothing to do with the police department. They informed him that he had to come up with seven hundred dollars (cash) to have the boot removed. Now seven hundred dollars is a lot of money, and he was not too happy. But, no cash, then no boot off. He paid it, got his car back and stormed back to the base. Our lady sergeant wasn't upset and felt someone else must have failed to do their job because she thought she took care of it. My poor partner is out seven hundred dollars, and she thought she took care of it. Well, the unit couldn't give him seven hundred dollars, so he was paid overtime in small segments until his money was reimbursed.

It's unbelievable that parking enforcement in this city just couldn't quit writing tickets around our building. They continued to write them the entire time we were working out of that location.

One night, one of the officers had parked directly in front our base doors. Six of us were heading out to make an arrest, and were all dressed in tactical gear. We exited the front doors, as he talked about possibly having a ticket flapping on his windshield. The pickup had a cap over the bed, and we could see the rear door of it was in the open position, and the officer said he hadn't left it that way.

We all looked at each other and peered into the truck bed. Here was Joe criminal, digging through the officer's property. I wish I had a camera to capture the look on that poor guy's face. He must have been thinking, "How in the hell did six tactical officers respond to this run so quickly?"

He didn't say a word as he slowly slipped over the tailgate and got out. He stood up, and said, "Just beat me. That was a straight up crack-head move."

He didn't get beaten, but he was arrested. Talk about bad luck — I felt sorry for him.

A 'HOLY SHIT!' COUPLE OF SECONDS

One of my closest calls was while I was working this unit. We were running surveillance on a gang that was running a slick check scam. We were on the east side of town and had just been relieved by a couple of our guys. I told my sergeant I would meet him in a school parking lot about five blocks away. He was waiting in his car as I pulled into the lot. It was a big parking area that was about eighty yards long.

His vehicle was positioned near the entrance, and I pulled up next to him. Our passenger doors were side by side, which had our vehicles pointing in opposite directions. I began to open my door, with the intention of standing in the open door to talk to him. It had just started to drizzle, and I sat back in my car, shutting the door. I rolled the passenger window down as he was doing the same. I didn't get a word out, when I was broadsided by a green minivan.

The impact threw me to the passenger side of the car, and I recovered quickly and instinctively drew my gun. I rolled back to the driver side, just in time to see the minivan pulling off. I jammed my car into gear, went about a foot, and the right front tire fell off. The van sped out of the lot as I got out to assess the damage. I seemed to be OK physically, but did have a little gimp in my right knee. My car was destroyed.

The sergeant quickly notified the rest of the crew via radio about what had just happened. They eventually caught four juveniles inside the van, which was stolen. Apparently, it was parked at the far end of the lot when I pulled in. They had traveled the length of the lot in reverse, and hit me at about forty miles an hour. The initial impact point was the center of my door. This was the luck portion again of my job. If it hadn't started to drizzle, I would have been standing outside and I would have been the impact point. If it didn't kill me, I would have had a very long hospital stay.

I had that "Holy shit" couple of seconds, and went back to work.

LESSON LEARNED

Police work is all about experience. I've said it a thousand times. The more experience the better the officer. Doesn't mean they will be a great officer just a better one. Easiest way to explain this is by example. If an officer responds to a police run, and kicks the front door in, someone may shoot at him. If someone shoots at him and misses, I guarantee the officer will not kick the door in on his next run. We call that experience. Now with experience come two things, confidence and a bit of cockiness. Every now and then we need someone to reground us and remove that cockiness. Oh it will come back, but every now and then we need a reality check.

While at this unit my squad had been working a case where a lone suspect had robbed nine separate victims on the street. The suspect was of the worse type, targeting only elderly victims. He even had pistol-whipped a victim who needed the aid of a walker. Several hours later, the suspect was at a pawnshop, cashing in the pawn receipts and taking possession of the victim's jewelry. This guy was a real low life.

The suspect's vehicle was a rather elaborately painted conversion van. In one of the incidents, the victim had acquired the license plate.

I completed an intelligence work-up on the plate, discovering it did indeed belong on a conversion van. The registered owner was a female, whose age matched that of our suspect. I figured it was either his wife or girlfriend's vehicle. The next step was a work-up on the address of the girl. This was my big break, as I discovered a male, matching the age and physical description of my suspect living with her. He had a lengthy criminal history, including armed robbery. He also was wanted on warrants, which made my job easy. I'll grab a body and head over to arrest him. All of my crewmembers were off for the day, so I poached an officer from another squad. This guy was green and new to the Task Force. I informed him of the case, and told him to pay attention as he was going to learn something.

With my eager and attentive partner, I headed to the east side. I was flush with confidence, as I knew I had my man — I just hoped he would be home. As we turned up the identified street, we immediately saw the conversion van parked in the driveway. Both our hearts were racing as I pulled to the curb, several houses south of the address. Now comes the tricky part. The van is there and he most probably is there too. If we knock on the door, he will simply ignore it. Let's find out if he is home first.

I ask my trainee what we should do. His answer is "Go in and get him."

I brief him on the legality issues, which sometimes get in the way of police work. I tell him we will check to see if he is home first. How are we going to do that without knocking on the door? I was waiting for that, and smile and tell him, "Watch this kid."

I reach down into the large box, containing the extensive files I had on the case. I find the phone number for the female the vehicle is registered to. I show it to my partner, and he looks puzzled.

"If you call them on the phone, and ask for him, we are still in the same boat," he cries.

"Just watch," I tell him.

I dial, and as hoped, the female answers. I identify myself as Gary Carson from the Veterans of Foreign War. I tell her I am looking for donations. I know Michael Grant lives there and is a veteran. I had done my homework and knew my suspect was a veteran. I'm smiling and speaking extra loud so my partner can hear. I can see his mind clicking and he begins to smile. Oh what a tangled web I weave. The female on the other end of the line responds quickly.

"He is dead," she tells me.

Dead? Okay, I've had many a felon try to avoid capture using the "I'm dead" ploy. I've clicked on to speed investigation mode, and fire back.

"I'm sorry to hear that ma'am. The VFW would like to get the information on the cemetery and plot, as we will provide complimentary flowers every memorial day," I say.

She releases a second salvo that hits hard. He is buried at Pinehurst cemetery, plot 39. He has been dead about five years.

My voice now loses all its thundering volume. I pause for a long minute, then I express my condolences, and wish her a good day. I hang up, and my partner immediately asks "Is he in there? Let's go get him."

He can see my face, and knows something is up.

"What?" he asks. "What is it?"

There's no way to get around it.

"Uhmm, he is dead," I say.

"Dead, what do you mean he is dead" he yells.

"Dead as in no longer alive," I reply.

Just moments before, I had been puffed up like a Thanksgiving turkey. I now was a plucked ostrich, trying to burrow my head into the sand.

"Come with me; learn something," my partner chatters, rolling his eyes.

Lucky for me, I did have enough experience to recover. I called for two additional units, and gave the ghetto knock. I pounded on the door, long and loud enough for him to answer. He refused to open the door and I told him that was okay. I had something on the way that would open the door, and his girlfriend would be pretty upset when she returned home.

Well he must have been more afraid of her than us, because he opened up. We immediately arrested him, and held the location until the search warrant arrived. We recovered property from six victims and the weapon he had been using from his bedroom.

We had the right van, right address and right girl. The suspect I had identified was her ex-boyfriend, who was indeed dead. Her new boyfriend was an exact duplicate of her first. His height, weight, age and bald head all matched. The totality of the arrest and recovery of property took some of the sting out of my lesson gone bad.

My partner was so excited; it took him hours before he started his version of the story. The bottom line is, I learned my lesson but it threw one more tool in my law enforcement toolbox. Always make sure your primary suspect is among the living.

CHANGE IS A COMING

We worked a number of good crews, and made a bunch of significant arrests. I thoroughly was enjoying what I was doing, but I knew a change was coming. I had taken the last promotional test, and now was on the established sergeant list. Rumor was they were going to promote and if they did, I was gone. The policy was that once you got promoted, you didn't go back to your former command. They claimed it was a respect thing. I knew that meant only one thing for Bubble. It meant a return to precinct life and from past experience, I knew that wasn't good.

SERGEANT SCHOOL

My promotion came through, and I got the call at home to report to the academy. They were going to teach me how to be a supervisor in two weeks.

You can see where there might be some issues. You better have an extensive street resume or you were going to be eaten up. So, off to sergeant's school I went. This class would include six investigators, who were promoted for simply being investigators. The department was trying to eliminate their position. This rank is basically a cross between a police officer and a sergeant. A little more pay than an officer, but less than a sergeant. They were our detective-portion of the job.

There are two unions in Detroit. The DPOA represents rank and file cops and the Detroit Lieutenants and Sergeants Union represents those promoted above the regular police officer position. The investigators fell under the lieutenants and sergeants union. This union had negotiated their promotion to the rank of sergeant. To be a sergeant, you had to pass a number of tests and have a certain number of college credit hours.

The investigators had been awarded the rank and pay, all with no test and no required college credit hours. How do you think that made the rest of us feel? We studied our butts off and enrolled in college to get the required credits for this promotion. It's a great union, when you think about it. The funny part was most of the investigators didn't want the responsibility, as they had it pretty soft working at the rank of investigator. So, now I'm upset that I had to go back to college and pass the test while these guys who didn't have to do any of that are bitching about getting promoted.

It created an uncomfortable atmosphere in the classroom. The first thing they tell us is that there is no hope of us going back to our former commands. Each and every one of us was going to the street. Precincts needed sergeants, and that is where we were going, according to our chief. There would be no exceptions. I figured that is where I was going anyway, so it was no big deal to me. But it caused a whole bunch of grumbling amongst my classmates.

We started learning, and within an hour, we were talking about barricaded gunmen and the department's procedure for handling it. Someone from our SWAT Team was conducting this portion of the class, and he had drawn a scenario on the board. It showed several city blocks and a residence where our suspect was holed up. The instructor is going to call each of us up to the board and allow us to demonstrate how we would handle the situation.

As soon as he is done saying this, the person next to me leans over and tells me, "I'm not going up there."

"What?" I replied.

"I'm not going up there, and they can't make me," he repeated.

I told him that he was going to be conducting roll call and training shift officers in a week, so he better get over that phobia.

"I'm still not going up there," he mumbled.

And he didn't. I could see the makings of a great supervisor written all over him.

As the classes progressed, I'm getting more and more upset, and truly beginning to understand the command structure of my department. It explained the ineptness some of the supervisors displayed on the street. They had two weeks of training with the hope they could be leaders.

Some would come up horribly short in that category.

THERE AIN'T NO BULLET IN THERE

One of the instructors asked if anyone was qualified for firearms inspection. I raised my hand. He asked if I could inspect everyone's weapon and make sure they were up to date on their qualification cards. Per general orders, you had to have your gun inspected every ninety days by a qualified weapons inspector. I had this qualification, and told him I would be in the garage on our next break. I hated checking other people's weapons. Most handled their weapons improperly, so you had to keep a very close eye on them. I was paranoid about being shot by an officer.

To conduct an inspection, the officer would have to unload his weapon, (this is the dangerous part), then field strip the gun for inspection. You are taught in inspection class that they have to field dress their own weapon, and I was a firm believer in that. I also was very strict, insisting that your weapon needed to be inspected, no matter what your rank. I had many command officers walk away pissed off when they presented their cards to be signed. I told them I would sign it as soon as they broke the weapon down, and I checked it. They must have figured their rank gave them a free pass.

Many officers tried a different tact. They would take the magazine out, remove the chambered round, and hand me the gun. I knew this was an indication that they couldn't break down their guns. I would hand it right back and tell them to take it apart. This would be followed by all kinds of pleas. My nails are too long, my gun is tough to strip, something is wrong with it. It didn't matter to me, I handed it back. Lots of officers despised me for it. I could never understand that. Don't you want to make sure your weapon is properly functioning? Your life depends on it and so does your partner's life. Amazingly, this was an environment the department had cultured.

I'm in the garage, and my first future sergeant asks if I will inspect her weapon. I watch closely as she removes her magazine and hands me her gun. I look at her, knowing she can't field strip it, but she can at least make it safe. I tell her to rack the round out of the chamber.

"There ain't no bullet in there," she says.

I assure her there is, and tell her to rack the round out.

"I'm telling you there ain't no bullet in there," she replies.

Again, I assure her that there is. Frustrated, I take the gun, rack it back three times and realize she is right: There ain't no bullet in there. I glare at her.

"You know you are walking around with no bullet in the chamber?" I ask her.

"That's right," she says. "That's how accidents happen."

This is a person who, in two weeks, is going to be a sergeant. I hand her back the weapon, and tell her that if she can field strip it, I will inspect it. I know I can't change stupid. She can't break the gun down, and replaces the clip.

I warn her that carrying her weapon like that is going to get someone killed. Does she realize she can pull the trigger all she wants and no bullets will come out? She would be better off carrying around a bowling ball. At least she could throw the ball at the suspect and it might do a little damage. She simply tells me again, that's how accidents happen.

I told her she may not care, but she needs to tell her partner that she doesn't have a round chambered. Department policy requires a round in the chamber so the weapon can be fired in an emergency. Maybe she didn't understand she was on a police department where the business of the day is about emergencies and danger.

I was going to give her a homicide story, but knew it was useless. I worked a case where a retired officer was being robbed inside a cleaners. She reached into her purse and pulled her gun, pointing it to the ceiling. The witnesses described this as odd (which it sure was). Why didn't she point it at the suspect? The suspect then shot her multiple times, killing her. Inspection of her weapon explained her actions. She didn't have a round in the chamber, and it cost her her life.

So, I'm sitting in sergeant's training class with, "They can't make me go up there" and "There ain't no bullet in there." And these characters were the future of the Detroit Police Department.

We completed sergeant's school and two days before we received our badges, the department decides they are not going to promote the investigators. Great, someone finally made a sensible decision.

The investigators are relieved, and then receive some additional good news: They won't get a promotion or any supervisory responsibility, but they will get sergeant's pay and all the benefits. Wow, why didn't they just award them the rank of lieutenant? Why did it always seem like the hard working officers got the short end of the stick?

9ᵀᴴ Command - Eleventh Precinct

A Piece of Work and Three Lazy Amigos

After graduation we all received our assignments. I got the 11ᵗʰ Precinct. The reputation of the 11ᵗʰ was only a tad better than the island of misfit toys at Number Ten. Six of my fellow graduates did not go to precincts. Several went to the chief's staff, and the others went to similar positions. Apparently, it was good to know someone. I guess that "No exceptions," was just for "regular sergeants."

I didn't know anyone and was a regular sergeant, so, off to the Eleventh Precinct I go. The first day at my new home, I report to the commander's office. Right off the bat, he kind of reminded me of El Duce. Little did I know at the time, that I would knock heads with this guy over and over as he rose to the rank of assistant chief. His first question is why I think I'm going to be such an asset to his precinct. I gave him the old, "I'm a worker and my reputation speaks for itself," routine. I have no idea if he liked that answer, but he tells me I'll be on midnights. Just like a rookie officer, I'm now at the bottom of the sergeant's seniority list. This means the worst furloughs, leave days and shift assignment. We were not off to a good start.

I reported for midnights and met my shift lieutenant. I've already asked around about him, and nothing I heard was good. He tells me he expects paperwork to be done on time, and to make sure officers answer runs. He informs me that is the commander's priority.

It sounds simple enough, and no matter what anyone says about him, I'll make my own judgment. He then introduces me to the other sergeants on the shift. There are two males and a female. The first couple of days, I'm feeling everyone out, as I'm sure they are doing the same. It's the old cat and mouse, is he a worker, or isn't he? My work ethic will affect everyone on the shift, which is good for some and bad for others. The one sergeant is in his late fifties, and has a tendency to fall asleep when you are talking to him. The female always appears to be missing in action when any work is to be done. My first week there, the last guy is late almost every day. This is definitely not my kind of crew, but I am going to try and make the best of it.

The shift itself is full of young and enthusiastic officers. Unfortunately, they don't have the bosses to match. As they are young, most of them are workers and haven't been tainted by the slugs in the department yet. It was good to see that enthusiasm again, which made me feel like a rookie again. I always liked being on the street, and would back them up on as many runs as possible. I knew this bothered them at first because, as an officer, you always felt like the supervisor was checking up on you. We were, but we also were providing another able body, which, at times, could be critical. After several weeks, they understood why I was there and welcomed it.

At the start of our shift, one of the sergeants would have to work the front desk. I hated this spot because it was boring. The other three sergeants loved it, so they had no problem when I volunteered daily to take the street assignments. This in itself told me a little something about my fellow supervisors.

I soon figured out the skinny on my co-workers. The old timer was basically harmless and sleepy. The only issue I had with him was that he never completed his paperwork. When this happened, I usually got stuck with it. Our late guy was just that: Late all the time. It made it easy for him to take the desk assignment. You certainly couldn't put him on the street if he wasn't there. There were several times that we had to call to get him out of bed and remind him he was scheduled to work that day. The female was an absolute slug. If she took the desk after midnight, she would turn off the lobby lights, fire up some incense sticks, take off her shoes, and go to sleep. What an outstanding example for the troops.

One night when I arrived back at the precinct, a young officer asked if I would approve his report. I asked why, and he told me he had been waiting thirty minutes for the female sergeant. They couldn't find her. Turns out, she was back in the detective bureau with the light off sleeping. I woke her up, and she got mad. So much for keeping Detroit safe.

The behavior of my three companion sergeants told me all I needed to know about the lieutenant. He was a real piece of work. He had allowed them all to operate this way for some time. He pulled me into the office after three weeks, and told me something I couldn't believe. He wanted me to review the officer's monthly production reports, and if they had not written any tickets, he wanted me to give them a disciplinary write-up.

I reminded him that he previously told me that he didn't want them to do anything but answer police runs. Well, now they need to write tickets, he said. I told him okay, I would let the officers know they needed ticket production. We couldn't just back door them without warning and start writing them up for not writing tickets. They have been doing exactly what I instructed them to do, which is exactly what the lieutenant ordered. I must admit I was a bit amazed when he agreed with me. I let the troops know of their new marching orders, and two days later, I went on furlough for three weeks.

WELCOME BACK

When I returned the shift was in an uproar. The lieutenant had ordered another sergeant from the shift to write-up all the officers for poor ticket production. This was the exact same thing he wanted me to do, and I refused. I was furious and confronted him about his actions. He informed me that they should have known that they have to write tickets. I got the chilling, "I'm in charge and you're not" vibe from him. I realized it was going to be near impossible to work with this guy. All those stories I had heard about him were dead on.

This supervision mess finally came to a head one morning. As usual, I couldn't find my female partner to check the shift off duty. I previously talked to the lieutenant about this, and he said he would correct the problem for me. I now confronted the lieutenant, and it wasn't done quietly.

I told him we had discussed this a number of times, and I was sick of it. He previously assured me that he would take of care of it and he hadn't. I screamed at him that if he couldn't handle it, I would find someone who could. There was no yelling on his part, and he tried to settle me down. I think I scared him because she showed up at every roll call until I left the precinct.

That was eight years ago, and the lieutenant still is running the same shift. Every time I think of it, I have pity for anyone who had to work for him — especially the officers on the street.

"CAUGHT WITH YOUR PANTS DOWN" FEELING

As usual, I had plenty of comical moments while at this command. My favorite incident happened on a homicide run. Dispatch had given a one-man car a run to check on a possible dead body. I volunteered to back up the responder, and we met at a vacant dwelling. Several persons were on scene as they had been contracted to demolish the home. One of them had gone to the basement and discovered it was flooded with a foot of standing water. From the bottom of the stairs, he believed he could see a human body.

We had ordered all the workers to exit the house, and I walked to the rear, where I located the basement entrance. From the bottom of the stairs, I could see what indeed appeared to be a human body partially submerged. It was about thirty feet from the stairway and all that was visible was the lower portion of the corpse's legs. I informed the young officer we would have to wade into that muck to get a good look. He didn't seem too happy with this, because he was wearing three-quarter length boots that came up to just above his ankles. I was wearing full-length high Danner boots that were waterproof. I told him not to worry, and I would do the checking, saving him a trip into the swamp. I rolled up my pant legs to just below the knees, and headed in, hoping the water would not go over my boots.

I waded deeper into the basement, and found a dead female with an apparent gunshot wound to the back. She couldn't have been there very long, maybe a day or two. I told the officer to make proper notification, and to let homicide know they had a case. I waded back out and gave him the details of the body. It now was a waiting game for us. Our job was to guard the scene until homicide arrived. It's not much of a job because there only was one entrance to the basement. Homicide showed up after about thirty minutes, which for them, is a very quick response time.

Because the house had vacant lots on both sides, we could see the homicide crew pull up with two other vehicles. One looked like a news truck, but it had no writing on it. The other was a non-descript newer car. Homicide always was easy to spot with their hats and ties.

Several people got out of the truck carrying large video cameras. Support personnel for the cameras exited the second vehicle. They were carrying several bags and a microphone. I pointed them out to the young officer as they walked up to the side of the house. Both of us straightened our hats and shirts. I asked one of the homicide officers what the camera crew was about, and he told me it was a new television program called the "The First 48."

It was a program that profiled local homicides and what happened in the first forty-eight hours of the investigation. Nice, I had been on TV before, and also in the newspaper. I'm practically a celebrity. We kind of hung in the back, while homicide and the cameras did their thing. It was all over in about forty-five minutes and I asked when the program would air. They handed us several cards that informed us we would be notified. It made my young officer and I feel pretty good. It was a huge change of pace, and maybe our family would get to see us on TV. We waved as they entered their vehicles and pulled off.

It only was when we walked out of the backyard that I realized I had forgotten something. A slight gust of wind had reminded me. I looked down, and could see my uniform pants were still rolled up to just below my knees. I had walked around like this for the past hour. If I was on tape, I was sure my rolled up pant legs and I would end up on the editing floor.

In typical senior guy fashion, I started yelling at the young officer. I told him he should have noticed my pants legs and warned me. I was testing him to see how cognizant he was of his surroundings. He didn't buy it, and told me I looked ridiculous and it was my own responsibility. I agreed with him, and we both laughed. It was a lesson learned for both of us.

AVOIDING THE EASY ROUTE

I can honestly say that when I first heard about my promotion, I was hoping the special skills I had developed would allow me to go back to my old command. I realized this wasn't going to happen. I constantly complained about the command structure and the promotional system. It was frustrating to see how some favored supervisors were led by the hand and given opportunities many people never would get. It bothered me that these connected policemen were promoted, even though they lacked experience. And, once promoted, they never would acquire the experience to make sound decisions in dangerous situations. Time on the job brought frustration, and I had plenty of it.

Now, here I was hoping I wouldn't have to deal with precinct life. I wanted the same things that I despised: The easy route. Learning to become a leader starts in the precinct. It involves the raw basics of supervising a police force. Once there, I knew it was the right place to be. You learned the ups and downs of the precinct operations. You had an opportunity to deal with every type of officer and supervisor. Just like police work, supervision is learned through experience.

You can read books and go to classes, but hands-on is the only way to do it. Sure, there are people who just don't have the ability to be in charge. It's not that they aren't intelligent; they just can't handle the responsibility. Some don't want to interact with the public, which is a big negative in our line of work. Some don't want to deal with police officers. It is much easier to avoid issues than tackle them. It takes a whole lot of diverse qualities to make a good boss. I learned quite a bit at the 11th Precinct, and it made me a better police officer (which I always knew, deep down, that it would).

After six months, I did have the opportunity to leave. I was offered two different jobs. One was at the Violent Crimes Task Force. The other was a complete new concept called the Criminal Investigations Bureau (CIB). This command would cover the investigative units in all the precincts. Now, violent crimes seemed like more my cup of tea. Their investigations covered the serial type crimes, and long- and short-term cases. The problem was that I didn't like many of the guys working that unit. They were a kind of a prima donna bunch. I had worked with both of the bosses at these units and would need to make a decision. On the Detroit Police Department, when someone opens that door for you, you better go through it because it can slam shut pretty quick.

When I talked to the CIB boss, he helped me make up my mind. All he wanted me to do was to come in and solve cases. The work involved all of the high-profile crimes that I had been involved with at surveillance. I would be working by myself, and he wanted results. It sounded like me and I took the position. In the long run, I was glad I did.

10TH COMMAND - CIB

IS THIS WHEN THEY JOIN THE CIRCUS?

It was a little sad when I left #11. I had grown close to the officers on my shift. I positively knew that I wouldn't miss any of my fellow supervisors, but I felt sorry for the rank and file guys working the street. When I was there, I felt it was my responsibility to make them better officers by teaching them what I had learned. Now their routine would return to the same old bullshit and the grind of being commanded by the incompetency that sometimes rises to the top.

I reported to my new command eager and ready to go. I had no idea whether my excitement was fueled by my escape from #11 or the prospect of a new challenge. It probably was a little of both. My new position came with a bunch of perks. My working hours were one of them. I would be working from 6 a.m. to 2 p.m., which gave me several hours to review and organize cases before the phone started ringing. The second perk was that I had weekends off. Coming off of a rookie sergeant position at Number 11 made the move seem like hitting the lottery. The third perk was the most important: I would have plenty of time to work open cases.

I got out of the gate quickly and had several significant case closures. At this point in my career, I found the department had a fatal flaw concerning investigations. No one talked to each other. Precincts didn't communicate and, at times, people inside the individual commands didn't communicate. You could have two people sitting at desks across from each other and they would not realize they were looking at the same suspects.

This is where I came in. I began to review all of the part-one crimes on a daily basis. These included homicides, rape, robbery, carjacking and any other peculiar crime like pigeon drops, frauds, gypsies, etc. I could monitor them citywide, try and identify the suspect or suspects, then turn the whole thing over to one of the investigative units. It all was the fun parts of police work, without being bogged down by paperwork or court. It was a dream job for me.

I only had been in my position for about three weeks when I had an opportunity to handle a case in the 11th Precinct. It involved a male and female crew who had robbed nine businesses at gunpoint. I had an opportunity to talk to a witness who had seen the suspects park a vehicle about a block from one of the crime scenes. I got a very thorough description from this witness, which included a partial license plate. I eventually identified the vehicle and a possible suspect, but couldn't locate either him or the car. The car had been through a second set of hands and my possible suspect had a narcotics problem. This meant he could be staying almost anywhere, including sleeping in the car. After a week of searching, I became frustrated and decided to go with the connect-the-dots plan. I was going to make it to all of the locations that had been robbed, one by one, in hopes of getting a better overall picture of this series.

Get in the car and get it done, I told myself. I really don't want to take any action, as I am alone. I'll be careful, I tell myself. It's funny how even with my time on the job, I still think young — way smarter, but still young.

I was en route to my first location when I was stopped by a traffic light. I looked over my right shoulder, and to my surprise, see my suspect's vehicle parked in a gas station. I swung across three lanes of traffic and quickly pulled behind several vehicles in the parking lot across the street. After a minute, I saw the suspect exit the station, enter the vehicle and pull off. I already had notified dispatch and pulled several cars behind the suspect as he proceeded east bound. After several minutes, backup units arrived, and arrested the suspect along with two females. Two handguns were recovered inside the car. The precinct was buzzing as I arrived to do my paperwork because this guy was a big deal for them. He was a big deal for the department.

As I walked down the hall, I saw the commander standing there with his arms folded. He still was reminding me of "El Duce." As I passed him, he said "nice work, wish you were still here."

I looked at him and said that I probably would have stayed if things were different.

This really bothered me because he was well aware of the issues involving my old shift, but he did nothing to fix it. He was in charge of the entire precinct, but allowed a few people to completely demoralize an entire platoon. Those officers would never forget it, nor would I.

Everyone was starting to buy into my intelligence communications thing. The upper command structure could see it was working. I began attending all of the crime analysis meetings. Detroit had gone to a data capturing reporting system. It was a great improvement from the past, but it still had some problems. The crime analysis unit organized all of its findings by gathering the compiled data from this system. The problem was it was raw and needed to be ciphered through. If the system said we had twenty robberies last night, that is what they would report.

The problem was that some of these reports were not robberies at all. Without reading them, you wouldn't know. In addition, some may be robberies, but could have been generated by other issues. For example, when there are reports of a victim being robbed of prescription drugs, you have to ask yourself did this really happen or do they need more drugs. The report never lists antacid, or blood thinners. Oxycodone or Vicodin or other similar narcotics usually are more like it. You needed a police report to re-up your prescription. This was a common report, and many of the supposed victims sold their scripts to finance their heroin or crack habits.

Another example is two buddies drinking, and one gets mad because the other didn't kick in for the liquor. He hits him on the head with a board, and takes two dollars. Yes this is a robbery, but more than likely, the victim is not going to prosecute. You get my drift. Now crime analysis would take in all this info, slap it on a map, show it to the heads of the department at the meeting and determine all our manpower needs for that area.

My job became convincing my bosses that the classification of crimes could be misleading. I could make my point because I knew the content of each incident. Why send officers where they weren't needed?

Believe it or not, a lot of senior officers attending these meetings based their decisions on what they had seen on TV police shows. I attended one meeting where one of our highest-ranking officials asked about a certain B&E report. In this incident, a dog was stolen. Keep in mind Detroit averages 1,200 shootings a year. He went on at length about how we could solve this one B&E.

He felt this was a rare dog, and we needed to check with the American kennel club. It probably ate special food and needed special care. A check should be made to where they board rare dogs. Hell, we couldn't spend that much time on a homicide case. I was just shaking my head. Rare dog my ass.

At another meeting, I had given a briefing on a gypsy confidence crew that was posing as water department employees. They would knock on the door of an elderly victim and claim to be from the water department. Dressed in reflective vests and hard hats, they would insist they needed to check the water pressure, and once inside, one would lead the victim to the basement, while the other looted the place.

About mid way through the briefing, a lieutenant raised his hand. The assistant chief interrupts me to call on him. He wants to bring it to everyone's attention that I shouldn't be saying gypsy. According to him, it is like using the word nigger. I'm shocked. I have worked a number or gypsy cases and knew there was a bit of controversy overseas about using the word gypsy. It had been generated by the media and died out soon after it came up. The majority of gypsies are proud of their heritage and only take offense if you get them mixed up with another gypsy family.

I thought about addressing it, but I knew better. It would be useless. This guy never worked a gypsy case in his life and knew nothing about them. Later, I found out the person sitting next to him had told him the whole n-word story. So this lieutenant was just talking so someone could hear him. Remember about moving up the promotional ladder? His next promotion would be an appointed one. I took a deep breath and decided just to finish the briefing. Before I could get another word out, another lieutenant raised his hand.

The assistant chief called on him and asked if he had something to add.

"Yeah," the lieutenant said. "When they are done robbing people, they join the circus."

For a brief second, I thought of pulling my gun and ending this madness. I thought better of it and completed the briefing. I sat down dejected. The "N word" lieutenant was promoted to inspector.

THE WORKERS GET THEIR CHANCE

These meetings proved that the major crimes and serial-type suspects could be identified and stopped. I convinced my boss to let me expand my one-man unit. With his approval, I picked two officers. One was a paperwork expert, and the other was a worker bee.

We made great strides, and after several months, I went to my boss again. I told him if he could give me four more officers we could do some great things. I had no personnel on the street, and the precincts could not effectively handle the cases I gave them. Most of the bigger cases jumped precinct boundaries, which just added to the confusion on who should handle what.

They say be mindful of what you wish for because it may come true. My inspector ran my suggestion by the deputy chief and he bought it. The next thing I knew, I was in the DC's office. I would be paired up with a lieutenant I had worked with at the Robbery Task Force. He was a great guy and a good cop. We sat down and briefed the deputy chief, pitching our plan.

He said he thought it was a great idea and really needed this team to work. Robberies were out of control, and someone needed to stop the hemorrhaging. He even was willing to give us his department car if it would help. I knew the only way this team would fail is if we had the wrong people in it. If the department picked the officers and sergeants, we were doomed. I had been through this a number of times and expected nothing less.

We pleaded our case with the DC concerning personnel, and he assured us they were going to let us hand pick our own people. I was thinking, finally, the department is getting desperate.

Knowing that this was a rarity, we jumped all over it. Usually, you were allowed to pick some people, but you always got a handful given to you (particularly family, friends, cronies etc.). It didn't matter what type of workers they were, they had an immediate position because of people they knew.

The lieutenant and I sat down to formulate our plan. The entire working end of the unit would be intelligence-based. We needed workers, but also good people who could interact smoothly with suspects, victims and fellow police officers. I didn't have to pick the four officers I requested because they were giving us a total of sixteen. We knew if we were to get our group approved, we would have to have a balance of race and gender. Yes, we would have limits because of this, but we did get to choose from the entire department.

We conducted more than a hundred interviews, and finally came up with our crew. There were two females, two Hispanic officers, six black officers, and six white officers. The group was approved and the department sent us only one officer. He seemed like a worker, but it really didn't matter. We didn't have a choice on that one. I was shocked, but excited. The workers were going to have their chance to show what they can do. We would be cut free of all the anchors the department usually attached to a unit of this type. We had talked the talk, now it was time to walk the walk. I was bubbling over with confidence.

11TH COMMAND - ROBBERY TEAM

SERIOUS BUSINESS

The job had now become a serious matter for me. I felt I had reached the pinnacle of my career. I had no aspirations to move any further up the promotional ladder, as I knew I wouldn't be able to stomach what came with it. From this point on, all the investigations, all the arrests and all the suspects would be the most dangerous law enforcement would have to deal with. I now was a supervisor and administrator. The street stories were grinding to a halt for me. I was forced to change, and wasn't liking it. I was starting to miss the streets.

THE A TEAM

So the new Robbery Team was formed and we began operations in the summer of 2006. We didn't disappoint the chief. This was a true testament to the officers we had chosen. They were the cream of the cream — self-motivated and dedicated. They all had investigative skills, but needed to learn the warrant process and the handling of cases all the way through the judicial system. This was going to be new to everyone, including myself. Everyone wanted to learn, which made this process flow smoothly. I had nineteen years on the job, and still was soaking it up.

Soon, the team was starting cases and finishing them. By this, I mean reading a robbery report, and being with it all the way until the end. This included conducting interviews, arrests and interrogations; obtaining warrants; attending court; and finally, having the perpetrators sentenced. I couldn't have been prouder.

My enthusiasm was gushing, and I was back to feeling like a rookie. I couldn't wait to come into work every day. We were closing an average of twenty-five to thirty robbery cases a month. Bad guys were going to prison at a record pace.

We were assigned a dedicated prosecutor, and their office bought into our program. They were elated with the ninety-five percent closure rate. The team had developed contacts with every major business, suburban agency, federal agency and the department of corrections.

With this impressive team working together, we couldn't fail. I thought, "leave us alone, and we can only get better."

LEAVE A GOOD THING BE

Whoops, what was I thinking? Eventually someone would start tinkering with the process, and I knew it. About six months into the operation, my lieutenant was offered a promotion to commander. I really don't know if the numbers put up by the Robbery Team made this possible, but it didn't hurt. He was a good cop, and more than qualified for the job. He would be a huge asset to the department. We talked about his move up the ladder, and he was hesitant. He knew what came with it.

It involved being quiet when the big boss made a decision. Remember, you are appointed and easily can be demoted back to your former rank. Money and retirement is what this offer was about, as far as I was concerned, and that's what I told him. Every worker on this job knew who the true cops were, and he would never lose that. Sure, he would have to kiss some ass, but who cares? He also could do some great things, and help change this department. He decided to accept the position.

The biggest problem I was going to have would be who they appointed as the new lieutenant. A connected guy could bring this whole thing down around us. This team had no egos, and we were just that: A team. Someone who wanted to toot their horn and wave flags wasn't what we needed.

I was lucky. Our present commander sat down with the chief and told him that I could run the team without a lieutenant. The numbers he presented didn't lie, and the chief agreed with my commander. I now was the officer in charge. The next few years were the best of my career. We continued at our current case closure pace, and eventually increased our numbers as we became more efficient.

We hit some speed bumps when my old commander retired and new bosses stepped in. We were a show case unit, and everyone trying to obtain rank knew this. We really could make a supervisor look good. This was our blessing and our curse.

Police Officer Charles Edward "Chuck" Armour
Detroit Police Department, Michigan
End of Watch: Saturday, June 11, 2011

Police Officer Chuck Armour succumbed to injuries sustained one week earlier when he was intentionally struck by a vehicle he had attempted to stop while on foot patrol in the Greektown area of Detroit. The driver of the vehicle was driving the wrong way down a one-way street and was yelling obscenities at pedestrians. Officer Armour instructed the man to stop when observed him driving the wrong way on St. Antoine Street, at Monroe Avenue, at about 12:30 a.m. Instead of stopping, the driver intentionally struck Officer Armour, and then turned the wrong way down another street. He was stopped by other officers and arrested on Monroe Street. Officer Armour was transported to a local hospital with several broken bones, and he passed away one week later from complications after undergoing surgery for his injuries.

In January 2012, the subject pleaded guilty to second-degree murder and was subsequently sentenced to eighteen to thirty-five years in prison.

CONGRATULATIONS, YOU DID YOUR JOB

I knew I now was neck deep in the political end of the job, and it was a balancing act to keep the unit running.

We had several incidents that were indicative of how the department operated. One of my guys was assigned out to work a detail in uniform. He actually was the one guy the department had sent us. He worked the detail, and about a week later, my commander told me to complete a meritorious write-up for this officer and his partner. He wanted the write-up on his desk that night.

I'm all for recognizing officers who do good work. I pulled the report and read it. The officers had spotted a carjacked vehicle sitting in the driveway of a house. When two suspects came out of the dwelling and got into the car, the officers pulled up and both suspects fled on foot. They arrested the passenger. It was pretty basic police work and nothing spectacular or out of the ordinary. I told the commander I was not going to do the write-up because I saw nothing meritorious about their actions. He told me I was going to write them up, as the order came from a higher authority. I wondered who the heck was recognizing this as a meritorious write-up?

I began arguing with him about it and asked, "Are you ordering me to do it?"

Most bosses are afraid of this statement because they know we can disobey it, if we have grounds. I knew what this was about, and didn't want to give in. Some boss who knows one of the officers wants him to get a ribbon. If anyone completes a write-up, that requesting boss can be assured the officers get a ribbon. My mind told me the officers did not deserve an award. I refused to do it, and told my boss to find someone else willing to ignore right and wrong.

After I walked out of the office, I started to think that if I don't do it, he simply is going to get someone else to do it. They didn't deserve it, and I had to think of a way to stop it. I hatched a plan where I quickly enter a positive counseling write-up into their file and approve it. That would be their award: Just a "good job, guys" thing on paper. The officers didn't even deserve that, but I sure didn't want them to get the medal of valor for a standard arrest.

I plopped down at my desk, banged it out, and submitted it. Once it is in the system, it stops the process of allowing any higher award. I marched back into his office and announced I had taken care of his request. He asked for the paperwork so he could sign and approve it, and then send it up to whoever wanted to give these guys a ribbon. I told him no need, as I had given the matter a counseling register entry electronically and it had been approved. I could see the look in his face. He knew he had been had. What was he going to say to the higher-up? How about the simple truth that this action didn't merit recognition?

Remember my favorite saying: Never be impressed by time rank or ribbons.

LIST SKIPPERS

At this time, our mayor was embroiled in a ton of controversy. This eventually would lead to a prison sentence for him. As he was on his way out, he did what every good mayor would do. He took care of his friends. He charter promoted sixteen sergeants. My unit was given one of these charters promotees. If you've forgotten, this is where the chief or the mayor can disregard the placement list and promote whomever they want. The first person on the list can be bypassed by the last person. The first day in the unit, I sit her down to brief her on our operation. It's obvious she is in over her head, and her main complaint is that she no longer can park her car in the department garage.

Everybody in the unit has a sour taste in their mouth over this charter promotion. I should correct that and say the majority of officers on the job had a problem with the promotions. How would you feel if you were number one on the promotional list and they bypassed you? Not only do I get a charter promoted sergeant, but my commander allowed several other officers to join our team.

This was his decision solely, and I assumed he knew I would resist his choices. We never discussed a thing, and he told me he thought they would be a great help. Anyone who ever has worked investigation knows these officer's reputations. They would be the last officers I would have ever picked. When we formed this team, our picks showed up with a shotgun and flak vest. One of our commander's picks showed up with a toaster oven and TV. Her first complaint was the building was too cold.

The easiest way to sum up the second guy is to talk about one of the first cases he was involved in. The crew was in court prosecuting a case, when one of their victims told them the second unidentified suspect who had carjacked him was in the court. Not only was he in court, he was testifying. The crew pulled the victim outside, where he was adamant that the guy testifying was the second suspect. His testimony was for a different case, and once he left the stand, the crew arrested him. There was no doubt in the crew's mind that this was their second suspect. Well, the new guy accompanies the suspect to the precinct where he interrogates him.

After the new guy returns to the base, I ask him what happened. He tells me he let the guy go. This was puzzling, but I was sure there was an answer — maybe a confirmed alibi, the guy was in jail or hospitalized. Nope. Nothing. The guy told him he didn't do it, so he let him go. I go ballistic. I tell him letting him go is not your choice — you have to have a reason. The victim positively identified him. No matter what the suspect says, you submit the warrant request and let the prosecutor make the decision. What if this suspect sees the victim on the street and shoots and kills him?

The third guy, well, I don't even want to get started.

The fourth I didn't have to deal with. He was suspended for failing his drug test and had charges pending for assaulting an airport officer. He was drunk at the time of the assault.

Now, whatever these new people do will be a direct reflection on the team. Three years of building our reputation and securing the confidence of other law enforcement agencies now is at risk. I was seeing the cracks, and where there are cracks, crab grass can get in with the wheat.

This was the beginning of a very dark time for me.

As I mentioned earlier, the mayor was on the way out because of bribes, scandals and affairs. I know what is coming when a new mayor is elected. It usually means a new chief and reorganization. Keep in mind that during my career, I had been through so many chiefs that I lost count. I was averaging about one every two years. It's hard to build any momentum, no matter what line of work you are in, with that type of turnover.

The new regime always wants to put more officers on the street. That always sounds good to the public because it gives the perception of safety. The problem is we don't have enough officers to make it safe.

When I was promoted and went to the precinct, my midnight crew, on average, would start with twenty to twenty-five priority one runs in the hole. It's not a good number to start with. If we doubled the police force, we might be able to service those police runs. There would be no police work, just police runs.

Seeing the changes on the horizon, I was playing the political game to the hilt. My mission was to keep the team together, and try to keep all the command officers happy. My personnel numbers had decreased, but our production had steadily risen, so I figured there was no way they would shut the team down. It was the best unit in the city. I was very, very wrong.

PAWNING IT OFF

We get our new mayor, and he appoints a new chief. This chief brings in his whole team of command officers, booting the guys who were kissing the last chief's ass. Now, our new chief has his own ass kissers, and all of the major meetings will be really loud because everyone wants the new chief to hear them talk.

Good system, right?

Almost immediately, my commander wants our stats and significant arrest sheets. I had to start fighting for my team's jobs. All the work we had done, everything we accomplished, and the reputation we had developed throughout the law enforcement community was going to disappear.

As the officer in charge of the unit, I got the call to go downtown to meet with the assistant chief. I arrived, finding him surrounded with a bunch of yes-men. He told me the team would stay intact, but now would concentrate on B&E's and pawnshops. He said pawnshops assisted in generating most of our crime. Really? I did not know that. Never one to mince words, I asked him if he was aware that to pawn an item, you needed a picture identification and a fingerprint. He replied yes. I asked him if he was aware that the majority of stolen items didn't end up in the pawnshop.

"Where does it end up?" he responded.

I told him gas stations, liquor stores and dope houses. Stolen jewelry usually is pawned, but the bad guy himself would have someone else do it so he wouldn't leave a paper trail. Even if he did, it would be very tough to prosecute. How could you prove he actually stole the item? I'm now teaching the assistant chief of Detroit the basics of police work.

He looked at me with this kind of blank stare. My innermost thought at that moment was wondering whether this guy ever has been in a police car or ever locked anyone up. This was the assistant chief of the city. All the yes-men began chirping in favor of the assistant chief, and I knew the battle was lost. I attempted to explain our accomplishments and the reduction in robberies. I was tired of fighting the fight. The department was winning, and I had to swallow it because it was obvious someone's mind already was made up.

The reward for my crew's dedication and sacrifice was getting back in uniform and answering police runs. They shut the greatest team of officers down, and spread them to the far reaches of the city — in uniform no less, not even considering the years of training and development they had concerning investigations.

What a waste of talent. I truly was ashamed to be a part of the department.

12TH Command - HIDTA

The Secret Squirrel

I knew I had ruffled some serious feathers, but I didn't care. I figured I was heading back to precinct life, scorned and banished. I did have an ace in the hole though: They knew I was valuable from my intelligence experience. The chief of police always needs to know what is going on, and I could provide that. I obtained a federal clearance, and they sent me downtown. I would be working as Detroit officers put it, "in a Secret Squirrel" capacity.

It was the same old thing I had been doing for years, I just didn't have a team to handle the cases. This didn't last long because the new chief of department decided he wanted to be a TV star. His show-boating and posturing rankled the new mayor. The topper came when the media discovered he was sleeping with his staff lieutenant. Her department history was horrible. She had incurred multiple lawsuits, and was accused of mistreating line officers.

The media discovered the indiscretions when this lieutenant attempted to wag her ass in front of other high level officers. She felt she was immune to the rules because she had a direct connection with the chief of the department. These command officers spilled the beans and our little Peyton Place became a shameful story about a moral calamity in a once-proud police department.

The mayor fired the chief, who immediately tried to sue everyone. The mayor appointed a new chief, and about a month later, the old chief claims the new chief was sleeping with the same lieutenant he was. The new chief goes on television news and admits he slept with the lieutenant and apologizes for his poor judgment. The current chief is married but, believe it or not, he kept his job. I'm not making this up. The chief sleeps with a subordinate and is fired. The new chief admits to sleeping with the same subordinate, and is not fired.

I have to admit I was feeling down in the dumps at this point. I entertained the thought of going forward and admitting that I slept with the lieutenant and the chief just to see how much bullshit the public could absorb.

Following the script, there is a juggling of command officers as the old ass kissers leave with the old chief and the new ass kissers come in with the new chief.

Where do I end up? Well, they had the nerve to ask me to set-up a new robbery team unit. No, thank you. I'll help anyone, but I won't fight that battle again. Someone could sleep with someone at any time, and upset the whole balance again. I continued to work in intelligence, and am assigned to a new HQSU. I realize at this point in my career, I have won most of the street fights, but have lost the battle with my own department. They have beaten me down and I'm tired.

13TH Command - HQSU

Twenty-five Years Later

My twenty-fifth year arrived so quickly. Where did the time go? It seems like I just graduated from the academy. I now have some decisions to make. Do I stay or do I go? I told myself I wouldn't give the department one extra minute, but now I'm torn. I truly love police work and the working officers, but I harbor a deep hatred for the department and the city. I know what the answer is, but I just don't want to face it.

I know you only have so many chances in life. Working as a police officer, you burn up a whole bunch of those. I survived and many didn't. Should I take that and run?

If I leave, how am I going to replace that daily adrenaline rush, the mind games, and pursuit of wanted suspects? Replace that with what — crossword puzzles and a couple of months in Florida? How will I ever gear down?

I have to search and search deep. I look back and reflect on all the ups and downs; the fights and injuries; car crashes and shootings; and the blood and the tears. Then there's the tragic loss of too many fellow officers. Is it worth continuing that?

I had taken a trip to Washington D.C. for National Law Enforcement week. We had lost an officer I had worked with. There was a quite a scene as a line of uniformed officers as far as the eye can see formed an honor guard for the families of deceased officers. I entered the memorial itself to find officers crying and embracing, kneeling at markers inscribed with the names of their lost brother or sister.

Something touches you when you see these heroes whimpering.

Police officers always must carry that emotional armor because we need it. I've never seen it stripped away so easily. As I searched for the name of my officer, I passed flowers and mementos. The memorial grounds were church-quiet, except for the whispers and tears. I knelt at the fallen Detroit officer's plaque. Next to it was a tan piece of wrinkled construction paper. A crayon drawing of a family holding hands stood over a simple message, "We miss you daddy." I began sobbing.

There are many deadly and dangerous professions. Law enforcement is unique in that it carries its dangers every second of every day. You never can let you guard down and you never can retire from it. I was off-duty and standing in line once at a large outside event. A voice boomed, "Officer Haig, how are you?" I turned to see man standing directly behind me. I did not recognize him, but he surely recognized me.

"Gary Hall." he said. "You locked me up in '89."

Both of his hands were in his pockets. The hair on the back of my neck was now standing, and my heart began racing. How much time would I have, maybe a second? Before I could react, he simply said "Thank You." He told me, I had locked him up in 1989 for a narcotics charge. He truly appreciated the way I treated him during his darkest days. It inspired him. He never would forget me, though I had surely forgotten him.

You are a target simply because you represent something: Law and order. So I'm asking myself, should I leave and lift this burden?

The kiss goodbye in the morning may truly be your last. Every contact on the job can be deadly. We are perceived as soldiers. Not only by the public, but by fellow officers. Unlike firefighters, when an officer is lost, it is accepted just like a soldier. A casualty. 9/11 was a good example. There were tons of stories about the loss of firefighters, but to this day, I have not seen one about the police officers. There were officers who had no fire equipment, but still entered those towers.

This isn't a bitch, just the reality of it. I never tell people about my profession. I love listening to them when they talk about cops. Never once have I heard a story about a hero — it's always about "that jackass who wrote me a ticket." To them, we are newspaper articles. Murderers caught. Pedophile identified and arrested. Serial rapist apprehended. Man who kills entire family is locked up. "Glad the cops caught them," is what you usually hear. Not the life or death struggle in some dark basement, when the suspect is armed with a knife.

The fact that an officer is willing to die for what he believes in goes without thanks. Yet most officers never ask for that thanks.

There also are families behind those badges. I have considered my family from the moment I was hired. They live with constant concern and the stress that comes with it. Does this really need to continue?

I tried to always leave the job at the station, and was very careful to bring home only the funny stories. I knew my family worried, but never knew how much until my daughter wrote a paper her senior year in high school. It was for a five hundred dollar scholarship offered by a retired department lieutenant. The story she wrote about was the incident where I broke three of my ribs. She was six years old at that time.

There was no way to hide the pain when I came home that day, and she must have overheard the story when I told my wife. I did not know until I read her paper that my six-year-old daughter had been terrified. Her strong daddy had been hurt, and he had been hurt by something terrible. She didn't want me to go back to work the next day. She didn't want me to go back to work ever. She never expressed her fears at that young age, and I wish I had taken time to explain things to her. We never talked about it, but now at 17 years old, I wondered how long she carried that with her. I had missed all of this until I read that essay that won her the scholarship.

How long had my mother carried her fears? How long did my friends and other family members carry theirs? I had made it a habit to immediately call a family member whenever an officer was injured. I wanted them to know I was okay, and to have them relay that to the rest of the family. Can you imagine the feeling of hearing a news report that two officers were shot and killed, but the media not releasing names, and you know that your husband, or wife, was on-duty that night? There's a lot more to this job than just a "jackass who wrote me a ticket."

What is keeping me here? I know it is the camaraderie. Is it worth it? I have said it many times that working officers do not care about medals or ribbons. They don't care about a thank-you in front of a news camera. If you sit down with a working cop, his stories will all be funny ones. Much like this book, they will keep the dangerous ones for themselves and their fellow soldiers. The only satisfaction they get is from their peers. It's that bond, that brotherhood, and that recognition of doing the job and doing it right. It's the courage and willingness to go into battle with someone — to crash through a door, not knowing what is behind it, and to risk your life for someone you don't know.

To have an officer risk their life to save yours takes something special. It takes someone special. You can't learn it from a book — it comes from deep inside.

How will I replace that?

THAT FINAL DOOR

As I reach this point, it reminds me of the voices from my past. I can hear those senior officers who told me to leave; leave before I have time invested. I often think about that, and I wonder how another department might have been the right choice — not only for me, but for my family.

Should I have gone?

My heart is telling me to stay, but my brain and body are screaming go. I think of those early days of bright eyes and innocence — and the fearless courage and the will to let that carry me. We were invincible, and knew it. I couldn't wait to go to work for fear of missing something. Catching criminals dominated my thoughts. Our choir practices were laced with pursuit stories. Like fighter pilots, we detailed every twist and turn. There never was a thought of losing the fight. The laughter and high fives never seemed to stop.

My fire is flickering.

My hair is now gray, my shoulders sag a bit, and I have a visible limp in the morning. A get-together with other officers usually is subdued. Complaints about pay and poor equipment are standard now. Talk of retirement and medical coverage always draws an argument. Quiet toasts to fallen officers always bring a few tears.

I now find it difficult to watch a training film where an officer is killed or shot. I think of the memorial and funerals. I think of embraced families screaming, "Why?"

I picture children touching flag-draped caskets and saying goodbye — their little chests rising and falling as they sob. I question how I survived and others didn't. I will carry this with me the rest of my days.

The decision is easy.

Battle scarred and worn, I will walk away from this job. My heart will be heavy, thinking of the coworkers who never will have that opportunity. I know they always will be with me, their faces crystal clear, full of life and dreams. They walk with me, whispering, "We got this. I have your back."

I smile, knowing that I'm ready to kick in one more door.